Obadiah Sedgwick

The parable of the prodigal

Containing The riotous prodigal

Obadiah Sedgwick

The parable of the prodigal
Containing The riotous prodigal

ISBN/EAN: 9783337279783

Hergestellt in Europa, USA, Kanada, Australien, Japan

Cover: Foto ©Andreas Hilbeck / pixelio.de

Weitere Bücher finden Sie auf **www.hansebooks.com**

THE
PARABLE
OF THE
PRODIGAL

CONTAINING,

The
- Riotous PRODIGAL, or the Sinners Aversion from *God*.
- Returning PRODIGAL, or the Penitents Conversion to *God*.
- PRODIGALS Acceptation, or Favourable Entertainment with *God*.

Delivered in divers Sermons on LUKE 15. from *Verf*. 11. to *Verf*. 24

By that Faithfull Servant of *Jesus Christ*
OBADIAH SEDGWICK, B.D.

Perfected by himself, and Perused by those whom He intrusted with the publishing of his Works.

London, Printed by *D. Maxwel*, for SA. GELLIBRAND, at the Ball in St. *Pauls* Church-yard. 1660.

CHRISTIAN READER,

GOds good Providence doth hand unto thee in this ensuing Treatise, The *whole Parable of the Prodigal Son*, both interpreted and improved, Doctrinally and Practically, for thy Spiritual Advantage, from the Pen of a workman, who needed not to be ashamed. Herein the Sinners *Aversion* from God, *Conversion* to God, and his *Acception* with God, are profitably unfolded & applied. Helps in these several Subjects, are well worth every Christians welcom, and time seriously spent in perusing such Discourses, will not be labor in vain. *Adam*, by forsaking God, lost his primitive Glory, which cannot possibly be repaired in his Posterity, but by returning to his Majesty. Man cometh into the World with his Back towards Heaven, and with strong Antipathies against God, yea, his constant course of life is a departing from the Lord, till his Highness by Omnipotent Grace doth change both his Heart and Way. And when the secure Sinner is well awakened to consider his wofull Apostacy, attended with the sad Consequents thereof, together with the impossibility of

A 2 all

all Creature succours to relieve him, then, and not till then, doth he seriously think of facing about towards God, whom he hath deserted with inexcusable neglect and dishonor.

Now the self-condemning Convict, in this dolefull condition, upon frequent self-reflexions, & aggravating his woful Apostacy, doth find it very difficult to hold up hope of gaining re-admission into the favor of slighted & forsaken Diety. This poor *Spira* did experience, as his tears, his torments, together with his desponding, despairing language doth demonstrate. But in this pitifull plight, the sinking soul may receive strong supports, by considering, with application, what loving Entertainment the guilty, worthless Prodigal received from his offended, forsaken Father. These particulars, which we do only hint at, are here largely handled for thy profit; the effecting whereof, is desired and prayed for, by

Novemb. 8. *Thy loving Friends, and*
1659. *faithfull Servants in Christ.*

HUMPH. CHAMBERS.
EDM. CALAMY.
SIM. ASHE.
ADONIRAM BYFIELD.

A Table of the Contents.

THe Scope of the Parable, pag. 2. The Parts of the Parable, pag. 4. Sin is a departing from God, p. 8. A Sinner doth voluntarily, of his own accord, depart from God, p. 9. The pleasures of sinning will quickly end, and the end of them is extreme misery, p. 9, The pleasures of sin are but short, proved, p. 10. Sin will end in many miseries, p. 12. Though sin brings men into straits, yet straits do not always bring men from sin, p. 22. An afflicted condition no infallible testimony of a safe condition, p. 26. The further men go on in sin, the worse work they shall find it to prove, p. 31. And the Reasons thereof, p. 34. And why we do not always see it so, p. 37. A sinner will try all wayes, and go through the utmost extremities, ere he will turn from his sins, p. 45. How it may appear to be true, p. 49. Why it should be thus, p. 51. Take heed of shuffling with God, p. 55. Means to prevent this shuffling, p. 59. Nothing shall avail this shuffling sinner till he return, but God will disapoint all his projects, p. 61. made to appear to be a Truth, p. 63. Why nothing shall avail the shuffling sinner till he repent, p. 64. A serious consideration, and right comparison of the miserable estate of a sinfull condition, and happy estate of a converted condition, are steps to true and speedy repentance, p. 69. How these two are prime steps to repentance, p. 71. Objections, That we are ignorant, not at leisure, it will make us despair, answered, p 77. How I may know whether my consideration be right, p. 78. Whether consideration of sin may be right, when there

are

The Contents.

are some sins that a man thinks not of, p. 83. Whether a single consideration of sin be sufficient to repentance, p. 84. Rules for right consideration, p. 86. Rules for comparison, p. 87. Sound Resolution is required to sound Reformation, p. 89. The properties of this Resolution, p. 90. Why it is requisite, p. 92. The benefits and comforts of a firm Resolution, p. 95. The Means to raise it, p. 97. and maintain it, p. 101. True Repentance for sin will bring forth true Confession of sin, p. 106. The Reasons of it, p. 111. Penitent persons are humble and lowly persons, p. 118. Humbleness described, p. 120. Why true Penitents are humble persons, p. 124. The means to become humble, p. 128. Personal Unworthiness is not prejudicial to spiritual Supplication, p. 129. Reasons for it, p. 131. How we may know that we are truly sensible of our Unworthiness, p. 136. Penitent intentions and resolutions should be accompanied with present executions and performances, p. 140. Reasons for it, p. 142. The Motives and Means for a present execution, p. 148. and The Helps, p. 154. The very initials of true Repentance are seen by God, p. 157. proved, p. 159. Evidences of true Repentance though initial, p. 163. God is very ready to shew all kinds of mercy to the truly Penitent, p. 165. Reasons of it, p. 169. By no means despair of mercy, p. 174. Objections answered, p. 175. Reasons why God makes not known his mercy presently, p. 179. How one shall be supported in the interim, p. 183. God is pleased not onely to be reconciled, but manifests himself so to be unto the penitent, p. 184. Reasons of it, p. 186. Motives to seek after the seals and tokens of Gods favour, p. 188. Means to attain them, p. 191. The kindest expressions of mercy do not hinder an humble confession of sin, p. 195. Reasons of it, p. 196. Motives to it, p. 198. God takes no
notice

The Contents.

notice of our sins upon our true Repentance, but expresseth himself wholly in love and kindness, p. 199. Reasons of it, p. 202. What is meant by the Robe, and the best Robe, p. 206. How we may know whether we have put it on, p. 211. God gives to the penitent person a precious Faith, by which he is espoused or married to Christ, p. 212. What tis to be married unto Christ, p. 213. How Faith marries us unto Christ, p. 216. Whether we have this Faith, p. 219. What is meant by Shoes on his Feet, p. 222. God doth enable the penitent person with Grace and strength for a better and singular course of life and obedience, p. 223. Reasons of it, p. 227. Every sinfull unconverted man is a lost man, p. 234. How a man may know that he is lost, p. 237. A lost sinner may be found, p. 238. How God finds a lost sinner, p. 238. Why God doth thus find a lost sinner, p. 241. Motives to a serious Trial, whether our lost souls be found, p. 242. An impenitent unconverted man is a dead man, p. 254. Reasons of it, p. 256. Trial, whether we be spiritually dead, p. 261. Every converted man is a living man, p. 265. How this may be evidenced, p. 268. Trial of our selves about our spiritual life, p. 269. Objections answered, p. 276. A very great and notorious sinner may be converted, p. 279. Who may be called so, p. 280. How it may appear great sinners may be converted, p. 281. Directions to such converted sinners, p. 288. Great afflictions are sometimes an occasion of great sinners conversion, p. 289. How it may appear, p. 290. There is an Almighty Power required to convert a sinner, p. 294. proved, 295. True Conversion is a very great, inward and universal change, p. 303. and demonstrated, to p. 312. How may a man know that God hath indeed changed his heart, p. 316. Comfort to those who are changed, p. 323. How may we know, this change is from converting Grace, and not from the power of a troubling Con-
scienee

The Contents.

science, p. 329. *Conversion brings the soul into a very joyfull condition, demonstrated* p. 333. *What kind of joy Conversion brings,* p. 336. *Why Conversion makes the souls condition so joyfull,* p. 339. *How can this condition be so joyfull, that is so exposed to afflictions,* p. 344. *and denies and abridges many delights,* p. 347. *Trial whether converted or no,* p. 359. *How converted persons should do, to walk joyfully,* p. 363.

The *Parable* of the PRODIGAL.

LUKE 15. 11, &c.

11. *A certain man had two Sons.*
12. *And the younger of them said to his Father, Father, give me the portion of goods that falleth to me. And he divided unto them his Living.*
13. *And not many days after, the younger Son gathered all together, and took his journy into a far Country, and there wasted his substance with riotous living.*
14. *And when he had spent all, there arose a mighty famine in that Land, and he began to be in want.*
15. *And he went and joined himself to a Citizen of that Countrey, and he sent him into his fields to feed swine*, &c.

His Chapter consists of three Parables, all of them tending to one scope and issue, though distinct in their special matter and object. The first Parable is of *a Sheep*, from *vers.* 4. to *vers.* 8. The second of *a piece of Silver*, from *vers.* 8. to *vers.* 11. The third of *a Child*, from *vers.* 11. to the end.

☞ All of these agree in two conditions; One, of *Loss*, the Sheep was lost, the Groat was lost, and the Child was lost: Se-condly,

Cyril.

condly of *Recovery*; the Sheep that wandred, is brought home; the Groat which was lost, is found out; and the Son who departed, is returned and accepted. There be who undertake the Reasons of these Parables or dark similitudes, under which Christ doth couch some special Lesson; as, why man is compared to a *Sheep, viz.* because of our Creation, wherein *God made us, and not we our selves*; *we are the sheep of his pasture*. Psal. 100. And why man is then compared to a *Groat*; because of that singular image of God which was stamped in man at his creation; as the royal image of a King is stamped upon such a piece of Coin. And then, why man is compared to a *Son*; because of that near relation which he had to God, being once able to call him Father. And then, why in every one of these, to a *lost* Sheep, a *lost* Groat, a *lost* Son, because of his revolt and departure from God by sin: Nay, and if it were lawfull to put and use free conceits on Parables, (as I am sure some of the Ancients do, as St. *Austin*, *Gregory*, &c.) what if in this threefold Parable, you might espie a threefold cause of mans fall. " In the sheep wandring, *Satans suggestion*; " In the Groat lost by the woman, *the womans yielding*; " In the Sons departing, *Adams voluntary revolting*, and spending of his happy estate and condition. But these and such like observations, though to some they seem more acute and pleasant, yet to me they are frothy and unprofitable.

The Scope of the Parable, with a division of the chief Heads thereof. Who are meant by the two Sons.

Touching the Parable therefore, concerning which I am to treat, there are several conjectures about the sense and intention of it. Concerning the *Father* of the two Sons, they all agree; but about the *two Sons*, they differ. Some by the two Sons understand *Angels* and *Men*: The *Angels*, they were the elder Son; *Man* the younger, being created after them. The Angels abode at home with their Father, Man had the stock put into his own hands, and in a quick time lost himself and it. This opinion you see hath some kind of Vicinity or correspondency; *sensus pius* (as *Aquinas* speaks of it) but not *proprius*. And there is one pregnant Reason against it in the Text; for that the elder Son in this place, is described to be grieved and sad at the acclamations and welcome testimonies of the younger Brothers return; but the Angels *rejoice* and are glad at *the conversion* or return *of a sinner*.

2. Others

2. Others by the two Sons understand the *Jews* and the *Gentiles*; the *Jews* were the elder, the *Gentiles* the younger; the *Jews* kept home, as it were; of all the Nations of the Earth, they seemed to be the inclosure for God and his service; and the *Gentiles* were as it were excluded, rejected, wandring sheep, a lost people; yet at length God through Christ looks after these lost sheep, (*the other sheep of his fold*, as Christ speaks, *Joh.* 19.) and returns and accepts of the Gentiles, which did much *provoke the Jew*, (as the elder Son was here provoked at the repentance and acceptance of the younger, and kept out,) they were *provoked to jealousie* by those who once were not a people. This interpretation pleaseth S. *Austin* and *Cyril*, and some others; and indeed it bears a fair congruity with the Parable in most respects.

2. But the third and general opinion is, that *by the elder Son* is meant the *Scribes and Pharisees*, (and under them any Justitiaries) persons too conceited and confident of their own works, service, righteousness, as this elder Son, who had been (as he said) *thus long in his Fathers house, and never transgressed any of his Commandments*, but served him carefully; which indeed was the opinion of the *Scribes* and *Pharisees*, who *trusted to*, and *boasted of their own righteousness*: And that by the *younger Son* is meant the *Publicans* and *Sinners*, persons more notoriously riotous and infamous in sinning, utterly forsaking of God, as it were, and living without him. And the end of this Parable was to convince the proud and envious *Scribes* and *Pharisees*, (who in *vers.* 1. and 2. of this Chapter, *murmured against Christ* for *receiving Publicans and Sinners:*) Now Christ tells them, that though these notorious sinners were despised by them, yet he *came to call them to repentance*, and that God would be most indulgent and gracious to them; though they had been great transgressors, yet now being penitent, he would receive them into singular mercy and favour, and that with much joy; and therefore little reason had they to snarl at his respect and desires towards Publicans and great sinners. Thus for the scope of the Parable, which is, *To declare the singular readiness of God in and through Christ, even to receive the most notorious sinners, proving penitent.*

The Parts of the Parable.

The Parts of the Parable. Now the Parable confists, or rather comprehends two eftates of the Prodigal Son.

1. Of *Sin* and *Luxury*, where are confiderable, 1. The *Occafion* of it, *v.* 12. *Father, give me the portion of goods that falleth to me.* He would have the eftate in his own hands: He loft himfelf, by defiring to be Lord of himfelf.

2. *The Sin it felf*, called *riotous living*, v. 13. lightly come, and lightly gone, which quickly wafted all the fubftance. Now whether this fubftance were thofe good Qualities in Creation, or good Gifts of mind or eftate afterward, it is fomewhat difputed; upon which I fhall confider in its time and place.

3. *The event of it*: That eftate being fpent, he bethinks of another courfe; indeed, now he fhould have thought of coming back to his Father, but he did not; nay, he tries all conclufions before he refolves on that: Therefore again obferve, upon the Lofs and confumption of his Eftate,

Firft, his *earthly policy*, *He joyns himfelf with a Citizen of that Countrey*, v. 15. By whom fome underftand the Devil; fo S. *Ambrofe, Civis ifte eft iftius mundi Princeps.* Others, fome kind of earthly or worldly employment: But being joyned with him, his fervice is fordid, for he is fent *into the fields* (no houfe fhall hold him who forfakes Gods houfe) *to feed the fwine*; he is made a fervant of the naftieft beaft, who would not continue the fervant of the beft Father and God. Secondly, his *extreme mifery*; this fhift did no way help him: Nothing fupplies, when God forfakes; and no way is comfortable, when we prove finfull. *He would fain have filled his belly with the husks which the fwine did eat, and no man gave him to eat.* v. 15. Ah, what a change doth fin make! Here is one, whiles he continued with his Father, enjoyed excellent fociety, tender love, compleat plenty; but now forfaking his Father, he keeps company with the fwine, is extremely pinched with hunger, glad would he have been ferved after the very hogs, and no man regarded him in this mifery and want; fo that now there is a lofs of all his happinefs, and a certainty of famifhing and perifhing, if he returns not, and hereupon comes forth.

2. The fecond eftate of him, which was of *his Converfion and Penitency*: Where you have three things obfervable.

1. His

1. His *Consultation*, set forth by a double act of reflection. 1. *Positively*. First, *of himself*, ver. 17. *He came to himself.* Secondly *of others*, his fathers servants, and their condition. 2. *Comparatively*, wherein he compares his present condition with theirs, in the utility or conveniency of it; *They have bread, but I have none*: Quantity of it, They have *bread enough, but I hunger*. Redundancy of it, They have enough, and to spare, but I perish with hunger: yea the meanest in my fathers house, the servants, the *hired servants*, yea all in my fathers house, though many, they have bread enough; what, and shall I a son famish and perish? Surely if my father hath bread enough for servants, he will have some for a child; and if he hath to spare for hired servants, he will have some to spare for a famishing child.

2. His *Resolution*; and indeed upon the sense of his own famishing misery, and his fathers bounty and clemency, he is resolved now what course to take. And me thinks he turns off an objection which might spring in his mind; yea, my father hath plenty at home, and for hired servants, but then they are obedient and careful, but I have been a wastful prodigal, a riotous spender, a departing and unkind child: To which hee gives answer; 'Tis true, yet for all that I am resolved to change this course, and I will home to my father. Nothing, no not the greatest sinnings must hinder our penitential turning to God our Father.

Now in this Resolution of his, there are four things which he did firmly purpose and intend:

1. *Aversion*, to relinquish and quit that base and miserable life and course, [ver. 18. *I will arise*] q. d. I will rest here, dwell here no longer; live thus, no, not a day more.

2. *Conversion*, to return to his father [*and go to my father*].

3. *Confession*, to acknowledge 1 His sin. 2. His unworthiness. If my father, thinks he, tell me that I have gone away from him, and have offended him, why and I will prevent him, I will confess as much; I will not defend, nor excuse, nor mitigate, nor mince the matter; I will say, *Father, I have sinned against heaven and before thee*, ver. 18. And if my father tell me, I deserve never to be looked on, and there is no reason on my part why hee should look on me as a son, or speak to me as a son; why, and I will

will confess that too, that my courses have been so sinful and vile, that I am not worthy to be called his son; not onely to be a son, but to be called a son.

4. *Supplication*; to intreat his Father, that yet he would look upon him, and own him, and accept of him.

Make me as one of thy hired servants. q. d. 'If I cannot obtain a sons place, yet I will beg hard for a servants place; and if I cannot get a choicer servants place, yet I will put in for an hired servants place; and if I cannot get any servants place, yet I will get to be as one of the servants, as one of the hired servants; which shewed the humility of his heart, and also the vehemency. When the heart is truly broken and humbled, any near relation to God, any owning from God will be acceptable to the soul; if God will look on the lowliness, on the unworthiness of the sinner, how pleasing is it to him

3. Thirdly follows the life of all, namely the *practical execution* of all this. This counsel enlarged it self to a resolution, and this resolution is crowned with an actual performance: for *verse* 20. *He arose, and came to his father.* Where again observe,

1. Some things or passages on his Fathers part, *viz.* 1. *His quick observation*; his *Father saw him,* ver. 20. nay, *he saw him when he was yet a great way off.* The very intentions and secret motions and close purposes of our Repentance are known to God: in this sense, he sees our thoughts afar off; many times God will not see the sinner quickly, but he will at all times quickly see the penitent. *I have seen him, and will heal him, &c.*

2. *His present commiseration,* [*His father saw him, and had compassion on him*] When *Ephraim* repented, and returned and lamented, why the Lord saith, *My bowels are troubled for him, I will surely have mercy on him:* So here, the father not only sees but compassionates. q. d. Look, the poor child is at length come back, he hath smarted enough, he shall be welcom, I will forgive him all.

3. *His gracious Acceptation,* expressed in three particulars:

One of *speedy readiness* [*The father ran.*] Mercy must speed to embrace a penitent: Swift are the feet of mercy to a returning sinner.

A second of *wonderful tenderness* [*The father fell on his neck*]. How open are the arms of mercy to take a penitent sinner into the

the bosom. Mercy hath not onely feet to meet us, but arms also to clasp and receive us, if we be penitent.

A third of *strong affectionatenefs* [*His Father kissed him*]. God hath not onely arms, but lips; he hath not naked mercies for a penitent, opening themselves in manifold promises onely; but also sugred mercies, mercies sealed with the kisses of his lips, with a sweet testimony that he doth accept of, and is reconciled to a penitent and returning soul.

2. Some things on the Childs part, which is *the real acting of his former resolution in an actual confession*, verf. 21. And here observe a strange interruption on his fathers part:

1. He staies not to hear all the confession and petition intended, though he have purposed to have said more [*and make me as one of thy hired servants*]. Why! the father stops him, prevents him; we propose a method many times, but God suddenly comes in with his mercies.

2. He cannot confess so much, but the father, though not in words, yet really doth much more; Fetch forth, saith he, 1. *The best robe*. 2. *The pretious ring*, and 3. *The comely shoo's*. We can bring nothing to God, but yet he can find enough for the whole soul: And 4. *The fatted Calf*. Ah! how infinitely different is the penitent condition from the impenitent: Now the child hath garments, hath ornaments, hath necessaries, hath comfortables; when we once truly turn to God, we shall find no lack; there is a complete happiness now come to this returning son, who adventured on the gracious disposition of his father: and there is a great gladness now in the father, for the penitential returning of his son. Our condition is best, and God is most pleased, when we turn penitents, *verf.* 21, 22. *Let us eat and be merry; for this my son was dead, and is alive again; he was lost, and is found.*

Thus briefly have you the sense of the Parable, with a division of the chief heads thereof: I will now proceed to pick out the moral observations which are couched in it, they may be reduced to three general head.

1. A *Sinners digression*, or aversion from God.
2. A *Penitents regression*, or conversion unto God.
3. A *Penitents acceptation* and favorable entertainment with God.

In the firſt, you ſee the ſinners going from God to miſery; In the ſecond, you ſee him returning unto himſelf by true penitency; In the third, you ſee God returning to him in mercy: In the firſt you ſee him loſing himſelf, in the ſecond you ſee him finding himſelf, in the third you ſee God finding of him. Sin loſes us, repentance finds us, and then God owns us.

I begin with the Sinners digreſſion or averſion from God, which is ſetforth unto us in *v.* 12, 13, 14, 15, 16. under the ſimilitude of a young man, who would have all in his own hands, and ſo he left his Father, took his pleaſure in Travels, ſoon conſumed all, and ſhortly brought himſelf to extreme neceſſiy and miſery. This is the literal part of the Parable: But the Moral part comprehends (if I miſtake not) theſe Propoſitions.

D. 1. *That Sin is a departing from God.*
Sin is a ſeparating from God

The young Prodigal, he muſt leave his Father, he muſt be gone, what doth it imply, but the ſinner is a departer? Sinning is a departing; we leave God when we betake our ſelves to a courſe of ſinning. Thus is it ſtiled in Scripture, *Eſai.* 1. 4. *Ah ſinfull Nation, a people laden with iniquity, a ſeed of evil doers, children that are corrupters; they have forſaken the Lord, they have gone away backward.* Here ſin is called a forſaking the Lord, and a going away, and a revolting, *ye will revolt more and more:* which is a falling off untruſtily from God. *Jer.* 2. 14. *They have forſaken me the fountain of living waters.* Heb. 3. 12. *An evil heart of unbelief, in departing from the living God.*

A two-fold departing.
Real.

Moral.

There is a two-fold Departing; One is *real*, when he turns away from the place or preſence of another, as *Jonathan aroſe and departed from his father Saul.* Thus no man can depart from God; for he being omnipreſent, is with us in every place: Another is *moral*, which is, when the heart or ſoul departs; and thus the ſinner departs from God, when his ſoul and affections leave him, and cleave to ſin. And it cannot be but that ſinning ſhould be ſuch a departing, for as much as God and ſin are moſt contrary, ſo that the ſoul cannot enjoy them both; if you will love and follow your ſins, you muſt leave God; and if you will love and follow the Lord, you muſt leave your ſins; for *what communion can*

can there be betwixt light and darkneß, God and sin.
  The Use of this may *inform us* of the *madneß and folly of a*   *Use.*
sinner, He will live in such or such a sin, and with greedineß he See the folly of
follows the inticements thereof: Well! thou enjoyest thy sin, the sinner,
but consider that thou losest thy God; and what doest thou get
in all thy delights, which are but *lying vanities,* whilest thou *for-*
sakest the God of thy mercies? Thy exchange is miserable, to
leave a God, and embrace a sin; to depart from the chiefest
good and happineß, and to make choice of the basest objects of
sin, which is worse then hell it self.
  A second moral observation is this, that *A sinner doth volunta-*   D. 2.
rily, of his own accord, depart from God. Here the Prodigal A sinner doth
makes choice of his own way and course, and desires to be left to voluntarily de-
himself, and to take his own course. God compels no man to a part from God.
sinfull course, nor is he the cause thereof, nor can Satan compel
the heart. A man in this regard is said to *tempt* and *entice him-*
self, and with *Ahab* to *sell himself to work wickedneß.*
  And therefore, The *sinner is utterly inexcusable* before God,   *Use.*
his mouth is for ever stopped, his sin and perdition is of himself. Therefore the
God is cleared in Judgment, who punishes the wicked who is sinner is inex-
the actor, contriver, and sole cause of his own sinnings. Take cusable.
any sinner who delights himself in a way of wickedneß, why!
he is voluntary in it: 'Tis true, in dispute he pretends an insuffi-
ciency or inability, but the real cause of his sinning is his own
will, for he *loves Darkneß rather then Light,* and had rather
serve his Lusts then God; he makes choice of them before God,
as the multitude did of *Barrabas* before *Christ*; and when Life
and Death, God and Sin are propounded, yea, and that with the
true rewards from the one, and severe wrath from the other, yet
he like *Issachar bowes down under the burthen, and loves rest*; he
had rather go on in his sins, and will not leave them: And therefore we alone are guilty of our own bloud, God is innocent as
well as just, our condemnation is but a due guerdon or paiment
for our own voluntary departings from God.
  A third moral Observation is this, that *The pleasures of sinning* Doct. 3.
will quickly end, and the end of them is extreme misery. The Pro- The pleasures
digal here will be gone, he must have pleasure, his Fathers house of sin will
was too strict; well, he begins his riotous living, but then you quickly end in
read that he quickly consumed and wasted all his substance, and misery.
                        C   brought

brought himself into such extreme necessities, that he became a servant to the swine, and fain would have fed his belly with the husks which they left, but none gave unto him. This point I intend more fully to press, which contains in it two branches: 1. *That the pleasures of sinning are but short.* 2. *That though delights and pleasures begin a sinfull course, yet extreme necessity and misery or streights do end it.*

The pleasures of sin are but short.

1. *The pleasures and delights of sinning are but short:* The riotous life of the Prodigal was a present consumption of his estate. The pleasure of sin is like a Candle, which in the very burning and lighting burns and consumes away. It is in Scripture compared to the *crackling of thorns*, which is but a speedy blaze; and to the Lightning, which is but a glance and a flash and away; and to a season, *the pleasures of sin for a season,* Heb. 11. which is a very inch of time, a τὸ νῦν, a little article of time; for though time be long, yet a season is but a short space. In *Job* the pleasure of sin is compared to *a sweet morsel*; a morsel is no great quantity, and though it be sweet, yet it slips quickly away from the tongue and palate. And the Apostle compares it to a *bait* wherewith a fish is taken; the fish looks on, and nibbles a little, and takes it down, and then away goes the bait. *Cain* pleased himself a while, but not long; for the sin of murther presently pursued and cried against him: And *Adam* before him, had but one taste of the forbidden tree, it quickly set his teeth on edge: *Gehazi's* gold and garments, and *Achan's* wedge, as they were stoln waters, and though sweet, yet short. So was it with *Ahab*, he got *Naboths vineyard* sinfully, but he scarce ever enjoyed it; he met with a mighty curse from God presently upon him.

In respect of estimation.

But here observe, that the pleasures of sin may be said to be short, 1. In respect of *estimation:* when the hearts of men judge of them as false, unlawfull, and short. Thus *Moses* esteemed of them, and therefore *refused the pleasures of sin, which were but for a season.*

In respect of duration.

2. In respect of *duration:* For if Life it self be not long, the pleasures of sin must needs be short. It is true, that as long as the impenitent soul hath a being, the guilt of his sin shall have a being and consistence in the soul, but at the utmost sinful pleasures extend not beyond our life, their date then of necessity must be expired, though usually they are extinguished or interrupted before

The Sinners Aversion from God.

before, and life is a very short tale, hour, moment. 3. *In com-* In comparison *parifon with eternity* ; though a man should live in the pleasures with eternity. of sin 20, 40, 60 years, yet what is that space of time to an eternity of sorrows and bitterness. Compare the longest time with eternity, it is scarce a considerable moment. But you may demand, Why should the pleasures of sin be so short ? *Sol.* Nay Reasons of it. you might rather demand, Why they should be at all ? for indeed real pleasure cannot arise out of sinful acts, yet a carnal and sensual pleasure there is, which is nevertheless short: Because

1. *Sin is never so pleasant, but it breeds that which is* Sin is never so *unpleasant* ; nay the more pleasure we find in it, the more pleasant but it displeasure it works ; like a draught of beer, which the more breeds that fully and pleasantly drops down, the more danger is added to the pleasant. patient: So is it with sin, it seems a delightful thing to you to follow your lusts, your evil waies ; but the more you sin, the more you increase your guilt ; and guilt is but a sword to cut the throat of your sinful pleasures ; It is like sweet poison, which goes down easily and delightfully, but it will suddenly disturb and crack the body.

2. *God hath cursed the waies of sin* ; and therefore though they God hath cursed the ways of sin. ged it with thorns, threatned all evil, miserable and judicial evil against it. And look as when a good man earnestly presses God upon his promises, his sorrowes shall not stay long, but sighs and tears shall flie away: So when a wicked man provoketh God by his sinnings, his pleasures shall be short, for the Lord will perform his threatnings against him.

3. *The pleasures of sin must necessarily be short, because consci-* Conscience *ence cannot be long quiet :* If you should wound and wound a man, cannot be long he will begin to feel, and to complain ; even your pleasant sin- quiet. nings are the most grievous woundings of conscience, and conscience will not bear, it will awake with blood trickling, and will be revenged of you with most bitter expostulations, severe accusations, unsufferable gnawings, and then where are the pleasures of your sins ? *Who can stand before envy ?* said *Solomon* ; so against conscience, the wounds thereof, yea and her woundings by it, *who can bear ?* thy delights will sink and flie off, yea thy heart will fail thee utterly, when conscience ariseth to accuse and condemn thy sinful pleasures.

C 2 4. *They*

The Riotous Prodigal, or

They raise up manifold afflictions. 4. They raise up manifold afflictions and calamities which shorten our pleasures and delights.

Sin will end in many miseries. But I proceed to the opening of the second branch, *viz.* the *endings of sin.* That though a sinful course may begin in many pleasures, yet *it shall end in many miseries, extremities, and straits.* There are diverse sorts of ending of things: some end by way of *annihilation*, as the souls of the beasts, they shall cease to be, they are resolved into nothing; some end by way of *perfection*, as the souls and waies of holy men, Glory and Salvation is their end; some end by way of *corruption*, as when the beauty of a thing is marred, or a goodly body is turned, and ends in a loathsome carkass, or sweet Wine turns to sharp Vineger. After this manner doth sin end, or a sinful course end: as it was with the day in which *Sodom* was destroied, it began with the *pleasant light of the Sun*, but it *ended in fire and brimstone*: Thus was it with those sinners, their delightful flames of lust ended in horrid flames of Vengeance. There are two sorts of sorrow and trouble: one *Penitential*, and the other *Judicial*; one of these sin must end in. *Achans* wedge pleased his eie, but it lost his life. *Ahabs* desire was satisfied to get *Naboths Vineyard*, but his blood paid for it in the *portion of Jezreel*. *Gehazi* obtained the *garments* and *talents*, and at the end a *Leprosie* to his dying day. *Judas* gets favour with the chief Priests, and money to betray his Master, but he got horrour of conscience, final despair and damnation for his treachery. *The young man* in the Proverbs is inticed with the filthy flattery of the Whore, her bed was perfumed with *Myrrhe*, but *her house is the way to hell, going down to the chambers of death*; those chambers of delight prove chambers of death.

Prov. 7. 17.

But to open this in some particulars:

Quest. 1. To what extreme miseries and streits may sin bring the sinner? *Sol.* 1. To those of *Body*; sin may be *rottenness of his bones*, and may infect him with the most nasty, irking, painful diseases, that he shall have no rest in his flesh: it may so poison his marrow, inflame his spirits, corrupt his humors, that many times the body, which was the instrument of sin, proves to be the great torment of the sinner. 2. To those of *Estate*; sinning may eat out a goodly estate, as the worm which is gnawing at the root of a tree, disrobes it, disflourishes it, pines and shrivels it: though a man hath quick parts, ample dealings, yet if he has secret waies of

Miseries of body.

Of estate.

The Sinners Aversion from God. 13

of sinning, his sins will blast him, they will be as the Moth which eats out the garment, or as the canker to the brass or iron. How many by such & such sinnings are quickly stript, laid low, brought to a morsel of bread, and are cloathed in rags, as the Prodigal here in the tex wasted himself out of all. 3. To those of *Name*, which is one of the three precious and tender things; *viz.* a mans *Eye*, a mans *Conscience*, and a mans *Name*. This is a precious ointment, a mans life is as his name is, yet sinning casts a flie into that ointment, a blur upon that copie, it procures reproach and shame, an hissing, a Proverb, a by-word, an odious name, a name that shall perish. 4. To those of *Conscience*, which are streits indeed, so that a man is almost distracted, knows not which way to turn himself either to God or man, day nor night, is weary of life, and yet afraid to die; he fears God, he fears man, he fears himself, he fears the shadows of things. 5. To those of the *imagining and thinking part of man*; a mans heart shall do nothing but meditate terrour, apprehend guilt; see the forms of bitter sinnings, and the Idea's of infinite wrath kindling from God against him, so that he shall be still amazed at the representation of his former sinnings, or at the expectation of future judgments. 6. To those of *the affecting part*: all his affections shall rise up as a tumult within him; burthens of cruel fear, tremblings of a fainting grief, and thick throws of hopeless despair.

Of name.
Fama,
Fides.
Oculus.
Of conscience.
Of the imagining and thinking part of man.
Of the affecting part.

Quest. 2. But why is it that sins, or sinful courses, end in such extreme miseries and streits? *Sol.* Reasons thereof are many: 1. *Because though the beginning of sin be from a deceived heart, yet the ending of sin is from a just God.* The corrupt heart begins sin, deluded thereto by sinful pleasure, but God puts a period to the sin in just judgment, in wrath and *tribulation upon every soul that does evil.* What we conceive about sin is one thing, and what God will do to the sinner is another thing; we make it sweet, but God will make it bitter at the latter end; The intentional way of theft is with delight, but the judicial end of theft is death; so is it in all sinnings, the intention of the sinner is to please his own corrupt heart, but the judicial end of it (which belongs to God, he being the righteous Judg offended) is misery. 2. *The true effects of sin must be made manifest.* Men would not onely question the Righteousness of God, but the unlawfulness of sin, if sinning should end peaceably. Well might they say with him,

Reasons of it.
The ending of sin is from a just God.

Finis. 1. operis.
2. operantis.

The true effects of sin must be made manifest.

him, *I have cleansed my heart in vain*, if sin should end in peace and blessing; but God by this doleful Catastrophe of sin doth convince man, that sin deceives them while it pretends so much pleasure, delight, contentment, and at length repays them with shame, loss, horrour and despair. 3. *Hereby men should learn that there is a difference twixt them who fear God, and such as fear him not.* For indeed, in this, among many other things, do godly ways and the ungodly differ: The Godly begin oft times in sorrow, in trouble, but the end of them is peace at the last; we see and meet with the worst of our journey at the first, as the Israelites did with the Wildernes and Sea, but they came to *Canaan* at length; but the Ungodly ways yield their best at first, their vanity, delights, like painted colours, fall off, and their worst is hidden, and appears at last: Alas, thou doest not imagine that hell which thy sinnings are kindlings, or that sword which it is unsheathing, or that death which it is breeding, or that horrour which it is maing within thee against thee; these are now hid from thy eyes, but yet they are the end of thy sinnings.

Use.

I now come to the application of this point. Is the entrance of sin pleasant, and is that pleasure but short, and ends that pleasure in miserable extremity, then 1. for

Information. All things are not safe which yet are pleasant.

1. *Information*; We may hence be informed, *That all things are not right and safe, which yet are pleasant. The ways of a man seem right in his own eyes*, said *Solomon*, and the motives of sin seem pleasant to our corrupt hearts; yet sinfull ways are false, and sinfull pleasures are nought and short. The first demand of any in point of opinion should be, *how true*, not how plausible; and of affection or action, should be, *How good*, and the next, how pleasant; not first how delightfull, but first how lawfull. We may not do about our moral acts, as we do in our civil, ask what fine Stuffs, but first, what good. The Apple, the forbidden Apple, which if tasted had death in it, was yet goodly to look on, *it was pleasant to the eyes*. And the Wine of which *Solomon* speaks, though it *bit like a Serpent, and stung like an Adder, yet it looked red, and gave its colour in the cup*. As all sins have after their commission something to back them, so they have before their commission something to enter them: After our sinning, there are corrupt defences and reasonings; and before our sinnings, there are corrupt pleasures and delights: As in the

Gen. 3. 6.

Pro. 23. 31, 32

the sewing of a Garment, there is a Needle to make way, and then a Thred to keep fast; so it is in the constitution of a sinfull course, there is pleasure to make way for the sin, and then there is love and defence which keeps fast the sin. Therefore we must in this be informed, not to entertain any thing becaufe it doth please and delight us, for usually that is sinfull which at first is delightfull; it is not how it pleaseth me, but how it pleaseth God: The soul of man naturally is very corrupt, and as it is with some stomacks which are foul, the worst diet is most delightfull, so it is with our souls being evil, therefore that which is evil suits bests with them and pleaseth them most. Pleasures of any thing must be judged by 1. *A Word of truth*; for if they be not good, as well as pleasant, they are sins factors; and 2. by *the respondency they have to a nature*, not as corrupt, but as *renewed*.

2. That *sin is not onely bad, but politick*; *not onely unlawfull,* but *deceitfull*. As it is with some faces which have natural wrinkles, these are dawbed over with painted glosses; or with some bodies which are crooked, these are bolstred out with secret stiffnings; or as with rotten wares, these are glazed over with gaudy dyings: So is it with sin, in it self a foul thing, a loathsome and odious thing (therefore in Scripture called an *abomination*, a *filthinefs*, a *vile thing*, a *disease*, a *rottennefs*, a *sore*, *putrifying sore*, &c.) yet it draws on the sinner by pleasure and delight. Sin doth not move us nakedly as sinfull, but cunningly as delightfull; it doth not tempt the young man to uncleannefs, and tell him, that *whoremongers and adulterers God will judge*; but *come, let us take our fill of love, I have perfumed my bed*, &c. as the strumpet in the Proverbs: It doth not tempt the person to drunkennefs, and tell him that no drunkard shall inherit the Kingdome of God, and that there is a woe belonging unto him; but it shews him the rednefs and colour of the Wine, and suggests the sweetnefs thereof unto him. So in sins of murther, it doth not shew that revenge which God threatens, but that acceptable revenge and way of ease which the sinner delightfully thinks on. As *Balak* sent to *Balaam* the rewards of Divination, and then desired him to curse *Israel*: And that *Apocalyptical whore* had in her hand *a golden cup*, and within that the *wine of fornication*: So deals our sin with us when it tempts us, it doth hide the hook, and shews the bait; it conceals the obliquity, and represents the

Sin is not onely unlawfull, but deceitfull.

beauty;

beauty; it covers the misery, and shews onely the pleasure, to draw and insnare our souls.

All sinners are extremely deluded.

3. *That all sinners are extremely mocked and deluded.* They may more safely say of their sins what *Esau* spake of *Jacob*; *Thy name is rightly called Jacob, for these two times thou hast deceived or supplamed me.* So may sinfull men say of their sins, Not twice or thrice, but always ye still mock and deceive me. I remember, that when *Josephs* brethren had cast him into the pit, *Reuben* anon returns thither, but finds him not; he was newly there, but he was quickly taken thence, and he said, *The child is not, and I, whither shall I go?* So may a man say of the pleasure of his sin, Even now they were, but now they are not: And instead of that pleasure, he may now be wringing of his hands, and cry out; 'The pleasure is gone and is not, the sin remains and here 'sticks; the draught is gone, but the poison is not gone; the 'delight is gone, but the guilt is present; the delight is fallen 'off, but the grief is present: And I, now I, whether shall I 'go? Conscience galls me, fears crush me, God abhors me, 'the world doth not help, friends cannot ease me; what I feel 'is bitter, and what I fear is worse: Ah my sins, you said I 'should have pleasures still, you said that I should not see misery, you said that God would be easily mercifull, you said these 'were nothing, you said that to morrow should be as to day, 'and much more abundantly: Ah that ever I trusted you, believed you, yielded unto you; you have deceived me; by a little 'pleasure I am now brought into, and left in the midst of all 'misery: Ah, you sins which were once so pleasant, can you 'not deliver me? can you not comfort me? do ye forsake me? 'is this your kindness? is this your delightfulness? where is 'it? I am bereaved of your pleasures, and by you, you alone, 'am I now sunk into the most soul-cutting and anguishing distresses.

Gen. 37. 29.

Sins, though temporally pleasant, yet are certainly dangerous.

4. *That though sins be temporally pleasant, yet they are certainly dangerous:* They end miserably, though they begin sweetly; like a River which begins in a quiet Spring, but ends in a tumultuous Sea. There are these dangers in the pleasures of Sin; 1. They are *apt to draw* and entice us, 2. *to bewitch* and entangle us. 3. *to enlarge the spirit of transgression within.* 4. *to hinder all true pleasures*, 5. *to sear up the ear and conscience against all holy counsel and remedy.* But

The Sinners Aversion from God.

But I pass to a second Use, which shall be of *Caution*, to take heed of being deluded any longer with the pleasures of sin : me thinks *Eliphaz* spake punctually, and to the purpose ; *Let not him that is deceived trust* (any more) *in vanity, for vanity shall be his recompence*. Though sin be a while pleasant, yet hearken not unto it, suffer not thy self to be deceived by it : *Wine is a mocker, and strong drink is raging, and whosoever is deceived thereby is not wise*. The like he speaks of the unclean woman, *whose heart is snares and nets*, (still dressing them to catch the bird) *and her hands are bands*. The same may be said of any sins whatsoever. But now to move and quicken your hearts to take heed of sinning, though mixt with pleasures and delights ; Consider these motives.

Use 2. Caution. Take heed of being deluded with the pleasures of sin. Job 15.31. Prov. 20.1. Eccl. 7.26.

Motives.

1. *What thing that is wherein thou doest take pleasure ?* Why ! what is it, O man, that hath enticed thee ? and what is it, O man, which in thee is so enticed ? It is *sin* that hath enticed thee, and it is *thy soul* which is thus enticed by sin. Sin enticeth thee, then which no evil is worse; thy soul is enticed, then which no part in thee is so precious. And wilt thou adventure that precious soul, that immortal soul, which must live for ever, wilt thou adventure it for a sin, for one draught of sinfull pleasure ? Wouldest thou adventure all thy earthly estate for one draught of Beer, (as *Esau* did his for *one mess of pottage* ?) Thou wouldest not : Yet wilt thou adventure the eternal being of thy soul for one minutes pleasure of sin. Though thy sins be pleasant in thine eyes, yet they are odious in Gods sight, though thy sins do delight thee, yet they do grieve him, they do incense and provoke him : Hast thou nothing to take pleasure in, but that which provokes thy God, and will damn thy so !

What is that wherein thou doest take pleasure.

2. *Thou mayest enjoy thy pleasures without sin.* Hast thou not a Wife to delight thee, an Husband, Children, many outward comforts, not a God, not a Promise, not a Christ, that thou longest onely for forbidden fruit ?

Thou mayest enjoy thy pleasures without sin.

3. *Is sin a thing to take pleasure in ? did it not shed the bloud of Christ ?* doth it not break a righteous Law ? transgress an holy Will ? grieve the Spirit of God ? cast the clouds of threatnings over our heads ? bring down all our Judgements on body ? kindle our terrours in Conscience ? heap up all our wrath against the day of wrath ? is this the thing of thy pleasure ? call you

Is sin a thing to take pleasure in ?

D this

this a delight! If one should say unto thee, Be drunk, commit filthiness, and within an hour after, thy whole body shall be roasted in a fire, or thy skin shall be flead off thee; or every bone in thy body should be distinctly broken in pieces, wouldst thou now sin? And what are these punishments to sins themselves? and what are these punishments to those of Conscience, or to that of Hell?

God can easily shorten thy pleasures of sin.

4. God can easily shorten thy pleasures of sin, and he hath many waies to do it. First, Is not his Word of mighty power? is it not a discerner of the thoughts and intentions of the heart? can it not divide twixt the marrow and the joint? Is it not a light, and a fire? Is it not the sword of God, a two-edged sword, able to pierce, and that with quickness, and that with sharpness? Or, Secondly, if yet thou be able to maintein thy sins, and by the strength of sensual pleasures to beat off the purest convictions, and revelations, and pursuits of the Word, cannot the *Spirit of God* drive home the sharp displeasure of God? cannot he break through the midst of all thy resolutions and delights, and so enter into thy conscience? can he not in a moment awaken that drouzie conscience? can he not inliven that seared conscience? can he not injoin it to stand up and act its accusing power, when he hath irresistably inlightned it, and set the great sins of thy delight before thee? and when conscience is deeply wounded, where then are all thy pleasures? O, it will be as bitter then unto thee as hell: the wrath of God felt, and the guilt of sin felt, and the terrors of Conscience felt, O how will they drown thy pleasures, sink thy spirits, and (if God be not the more merciful) confound thy soul! Yet this God can do, and he can easily do it; if he saith but the word, My wrath be upon him, Conscience arise and accuse him, it is done, and then where are thy delights? Those sins of thine, unto which thou hast been enticed by a little false pleasures, even they alone shall rise up, and be the sufficient punishment for all their pleasures. Or, *Thirdly*, He can shorten thy pleasures by *many Judgements*; he can lay such a disease upon thy body, or such a loss on thy estate, or such a rottenness on thy name, or such a vexation upon thy spirit, or such a madness in thy mind, or such a cross in thy delight, that thou shalt find no more pleasure in any thing. Or, *Fourthly*, Can he not send forth the *King of Fears*, that which thou least thinkest of,

and

The Sinners Aversion from God.

and which will make thy joynts to tremble, *Death it self* upon thee? Hath not He the Keys of Life and Death; and when life is gone, where then are the pleasures of thy sin? Sin makes way for death, and death to a wicked man, though it makes not an end of his sinning, yet it makes a full end of the pleasures of sinning; thou shalt never rejoyce in the way of thy wickedness more, thou shalt never taste delight more, neither lawfull delight, nor unlawfull delight. And cannot God do this suddenly? and art thou able to withstand him? art thou greater then he?

5. *Thy pleasures of sin will end in bitterness.* Read the Scripture, see whether it be not so, and I beseech thee tell me, hast thou not found it so already? canst thou not say, That thy sin *hath been an evil thing, and bitter?* Canst thou not say, *What fruit have I in those things whereof I am now ashamed?* Two things remember, There is a certainty of bitterness for former sinnings, *Eccl.* 11. 9. *Rejoyce O young man in thy youth, and let thy heart chear thee in the days of thy youth, and walk in the ways of thy heart, and in the sight of thine eyes; but know thou, that for all these things God will bring thee into judgment.* 2. *Thou knowest not the manner of that bitterness.* The sinning, that is thy work; but the punishing of thy sins, that is Gods work: thou hast taken the pleasures which sin delivered unto thee, and thou must now take the bitterness which God will inflict on thee. And canst thou tell. 1. *When* the Lord will begin to account with thee, either to night, or to morrow? thou art not secure a moment. Secondly, *How* the Lord will begin with thee, whether in thy body, or in thy soul, or in both, in conscience, or estate? Thirdly, *How far* the Lord will extend the cup unto thee; perhaps it shall be in thy hand a cup of fury, and trembling, and amazing horrour, and whether he will have thee to drink to the lowest dregs of his wrath, how knowest thou? This bitterness after thy pleasures may be purely judicial, which shall not be tempered with any comfort, nor yet at all with the hope of any mercy; it may be an endless displeasure from God.

Object. Yea, but we mean to repent hereafter, and so we will prevent all that bitterness.

Sol. 1. You cannot repent at pleasure, though you sin at pleasure; nay, the more pleasant thy sins are, the more they do disable thee to repent; for they by thy delights do hold thy affecti-

Thy pleasures of sin will end in bitterness.

How sudden.
How great.
How endless.

ons more firm, and increase thy sinfull acts more often; and both of these do cross repentance.

2. But suppose thou shouldest repent, yet must thy sins be bitter unto thee; though thou mayest believe with joy, yet thou must repent with sorrow: Repentance is a mourning weed, a sad lamentation, a reformation with tears.

3. And believe me, thy penitential work will be the more sowr, by how much the more sweet thy sinnings have been. In Physick (if I mistake not) they hold, that *Dulcia cito vertuntur in bilem*, the sweet meats are most easily turned into bitter choler; so shalt thou find experimentally, thy sweetest sins to prove (even if thou doest repent) thy sharpest burthens and griefs. *Davids* adultery cost him more tears, then any sin of his that we read of.

Use 3. Direction.

A third Use shall be of *Direction*: If any man of us hath been enticed, that we have taken the sweet bait, that sin hath insnared us by its pleasures, my advice is, Let him vomit up the morsels again, and no more to embrace the sin for the pleasure, but to abhor the pleasure for the sins sake. The rules which I would prescribe, are these,

Presently imbitter those sinfull pleasures.

1. *Presently to imbitter those sinfull pleasures:* Do you your self begin the work, defer it not to God; if you begin it in a penitential way, God will spare you in a judicial way. *Judge your selves, and ye shall not be judged of the Lord.* See and consider what thou hast done; True, I have had the pleasure, but by sinning God hath had the dishonour, much dishonour, great dishonour, frequent dishonour. Oh grieve for this, that thou shouldest ever delight in that which grieves thy God; that sin should be pleasant to thee, which is so dishonourable unto him: Afflict thy soul, and do this presently, take down thy sins the second time with bitter herbs, which at the first thou swallowedst down with sweet delights; or rather cast them out with hearty sorrow, which thou didst hastily take in with vain pleasure.

Think of the bitternefs of former sins, and that future sins will be more bitter.

2. *For time to come, let two thoughts lodge between thine eyes;* viz. 1. *Former sins have been bitter though pleasant;* 2 *Future sins, be they never so pleasant, will prove more bitter.* O let these be engraven in thy soul, never believe thy thoughts, thy hopes, thy confidences, nor Satan any more, nor thy own false heart; sin was pleasant heretofore, but it ended bitterly; if thou any more

The Sinners Averſion from God.

more hearken unto it, it will be leſs pleaſant; and much more terribly bitter; the ſecond ſurfeits of ſin do either breed more ſtupefaction, or more confuſion in the conſcience.

3. Study to find and taſte that pleaſure which ariſeth from an entire communion with God, and a converſation which is upright. Talk what thou wilt, the ſoul will have ſome pleaſure or other; if it pitcheth not on God, for it, it will ſtray aſide to ſin for it. Now then ſtrive to take pleaſure in the Lord, and in his work, and in his way, and in his Graces, and in his Chriſt: This ſhalt thou find of ſpiritual pleaſure *Study to find and taſte pleaſure in communion with God.*

1. *It is more ſweet a thouſand times then that of ſin:* One glaſs of Spring-water is more ſweet then a Caldron of Sea-water; though the Sea be larger, it is fouler and mixt. 2. *It is more laſting and durable:* Ah, thou needeſt not to repent of it; it is a Spring, and not a Puddle, and its foundation is conſtant; never forſake thy mercies, for lying vanities. 3. *It is more affecting then the other:* That of ſin goes not beyond the ſenſe and affections, but this of God enters into the conſcience, which is the ſeat of trueſt comfort or ſaddeſt miſery. 4. *It will drown your ſinfull pleaſures:* Oh, thou ſhalt find ſuch a real value, ſuch a ſurpaſſing excellency, ſuch a full contentment in the all-ſufficient God, that thou mayeſt well ſay as Ephraim, *What have I to do any more with Idols!* So thou with the vain, piercing, falſe, ſhort, pleaſures of ſin. Therefore ſet thy heart not on ſin, but holineſs; though it may fall out, that at the beginning the ways of God and holineſs may ſeem bitter unto thee, yet know, 1. This bitterneſs either is by reaſon of thy former pleaſant ſins, or thy preſent ſinfull nature: 2. That aſſuredly thy delights in holineſs will bring thee at laſt to that right hand where there are pleaſures for evermore; for as ſin, though pleaſant in entrance, is bitter in concluſion, ſo holineſs, though it ſets forth with a ſtorm, ſhall land ſafely in a calm.

And when he had ſpent all, there aroſe a mighty famine in that Land, and he began to be in want. Luke 15.14.
And he went and joyned himſelf to a Citizen of that Countrey, and he ſent him into his fields to feed ſwine. 15.

The Prodigal hath done with his *Eſtate*, and all the pleaſures of of it; now we are to confider him both in his *ftreights*, and in the immediate ufe which he made of them. Touching the former, I fhall fay little; onely you may obferve, 1. The occafion of it, *a great famine:* 2. His fence of it, *he began to be in want.* Touching the latter, you may obferve two things, 1. His practice under his ftreights, *And he went and joyned himfelf to a Citizen of that Countrey:* 2. His fuccefs or reward, *And he fent him into the field to feed fwine.* By the Citizen generally is expounded, the Divel; by the Countrey, the World; by Swine, wicked Men. There are two Prepofitions which I would hence obferve, *viz.*

1. That though fin brings men into ftraits, yet ftraits do not always bring men from fin.
2. That the further men go on in fin, the worfe work they fhall find it to prove.

1. Doct.
Though fin brings men into ftraits, yet ftraits do not always bring men from fin.
Diftinguifh betwixt Poffibility and Infallibility.
Reprefentation of fin, and Reformation of fin.
Impediment to fin, and amendment of fin.

That though fin brings men into ftraits, yet ftraits do not always bring men from fin. You fee here the prodigal is pincht with famine, and yet he comes not home to his Father, but goes on further in his own ways. For the opening of this Affertion a little, you muft diftinguifh betwixt,

1. Poffibility, *ut medium*, and Infallibility, *ut remedium.*
2. Betwixt *Reprefentation* of fin, and *Reformation* of fin. Straits and miferies are ordinarily the Looking-Glaffes, wherein we may fee the face of our finnings, but they are not always the Phyfick-Glaffes, wherein we find the cure of our fins; they are more often an eye-falve, than an heart-falve; they may be a cualm to bring fin to fence, when yet they are not a potion to bring off the finner from wandring.
3. Again, twixt *impediment* to fin, and twixt *amendment* of fin. Miferies and ftraits may be a Dam to ftop the Current, when yet they are not like the Prophets falt, effectual to heal the waters. A Lock may ftop a Thief, but not alter him. When the the Prophet *Eliah* met *Ahab* with a fharp meffage about *Naboth*'s bloud and Vineyard, it made him go foftly, it cooled his fpirit, but did not change it. Miferies more ordinarily (for the prefent) make men lefs forward and bold in fin (as *Jupiter's* Log did quafh the noife of the Frogs) when yet they make them not fo good as to turn them from fin: They do (like a fhower of rain and hail) make the Traveller to ftand a while under the Tree, who yet intends to hold on his journey again.

4. Again,

4. Again, twixt *Declamation* and *Declination*. A sinner under misery may play the Oratour, and yet never prove the Penitentiary; he may both indite and accuse the sin, which yet by no means he intends to condemn and execute. It is one thing to confess, that my sins do now hold me in bonds of affliction, and thereupon to profess a discharge of such inmates; and it is ano'her thing, really to repent and to forsake those sins, yea, the very those which a man more then suspects as patrons of his misery. So that straits may bring sin to sight, and the sinner to a stand, and to a confession, yet not always to repentance and to conversion; which is true, *Declamation and Declination. This is true.*

1. Of *inward straits*; those manacling and severe fetters of conscience, to which no distresses are comparable. The boylings of conscience may be but like the boylings of the Sea: a person may have many guilts fretting there like a Leprosie, and gnawing there like death, and flaming there like hell itself, and yet not be brought off from sin. As *Judas*, who betrayed his Master (O think of that sin!) and fell into quick horrours of conscience, and these cured him not, but he proceeded to despair, and then to self-murther. *Of Inward straits.*

2. Of *outward straits*; which do never come without cause, but many times go off without remedy; they may in all the sorts of them say oft times, as they did of *Babylon*, *We would have healed Babylon, and she would not be healed*. They find us evil, and they leave us worse, as we do our friends upon their dying-beds; *Ye revolt more and more, why should ye be smitten any more?* Isa. 1. 5. This is evident in *Pharaoh*, whose hardnings increased (like the iron) with the strokes. Or like the Snake which, *Salvian* spake, did multiply by occision. It was no better with *Saul* and *Ahab*, nor with that King *Ahaz*, who is blackt and fingred out amongst all the Kings of *Judah*, because he *sought not to the Lord in his distress, but trespassed yet more against the Lord; This is that King Ahaz.* 2 Chron. 28. 22. Thus it was with the *Israelites* many a time, who felt the scourge, but mended not their work, but with bleeding shoulders oft times went away to sin; and no sooner were the Assizes past, but they adventured the way to the prison again. *Of Outward straits.*

If you now demand the *Reasons* why straits or miseries do not always bring men off from sins? I answer, *Reasons of it.*

1. Be--

Onely true grace brings men off from sin.

1. Because, *that onely true Grace is it which brings men off from sins.* Afflictions may be considered two ways, either *immediately* and solitarily, so they are not forcible to bring any man off from his sinfull course; no punishment whatsoever is an immediate Agent, and sufficient to turn a sinner. *Mediately* and concomitantly as they are sanctified, (*i.*) either as they light upon an heart sanctified, or as sanctifying Grace, with them, or by them is wrought in the soul, and so they may bring off the heart from sin; not the naked afflictions, but grace in the heart afflicted, turns the heart; for nothing turns the heart from sin, but that which is contrary unto sin: now though miseries are contrary to the *sinner*, yet not to the *sin*; they are contrary to the sinners ease and way, but not to the affection and delight of sin, which may, and oft times doth live and remain even under extreme miseries. Now then, many men are in miseries by reason of sin, yet they turn not from sin, because they want true grace, by the strength of which alone men come off from sin, for that it is which changeth the sinfull heart. You know that Physick ordinarily works as the body is, into which it is received; there must be some strength of nature to help it, else it will not work; the Philosophers rule being true, *Quicquid recipitur, recipitur ad modum recipientis*. The heat which melts the wax, hardens the clay; and the juice which goes into the Rose makes it sweet, but that which goes into the Nettle makes it stink; so it is with miseries, they work as he is on whom they fall; if true grace be not in the heart, what good use can an evil heart make of them?

Straits are sometimes meerly judicial.

2. Secondly, *Because straits and miseries are sometimes meerly judicial*, onely the strokes of revenging Justice. You know, that there is a great deal of difference 'twixt a whip which causeth smart, and a plaister which causeth healing: All miseries which befall us are not healing plaisters, sometimes they are judicial lashes, they are not the wounds of a friend, but of an enemy. God is said in *Job*, to *distribute sorrows in wrath*, and then they are not remedial effects, but exitial; they come not then with their teaching and recovering assistance, but are the beginnings of a greater judgment yet to come. You know that God plagued *Pharaoh* in a judicial way, the miseries which befel him were as sharp, and great, and many, and came as thick as most that ever befel any man of whom we ever read; nevertheless they were so far from

reclaiming

reclaiming of him from his sins, that still he hardned his heart, and exalted himself; If you should demand why it should be thus with him, that no, not quick, nor great, nor many plagues did him any good? I answer, One cause, amongst many, is this, Because they came onely in a judicial way; they did not come out of the hand of a mercifull Father, but of a provoked and revenging Judge: If there be not grace in the heart to joyn with, and to improve the affliction, and if there be not mercy to send out and bless the affliction, it will then never do us good, it will not turn us from our Sins.

3. Thirdly, *The Heart of a Sinner may be above his miseries*: There is not such a power in miseries alone, as to over-rule the heart, or to mend it. As it was with *Gallio*, when the Jews did beat *Sosthenes*, and kept a stir, the Text saith, *He cared not for any of those things*: (*i.*) they made no prevailing impression on him, so as to divert his purpose: In like manner may it be with the miseries which personally befal a man, his heart (notwithstanding) may not regard them, neither may he lay things to heart, they may be thrown off, in respect of any beneficial impression, as water from a rock; as is evident in *Pharaoh*, and in the Jews, see *Isa.* 42. 25. *He hath powred upon him the fury of his anger, and the strength of battel, and it hath set him on fire round about, yet he knew it not; and it burned him, yet he laid it not to heart*. Here was anger, and fury of anger, and poured out, and so as to set him on fire, and to burn him, yet he laid it not to heart. If you should take dross and corrupt stuff, and put it into the fire, you shall never refine it, it is to no purpose, the founder in such a case would melt but in vain, *Jer.* 6. 29. so in this case: For the proper operation of all miseries is onely moral, and rather representative then effective (*i.*) they can of themselves do nothing; perhaps they may point a man to his sins, but his heart may effectually resist that evidence of sin by the rod of God, as well as by the word of God. Look as it is with the Light of the Sun, though great and gentle, yet it never opened a blind mans eyes; nor yet the Lightning, which runs swiftly in the time of Thunder: For that natural privation exceeds the strength of such Agents. So it is with a sinner, his heart may so cleave to sin, that neither the Light of the Sun, I mean the blessed Word of God, nor yet the Lightnings and Thunders of afflictions may di-

The heart of a sinner may be above his miseries.

E   vorce

vorce him; so great may the power of sinfull love be, that not the kindest mercies, nor the sharpest miseries (alone) shall ever be able to melt him, or turn him. The love of sin may increase even an incorrigible and desperate perversness in the Will; such perversness, that the afflicted sinner (possibly) may be so far from leaving his sins, that therefore he will cleave to his sins the more, and in a proud despite will forsake God; as that prophane person, *This evil is of the Lord, why should he wait for him any longer?* 2 Kin. 6. 33.

Men hate holi-
ness more then
miseries.

4. Lastly, Miseries do not always bring men off from their sins, because *Men hate holiness and a godly life, more then miseries:* (i.) There is a greater contrariety twixt their sinfull natures and holiness, then twixt them and miseries; it is confessed, that misery, in some respect, is contrary to nature, at least to the peace and ease of nature; yet misery is not so distastfully contrary to a wicked nature, as holiness and godliness. Sin can live and rule whiles the sinner is under misery, but it never can do so when he is under grace. You know that a man never can turn from sin, but when he loves holiness; now holiness is that which many a sinfull heart, like *Paul* before his conversion, persecutes to the death. Why! if some sinfull hearts will venure the loss of heaven, rather then they will be holy, will they not rather then endure the loss of friends and estate? &c. and if they will adventure the pains of hell rather then they will come off unto an holy life, will they not rather endure some temporal distresses? &c. and doth not this shew, that some had rather be passive in misery, then active in holiness?

Use 1.
Information.

Now I proceed to the usefull Applications of all this to our selves: Where 1. for *Information*. Do not straits and miseries always bring men off from their sins? then

An afflicted
condition no
infallible testi-
mony of a safe
condition.

1. *An afflicted condition is no infallible testimony of a safe condition.* Some people are of an opinion, that if God doth punish them in this life, in crosses, losses, sicknesses, penuries, &c. they have all their portion of misery already, and undoubtedly shall be saved. To which I reply, 1. Though as the *Israelites* came at length to *Canaan* through the Red Sea, and through the wilderness; so a person may after many afflictions and miseries come to heaven: Heaven can admit of a poor *Lazarus,* and of a distressed *Job,* and of a pursued *David.* 2. Yet it is not always so:

A.

A perfon may be under many miferies, and notwithftanding them, he may never be happy: the meer prefence of miferies is of common providence, and not a diftinguifhing priviledge; by what is before us, whether outward good, or outward evil, we can know neither love nor hatred; but as it is with the Ships at fea, whether of the Kings Loyal fubjects, or of hoftile pirats, either of them are expofed to winds and ftorms, to leaks and rocks, and fands; fo is it with good men and bad men, each of them are expofed to outward calamities, as each of them are capable of outward mercies; there may be a change in their outward condition, when yet there is no change in their inward difpofitions. *Job* may hold faft his uprightnefs under all his miferies, and *Pharaoh* may retain his hardnefs under all his Judgments. And where the finful affection and practice is ftill retained, he fhall not be free, becaufe of his prefent miferies, but for ever rejected, becaufe of his continued iniquity.

2. *That the Conjunction twixt Sin and the finful foul is very ftrong*: For as much as very great ftraits and miferies effect nothing many times. You fee here, that though the Prodigal had fpent all, and a famine, yea, a great famine arofe over the Land in which he was, yet he is fo far from returning and giving over his finful courfe, that he does not fo much as think of it or mind it: affuredly, the Covenant of affection is very firm, which cannot be untied with the faireft promifes, nor with the fevereft indurances. When the Lord fhall come to a finner, meet him in his courfe and way, and becaufe of his contempts and rebellions, diftrein his eftate and goods, and then lay an Attachment of ficknefs on his body, and more then this, indite him for his life by the fummons of death; And yet neither the lofs of all the Mercies which once he had, nor the prefence of all the Evils which now he feels; neither the poverty of his Table, nor the rags on his Back, nor fhivering in his Bones, nor anguifh in his Confcience, no, nor appearance of Death, nor yet the reprefentations of Hell, do turn him from his finful affections and courfes; judge, whether the tree be not tough, which no Wedge can cleave; and the difeafe be not deep, which no Potion can remove; and fin doth not fit clofe and ftrong to the heart, which no not extreme miferies can occafionally and effectually difcharge and quit. There are no penalties fo grievoufly and unfpeakably afflicting

The Conjunction betwixt fin and the foul is very ftrong.

and miserable as those in Hell, which cause weeping and gnashing of teeth; and yet these, though highest for intention, and endless for duration, never are able to turn the sinning soul: so madly and excessively is the person enthralled, that the greatest Calamities effectually avail not to bring him off from the least course of Iniquities.

Wonder not if some men Revolt after miseries. 3. *Not to wonder if some men make ordinary Revolts after ordinary miseries:* Some persons may (like some stones which yield a sweat in change of weather) somewhat reflect on themselves, and relent, and confess, and profess what they will be and do if God will take off his heavy hand. And may I not appeal to many of you this day, whose hearts have been visited with the plague, that thus then it was with you, &c. Yet when the plague is off, and the smart and fear gone, the bitterness of death is past, that health succeeds the sickness, and plenty succeeds the want, and strength succeeds the weakness, good Lord! what are they? how live they? what do they? what mind they? what affect they? what work they? Do they leave their sins? ah, as the Pharisees made their proselites twice as much more the children of the Devil then before, so these men become more vile, more profane, more careless, more rebellious against the truth of God, more earthly, sensual then ever. Brethren, if as *Solomon* spake in another case, *when thou seest a violent perverting of judgment and justice in a Province, marvel not at the matter:* So, if thou seest a man to pervert the judgments of the Lord, to pervert his afflicting hand, to go on in his sins after he is punished for his sins; I say, in this case do not much marvel at the matter, for miseries alone cannot make any saving impression, or sanctified alterations. If men may hold fast their sins even under their miseries (as a Thief may steal under the Gallows) what marvel then if they go on in their sins after their miseries? And what cause have we to think, that any pious semblances and pretences should hold long, which did owe themselves to such temporary causes, as were never able to alter the sinners heart, though they were in some degree able to stop the sinning person?

Eccl. 5. 8

Use 2.
Reflect upon our own hearts. But I proceed to a second Use, which shall be a little to reflect on our own hearts and wayes, and to enquire how it is with us, notwithstanding the miseries and straits that are upon us, as *Solomon*

mon spake concerning sin, *Who can say, My heart is clean?* that I may speak this day concerning punishment of sin, Who can say, I have been free? As it was in *Egypt*, upon the departure of the Israelites, so it hath been of late with most of us, there is scarce an house of us where at least one hath not been dead. I may confidently affirm, That either death in opposition to Life, or death in opposition to Livelihood, to some one kind or degree of outward comfort, hath within this year befallen most of us that are now here this day. Nevertheless, I pray you tell me, Can you shew your repentance yet, as you can relate your straits and miseries still? Have not we, the Ministers of God, faithfully and plainly told you of your sins? have not your miseries and straits been clear Glasses to represent your sins? have not your Consciences delivered up your sins, and said as *Jonah, I know that for my sake* (so they for our sake) *this great Tempest is upon you,* Jon. 1. 12. Were you not in great fears, in great griefs and troubles of mind? need I say, in great Protestations and Purposes? But now I demand of you, Have your great straits brought you off from your great sins? did they not find thee in a sinful way, and do they not now leave thee walking in that path? Ah! and must the Lord say of you, They refuse to receive instruction? *they turn not to him that smites, yet have they not returned to me; they will know no shame; they are reprobate silver; they are not refined nor purged; their scum is not departed; wherefore should they be smitten any more? they revolt more and more.* Well, if it be thus with thee, yet remember, 1. That this continuance in sin (notwithstanding our miseries) may give us just suspicion to fear that our Corrections come not from mercy, because they go off with impenitency. You need not ascend into heaven, to pry whether your chastisements come out of the land of Indulgence or of Vengeance: when they come from a merciful hand, they are assisted with some recovering and curing blessing. The Prophet saith, *That the Lord did not smite his people as he smote others*: and in two respects he manifests the difference; one of Proportion, *He did debate with them in measure,* ver. 8. Another of Operation, v. 9. *By this shall the iniquities of* Jacob *be purged; and this is all the fruit to take away his sins.* God never strikes in mercy, but he in some measure betters the sinner. Look as every outward good, if it comes in mercy,

If we continue in sin after miseries.

We may suspect our corrections cemes not from mercy.

Isa. 27. 7.

it

it proves a step unto more holiness; so every outward misery, if it come in mercy, it proves a stop, nay an abatement of more sinfulness. 2. *We may justly fear that our hearts are hardned;* for the soft heart will tremble with *Josiah,* at a correction in a threatning, and much more will it melt and amend when it is in execution, as he in *Job* 34. 31. *I have born chastisement, I will not offend any more.* But when the heart can feel wrath, as well as hear of it; and receive the stroaks with stoutness, and strike God by sinning, when God strikes it by punishing; is it not hardned, unsensible, I had almost said, desperate? And is an hardned condition, a good or safe condition? 3. *Do we not treble our accounts unto God by not coming off from sins which have brought on our miseries?* Now we must answer 1. For the sins which brought down our corrections: 2. For the continuing in those sins still. 3. For doing this, being corrected thus for our sins; not onely thy sins, but Gods punishments (being thus abused) come into the account, the Vineyard was reckoned with for the *pruning*, as well as the *withering*. 4. And lastly, *What can we look for from God, when former miseries bring us not off from former sins?* Christ said, *Sin no more, least a worse thing befall thee;* and will not a worse judgment then attend us for worse sinnings? It is with divine punishments, as with the messengers of a displeased King, who in his name summons us to yield and become loial; and if you despise a few messengers, they indeed may return, but then more and greater are sent, perhaps not to parley, but to destroy: If one punishment brings not off from sin, it doth onely go back to fetch a greater; and thou canst not tell but that the next messenger may be death it self, and then somthing worse then death.

Use 3. Apply our selvs to such waies under our miseries, as may bring us off from our sins. In general. A sanctified heart. A sanctified use In particular Repentance.

The last use which I will observe from this point, is, since miseries do not alwaies bring men orf from sins, therefore to *apply our selves to such waies,* and to get those things *under our miseries, which may bring us off from our sins.* In the general, two things available hereto: 1. *A sanctified heart*; until the heart be sanctified, can it possibly break off from sin? 2. *A sanctified use*; you must not be senseless, nor yet impatient, but under every hand of God seek for direction and blessing from God: Secondly, in particular, I conjecture these things mainly conduce: 1. *Repentance,* which you know takes into it these branches: 1. Serious consideration of the present condition, and of the end of present afflictions.

We may fear our hearts are hardned.

We treble our accounts to God.

What can we look for from God, when miseries do not bring us off from our sins?

The Sinners Aversion from God. 31

ons. 2. Solid humiliation. 3. Earnest praier. 4. Effectual reformation 2. *Love of God*, and more intire communion and delight in him, and with him. Afflictions will drive you oft from God, unless you love him. Even a small stroke is enough to mend and bring in a loving child. 3. *Faith* to believe our pardon and acceptance. Nothing more avails with the soul to leave the course of sin, then when it can be assured if it comes back to God it shall receive the pardon of sin. Therefore God generally propounds to his afflicted people, an hope of mercy, as the great motive to bring them home from sin to himself by true repentance, *Joel*, 2, &c. All which are wrought by the Spirit of God in the use of the Word, and shall be given unto us, if under our miseries and straits we do earnestly crie and pray unto the Lord.

Love of God.

Faith.

And he sent him into his fields to feed Swine.] You have heard of the Prodigals design under his misery to relieve himself; he did not return to his father, but *joined himself to a citizen of a far country*. Now yee are to hear of the success of this design, how much it mended his poor and famished condition, viz. nothing at all; and that will appear in two particulars : One *in the basestness of his service*. That *citizen sent him into his fields to feed swine*. Of all creatures the most nasty and filthy, these must he serve, and none but these: his whole service was to be base, and therefore he is sent into the fields to perform it; any houshold-service and home-service (though mean) had been tolerable. Another, in *the nothingness of his reward* or wages; he did the basest service, and without the least husk of paiment: for it follows in *vers.* 16. *That he fain would have filled his belly with the husks that the swine did eat, and no man gave unto him.* If he had had any thing afforded, either to have nourished, or to have procured nourishment, though it had been but mean, nay the meanest; but to have nothing at all, for the sordidest service of all; yet this was the fruit of his sinful design, that he was set upon a most base work, and without any profit or relief at all; whence I conjecture we may observe this second conclusion, *That the further men go on in sin, the worse work they shall find it to prove.* You see it a manifest truth here in the Prodigal, his sin drew down his penury; notwithstanding this, he proceeds to his sins, and now he is sent to the Swine, &c. For the better opening of this Assertion, premise with me some few particulars.

Doct. 2.
The further men go on in sin, the worse work it will prove.
Here is premised.

1. A

The Riotous Prodigal, or

A Suppofition.
Wicked men ufe to go on in fin.

1. *A fuppofition*, viz. *That wicked men do ufe to go on in fin.* They are faid in Scripture to proceed from evil to worfe, and to add *drunkenneß to thirft*, and to *fill up the meafure of iniquity*, and to *know no fhame*, and to *revolt more and more*, and to grow worfe and worfe, 2 *Tim.* 3. 13. therefore is fin in them compared to a *Canker*, which frets from place to place, or eats up from part to part; and to a *fretting Leprofie*, which difrufeth it felf from a leffer to a larger compafs; and to a *Plague*, which by degrees feizeth on all the fpirits; and to *Leaven*, which fpreads over all the lump. And this is verified of them every way, whether they live in eafe, or live in mifery; profperity and eafe do but flefh them the more, adverfity and punifhments do not turn them at all; fmiles or frowns, word or rod, mercy or mifery, neither of them do alter, but after both they yet put forth, they will lanch further: As he in the Proverbs concerning his Wine, *When I fhall awake, I will feek it yet again*, that may be faid of evil men; though they have felt many a fmart blow from God for their finnings already, yet they will look back to this trade again, they will ftill deal unjuftly: What *David* fpake in another cafe, they will fully act in this of Sin, *I will be yet more vile*.

1 Tim. 2. 17.
Levit. 13. 8.
1 Kin. 8. 38.
1 Cor. 5. 6.

P. or. 23. 35.

A Pofition.
Though after punifhment men be progreffive in fin, yet they fhall never be fuccefsfull.

2. A Pofition, which is this, *Though after punifhment they will be progreffive in fin, yet they fhall never be fuccefsfull in fin:* They may renew their work, but they fhall never amend their wages; they may fet up again, but they fhall break again; if they, after fo great a fhaking, will build upon the fame foundation, they fhall find their future labours to end in the fame ruine: Nay, that's not all; but as *Jofhuah's* curfe upon the man who fhould again build the City *Jericho*, was, that *He fhould lay the foundation thereof in his firft-born, and in his youngeft fon he fet up the gates of it*, Jof. 6. 26. So will it prove to the perfon whofe fins God did ftrive to demolifh, and overthrow by former punifhments, if he again will prefume to fet up the gates of them, recover them to their ftrength by future love, and further progrefs; he fhall be fo far from being hereby more fuccefsfull, that his condition doth become more fearfull; he doth lay his foundation again in the ruine of his foul, and fhall build up the gates with a greater curfe from God. Therefore you read of fuch who are entangled again, *That their latter end is worfe then their*

their beginning. 2 Pet. 2. 20. Men are entangled again, when (either by the vigour of conscience, or sharpness of affliction, &c.) they have made a pause or stop; but, like the restrained River, which climbs over the Dam, so they get over these, unto their course of sinning again: Now saith the Apostle, these men shall never better their estates, nay, they make them the worse; the latter end of them, or with them, is worse then the beginning.

Thirdly, know, That by progress in sin, after punishment, the estate is worse, *Formally, Judicially, Eventually.* 1. *Formally worse:* For, if sin be it which makes the estate bad, then more sinning must needs be that which makes the estate worse; as on the contrary, the additionals and incrementals of Grace, (i.) when a man doth add one degree of grace to another, and riseth in a better, and a stronger, and fuller acting of grace, hereby the moral perfection of his soul is much more bettered and perfected; so when the habits of sin admit of more love of sin, more exercise of sin, that a man doth go on from one sin to another, by way of addition, or in the frequent practise of the same sins, by way of iteration, he cannot but make his sinfull nature much more sinfull, more filthy, and more vile; as, when a man doth twine one thread upon another, or one cord upon another, he adds a greater strength unto it; so, when a man shall rowl and file one sin upon another, &c. by further progress in sin, the very pollutions are more spread, and more established, and more enlarged, by it a man is always more under the pollution of sin, and more under the dominion of sin, as the Proselytes were made ten times more the children of the Devil.

Progress in sin makes the estate worse Formally.

2. *Judicially worse*; which appears in two particulars, *viz.* 1. In a *Dereliction on Gods part*; he doth more sadly leave such a soul, give it up to its own lusts, and its own vile affections, and unto Satan, to rule mightily and efficaciously in such a child of disobedience, who loves to adventure in a known way of curse and misery, so that the Lord may withdraw himself, and desert that progressively sinning soul, and not aid and assist it in case of most horrible lusts, or of most hideous temptations. 2. In *Condemnation on Consciences part:* For the progress in sinnings, as at any time, so after the time of punishment for sin, will make and raise a louder cry, and a fiercer sentence from the conscience. A man who will not repent for the lashes on his back, shall by his conti-

Judicially. In a Dereliction on Gods part.

In Condemnation on Consciences part.

F nuance

nuance in sin, quickly feel the lashes of Scorpions in his soul; as more guilt doth arise from sinfull practices, so more horrour doth ensue upon more guilt; more guilt is but like a great storm at Sea, or like a great raging of a disease.

Eventually. 3. *Eventually worse:* My meaning is, that by his continued sinnings, he shall not onely continue, but much more enlarge his outward miseries, and straits, and punishments. *I will punish you yet seven times more.* Levit. 26. *Pharaoh* still hardned his heart,

Verbs.
Verbera.
Vulnera.

but God still followed him with sorer Judgments, destruction of his fields, and then of his cattel, and then of his children, and at length of his own life. As it is with a Bird in a Net, the more she flutters and stirs, the more is she hamper'd and involved; so it is with the sinner, the more he stirs on in a sinfull way, the more doth he enwrap, and intrap too, himself with greater mischief. The *Israelites* did begin to murmur against God, and God then as it were did privately correct and chastize them; afterwards they did revolt from God, and then he did let loose some of the *Canaanites* and *Midianites* upon them, who did greatly distress them; at length they grew common in Idolatry, and very audacious in their Rebellions against God, and then they were carried away captive by the *Babylonian Armies:* So that if you read the History of them, you shall evidently discern, that every further sinning of theirs, was nothing else but a further engaging of themselves unto greater calamities, and as it were an adding to more cords wherewith they were more held and beaten.

Reasons. If you now demand the Reasons, or causes, why that the further men go on in their sinning after punishment, the worse work they shall find it to prove. I answer, the Reasons thereof may be

Sin is a barren and unprosperous thing.

these. 1. *Sin is a most barren and unprosperous thing. Who hath hardned himself against God, and prospered?* said *Job* 9. 4. his meaning is this, that sinning is no prosperous and thriving way. It cannot be, that a man should go on in sin, and yet meet with prosperity and good success; and therefore *Solomon* saith expresly, *He that hardneth his heart, shall fall into mischief.* Pro. 28. 14. So that sinning is not onely not prosperous, but it is also mischievous; it will do a man a mischief sometime or other. *Can a man gather grapes of thistles?* said our Saviour: It cannot be; for thistles produce blossomes according to their kind, of a filthy and sharp quality:

quality: But as for Grapes, which are of a sweet and refreshing and delighting nature and virtue, they come not from such a root as a Thistle. Comfort, and blessing, and peace, and prosperity, and good success, these cannot grow from a sinfull course; the land of sin is alwayes a land of famine and barrennefs, and watered onely with clouds of wrath, and set with thorns of vengeance, a land wherein a person must not look to see good. So that what the Lord said of *Coniah*, *Write that man childleſs*, the same may be affirmed of every sinfull way; It is a barren, an accursed, an unprofitable, an unsuccessfull way: No way to better, but the onely way to increase wrath and punishment to the sinner.

2. Nay, sin is not onely a barren thing, unable to produce any good or blessing, but sin is also a *very wicked thing*, and provoking. The sinnings of men, are the provocations of God to wrath and punishment, and the more sinnings, are still the greater provocations. *How long* (saith God to *Moses* of the *Israelites*) *Will they provoke me?* Look as the froward and perverse walking of a child provokes the parent (*i.*) stirs up his displeasure and anger: So the sinnings of men, they do provoke the Lord by them unto jealousie and wrath, and stir up his displeasure against them; therefore it cannot be, but that if men go on further in sinning, they should find a worse thing of it; for every sinning is but as it were a further kindling of the fire, and a new incensing and provoking of the Lord; and the more that the Lord is provoked against a sinner, the more misery and punishment is the sinner like to feel from God.

Sin is a very provoking thing.

3. *No punishment which any sinner hath already felt, is a discharge, but onely a part of greater punishment yet due unto him.* As the first-fruits were a pledge of the crop. We may not think, that because God doth for precedent sinnings afflict and judge the sinner in some particular kind, therefore he is now secured and discharged for the time to come, as if God did not intend to reckon with him for after sinnings: But this we must know, *viz.* 1. That infinite and full wrath is the due debt of the transgressing soul; not one or two punishments, but all the testimonies and degrees of wrath. 2. That particular demonstrations of Gods wrath, are no acquittances, but rather certificates of a fuller writ yet behind. *If ye yet shall walk contrary unto me* (saith God to the *Israelites*, *Lev.* 26. 21.) *I will*

Punishments already felt is no discharge from greater to be inflicted.

will punish you seven times more for your sins. q. d. If ye will go on in sinning, I will surely rise higher in punishing, I have greater punishments yet behind; so that if you consider that debt unto sin, which is the full latitude of punishment, it must be, that if the sinner goes on in sin, he shall not thrive, but still become more miserable.

The Nature of Divine Justice. 4. Nay, do but consider the *Nature of divine Justice*, and this will clear it to be so. Divine Justice appears in two things, one in an *Homogeneous Retribution*, if I may so phrase it, *according to the quality of actions and persons. If thou dost well, shalt thou not be accepted? and if thou dost ill, sin lyeth at the door*, said God to *Cain*; there is an acceptance upon well doing, and vengeance for evil doing. The just God will recompence every man according to the quality of his work; so that in this regard the sinning person, who doth not change his sinful work, must look for no other pay from God at any time, but the wages for sinful work, which the Apostle assures us in *Rom.* 2. is tribulation and anguish. Another is, *A proportionable Retribution according to the extension of actions or works*; and therefore you read of more stripes, according to the greatness of the fault in the knowingly disobedient servant. Now, as it were against the natural retribution of Justice, to give unto the wicked as unto the righteous; so it were against the proportionable retribution of Justice, to repay either no punishment to a greater sinner, or less punishment for greater sinnings; That when he continues worse in sinning, he should either prosper at all, or that the punishment should be more mittigated, when the offence is more raised and aggravated.

To teach that no time is safe to sin. 5. Lastly, *God would hereby teach all men, that no time, whatsoever, is safe to sin:* Before punishment come, it is not safe to sin; for we see that sinners do pluck down punishments, and as it is with the winds, which bring the clouds, and fly away; yet the clouds pour themselves down on the earth; so the sins which bring out the threatnings of God, though in respect of particular facts, they are gone, yet the threatnings pour down many a curse and misery upon sinners: and when punishments are off, it is not a safe time to sin, forasmuch as God is still as ready to punish, as men are forward to sin; as we may see in the Israelites, whose *pride and murmuring* caused the *earth to open her mouth*, and to *swallow up Corah, Dathan,* &c. And the next day when they *murmured* again, God presently

The Sinners Averſion from God.

fently ſent the *Plague* amongſt them, which ſwept away many thouſands of them; for as time is not allowed to ſin, ſo no time can at all ſecure the ſinner from puniſhment.

Object. But now againſt all this truth it may be objected, *That we do not allwayes ſee it ſo*: that men after puniſhment, making progreſs in ſin, find it to prove a worſe work, in reſpect of greater miſeries and ſtraits. Nay, Secondly, We ſee oftentimes the contrary.

Sol. I anſwer to the firſt part of the Objection, That you muſt diſtinguiſh,

1. 'Twixt *immediate puniſhment*, and twixt *certain puniſhment*: It cannot be denyed, but granted, that a worſe puniſhment commeth not alwayes immediately unto the adventurous ſinner: Indeed ſometimes God doth ſhoot an other arrow of puniſhment, as ſoon as the ſinner ſhoots up a ſecond arrow of rebellion; as you read in the Iſraelites caſe of murmuring; I ſay, ſometimes God doth thus, but alwayes he doth not ſo. Sometimes he doth ſo, that ſinners might know his Juſtice can be quickly even, and meet with a daring ſinner; but alwayes he doth not ſo, becauſe that even great ſinners might confeſs ſomewhat of his great patience. Neverthelefs, there is a certainty of a worſe miſery unto the progreſſive ſinner; for as when God defers a Mercy, it uſually comes down in a cluſter; ſo when God defers a Judgment, it ordinarily falls down in a thunder: he is therefore in the Pſalms ſaid to *whet his ſword*. The whetting of the ſword is but a time of preparation, and a putting on a ſharper edge to give the deeper wound; ſo, &c. and he is ſaid to be righteous in recompenſing vengeance, therefore there is a certainty of a worſe puniſhment.

2. Twixt *Viſible* puniſhment, and *Real* puniſhment: though to the eye of others, a man may ſeem either not to be puniſhed at all, or leſs now in his continued ſinnings then before: yet the perſon may be more really puniſhed then before; the miſery upon him may be a greater miſery, not for the quantity of the thing, but for the quality of his affection to the thing; for that evil is alwayes moſt grievouſly miſerable unto us, which meets us in our higheſt way of Love, or cloſeſt ſuſpicion of fear. And again, the greatneſs of the puniſhment is as God mingles more wrath in the conſcience at the time. Even a little outward miſery, if it be joyned with a greatly accuſing and condemning conſcience,

ence, is a misery, more then all other miseries besides.

Obj. But we see the contrary.

Object. Yea, but *we do see,* that wicked men, who do continue their sinnings more after their punishment, *that their conditions are so far from being worse, that they are most merry and prosper?*

Sol. This is not always true. This argues the sorer wrath. First or last they shall find it true.

Sol. 1. *This is not always true,* but onely in some, and but for some time. 2. These very *things prove to them very sore judgments*; for by the abuse of them (like an ill stomach, which gathers a surfeit upon good meats) they do more increase their sinnings, and the wrath of God. 3. *First or last they shall know that it shall not be well with the wicked,* and that between a former punishment and a greater there may step in many mercies, as twixt the fits of a Fever, some real slumbers and pauses.

Use. Conviction of The vanity and deluding presumption of the sinner.

Now I proceed to the Application of this Point, which shall be for *Conviction.* 1. Of the *vanity and deluding presumption in the heart of sinners,* who imagine, that worse they cannot be, and as much misery is befallen them as can be, and therefore they will on to their sins again. Let us not deceive our selves; that God with whom we are to deal, is of infinite power and wrath, and the conscience of a guilty sinner is capable of infinitely many miserable impressions. The Bee may leave her sting in the flesh, and so be disabled, &c. Therefore let no man say as *Agag, Surely the bitterness of death is past*; you know *Samuel* presently *hewed him in pieces before the Lord in Gilgal.* Alas! thou knowest not the wrath which is yet behind. God doth never fully manifest his wrath upon any sinner in this life; nor doth he punish him so in any kind, but that a greater judgement, *a worse thing,* as Christ spake to him in the Gospel, may yet befal him. Consider, that as greater judgments are yet behind all the punishments which we have felt; so it is Gods method to begin low, but to end his work of Judgement heavily: he doth by some lighter afflictions skirmish with a person, or a Nation, and if they yield not, then he will bring the great Army of his Plagues and Judgements. And again, know, that multiplication of sins is a just cause for the addition of Judgements. Renewed sinnings are alwayes the more hainous, and strong in deserts; but renewed sinnings after punishment for sin, are yet of a deeper dye, because *They relish much of Presumption*; though God hath already testified his displeasure, yet the sinner will

The Sinners Aversion from God.

will adventure on his wrath, and provoke him again. They *receive universal condemnation*, the finner now fins againft all the waies of recovery; the *Word of God* which called upon him to be wife, and to receive inftruction, and to return unto him that fmote; *The punifhment or rod*, which did tender him the fins which brought this upon his back; The *mercy* of God which drew off the wrath, and though it might have been a deftroying fword at once, that deftruction fhould not have rifen up the fecond time, yet it fo wrought with the matter, that he would try the finner yet a little longer, thou mightft have been among the dead, yea among the damned for thy former finnings, yet mercy hath fo tempered juftice, that time is left thee to repent, and this fpace thou abufeft to fin again; yea, though juftice met with thee for them already, yea though mercy releafed thee yet a little longer, yea though thou didft confefs thefe fins, yea though thou wert greatly troubled for thefe fins, yea though thou didft refolve againft thefe fins; and if thou thus finneft more, will not thy punifhment be greater? Doth not God hate fins now as well as then? Or if thou be greater in tranfgreffions, will he be lefs in juftice? Canft thou expect mercy fhould come more eafily, when fin is raifed more deeply. *He that being often reproved hardneth his neck* (faith Solomon, *Prov.* 29. 1.) *fhall fuddenly be deftroied, and that without remedy:* The fame may be affirmed of being punifhed; ufually perfeverance in fin after punifhment, brings a fudden and a fore deftruction. God hath many arrows which flie over the heads, and after that hee hath arrows to wound the hearts of his enemies. You know that there be not onely warning-pieces, but murdering-pieces in the roial artillery. The punifhment which a man hath already felt for his fins, are but fo many warning-pieces to repent, to return from fin; but if men will harden their hearts, there are murdering-pieces; God can fo deeply ftrike, that deftruction fhall not rife up the fecond time.

2. The fecond conviction fhall be of *Duty*: If the further men go on in fin, the worfe they fhall fpeed; then let us learn a double duty; 1. To avoid fuch things as will occafion a further progrefs in fin after punifhment. 2. To apply our felves to fuch waies as may take us off from finning being punifhed. 1. *Vitanda*, The things which we muft avoid as occafioning a further progrefs in fin are thefe 1. *Ignorant Mifconftruction*; as if Gods arrows did flye out as his, who fhot at an adventure, and lighted

Coviction of duty.

Avoid,

Ignorant mifconftruction,

on

on *Ahab*, so that our punishments are but meer casual things; naked acts, but no lessons. Nay brethren, if we had but an ear to hear, every affliction and punishment hath a voice to speak; this may be said of every punishment, what *Ehud* said to *Eglon*; *I have a message unto thee from God.* 2. *Atheistical pride*; as *Pharaoh, Who is the Lord, that I should let Israel go*? When a person will exalt himself in the times of wrath, and will not tremble nor fear before the Lord, but slights the operation of his hands, and for all this will not lay to heart the hand of God, alas, this makes way for sinning.

Atheistical pride.

3. *Froward Impatience*: when persons are sensible of punishment, but vex against God, who strikes so close, yea and like that King in the strait, *This evil is of the Lord, why should I wait on the Lord any longer?* When men will forsake God because hee doth punish them, this is a further sin, and makes way for more sinning. The soul, which is most apt through a murmuring impatience to question God, will be apt through a presumptuous confidence to sin against God; in the dead sea there is least sailing, and in the raging sea, there is most ship-wracking.

Froward impatience.

4. *Empty confessions*, when persons satisfie themselvs with words, and a meer form of Repentance, putting on for the time a grave countenance, and fetching a sigh, and dropping a tear, and acknowledging that all is not well; but all this while they search not to the root, they do not strive to examine their hearts, to humble them, to cleanse and reform them; and what then can be expected, but upon some convenient occasion the old heart should return to its old waies and courses? *Pharaoh* confessed *that he and his people had sinned*, but still he hardned his heart, and would not let Israel go: Hypocritical humiliation or repentance, because rising from mutable causes, lasts not long, nor changes the disposition of the soul. The sore which is but covered and not cured, will break out again.

Empty confessions.

5. *Negligent remissions*: An heart which likes not to change its course, may yet for the obtaining some special good, give out unto the doing of much good, and for the removal of some evil, make a stop of much sin. You may observe, that sometimes in the heat of a punishment, how our hearts (perhaps) fall down before the Lord, and we are very urgent on him, and very diligent; spend much time in his service, and a kind

Negligent remissions.

The Sinners Aversion from God.

kind of watchful tenderness is come upon us against sin, but then we let fall our hands, and our candle quickly burns more dimly, our task abates, our affections grow slack, our purposes, our services wear away, and we begin to grow as forward to our sins as before: the liking of God, and of his waies and services cool, and sinful occasions grow as pleasing and acceptable. Remember it, that man will be quickly bad, who grows negligently good, and the soul which is weary of Gods service, is ready for sins work.

6. *Partial reservations;* when men in or after punishment will profess against the great bulks of sin; and as *Pharaoh* (at length) was willing to let the people go, but to stay the little children, so we wil bid defiance, and seem to take resolution against our former great iniquities, in the greatness of them, but yet we will keep back and not part with such and such things, which perhaps formally are not sinful, but occasionally they may (to our corrupt affections) prove so. Why! how can it be but such a soul should make yet a progress in sin, who reservs still an incendiary motive, a quick and captivating incentive unto sin? The river will quickly over-spread and fill the channel if you give it way: spare but your self in occasions, and they will bring on first the lesser trials of sin, and the lesser trials will quickly ingage you to greater adventurings, and some adventurings will easily bring you to your old courses. *Partial Reservations.*

In the second place let us *apply our selvs to such waies as may take us off from sinning, yet more after punishment*, which you have heard doth make the condition yet worse. The directions which I would commend unto you, are these: *Directions.*

1. *In all punishment for sinning follow the writ, open it, and see whose name is in it*; my meaning is, enquire into thy self, search diligently for whose sake this evil befals thee; as the *Mariners* in *Jonah* concerning the tempest, they did cast lots, that they might know for whose cause that evil was upon them; so should we in the presence of our punishment, when Gods hand is in any kind upon us, search and lift up our hands unto God, to shew us the special reasons of his wrath and indignation; for though earthly parents do many times inconsiderately in passion chastize their children after their own pleasure, yet God doth it wisely and never without cause; we may say of all our punishment what the Prophet saith to the Israelites, *Jer.* 4.18. *Thy way and thy doings have procured* In all punishment for sin, search out the Cause.

G

cured these things unto thee, this is thy wickedness, &c. Punishments never prove reformations, until first they be informations; they never cure the heart, unless first they clear the eye: We must first spell the Lesson, before we can take it forth; therefore this do, if thou canst not find the specialty of thy provocations, 1. Look thy afflictions and punishments well in the face; perhaps thou mayest in them see the very feature of thy sin which hath caused God to punish thee; very usually, that punishment which is a Rod, is also a Glass, it shews us the fault for which we are lashed. 2. Observe thy self in the estate when thy punishment doth come; do but recal thy bent of heart, course, ways, imagination, devices; sometimes a man is taken by the punishment, when he is dealing in a way which doth more especially provoke God. 3. Peruse the Word, and well consider what sins have brought down such kind of punishment. God doth many times keep his course of the same punishments with the same sins; else the Apostles dehortation of the *Corinthians* from Idolatry and Uncleanness, which was the *Israelites* sins, for fear of the like punishments, were somwhat vain. 4. Lastly, Regard the first and more frequent verdicts of thy own conscience. There are two times when Conscience deals more home and faithfully with us: One is, when we are to die; Another is, when we are to suffer; in a time of judgment and affliction, we find, as *Josephs brethren* did, the remembrance of former evils, *Surely this is befallen us because of our brother,* &c. said they: So our hearts tell us, Well, assuredly this comes upon me for my Swearing, for my Drunkenness, for my Uncleanness, for my Covetousness, &c.

Pares culpæ. Pares pœnæ.

When the sin is discovered, go to God in an humble confession of it.

2. When your sins are brought to light, that you can say, Here is my punishment, and there are my sins; then go to God with them, to him that smote thee, *By most humble and broken Confession,* that thou hast done wickedly, but the Lord hath dealt most righteously; acquit him, but condemn thy self: Accuse and indite thy sinning soul; O Lord, thus and thus have I sinned and provoked thee, &c. Deal ingenuously with the Lord, and freely confess unto him, and never leave, until thy soul be afflicted for sinning, as well as thy body; until thou canst grieve a thousand times more for thy sins, than for thy punishment; for the dishonour which God hath felt by thy sinnings, than for

the

The Sinners Averſion from God.

the ſmart which thou feeleſt under thy puniſhments. *By moſt vehement and conſtant Petition*; and that for two things eſpecially, viz.

1. *Reconciliation with that God whom thou haſt ſo much provoked by thy ſinnings*: As *Moſes* ſaid to *Aaron, Take a Cenſer, and put fire therein from off the Altar, and go quickly to the Congregation, and make an attonement*: So let us ſpeedily ſtrive to reconcile our ſelves unto the Lord, beſeeching him to love us freely, to receive us gracioully, to pardon us for his own ſake, to remember our ſins no more, not to contend with us for ever, but to caſt our ſins into the depths of the Sea, and mercifully to be our God. And in this buſineſs of reconciling our ſelves with God, take notice, 1. Of the *meritorious cauſe of it*, which is the bloud of Chriſt, called therefore our *attonement*, Rom. 5. and our *Propitiation*, 1 Joh. 2. 1. Now beſeech the Lord to look on thee in Chriſt, and to remember the bloud of the everlaſting Covenant, which was ſhed for the remiſſion of ſins, and to make peace: Beſeech him to be reconciled unto thee in and through Chriſt, and do thou ſtedfaſtly truſt unto him by faith for it. 2. *Of the means of it*. To the Word, to Prayer: O be earneſt for ſuch diſpoſitions upon which the Lord will ſeal mercy and forgiveneſs. He will be gracious to the cry of the mournfull ſoul, *Iſa*. 30. 19. and to the penitent, 2 *Chron*. 7. 14.

2. *Sanctification*: Alas, if the Lord ſhould lay upon thee as many and as great plagues as he did on *Pharaoh*, and ſhould they come as thick on thee as on him, or any that ever thou didſt read of; yet if the Lord did not give thee a ſanctified heart, or if the Lord did not co-operate with the afflictions in a ſanctifying way, thou wilt be ſo far from deſiſting, that thy heart after a while will grow as wicked as before. It is not abſolutely the puniſhed ſoul, nor is it abſolutely the troubled conſcience, nor is it abſolutely all that we can ſee or ſay which will divert our future courſe of ſinning; but it is the ſanctified heart, the new heart, which will make us to leave old ſins, and live new lives: Therefore to the Lord muſt we go under our afflictions, and beſeech him to open our ear to diſcipline, and to purge away our iniquities, and to make us partakers of his holineſs, and ſo to cauſe us to bring forth the more peaceable

Go to God by earneſt petition for Reconciliation. Numb. 16. 45.

Sanctification.

able fruits of righteousness: and note this, That all this must be done not in a fit, for a little time, but habitually; we must not cease confessing, until we can heartily mourn; we must not cease confessing, mourning, praying, until we find the Lord reconciled unto us, and our hearts changed and renewed. Now those sanctified Qualities, which more specially a punished sinner should beg, to divert him from progress in sin, and to turn him off from sin, I conjecture are these; 1. *Hearty contrition for sins past:* He who is a merry Penitent, proves an easie Delinquent; if former sinnings be no Grief, future sinnings will be no Fear; he will never with stedfastness learn a good Course, who can without mournfulness come off from a bad Way. Beg of God for ever to make thee sensible and mournful. 2. *Real Conversion:* That the very frame of the Mind, Will and Affections be changed; the Frame more then the Form: that thou become a new Creature, get a new heart and Spirit. 3. *A sincere love of God:* If thy heart knows not yet how to love God, it never forgat how to go on in Sin; there is nothing which heals the Soul of Sin, so as the Love of God: this sets the heart on him and makes it to cleave unto him, and tender to please him. 4. *Solid fear of God:* A reverent awe, both of his goodness and of his greatness; this will strike off security, and hardness, and presumption, and set us in Gods presence, and keep the conscience tender, and increase humbleness, &c. 5. *Watchfulness over our special corruptions*; which, if any, will make us to halt soonest. Do not forget how much they did provoke God already, and how assuredly bitter they will prove, if thou dost resume them.

Sanctified Qualities to be begged.
Hearty Contrition for sins past.

Real Conversion.

A sincere Love to God.

Solid Fear of God.

Watchfulness over our speciall Corruptions.

Vers. 16. *And he fain would have filled his belly with the husks that the Swine did eat, and no man gave unto him.*

These words comprehend in them two things,

First, The utmost design of the sinful Prodigal, *He would fain have filled his belly with the husks that the Swine did eat.*

Secondly, The utmost disappointment, of that utmost design, *And no man gave unto him.* According to either of these, there are two Propositions observable by us; *viz.* That a sinner will go through, and try the utmost extremities and wayes ere he will return

The Sinners Aversion from God.

return from his sins. 2. That nothing shall avail the shuffling and trying sinner, untill he doth return from his sins. When the Lord forsakes a man, nothing avails to help a man.

That a sinner will try all wayes, and go through the utmost extremities, ere he will return from his sins. The Prodigal here spends all, yet he returns not; he is *pinched with famine*, yet he returns not; *he joyns himself with a Citizen*, and he sends him *to feed Swine*, yet doth he not return: if he could have got but the husks which the *Swine* did eat; husks are but poor, empty, light things, miserable nourishment; but if he could have made any shift, any way to have supported himself, he would not have returned unto his Father. Thus you read of *Pharaoh*, that though there were a Climax of plagues upon him, and wonders of ruine upon his Land, and Cattel, and Servants, rising like a Tide and Flood, yet till it came to his first-born, and the next stroke was to reach his own life, he would not obey the Voice of the Lord in letting of Israel go; like obstinate defendants in a City, which will lose one Outwork after another, and suffer the Undermining of their Walls, ere they will come to terms of Capitulation. So we read of the Israelites before the Captivity, how extremely they did endure a very succession of Judgments, and variety of strange punishments before they would return? Amos 4. 6. *Cleanness of teeth, and want of bread; yet have they not returned to me, saith the Lord.* Ver. 7. *Rain was withheld*, and great scarcity was there of water; yet, Ver. 8. *Have ye not returned to me.* Ver. 9. *Smiting, with blasting, and mildew, and the Palmer worm, yet,* &c. Ver. 10. *Pestilence after the manner of Egypt, and the Sword; yet have ye not returned.* Ver. 11. *Overthrowing some of them as God overthrew Sodom and Gomorrha, and pulling some of them as a firebrand out of the burning; yet have ye not returned unto me, saith the Lord.* And thus was it with them after the Captivity, all the famine and miseries, which they suffered in the Siege, where the *mothers were forced to eat their children of a span long.* Lam. 2. And all the mercilefs devourings of the sword, and all the kinds of destroying sicknesses, did not turn them to the Lord against whom they had sinned; but after all, they spend the utmost of their pollicies for safety, running into *Egypt*, flying unto *Ashur*; they tryed all sorts of fruitless confidences, before they would return unto the Lord;

Doct. 1. A sinner will try all wayes, to the utmost extremities ere he will return from his sins.

Lord, therefore doth the Lord threaten to *hedge their ways with thorns, and to make a wall that they shall not find their paths.* Hof. 2. 6. (i.) he would cast them upon such a condition that they should not go any further, or if they did, they should have little ease, they should walk as upon thorns, upon continual prickings and woundings; and all this must be done before they will *return to their first husband,* verf. 7. Now for the clearer opening of this Assertion, consider of these particulars:

<small>This is to be understood of the natural temper of the sinner.</small>

1. *That it is to be understood of the natural temper of the sinner.* The sinner may be considered two wayes under extremities: *As effectually assisted by the preventing grace of God,* which is of surpassing vertue to renew the soul, and to conquer its stubbornness and aversness, and effectually to persivade and draw in the heart to yield unto God, and to give up its weapons of lusts. The which grace (if God infuseth) at any time whether before, or under, or after afflictions, then the sinner doth not wander in the paths of perversness, nor doth he hold out so long, but in stead of trying all ways to continue in his sins, he will speedily assay all the ways to be freed from them. *As left unto his own corrupt spirit,* and the projects, contrivances and ways thereof. And thus it is with him, like a besieged enemy, which will retreat from hold to hold, and dispute every inch of ground, before he will give up the City: So is it with the sinner, his heart will devise one defence after another, and he hath yet another shift, though he be many times hardly beset in his name, or in his estate, or in his body, yea, or in his conscience. And God doth narrowly watch over him, and doth spoil him of his many false confidences, and deals more smartingly with him to yield and return; yet he hath not onely much subtilty of spirit behind to delude all, but also he hath exceeding stubbornness of spirit to oppose all the means which are used for his conversion.

<small>Distinguish of the wayes whereby God doth deal with a sinner.</small>

2. *We must distinguish of the ways whereby God doth deal with a sinner;* which are of two sorts: Some are *Victorious ways,* wherein the Lord undertakes the conquest of the heart himself by the immediate power of his own grace, to pluck down strong holds, and to cast down high imaginations; upon which, as the conversion of a sinner doth infallibly ensue, so likewise presently and speedily; for this way exceeds the strength

strength of rebellion in sin, and in despite of it overcomes the heart. It is the stronger man dispossessing, and the stronger hand pulling us out of the powers of darkness. Others are *Moral wayes*, which consist onely in external means; not in the infusing of grace, but rather in the proposal of it, and invitations thereto by counsel, reproof, threats, rewards, and seconding this proposal with some or many miseries: the Proposition, *That a sinner will use all the wayes and methods ere he will return from his sins,* is to be understood onely, when God deals with him in a moral way, by the presence of means onely, (not otherwise) for which his corrupt heart may be too strong.

3. *We must distinguish of turning from sin:* It is two-fold, either *Hypocritical*, and feigned; and thus many times at the first, upon the very denunciation of a Judgement, as *Ahab*; or upon the perception of it, as *Jeroboam*, when his hand was struck; evil men may seem to confess, and to grieve, and to forsake sin, and to seek unto the Lord, and pretend to serve him. *Real*, and solid; when the heart is truly affected with a sound detestation of sin, and the occasions thereof; and with a sincere affection of love to God, and endeavour of new obedience. Though the former may be acted by the sinner without the applying of himself to the utmost extremities, yet the latter is not.

_{Distinguish of turning from sin.}

4. There are *two sorts of sins in a person*: Some which are more *useless*, either for the profit, or for the pleasure of the sinner; they are not the favourites: Others are more *special*, which are wrought into singular affection; the custome of practise, and the much experience of their damnable delights and revenues have exceedingly indeared the soul unto them. Though a sinner might more easily be upon parting terms with an unprofitable servant, an unserviceable sin; yet when the divorce is to be made twixt him and his special lust, the sin of his love and affection, the sin which lies in his bosome, this he will not easily part with. A man will endure much pain ere he will part with his right hand, or suffer his right eye to be pluckt out; he will stir much, and rage much, and project much, and adventure much, ere he will be perswaded to let this *Benjamin* go from him.

_{There are two sorts of sins in a person.}

5. *There are two kinds of subsistence:* One is *comfortable*, wherein a person hath many supports, even of a chearfull and a plentifull

_{There are two kinds of subsistence.}

full living, his cup runs over, and his head is anointed with oil. Another is *absolute*, when there is no more then to keep soul and body together: The proposition is true, even in this latter sense, That a sinner, though God doth shave off and suspend all the comforts of his life, and doth reduce him so short, that there remains no more then upon what he can live, if there remains but any one sprig on which he can take hold, if he can devise any one method of safety, so that he may imagin I shall yet live and be safe, though I go on in sin, he will not turn in unto God now, and leave his sins, but will live the basest of lives, rather then he will relinquish the worst of lives (a sinful life) he will walk in rags, and beg his bread, and leave all his friends, and become an out-cast, and a companion of the most ignoble and infamous wretches, rather then, &c.

<small>This true of all sorts of Extremities.</small> 6. This proposition *holds true of all sorts of extremities*: *Inward*, in those of conscience; a sinner oft-times will rather endure the sharp edge of the Word, which speaks nothing but wrath and bitterness, yea he will live under the galling Items, severe frowns, bitter accusations, intolerable scourgings, and terrours and condemnations of his conscience, though his conscience many times upbraids him in society, amazeth him asleep, terrifies him in the dark, condemns him for a wretch, and claps on him the apprehensions of Hell, which makes the foundation of his soul to quake, yet it falls out frequently that he will not turn from his sinful course. *Outward* in all the kinds of misery. A mans sinful wayes may be like the putrifyings of the body which beget the worms, that eat it out, and consume it: so the sinnings of a person many times do rot and consume his name, yea, all his estate; yea, all his amity; yea, all his strength, and yet through the affectionate combination of his heart with sin, he may rather indure infamy, scorns, poverty, desertion of friends, famine and nakedness, any thing rather then he will leave his sin; the wicked know no shame. *Pharaoh* did not set his heart for all this, &c.

<small>This true not only in a transient and passionate sense, But in a more permanent and deliberate sens.</small> 7. Lastly, This is true not only in a *transcient and passionate sense*, when through the rage of some present distemper and fury, a person will hear no counsel (this is true of Nations as well as Persons) nor regard any dealing, but is violently on a sudden carried away with the strong tide, or storm rather, of his foolish mind and passions: But it holds true likewise in *a more permanent and deliberate*

sense

The Sinners Aversion from God. 49

sense : When a sinner is exempted from the times of rashness, and is able to see and judge of his wayes and courses to be sinful. Yet is it possible, that he may suffer not a little, but much evil; not in one kind, but in manifold kinds; not for a short time, but for some long duration; many weeks, yea, perhaps many years, ere his heart doth yield to return from his sinful wayes to God. Thus briefly have you the Explication of the Assertion. Now I will touch two things more, and so proceed to the Application. One, how this may be manifested to be true: Another, why it is, or should be thus with a sinful heart.

Quest. 1. *How it may appear, that a sinful person will try all,* &c. *ere he will return?* — How this may appear to be true.

Sol. It may manifestly appear, if you consider these particulars.

1. *The patient continuation of spiritual means, without any fruit of Conversion:* God hath used incessant means, and followed and pressed upon sinners by his Servants, the Messengers of his Word many times, and for a long time, yet they repented not, nor turned from their sins. 2 Chr. 36. 15. *The Lord God of their fathers sent to them by his Messengers, rising up betimes and sending :* he did send, and send again. Ver. 16. *But they mocked the Messengers of God, and despised his words, and misused his Prophets, until there was no remedy.* So Matth. 23. 37. *O Jerusalem, Jerusalem, thou that killest the Prophets, and stonest them which are sent unto thee ; how often would I have gathered thy children together, even as an Hen gathereth her chickens under her wings, and ye would not ?* Rom. 10. 21. *And to Israel he saith, All the day long I have stretched forth my hands unto a disobedient and gainsaying people.* — By the continuance of Spiritual means without any fruit of Conversion.

2. *The large expectations of God, for the returning of sinners, without any success :* Luke 13. 7. *Behold, these three years I come seeking fruit on this figtree, and find none.* Num. 14. 11. *The Lord said unto Moses, How long will this people provoke me ? and how long will it be ere they believe me, for all the signes which I have shewed among them ?* Ver. 27. *How long shall I bear with this evil Congregation which murmur against me ?* Jer. 4. 14. *O Jerusalem, wash thine heart from wickedness, that thou mayest be saved ; how long shall thy vain thoughts lodge within thee.* Hos. 8. 5. *How long will it be ere they attain to innocency ?* Jer. 13. 27. — By the large expectations of God for the return of sinners without success.

H   *O Je-*

O Jerusalem, wilt thou not be made clean? when shall it once be?

By the long and exceeding complaints of God concerning sinners.

3. *The long and exceeding complaints of God concerning sinners:* That he is forced still to bear with them; insomuch that their continual sinnings have grown (as it were exceeding of Gods patience) too much for God to bear any longer; Amos 2.13. *I am pressed under you, as a Cart is pressed that is full of Sheaves.* Jer. 15. 6. *Thou hast forsaken me, saith the Lord; thou art gone backward, therefore will I stretch out my hand against thee; I am weary of repenting.* Isa. 43. 24. *Thou hast made me to serve with thy sins; thou hast wearied me with thine iniquities.*

By the non-plusses that obstinate sinners have put God unto.

4. *The Non-plusses* (if I may so phrase it) that wicked and obstinate persons, by continuing in their sins, have put God unto: Hos. 6. 4. *O Ephraim, what shall I do unto thee? O Judah, what shall I do unto thee? for your goodness is as a morning cloud, and as the early dew it goeth away.* This is an Antropopathy, a speech after the manner of men. Not that God doth not know what to do; but he expresseth himself after the manner of a person who hath used all the wayes and means to reclaim another, and yet the other, though sometimes cunningly he pretends a reformation, falls away again. Now, saith a father, such and such wayes have I used, and such wayes, and nothing doth avail; my son still is wicked, he runs on from evil to worse; I know not what to do with him, I can think of no course, &c. So, Isa. 5. 4. *What could have been done more to my Vineyard, that I have not done in it? wherefore when I looked for grapes, brought it forth wild grapes.*

By the Despair which God hath conceived, after many dealings to do any good.

5. Nay, the *kinds of Despair* (as it were) *which God hath conceived after many dealings, to do any good, or to reclaim them from sinful wayes:* Hos. 5. 15. *I will go and return to my place.* Isa. 1. 5. *Why should ye be stricken any more, ye will revolt more and more?* Jer. 23. 39. *I will utterly forget you, and I will forsake you; reprobate silver shall men call them.*

By those farewel wishes and resolutions of God because of their Impenitency.

6. Yea, those *dying knells and farewel wishes* and resolutions of God, because of the impenitency of persons, demonstrates this truth. Expostulations upon utmost terms, *Why will ye dye?* And, *You shall dye in your sins; and I will forsake you; and I will utterly destroy you.* Luke 19. 41. *He beheld the City, and*

wept

The Sinners Aversion from God.

wept over it; Ver. 42. *O that thou hadst known, even thou, at the least in this thy day, the things which belong unto thy peace: but now they are hid from thine eyes.* Gen. 6. 3. *My Spirit shall not alwayes strive with him.*

7. Lastly, It may appear that sinners will try all wayes ere they turn, and endure much, *By the multiplication of many Judgments*, and repetition of manifold calamities. The many wedges which are knockt in one after another, shew that the wood is tough and unyielding : this giving pill after pill, shews that the corrupt humor is strongly rooted, *Mic.* 6. 13. *I will make thee sick in smiting thee, because of thy sins.* So that when all is done and suffered, God must say and do what he promises in *Isa.* 57. 17. *I was wroth with him, and smote him, I hid me, and was wroth, and he went on frowardly in the way of his heart.* Ver. 18. *I have seen his wayes and will heal him.* When all is done, one thing more God must do, he must come into the heart, and over-rule, and heal, and turn it, and then it shall be turned. *By the multiplication of many Judgments.*

Qu. 2. Now for the second Question, Why it should be thus, that sinners should try all the wayes, and indure to the utmost rather then to turn from their sinful courses? *Why it is thus.*

I answer, It is not either, 1. Because sin is such an *Excellent thing*, or really beneficial to the soul; by reason of which excellency and use, a man might be moved to endure much in his body, for the preservation and defence of it: for sin is an evil thing, and therefore worthless. Or, 2. Because any sin is less evil then misery; and therefore this shall be endured rather then that shall be forsaken. But, 1. *The sinner doth exceedingly love his sin*: The heart of a sinner is set on his sin; he hath made a *Covenant with death, and an agreement with hell.* He loves darkness, and is held fast with the bonds and cords of his sinful affections. A person doth many times suffer pains sharper then death, because he doth exceedingly love life : Why ? a sinner loves his sin as he loves his life ; nay, more then his life, the which he doth often hazard for ever to preserve his sin. 2. *The sinner is a Fool :* Put a fool never so oft in the Stocks, it doth him no good ; he understands not the cause nor end of it. Evil men are chastized and punished by God, but they know not nor understand; they know not that their sins are the cause thereof, and that *It is not, Because sin is really beneficial to the soul. Nor because any sin is less evil then misery. But because, The sinner doth exceedingly love his sin. The sinner is a Fool.*

There is a stout spirit of pride in a sinner.

From a vaine presumption, that yet their sinful wayes shall be well at last.

From the Contrariety betwixt the wayes of God and the Sinners heart.

From unbeliefe.

From the Vanity of a corrupt Judgment.

Use 1. Conviction. It is no easie work to Repent.

that Conversion from sin is the end thereof. 3. *There is a marvellous stout Spirit of pride in the sinner*; who is therefore said to fight against God, and to resist him; and though he be smitten, yet to refuse to return, and wilfully to transgress, and that they will not hearken. Stifnecked are they called; and foreheads have they which cannot be ashamed, and faces that cannot blush. 4. *A vain presumption, that yet their sinful wayes shall be well at last*: It is but bearing a while, and at length their calamities will off. He who goes on in a sinful way, is never without some sinful project and chimeraes; silly fancies of some good, and some support and wearing out of his troubles, &c. 5. *There is a bitter contrariety twixt the wayes of God and the sinners heart.* Light and darkness are not more opposite; hence is it that in *Job* they say unto God, *Depart from us, we desire not the knowledg of the Almighty*. And in Psal. 2. *They break the cords in sunder.* And Heb. 10. *They are said to offer despight unto the Spirit of Grace.* Holiness and holy walking, ah! it is that which their hearts hate more then hell; they will adventure their damnation, before they will affect and practice holiness; no greater burden and torment to them then it. 6. And sometimes *Unbelief* may be a special cause, why a sinner doth thus shift and try. The guilt of his sins under his afflictions may lie heavy upon his conscience, and he may be so wholly taken up with the apprehension of wrath and judgment and an implacability in God towards him, that God will never shew him mercy, who hath been so much and so long provoked, that it is in vain to return, now there is no hope. 7. *The Vanity of a corrupt Judgment*, which deludes the sinner, as if he could be sinful and safe; or that he could subsist well enough without returning to God.

Now I proceed to the Application of this point; the Uses are many, 1. For *Conviction of Error* in Judgment.

1. *That it is an easie work to Repent, and to leave sin.* When I am sick, or come to dy, then I will think of that work. No, brethren, if the heart of man be of so subtil a temper, and so perverse a frame, can afflictions do it of themselves? if the love of sin be so strongly in grain, that many waters of afflictions cannot wash it out, nor many beams of mercy melt and turn it; you must then imagine it not to be an easie work to turn the heart from sin, if it will adventure the loss of heaven, and the endurance of hell, and the actual presence of many sore calamities; confess then, That the descents into

The Sinners Aversion from God. 53

into sin are easie, but the returns from it are not ordinary or facile. Where all the means, tending to the Conversion of a sinner, are opposed, and, as it were, wholly defeated and frustrated, there the heart is not so easily wrought upon to return. 2. *That no more is required to Convert a sinner, but External and Congruous Grace*; as if the heart were like a Fish upon the hook, which might be drawn at pleasure to the shore; or, like Wax prepared, and it were no more but to put on the Seal: or, as if to Convert a sinne, were no more then to report a History, or to offer a man a Purchase. Nay, but there must be likewise *Impressions* as well as *Invitations*; not only Means, but Grace it self; not only the Rod and Word, but likewise the Spirit of God, and his mighty Operation; not only a Voice saying, *This is the way*, but also the Spirit of God which must *cause us to walk in that way:* there must be healing Medicines put within the Soul by the hand of God himself, or else all the means in the world, the Word, the Sacraments, the afflictions, and miseries, and examples may say and complain with the Prophet, *Isa.* 49.4. *I have laboured in vain: I have spent my strength for nought.*

Faciles aditus Dificiles exitus, saith S^t. *Austin.* More is required to Convert, then External and Congruous Grace.

2. For *Information*. 1. *Of that excessive stubbornness and madness in the hearts of us sinners.* Good Lord! what an hand hath sin over us. That terrors should arise like an horrible tempest within the conscience for sinning, and drive a man to his feet; yea, to the dust; yea, almost as low as hell. That his sinning should pull down one calamity after another; take away the dayes of peace, of plenty, of safety, of health, and darken them with war, and tumults; with scarcity, and indigence; with danger, and trouble; with losses, and diseases; cloath a mans body with rags, fill a mans body witth rottenness, obscure a mans name with infamy, and yet, yet after all, and under all that a person should hold fast his wickedness, which is the cause of all and will not let it go, he will not be weaned from it, nor charmed. No Mercy, nor Justice, nothing can dissolve the Covenant tvixt his heart and sin; but like that *Athenian* Commander (if I forget not the story) who when he was threatned to let go the Ship, held it; when one hand was cut off, he held it with the other; when both were cut off, he held it with his teeth. The Lord be merciful to us, thus is it with us, though God threatens, yet we sin; though he strikes us in one kiud, yet we sin; though in many kinds, yet we sin; though losses though crosses, though death be in our doors, though it riseth on our bodies,

Information. Of the excessive stubbornness of the hearts of sinners.

bodies, though we lose earth, life, heaven, all, yet we still sin, and return not, but stand it out, 2. *Of the admirable patience and goodness of God.* Not without reason is he stiled a *God of long-suffering*, and *to endure with much long-suffering the vessels of wrath*: and his Goodness, *the riches of Goodness.* Rom. 9. 22. Rom. 2, 4. That he should look after a sinner, nay, speak, nay, strike, nay, wound, nay, almost take away his life to save his life; that he should run after a proud and resisting sinner, though a sinner doth contrive the ways of opposing, and cunningly strives against all the methods of mercy; yet that God should not desert him, and give him over, but try again and again, and be actively ready to give grace to an unwilling, to a resisting, to an obstinate, foolish sinner! who but a vile sinner would obstinately abuse such great mercy? who but a God would endure the same with so much patience? It is not that the Lord seeth not the ways of a sinner (for he is *Omniscient*;) It is not that he approves or likes the ways of a sinner, (for he is *most Holy*;) It is not that he will not recompence the ways of a sinner, (for he is *most Just*;) It is not that he wants power to execute his wrath and displeasure, (for he is *Almighty:*) No, no, that he all this while spares and holds up, ariseth onely from his nature, which is delighted rather to shew mercy, and which is slow to wrath, and of much long-suffering. 3. *Of the freeness of Gods grace. It is not of him that willeth, nor of him that runneth, but of God that sheweth mercy,* Rom. 9. 16. Alas! what is it that the Pelagians scribled of Merits, and Papists of Deserts and Congruities? Lo here! naturally we run from God, and naturally we are fighters against God, we resist the motions of his Spirit, the counsels of his Word, the lessons of many Afflictions; and could we any how subsist, we would never lay down our weapons. Did not the Lord shew more compassion to us, then we do unto our selves; did he not enquire after us, and follow us, and as it were beset us on every side, and in a sort surprize us by the goodness and strength of his own Grace, we should perish in our bloud, die in our folly, and be lost for ever; but this commends the exceeding graciousness of his Grace towards us, that though we be not onely enemies by nature, but rebellious also by practice, yet the Lord shews pity to our wandring souls, will forgive our proud rebellions, and will heal our

foolish

Of the admirable patience and goodness of God.

Habet in potestate vindictam, mavult tamen diu tenere patientiam, &c. Cyprian.

Of the freeness of Gods grace.

The Sinners Aversion from God.

foolish and gainsaying hearts. It is great mercy for him to spare us, who might for our manifold sinnings so often have condemned us; and it is the greatest mercy, that he doth not onely not leave and damn us, but pities, converts, and saves us.

3. For *Caution*: And this is the main Use which I desire to insist on, *To take heed of shuffling with God*, and digging after pits, which will hold no water, when God calls upon us by his Word, or by his Corrections, to return from our sins unto him, and not to hold them fast, or to withstand the Lord, and hold him off. Here I shall propound two things: 1. Some Motives, or Arguments to hearken unto this; 2. Some Rules and Directions to guide us. The Motives may respect us either, 1. in the evil of thus shuffling with, and delaying of God, 2. in the good on the contrary. I will mingle them together. Consider therefore,

For Caution.
Take heed of shuffling with God.

Motives.

1. *It is a most precious thing which the Lord offers unto us, when at first he calls upon us to leave our sins, and to return unto him.* A thing may be reputed precious, partly, in respect of the *necessity of it*, when it doth so nearly concern us, that we are undone without it. Now what shall become of us, unless we come off from our sins? What is it that we so shuffle for, and will not let it go? What! is it a good in itself, or a cause of good to us? and what is it that we so hold off from? is it not Grace and Salvation? *I shall perish with hunger*, saith the Prodigal. So mayest thou truly say, Unless I do accept of this offer of Grace, if I do thus hold on in my sinfull ways, if I shuffle never so long, yet if I continue thus, I shall at length perish for ever, *Exod.* 10.7. *Knowest thou not that Egypt is destroyed?* so, &c. to go on thus is the way of death, to return and submit is the onely way of life: I cannot be saved unless I repent: It is not a vain thing for which the Lord strives with me, it is to give grace and life to my poor soul. In respect *of the excellency of it:* Excellent things are truly precious. Now every grace is excellent, it hath a native beauty in it, and makes us a choice and estimable people. Do throughly weigh a penitent and converted condition, how in it we are partakers of the Divine nature; what a communion we have thereby with God; what a fellowship with Jesus Christ; how we pass from death to life, are made the sons of God, and become

It is a most precious thing the Lord offers to us, when at first he calls upon us to return.

become the heirs of glory, and will we then thus devise and flie from our best good ; Why! when the Lord offers grace to a sinner, what doth he therein but offer himself to be his God, offer Christ to be his Saviour, offer the pardon of all his sins, offer all the comforts of his Spirit, the blessings of his promises, and the hopes of eternal life ; and if this be not an excellent thing, what is ? can a better or greater matter be tendred to you.

The Lord will not alwaies be calling upon us. 2. *The Lord will not alwaies be calling upon us, nor tendring repentance unto life,* and which brings forth salvation, as the Apostle speaks ; *My Spirit shall not alwaies strive,* saith God, *Gen.* 6. God strives, when he comes close in any means. 2. When hee continueth and multiplieth means. And *to day if ye will hear his voice, harden not your hearts, as in the provocation,* Heb. 3. God did deal often with the Israelites by wonders, by words, by corrections ; but you know that though he bore long with them, yet he did not bear for ever; at length he consumed and made an end of them, he would not continue to seek after them for ever. *I will ease me of mine adversaries* ; Cut it down, why cumbers it the ground. If we will not become obedient, he can quickly destroy us for our disobedience. There is a day wherein God offers himself to be ours in grace and peace, how long or how short that day is, I cannot justly determine ; onely of this we may bee sure, that God may in justice refuse us for ever, if we refuse him once. Note these Scriptures, and they may perhaps awaken and recall us, *Ezek.* 24. 12. *She hath wearied her self with lies, and her great scum went not forth out of her, her scum shall be in the fire.* v. 13. *In thy filthiness is lewdness, because I have purged thee* (by afflictions,) *and thou wast not purged* (by repentance,) *thou shalt not be purged from thy filthiness any more, till I have caused my fury to rest upon thee* Ver. 14. *I the Lord have spoken it, it shall come to pass, and I will do it, I will not go back, neither will I spare, neither will I repent : according to thy waies, and according to thy doings shall they judge thee, faith the Lord God,*Luke 19. ver. 42. *Oh! if thou hadst known, even thou at the least in this thy day the things which belong unto thy peace, but now they are hid from thine eies.* Hebr. 3. ver. 10. *I was grieved with that generation, and said, they do alwaies err in their hears, and they have not known my waies.* Verf. 11. *So I sware in my wrath, they shall not enter into my rest.* Psal. 81. ver. 11. *But my people would*

The Sinners Averſion from God.

would not hearken to my voice, and Iſrael would none of me. v.12. *So I gave them up to their own hearts luſts, and they walked in their own counſels.* Theſe four places do afford us four ſad things, which may befal perſons refuſing to return from their ſins, and deluding that work. 1. That the Lord will not ſtill be uſing of means. 2. That he will draw off the means. 3. He will leave ſuch ſinners, and give them up to themſelves. 4. They ſhall never enter into his reſt; and this the Lord binds with an Oath. Every one of theſe is a Judgment ſufficiently fearfull; for, what ſhall become of the ſinner, when the Lord ſhall (judicially) draw off the means of his Converſion? or if the means be continued in common to others, yet he will not work any more upon that perſon through them; but he ſhall deſpiſe the counſels of the Word, and ſlight the meſſage of all Afflictions; and that a perſon ſhould run ſo far and ſo high in a way of wickedneſs, that the Lord gives him over as a deſperate, hopeleſs, and forlorn wretch, to walk in his own counſels, and after the luſts of his own heart; and when the Lord ſeals him up by his Oath, that this is a perſon who ſhall never ſee my face; though many a ſinner ſhall be pardoned and ſaved, yet this ſinfull Tranſgreſſor ſhall never enter into my reſt: Now what doth the ſinner know, who ſeeks new ways to ſecure his ſinning, and oppoſeth thereby all the ways which God uſeth for his converting, I ſay, how doth he know, but that the Lord will deal thus with him. God hath dealt ſo with ſome, for dealing thus with him; he cloſed up the day upon *Jeruſalem*, and left the *Iſraelites* to their own hearts luſts, and never anſwered *Saul* any more, neither by Prophets, nor by Dreams, and threatens to remove the Candleſtick, *Revel.* 2.

3. Conſider, That if the Lord ſhould ſhew almoſt the Miracle of his Goodneſs towards ſuch a ſhuffling ſinner, his Converſion will be 1. the Harder, 2. the more Bitter. It will be *the Harder*, for as much as all further degrees and ſteps in ſinning, do engage the heart more to the love of ſin, and naturally infers more hardneſs of heart, and reſiſtance againſt the motions of Grace. When a Skaine of Thread is more and more clotted and entangled, it will be the harder to clear it; and a Cord may be ſo knotted, that you cannot undo it, but by cutting it aſunder: Though the work of Converſion

The converſion of ſuch a one will be,
The Harder.

verſion be not difficult to God, yet the far running ſinner ſhall find it, for his part, a more intricate and hitching thing, to wind his heart from thoſe acts and paths of iniquity, into which it hath been ſo long accuſtomed. However, it will *be the Harſher*; the child which ſticks ſo often in the birth, cauſeth the birth to be more ſharp and dolorous. Uſually, the more ſinfull a man hath been, and the longer he hath held off God, his ſoul is more cut; partly with *Fears*, for now he hath many doors to unlock ere he can faſten on grounds of comfort; not onely that he hath held on a courſe of ſin ſo long, but alſo that he hath ſo ſubtilly and frequently withſtood the tenders of grace, and Gods manifold dealings with him already. Though the perſon may have grace truly wrought in him, to make him ſee all this vileneſs, yet it may be long ere his faith ſhall be able comfortably to apprehend Gods mercy to forgive it. He may have doubts, not onely of mercy, but of the truth of his converſion, as if it ſeemed rather to be compulſive; God may long withhold from him the teſtimony of his love, who hath a long time perverſly withheld the conſent of his heart from returning unto him. Partly with *Shame*: It will be an exceeding reproach and confuſion of face unto this perſon, when ever the Lord converts him, that he ſhould deal with the Lord thus, reſiſt his Spirit ſo much, and withſtand that great kindneſs of God intended to him by the many means which he hath uſed. *Surely, after that I was turned, I repented,* ſaith *Ephraim,* and *after that I was inſtructed I ſmote upon my thigh, I was aſhamed, yea, even confounded, becauſe I did bear the reproach of my youth,* Jer. 31. 19. *Then ſhall ye remember your own evil ways, and your doings that were not good, and ſhall loath your ſelves in your own ſight, for your iniquities, and for your abominations.* Ezek. 36. 31. Ah! how it will rent and preſs the ſoul! Such a fool, ſuch a beaſt was I, to purſue my own ruine, to reject my own mercies, to ſlight ſo great ſalvation, to vex ſo good a God, and to be ſo infinitely unthankfully baſe, that if I could have found any means of ſupport, I would never have ſubmitted unto him, and left my ſinfull courſe: Ah! how doth the Lord take this at my hands? how unacceptable may my returning now be, which may ſeem rather to be forced through extremity, than to ſpring out of any ingenuity. So that you ſee, by our ſinfull ſhiftings, either God may deny us converting grace,

Or the harſher.

The Sinners Aversion from God.

grace, or elſe we ſhall make our Converſion much leſs eaſie and comfortable.

Object. But ſome may ſay, What can we help it? can we turn our own hearts? it muſt be the Lord who muſt do that; and he might do it at the firſt as well at the laſt, if he would. — We cannot convert our ſelves.

Sol. And is this excuſe to paſs for currant? hath not God dealt with thee often? didſt not thou more often harden thine own heart, willingly withdraw thy ſelf, and all out of a love to ſin? 2. Though thou couldſt not convert thine own heart yet this thou mighteſt have done in the times of afflictions, &c. conſidered, what might move the Lord thus to deal with thee; all, or ſome of the cauſes which thy own conſcience did freely ſuggeſt, and the ends which God pointed thee to, to reform them; And then to have gone to him by vehement prayer, to convert thy heart from thy ſins, to teach it righteouſneſs, to ſubmit to his inſtructions: Thou mightſt thus have gone to him who can convert, and have waited on him in the means of converſion; but thou didſt nor deſire after him, nor delightedſt to ſeek him, &c. — Anſwered.

2. But *What may we do to prevent this ſhuffling*, and aſſaying of means to ſupport us in ſinning, when the Lord deals with us, and calls upon us for the leaving of ſin? — Means to prevent this ſhuffling.

Sol. I would commend theſe five Directions. 1. Strive to be *convinced of this, That as long as the Courſe is a ſinfull Courſe, it can never be a ſafe Courſe.* We may weary our ſelves in the multitude of our imaginations and ways, but run what courſe you pleaſe, and purſue your own devices, yet this ye ſhall reap of the Lord, you ſhall lie down in your ſhame and ſorrow; you may run to new experiments, but miſery will follow your ſins the next time as well as this, and in every way as well as one way: *Your ſins will find you out*; and as long as you carry your ſins with you, you cannot keep off calamities from you. — Be convinced of this, That a ſinfull courſe cannot be a ſafe courſe.

2. Of neceſſity *you muſt return or periſh:* Your ſinfull courſe is a by-path, and leads to death. It is ſinfull, and you know it; and being ſinfull, it muſt be miſerable. To what end doth the Patient excuſe the taking of the Receipt, the wholſome Balm? he muſt die if he doth not receive it: So conſider, To what end do I thus vary my paths, and ſhuffle and ſeek ſupports? there is nothing ſtrong enough to ſecure a ſinner; and let me ſadly conſider, that I muſt one time or other leave theſe ſinnings, or elſe farewel my Soul and Salvation. — You muſt return or periſh.

It

3. *It cannot but be best, the sooner it is*: I must return, or perish; too soon I cannot return, and the sooner the better. A Souldier of a middle age, a Counsellor of a grave age, and a Penitent of a young age, are still the best. The work which must be done, is best done when soonest: Best, *for Safety*; for, thy life is very uncertain; and if thou doest not leave thy sins to day, thou mayest be in Hell. (for ought thou knowest) for thy sins to morrow: *For Acceptance*; the Lord likes it best, when one word of Mercy can cause us to trust, and one shaking of the Rod can cause us to tremble, and when one command sufficeth to turn us; when upon the first Arrest, we give up our Weapons, it pleaseth Soveraignty best: *For Quietness*; for we do hereby deliver not onely our Souls, but Bodies also, from many troubles, the sooner we do repent, and plainly yield; why! Conscience speaks peace the sooner, and God commands mercies the faster; strong Sins, breed long afflictions; but give up the Sins, and God gives up the Quarrel; throw over *Bichri's* head to *Joab*, and he will presently remove the siege. If a man had health, he might take sleep the better; but as long as the body is diseased, it is unquiet.

Our Return is best, the sooner it is.
For Safety.
For Acceptance.
For Quietness.

4. *Strive against those diverting Principles,* which do draw thee from the right and onely way, and put thee on by-thoughts and by-paths, and a vain assayment of means to support us: As 1. *Presumption,* either of *Mercy*, though thou doest add drunkenness to thirst, and still findest out thine own inventions; or *thine own Power*: Thou mayest be hindred of the time which thou doest project, and mayest want strength to execute thy purposes: For sinfull practises do altogether weaken our power, whilest they delude us with a conceit of strength hereafter. 2. *Stoutness and pride of spirit*: Do not, in a bravery of villany, dispute with the Almighty God; it may prove a sad Victory to thee, that thou art able to reject good counsel, and to quench all good motions. 3. *Delight in sin,* which drowns the errand of all afflictions, *&c.*

Strive against diverting Principles, as
Presumption of Mercy,
Or of thy own Power.
Stoutness and pride of spirit.
Delight in sin.

5. *Beseech the Lord, at the very first, to circumcise the stubbornness of your hearts,* and to give you the understanding ear, and the obedient spirit; that when in the Word he calls upon you to turn from your sins, your hearts may fall down, and cry out, O Lord, turn me; and when by afflictions he calls upon you to turn, you may presently humble your hearts, and cry out, O Lord, pardon

Beseech the Lord to circumcise the stubbornness of your hearts.

The Sinners Aversion from God.

don me ; O Lord, heal me ; O Lord, turn and save me : Let us all think of this ; You know that the Lord is displeased with us, and we have hitherto hardened our hearts against the Lord ; God hath dealt with us once, twice, often, in publick, in private ways, and still we seek our own ways, delude the work of Repentance, set nothing to heart, nor repent of our evil doings.

II. Now I proceed to the Second thing, which is, *The final disappointment of the Prodigals assays and designs*, in these words, [*And no man gave unto him.*] Whence I observe,

That nothing shall avail the shuffling sinner, until he doth turn from his sins ; but God will disappoint all his projects, batter down all his confidences, frustrate all his expectations, drive him out of all his harbours, and overthrow all the means and ways which he flies unto. Before I confirm this Assertion, let me premise a few particulars, that so you may rightly conceive the scope of it. Thus then.

1. I intend the Assertion, of a sinner whom God doth intend to convert ; others he may leave to prosper in their imaginations : For you see it raised from the disappointment of a Prodigal, one whose conversion at length attended his manifold afflictions, and as manifold contrivances to keep up his sinfull conversation : though such a person knows not it, nor thinks on it, yet God is secretly against him, and thrusts him off from all the Cities of Refuge, unto which he flies ; which way soever he turns, and what course soever he applies himself unto, whatsoever vessel he puts himself into, it shall be like *Jonah's ship*, which will not be quiet until he be cast out, until he doth come to consider of his doings, and return.

2. I intend the Assertion, *of an eventual, not of an instantaneous disappointment* : (1.) Though for the present, and some short space, the cunning sinner may quietly possess the fruits of his projects, and solace himself in some carnal securities ; yet at length, sooner or later, God will again besiege him, and take him off. As it was with *Adonijahs guests*, though for some minutes they did feast and rejoyce, yet on a sudden they were all amazed, fled and dispersed ; or as it is with the Fowls which are pursued, though they light, as they think, upon a prey, yet the Piece is discharged, and they are all driven away : So is it with the sinner (whom God intends to convert) though he may contrive a way (as he thinks) and quietly and safely go on in his sinfull course,

The final disappointment of all the Prodigals designs.

Doct. 2. Nothing shall avail the shuffling sinner, till he return, but God will disappoint all his projects.

Some things premised. This is meant of a sinner whom God intends to convert.

It is intended of an eventual, and not of an instantaneous disappointment.

course, and begin to sit down, yet thither also will the Hue and Cry come, and he shall be forced away; all that also shall be dashed in pieces; there will come down a Writ of Ejection, and cast him out of the house, as it did *Ahab* out of *the Vineyard* which he had unjustly possessed; so that he shall not settle long upon any way or course, without some special and effectual disturbance from God.

The shuffling projects of a sinner shall be invalid several ways.

3. *The shuffling projects of a sinner may be reputed invalid, either, when that every thing or way which he contrives is rased and slighted*: As a Castle, unto which the Souldiers fly, is demolished; so when the Lord takes off that Friend, or utterly blasts that course of Living, that way of Trade and Imployment wherein a sinner trusted all his hopes with: Or, *when that which the sinner contrived as his help and strength, shall shut the gate against him, not admit him into harbour*: Or, when that *which he hath with much art and pains contrived, is so far from proving an help, that it augments his grief and trouble*: There is, as it were, an evil spirit, put in twixt the plotting heart, and the obtained help, so that it proves a bitter enemy instead of a friend, and a further misery instead of a comfort. One of these ways doth God make the shuffling projects of a sinner unavailable; either by blasting that vain Gourd which delightfully shadowed him; or by turning off the sinner from the Horns of those Altars, unto which he flies in times of misery; or else by making the land of Egypt, into which he flies for Bread and Corn, to become an House of cruel Bondage; I mean, by turning his desires into, if not Curses, yet intollerable Crosses.

The shuffling sinner shall neither keep down strokes of conscience, nor keep off afflictions.

4. Whether the *cause* why *the sinner doth shuffle*, be *inward*, or whether it be *outward*; whether it be *the strokes of Conscience*, or whether it be *the stripes of Affliction*; he shall neither *keep down the one*, nor *keep off the other*, but the inward wounds shall ever and anon be renewed. As all the endeavours of the Mariners could not calm the Sea, until *Jonah* was cast out of the ship; so until the sinner forsakes his evil ways, there is no escaping the one or the other.

The Proposition being thus explicated, I shall briefly confirm it, by resolving two things; 1. How it may appear to be true? 2. Why it is so?

How this may appear to be true.

Quest. 1. *How it may appear to be a truth*, that nothing shall avail

The Sinners Aversion from God.

avail the shuffling sinner, until he returns from his sins?

Sol. Thus: 1. The Lord doth many times make all the helps and means which the sinner useth, to be vain, and unable, and insufficient. This is imported in that phrase, *Jer.* 3. 23. *Truly in vain is salvation hoped for from the hills, and from the multitude of mountains.* The *Israelites* were distressed by reason of their sins, they were besieged and surprized by the *Babylonians*; their proper work now had been to have returned unto the Lord: But they still go on, and think to salve and secure themselves by the help of *Syria*; but all in vain, they could not preserve them, they were not able. So the Prophet, *Hos.* 5. 13. *When Ephraim saw his sickness, and Judah his wound, then went Ephraim to the Assyrian, and sent to King Jarib, yet could he not heal you, nor cure you of your wound.* He alludes to a sick patient, and an impotent Physitian, who cannot possibly heal. See, all the strength unto which they repaired, could not deliver or secure them; though they did undertake the cure, the safety, yet they could not perform it. 2. *That shame which hath covered the faces of sinners after all their cunning experiments,* confirms this truth also, That nothing avails, *&c.* The *Israelites* tried the help of *Assyria,* but that was too weak a Bow; then they have another project, they will make use of *Egypt;* nor should this prosper, when they had tried it, they *were ashamed of it*; they had propounded great matters, and boasted much, how able they should now be, and how safe; but when all came to all, nothing at all came of it. *Jer.* 2. 36. *Why gaddest thou about so much to change thy way? thou also shalt be ashamed of Egypt, as thou wast ashamed of Assyria.* v. 37. *Yea, thou shalt go forth from him, and thine hands upon thy head; for the Lord hath rejected thy confidences, and thou shalt not prosper in them.* 3. *The Lord hath pulled the sinners out of their sanctuaries and helps unto which they have fled*; yea, hath pulled them out *like sheep, Jer.* 12. 3. and taken them away *as with fish-hooks, Amos* 4. 2. 4. *He hath dashed in pieces the refuges on which they trusted*; blown down the house which they took up to lodge in; as is evident in the cracking of the *King of* Egypt, unto whom the *Israelites* in their captivities fled; but the Lord brought on him the *Army of the Chaldeans,* which utterly overthrew him. As it was with *Jonah,* who fled from the Lord, and got into a *ship for Tarshish*; the Lord sent

[margin: God many times makes all their helps and means insufficient.]

[margin: Shame hath covered the faces of sinners after all their cunning experiments.]

[margin: The Lord hath pull'd sinners out of the sanctuaries to which they have fled. He hath dashed in pieces the refuges on which they trusted.]

sent a wind and *storm*, which did never leave working, till it purged *Jonah* out of the ship. So that strength, and secure defence, unto which the sinner betakes himself, God doth as it were besiege him therein, and never leaves, until he hath demolished it, and brought him to terms of capitulation afresh.   5. *By making his sinfull contrivances to prove his stronger and harder fetters*; that that way, and that comfort which the sinner took up as a shadow from the storm and heat, hath (like some hired Souldiers in the day of battel) wheel'd about, and become the strongest snare, and bitterest burden. As *David* complained of some of his friends, that they did prove his most enraged and cutting enemies; Or as the Prophet speaks, *The men of thy Confederacy have brought thee even to the border; the men that were at peace with thee, have deceived thee; they that did eat thy bread, have laid a wound under thee*. Obad. 7. So the Lord hath so over-ruled it, that he hath driven the sinner to a miserable stand, even when he hath pursued the wyaes (as he thought) of his own contentment; in the pursuing whereof, he hath onely followed a smiling River, into a most unquiet and troublesome Sea.   6. *By a most perfect beleagring* (as it were) *of a projecting sinner*: hedging up all his ways with thorns, or immuring of him as in a Castle, *Hos.* 2. and shutting of him up, that there shall be no going out or coming in.

Quest. 2.
Reasons of it.

Now for the second Question, Why nothing shall avail the shuffling sinner, until he repents?

Sol.

I conjecture these Reasons may be rendred. 1. *That unhappy quality of sin which makes every way unsuccessfull*. It is like some weeds which mar every dish they come into; or like some servants, under whose hand nothing prospers: So is it with sin; it is an unprosperous thing, and mars all ; the worm in our gourd, arms every creature against us, it alone were enough to batter down the strongest Castle, and to blast our sweetest comforts ; it thrusts in a secret curse upon all our undertakings. 2. *Whiles the Lord is against a man, nothing can be sufficient to help him*. What can prove a friend, while the Lord is an enemy? all things come on, or fall off, as God draws near, or stands off from us; we can never establish our selves by our own hand, nor against Gods. You may read in *Hos.* 5. 13. that *Ephraim and Judah in their distress betook them to the Assyrians, but they could do them no good*. V. 14. *For I will be unto Ephraim as a Lion, and as a young Lion to the house of Judah; I, even I, will tear, and*

He makes his sinfull contrivances to be his stronger fetters.

By the beleagring of a projecting sinner.

Quest. 2.
Reasons of it.

Sol.
The unhappy quality of sin.

Whilest the Lord is against a man, nothing is sufficient to help him.

go

The Sinners Converſion to God.

go away; I will take away, and none ſhall reſcue him. But now whiles a man goes on, ſhuffling, in a ſinful way, the Lord is againſt him. 3. *The ſinner would never turn to God, if any of his own waies could avail.* If the ſhip could any way hold out, the men would not come to ſhore; but when it is all ſplit, and they muſt periſh if they ſwim not, now they make to the ſhore: So is it here; the Lord muſt wholly unbottom the ſinner, he muſt ſtrip him of all hopes and confidences, yea he muſt hold him as it were over the flames of hell, before he will turn unto him; Oh! the heart of a ſinner hath made a covenant with ſin, which will not eaſily be diſannulied; ordinarily, till the very life comes to it, that a man ſees he muſt preſently be damned, if he doth not repent, he will ſtand it out againſt God.

marginal: The ſinner would never turn to God, it any of his own waies could avail him.

Now to proceed to the Application of this: Shall nothing help the ſhuffling ſinner till he repents? *then certainly the Lord ſhews great mercy unto him;* it is one of the greateſt judgments, when the Lord lets the ſinner alone, to go on and proſper; a miſerable thing it is, when the patient is given over, and no Phyſician will meddle with him; ſo on the contrary, It is a great mercy, when the Lord doth not give over the ſinner, but ſtill follows him, and ſtill diſappoints his counſels, and undermines as it were his projects, and is too hard for him in all his waies. Thou doeſt oft times take it heavily, that the Lord ſhould ſtand againſt thee thus, and pull away this comfort, and ſtop up that way, and diſappoint and defeat one enterpriſe after another: Why! now conſider, were it kindneſs to let thee make up thy works to hold out againſt God? Were it a mercy to thee, to let thee grow ſtrong in a way of damnation? The Lord is ſtill againſt me, ſaieſt thou, I can ſet on no way, but I find him my adverſary; I cannot ſettle on any thing, but he plucks it off: I anſwer, The Lord is not ſo much againſt thee, as thou art againſt thy ſelf; it is true, the Lord hath not yet done with thee; Why! becauſe thou haſt not yet done with ſin? and his hand is ſtill ſtretched out againſt thee, Why? becauſe thy hand is ſtill ſtretched out againſt him; he doth by variety of afflictions and croſſes ſtill purſue thee; but let me tell thee one thing, It is better he ſhould purſue thy ſins, then thy ſoul; let the afflictions be what they will, they are better then damnation; all that God intends unto thee is onely this, he will never leave thee, untill he hath overcome thee; as they in the war take one

marginal: Uſe. Then the Lord ſhews great mercy to ſuch a ſinner.

K out-

out-work after another, untill the besieged do yield up: So is it with the Lord, he will drive thee out of all thy holds, as he did *Nebuchadnezzar* out of his Kingdom, untill he hath brought thee to humble thy self for thy sins, and repent. And what is all this, but a most tender mercy which doth thus pursue thee, onely that it may save thee.

It is in vain to strive against God.

2. Then *it is in vain to strive against God*, to hold out, for nothing shall avail: *Are we stronger then he*, said the Apostle? Can our counsels lie hid from his wisdome? or can we set upon the waies where his eie cannot find us? Can we grasp the comfort at all, which his hand cannot instantly pull from us? Can we command our own safeties, whilst he is displeased with us? or prosper at all while he saies, Cursed is every fruit of thy labour? Can any way of thine enable thee against him who can crack a whole world at once? thou canst repose thy self on none but creatures, and hadst thou them all, what were they, could they secure thee against their Lord? Is there any creature a Castle strong enough to retein a sinful traitor against God.

Let us speedily return.

3. Lastly, then *let us speedily return*, and at once take forth the lesson of all Gods dealing with us; that which he aims at is our repentance; Let former times and denials and subtilties suffice us; doth God strike off all thy friends, and lay them aside? doth he pull thee out of every harbor? do all the means on which thou trustedst forsake and fail thee? O then return unto the Lord; all this befalls thee, purposely to bring thee home to thy father; It is because the Lord would have thy heart, thy love, thy joy, thy fear, thy hope, thy confidence, thy obedience, &c.

Luke 15. 17. *And when hee came to himself, he said, How many hired servants of my father have bread enough, and to spare, and I perish with hunger?* ver. 18. *I will arise and go to my father, &c.* These words contain in them the happy fruits of sharp afflictions, the dawning of the day after a stormy night, the quicknings of a dead man, the penitential recovery of a sinful Prodigal. We must not despair of men, though they be great sinners; a prodigal, riotous, luxurious person begins here to return; not must we be quick and peremptory in our final censures of them, though (like a ship in many storms) they hold on their sinful courses after many dealings, for the power which converts is mighty, and the season to convert is different; God

doth

doth as it were nurse up some from their youth in grace, others he leaves to conquer in battel; when their defeates are grown to age and strength, yet he can over-master and heal them, as here the Prodigal. Concerning whose *penitent estate* (which was the second General) you may he pleased to consider a double act: 1. One of his Judgment, described in this *verf.* 17. 2. Another of his Will, described in *verf.* 18. the former is an act of inspection, in the viewing of his bad life; the other is an act of resolution, to change and leave it; that is, (if I may so call it) the *fundamental* work of Repentance, and this is the *formal* work of it; the one is the framing, the other is the launching of the ship.

II. The division of th. Text.

I must treat next on the first work, which is the *judgment of the Prodigal.* Some call it an *act of Consideration,* which is such an effect of right reason, whereby we rightly understand and judge of things; Others conjecture it an *act of Consultation,* wherein he did deliberate and debate his way and condition throughly in his mind, in comparing it with another opposite condition; so then in this judicious working of his you have:

The judgment of the Prodigal expressed in

First, A serious consideration [*he came to himself*] (i.) now he began to bethink where he was, and what he had done; like a mad man before he still raged, and ran on, never minded any thing but his sins, but now his reason comes into joint again, hee soberly and in good earnest considers of his course and estate.

A serious consideration:

Secondly, A wise consultation: Ah! thinks he, I have brought my self into a miserable condition, I am even ready to perish with hunger; I have gone on so far in sin, that if I return not, I am lost for ever; I have tried all the waies that I can imagin, but they prosper not; die and perish I would not, is life to be had no where? Where might such a poor famisht creature find a bit of bread to save his life; Now I think on it, I have a father living, and he hath bread enough, even his meanest servants have enough, and to spare; he hath bread for servants, will he have none for a child? they have enough, I have none at all; they have to spare, and I hunger, I perish with hunger, my condition is most miserable, their condition is most plentiful; Well! thus I will not rest, I will arise and go to him, &c. Before I handle that Assertion which the text will immediately afford, there may be many

A wife consultation.

K 2   not

The Returning Prodigal, or

not unuseful observations, which occasionally and collaterally fall in: I will but mention them unto you, and then fit down upon the principal intention of the Verse.

Great Afflictions may end in a sweet Conversion.

1. *That great afflictions may end in a sweet conversion; or, the sharpest miseries, may prove a means to bring us to the sweetest mercies*: Storms, though they be to some shipwracks, yet they land some; the prodigal met with famine, and that brought him back to his fathers house for bread. *I had perish'd*, said one, *unless I had perished*; so may many a man say, Had I not been afflicted, I had been damned; my great losses have proved my greatest gain; I never fell into the love of God, untill I came under the scourge of God.

A Great Sinner is not uncapable of mercy.

2. *That even a great sinner is not uncapable of mercy or grace*; a luxurious prodigal, who spent all among Harlots, is now returning home to his father, a penitent and grieved child: and the reason is this; Though the sins of a man be great, yet the mercies of a God be free, and mercy advanceth its own glory, when it shines on the greatest sinners. Sin is great, but grace is stronger, it can quicken dead men. As the knottiest wood, when it is squared, proves of strongest service; so the vilest sinner, once converted, proves the faithfullest and activest instrument of glory to God; and lastly, God doth extend grace to great sinners, that no sinners might despair.

God sometimes permits the Sinner to try the utmost, and then converts him.

3. *That God doth many times permit the sinner to try to the utmost, and then converts him.* A long season ere some return: as *Paul* to breath out persecutions, and to get authority to bind all, &c. and then he is struck down; hereby he magnifies his patience, and more demonstrates his mercies and goodness, that after all, hee will yet accept of such a sinner, and pardon him.

An Unconverted man, is a mad-man.

4. *That an Unconverted man is a mad man*, he is besides himself. Sin bereavs the sinner of the right use of reason, and he never comes to be sober, to be himself, until he doth repent; whatsoever fury of spirit, wildness of fancies, rendings of cloaths, tearings of bonds, untameableness, ragings, inconsiderations, are extant in madness, the same are to be found in a meer sinful heart and life: all these propositions are observable and useful, but that which I intend to insist on, is this:

That

The Sinners Conversion to God.

That a serious Consideration, and the right Comparison of the miserable estate of a sinful Condition, with the happy estate of a Converted condition, are the prime steps and occasions of a true and speedy Repentance. For the Explication of this point, I must open some particulars; 1. Concerning a *Serious Consideration of a Sinful Condition*: It is an *Intentive work of the Judgment*, wherein it doth *narrowly and diligently meditate on the whole estate of sin*. It is called in Scripture, a remembring of our wayes; and sometimes a bethinking of our selves, and a seeing what we have done, a pondring of our paths. It is opposed not only to Ignorance and Nescience, but also to Negligence; yea, to rashness and suddenness; and indeed it is a very deep searching, and minding, and weighing of matters: When a man sits down and museth, so that his mind and thoughts are throughly imployed, he makes it a special business, he bends all his strength rightly to inform himself, to bring himself to a right understanding of his estate; this is a proper consideration. There be two kinds of thoughts and mindings: some are only *Intuitive*; they are but the cast of the eye, a glancing, lightning motion. Others are *Discursive*, fully searching; the mind in them doth throughly insist on the Natures, Kinds, Circumstances, Occurrences and Issues of things, it is taken up with it as a business. The serious consideration of a mans sinfulness, falls into this latter; it is not a confused work, or a light overly sight of sin, it is a setled and deep pondering of the estate in the Qualities, Acts and Fruits of it; Nature, Number, Circumstances, Danger:

"*v. g.* When I seriously consider of my sinful estate, I reflect
"on my self, what kind of life I lead, what are those qualities,
"what those wayes which I find and walk in: my Thoughts,
"my Affections, my Speeches have been thus; and thus my acti-
"ons, and thus my course of Life. I have many bonds upon
"me to serve the Lord, and not to sin against him; but, Wretch
"that I am, I see all my wayes (which I took for pleasures and
"profits) have been sinful and vile. By them all I have violated
"a righteous Will, dishonored and provoked a great God (whose
"wrath is a consuming fire) I have (to satisfie them) lost all my
"comforts, caused many evils to others, brought many miseries
"on my self, put Christ to death, and, if God be not mer-
"ciful, lost my miserable soul for ever. These wayes (will I
"not

Doct.
A serious Consideration, and right Comparison of the miserable state of a sinful Condition, and happy state of a Converted Condition, are steps to true and speedy Repentance. What this Serious Consideration is.

" not believe mine own eyes?) are extremely sinful, and there-
" fore (should I not believe the Scriptures) are damnable: many
" a year have I run this course, and oftentimes under checks of
" Conscience; very much evil hath already been upon me, and
" all for sin; some troubles of Conscience: And that wrath
" which God threatens and is behind, is terrible. If I go on
" thus, I perish for ever; for whilst I keep my sins, the least sin
" of them, I must necessarily part with God, and lose my soul.
" Tell me, O my vainly deluded soul, can that be good which
" God hates, or safe, which God doth curse? Wouldst thou
" dye thus? O then thou dyest for ever; and why then wilt thou
" live thus any longer? O thou hast presumed too far already;
" perhaps Patience will bear no longer, and Mercy being often
" abused, may be for ever recalled; and then, thou, O my Soul,
" then whither wilt thou go? No, no, we must no more of these
" forbidden fruits, and no longer must we trade in the paths of
" death; there is a God who hath lookt on thee all this while,
" and hates thy wayes, and hath sealed his implacable wrath with
" an Oath if thou return not: Come, my soul, think aright of
" God, of thy past acts, of thy present estate, of thy future
" condition; believe me, thy Guilts are many, thy Accounts will
" be bitter; God hath been still dishonoured, he will not be
" mocked; let us return, for we are out of the way of Heaven, and
" are even upon the brink of Hell.

What this right Comparison is Opposita juxta se posita, &c.

2. Concerning the *right Comparison of the miserableness of a sinful, with the happiness of a penitent Condition*, I need say but little: It is nothing else, but after a distinct view of either, to set the one against the other in the Nature, Kinds, Qualities, Concomitants, Ends and Issues, *v. g.* " Thus base and foul is an
" Impenitent estate; thus excellent and glorious is a Converted
" estate; That how opposite to God, This how suitable; That
" how odious to God, This how acceptable; That how covered
" with threats, This how inriched with promises; That is a cloud
" of thunder, This a river of delight; That is a path of misery,
" This a way of mercy: in that God Abhors me, in this God
" loves me; in that I feel his Frowns and strokes, in this I feel
" his Smiles and comforts; that brings down all Curses on me,
" this all Blessings on me; In that I shew my self a Rebel, and
" do nothing but dishonour God, in this a Servant, and in some
" measure

" meafure bring him Glory;if I continue in that,farewell all Mer-
" cy and happineſs,I perifh with hunger,I am loſt for ever; if I at-
" tain to this,God is mine,Chriſt is mine,Mercy,Pardon,Favour,
" Comfort, Grace, Heaven, Happineſs, I ſhal be ſaved for ever.
" Now,O my Soul,thou feeſt both Eſtates in their Nature,in their
" Fruits,in their Ends;yea,thou haſt felt the bitterneſs of the one,
" ſay, Is not Mercy better then Miſery ? is not God better then
" Sin ? is not Heaven better then Hell ? is not Plenty better then
" Famine ? Life, then Death ? O then, ariſe, up, be gone, re-
" linquiſh thy courſe of Sin, of Miſery, of Death, of Hell,
" and ariſe and go by true Repentance unto God, unto Chriſt,
" unto Grace, unto new Obedience, unto Mercy, unto Joy, un-
" to Bleſſing, unto Life, unto Eternal Life, and that moſt hap-
" py, &c.

3. The third thing is to clear it, *How theſe two are prime ſteps* How theſe are
to Repentance ; *viz.* A Conſideration that a ſinful courſe is moſt prime ſteps to
miſerable, and a penitent is, moſt happy and comfortable; are Repentance.
ſteps, &c. Only premiſe a difference twixt a *Cauſe*, and twixt
an *Occaſion* of Repentance. The Spirit of God is the *Cauſe*,
theſe conſiderations are *Occaſions*, and *work by way of argument*
or means.
They work by
1. That they do ſo, *appears by Scripture*, 1.King.8.47. *If* way of Argu-
they ſhall bethink themſelves in the Land whither they were car- ment or Means
ried,Captive, and repent. Ezek. 18. 28. *Becauſe he conſidereth* proved,
and turneth away from all his Tranſgreſſions, &c. Nay,if in- By Scripture.
conſideration be given as a proper reaſon,why ſome repented not
(*no man repented*, *ſaying*, *What have I done* ?) then é contra,
Conſideration of our ſins muſt be a right ſtep unto Repentance:
Here you ſee clearly, that ſolid conſideration is, as it were, the
Foundation of true Converſion ; there it begins, and takes
riſe ; there is a Bethinking, of ſin, before a Repenting from
ſin.

2. Nay, and it is evident in *Example* too : *I thought on my*
wayes (ſaid *David*, Pſal. 119. 59.) *and turned my feet unto thy* By Example.
Teſtimonies : Like a Traveller, who in a Journey ſtands ſtill,and
conſiders with himſelf, ſurely this way is wrong, I am out of my
way, and then he turns about and gets him into the right way
again. So in this caſe, the like may be ſaid for compariſon of
an Unconverted courſe, with the happineſs of a Converted and
peni-

penitent condition, *Hof.* 2. 7. *The shall she say, I will go and return to my first husband, for then was it better with me then now.* The condition in which the Church then was, was a condition of much misery and affliction; her way of sin was *hedged up with thorns,* verf. 6. and the way of obedience she considered of to be a path of mercy, and much prosperity; and comparing the one condition with the other, hereupon resolvs, to *return to her first husband* (i.) to turn unto God by true Repentance.

By Argument.

3. It may be cleared *by Argument* and *Reason,* that thefe two, *viz.* Solid Confideration, and Right Comparifon, are fteps unto Repentance.

For folid Confideration.

1, For *Solid Confideration,* thus: If *inconfideration be the caufe of impenitency* (or of going on in a finful courfe) then *Confideration is a proper means and way for Repentance* ; for as much as thefe two are contraries, and contrary caufes produce contrary effects; but inconfideration is a caufe of impenitency, fo the Prophet, *Jer.* 8. 6. *No man repented him of his Wickednefs, faying, What have I done ? every one turned to his courfe, as the horfe rufheth into the battel.* They minded not what they did, whether lawful, or unlawful, or what would be the iffue of thefe things; but like the horfe, which without fear or wit rufheth into the battel among fwords and pikes.

If inconfideration be the caufe of impenitency, then confideration is a proper means for Repentance.

Confideration of fin removes many qualities of fin, which keep the heart in impenitency, as,

2. *Confideration of fin, removes many qualities which keep the heart in impenitency*; therefore it is a good ftep and way unto Repentance. There are three qualities which hold faft the foul from returning :

Ignorance.

1. *Ignorance*; therefore *darkned underftandings,* and *hearts alienated from the life of God,* are conjoined, *Eph.* 4. 18. a blind mind, and a wicked life, are infeparable ; yea, greedinefs to fin, and ignorance, are there alfo coupled, verf. 18, 19. no man fo forward to fin, as he who knows it not. Now folid Confideration removes ignorance, it opens the eies of our underftanding, and makes us to fee and behold that evil in fin which we never faw before ; in a right confideration there is 1. *Lumen fcientia.* 2. *Confcientia.* 3. *Experientia.*

Security.

2. *Security* ; for prefumptuous men will never leave fin, if they may be fafe. He who fears not miferable evil, will not be perfwaded to forfake his finful evil : He who thinks that he may be wicked and fafe, will be wicked ftill ; nay, he adds drunkennefs

to

The Sinners Conversion to God.

to thirst who presumes of peace. No evill shall befall us, said they who despised all warnings to Repentance; but solid consideration removes this security and presumption; it makes the soul to see, that as sin is an evil thing, so it will prove a bitter thing; and that the way which is sinful (of all wayes) is the most fearful: it makes the sinner to behold the Angel with the sword drawn in the way of sin; my meaning is, to behold God exceedingly displeased, the Wrath of God revealed against all Unrighteousness, severely threatning, and one who will assuredly execute his wrath to the utmost, if sinners will not hearken and return; by no means acquiting the guilty: Except ye repent ye shall perish. 3. *Hardness of heart:* That brawny Rockiness which is ever accompanyed with an impudent resolution, casting off, and sligh ing all means, and which is gainsaying, or frustrating all the Lessons of Mercies, Afflictions, Ordinances, &c. they made *their hearts as an Adamant stone*, least they should hear the Law, &c. Zach. 7. 12. But solid consideration helps much against this unsensible temper; it is of great force towards the melting of the heart, working strongly upon the affections, *as Peter thought thereon and wept bitterly. Then shall ye remember your wayes, and shall loath your selves:* For now a man sees indeed that he is in a very evil condition, and lost for ever, if the Lord be not the more merciful to him; and this will startle him somewhat, pierce him, make him, with them in *Acts* 2. cry out, *Men and brethren, what shall I do?*

_{Hardness of Heart.}

3. *Solid Consideration of sin, makes sin appear to the soul in its own proper nature, colours and effects:* As we are drawn to commit sin, so likewise to continue in it: through falshood and error, we are deceived and err in our hearts, and therefore we continue in sinful wayes; but as Truth doth rise in the mind, so Reformation will appear in our hearts and wayes; know therefore that sin appears unto us two wayes; either *Erroneously*, as invested and clothed with pleasures, profits, much serviceableness to our ends, and as satisfactions of our desires; as *Judas* lookt on his sin in the money, and went on; and thus they tend to impenitency, they keep us fast in an evil way, because of sensible sweetness. Or, *Properly*, and nakedly as sin; as the Violation of a most holy Will, dishonour of a great God, and separation from a good God, and as exposing us to the wrath of God,

Solid Consideration makes Sin appear in in its own proper Nature.

L curse

The Riotous Prodigal, or

curse of the Law, and pains of Hell and all outward Calamities. And thus apprehended, new Arguments and Reasons of hatred and Detestation arise within the Soul: Should I love that, or live in that, which is Gods dishonour, and will prove mine own damnation? My troubles, losses, fears come all from my sins; these are my sins and my doings, they are the cause of all this trouble, inward and outward: But solid consideration makes sin to appear as sin in its own nature and true effects; therefore it occasioneth hatred of sin, and consequently Repentance.

Comparison of the misery of a sinful, with the happiness of a penitent condition, a step to Repentance.

For, This breeds found Judgment of things that differ.

2. For Comparison of the misery of a sinful, with the happiness of a penitent and converted condition; that this likewise is a stept and way to Repentance, may be thus proved:

1. *This Comparison breeds sound Judgment in us of things that differ:* All corrupt works are rooted in a corrupted mind; like ill rhumes in the Head, which come from ill qualities in the Stomack; or rather like some ill diseases and irregularities in the Limbs, Arms and Feet, which come from unsound humours in the Brain. So it is in this case, men go on confidently in sin, and are taken excessively with those poor baits of sensual pleasure and profit, as if there were no other pleasure, delight, gain, acquirable, or to be found, but in the wayes and service of sin; as they in hell, think there is no other heaven: Or as foolish children, who conceive no other sport or delight like a rattle or dirting their hands, &c. But now, when by a comparison and true survey of either estate, it shall appear unto the soul that all these sinful pleasures and profits are but stolen waters, and at the best but for a season, they will end bitterly; and on the contrary, That Repentance from sin makes way for the most precious fountains of the most living comforts; that it enables a man for a nearer conjunction with the truest happiness, an Heiress of most infinite goodness, and lets in to such pleasures and joyes which pass all understanding, &c. Now the soul is reduced to a right judgment, and begins to contemn those false, vain, deluding temptations by sin, and is carried off to another course or way which will afford the real, solid, superlative advantages in happiness and comfort, &c.

This wins our love to a converted condition.

2. This Comparison *will win our love and affection to a Converted and penitent condition:* It is true, that as long as the heart loves sin, it will never leave it; for love is an iron clasp, a strengthning quality, a strong and tenacious quality; but if a mans love be changed,

changed, then his sinfull wayes will quickly be changed; for that way doth the heart and life go, that love do h go; they are not out who say that *Amor is Radix actionum,* as well as *Passionum.* Now by a right comparison of estates, there will appear in a converted and penitent condition the sole and sufficient causes of Love; *viz.* Good, and the best good, and only good, and most proper and sutable good; all which is apt to draw love, and consequently Repentance, for as much as Conversion from sin, begins in love to God.

3. This comparing of estates, in the wofulness of the one, and in the happiness of the other; that the one is death, and the other is life (as *Moses* propounds it to the Israelites) *occasionally stirs up the heart to fly unto God by prayer, and in the use of other means,* for grace and ability to leave the paths of death, and to walk in the wayes of life; for naturally men do affect life and happiness, and are afraid of death and misery.

This occasionally stirs up the heart to fly to God by Prayer, and in the use of meanes.

The first Use which I would make of this shall be for *Information.* You here see the *Cause why many are yet in their sins;* that they repent not, though we preach, though God punisheth, though man counsels. Surely they never yet did search their hearts and wayes, they never did consider of what they have done; they are like the *Laodiceans,* who thought themselves to be *rich and increased, and to stand in need of nothing;* but they never yet saw their *blindness, nakedness, and extreme poverty and misery.* There are many duties unto which men will be perswaded, as to hear the Word, receive the Sacrament, give some Almes, say some Prayers, and now and then to confer of some good; but of all the duties which do so nearly concern them, they are hardly perswaded to this, *viz.* to consider of their sins: 'tis true, they will confess, That all men are sinners, and themselves too, but as some do with their debts, they care not to see and view them; so many with their spiritual estates, they have no mind to search into them, to look them over, to meditate of the Vileness of them.

Use
For information.
Of the cause why many are yet in their sins.

Consider these things, 1. *That this inconsideration leaves many a sin already committed upon a sad account.* God doth consider them, though we will not; they are in his book and before his eye, though we will not think and look on them. 2. *That it ripens sin exceedingly:* The heart which will not consider of past, will break

Considerations to such as doe not Consider their wayes.

break out into sin future; it will be high in sinning, if negligent in considering; he will venture deeply, who knows not the nature nor the merit of sinning. 3. *All the work of Repentance will lye flat and dead*: Why? where can be that brokenness of heart? that filial lamentation for sinning? that remorse of spirit? that indignation, that detestation of it? that resolution against it? that watchfulness and fear? until by a sound consideration we come to see the vileness and miserableness of sinning, &c. He who thinks his way right, will not turn aside; and that man who knows no better, will never leave, or change, a bad course. 4. *You advantage Temptations exceedingly*: You are under the edge and power of them all, for you see nothing to hinder you; the motions to sin will pass without any contradiction, for you know not the evil nor misery of being impenitent. Great sins will seem but little, little will seem none; how easie is he to sin, who considers not the great evil in sin? 5. *All the edge of the Ordinances is blunted and dulled by inconsideration*; they are but water on the Tiles, which passe away: For what are *Threatnings* against sin? what operation have they on us to make us tremble and humble our hearts, whiles we hear them as Pieces discharged at others, not at our selves? And so, what force have the *Precepts* for new Obedience, or the *Promises* for much mercy to the Penitent, until we see that we are the men (as *Nathan* said to *David*) whom all this concerns. 6. *You will never prize Christ aright, nor the love of God in giving of Christ*, nor will you ever seek him to purpose (with hungrings and thirstings) until you do seriously consider of your sinful estates: A man, if whole, will not seek to the Physician, and if he hath but a scratch, will not send to the Chyrurgion: No, sense, or slight sense of sin, hath no influence on our affections; but let a man sadly view and find out that he is bad indeed, out with God, ready for Hell, must perish for sin, this man will cry out, *Is there no Balm in Gilead*? is there no hope for us sinners? He will enquire for a Saviour, and when he knows him, he will with tears beseech him (*O the hope of Israel and the Saviour thereof in the time of* Trouble!) Master, have mercy on me or else I perish: if thou canst do any thing, save me. 7. *You will never come to any true setledness, nor grounded assurance of peace with God,*

The Sinners Conversion to God.

God, nor in your own Consciences, until you do throughly consider of your sinful conditions and estates: For how know you whether you be good or bad? in Covenant, or out of Covenant with God? that he will save you or condemn you? what shall become of you when you die? Untill you by solid Consideration find out the vileness and miserableness of your sinful condition, out of which you must indeed be translated, if ever you would be saved, or know assuredly that you shall be saved. 8. *You will not know how to make special requests unto God:* For you know not the nature nor danger of that pride, of that hypocrisie, of that uncleanness, of that envy and malice, &c. which are in you: When we do not know what our selves are, what our estates are, we can never make special requests for the supply of special wants; either we make no prayers at all, or only general, and faint, and flat Petitions. 9. Lastly, *If you will not think on your wayes with a Penitential Consideration, you must one day think on them with a Judicial Consideration*: Tis better to consider of them now and Repent, then to feel them and find them in Hell and be Damned.

Object. But you'l say, We are *Ignorant*, and it belongs to such as *have Learning to consider throughly of their sinful estates.* This belongs to such as have learning.

Sol. 1. *It doth indeed belong to the Learned, but not only to them:* A learned conscience is necessary for every sinner, though not a learned head: the Subject who should consider, is not the learned man, but the lamed sinner; art not thou one? 2. *God hath given thee a Reflexive Faculty,* a conscience, a memory inabling thee to review what hath been done; thou hast these still in thee, and thou canst make use of them for other businesses; why not in this? 3. But then, study the *Word* more, that thou mayest thence be inlightned to conceive of sin aright, &c. get knowledg, get understanding, &c. Answered.

Obj. But we *are not at Leisure*, we have so much businefs to do, &c. We are not at leisure.

Sol. 1. *This is a most necessary work*, it deserves thy pains and time: What, not at leisure to save thy soul? at leisure to eate, to drink, to play, to be idle, to sin, and not at leisure to consider of sin? to repent of sin? to save thy self from sin? Answered.

sin? Have you leisure to go to Hell, and none to goe to Heaven? 2. *It is a most Beneficial work*: it will deliver thee from Hell, and make way for Heaven. 3. *It is the most excellent work* that thou canst spend time upon, the change of thee from Sin, to Grace; from a sinful, to an holy condition; it is a glorious change, even into the Image of God in Christ.

Object.
It will make me mourne, despair, and feare.
Answered.

Object. But it will make me nothing but mourn, and sigh, and despair, and fear.

Sol. 1. So *Satan tells thee*; so doth not God nor his Word tell thee. 2. *If consideration of Sin, breeds godly sorrow for Sin;* and *Godly sorrow, Repentance unto Salvation,* thou hast little cause to grieve to be thus grieved. 3. Nay, *the neglect of timely consideration, that is the cause indeed of such fear and despair.* O, say men! had we thought of this course, known this heretofore, we had never run on so, we had never come into this extremity of horror, &c. It is with sin as it is with diseases, if taken or not taken in time.

Use 2.
To settle and Relieve Troubled Souls.

Another Use which I would make of this Point, shall be of *Satisfaction to settle and relieve troubled Souls,* who fear much whether they have ever throughly and rightly considered thus of sin or no; and consequently, fear the truth of their Repentance. For the fuller satisfying of them I will propound some Cases, the Resolution of which may afford more clear light:

Some Cases Resolved for Satisfaction.

Case 1.
How a man may know his Consideration is Right.
If it work in him a Condemnation of Sin.

1. How a Christian may know that his consideration of sin is right and penitential? I conjecture thus,

1. *If it work in him a Condemnation of sin*: Before a man consider aright of sin, he is ready to call the proud happy; he knows how to commit sin, and to approve it, and defend it, and plead for it. Sin seems his daintiest bit, and choicest bait; as if nothing else bore delight and contentment but sin: but when the heart is brought rightly to ponder and to consider of sin, he is enabled not only to condemn sin in the general, (thus, sin is an evil thing;) but also in particular (these my sins are vile and evil things; *I have done exceeding foolishly,* said *David*;) O that I should ever open my mouth for them, that ever I should love them, follow them as I have done; I now behold them as the only dishonour of God, grief of his Spirit, Violations of his Righteousness, Injuries of his

Pa-

The Sinners Averſion from God.

patience, abuſes of his goodneſs and mercies ; the ſpeares in the heart of Chriſt, the ſpots in my ſoul, the wounds in my conſcience, &c. It is one thing to look upon ſin as a *meer Object*, and it is another thing to look upon ſin as a *vile Object*: to look on ſin as a meer Object, this is but the natural act of the underſtanding, which, like the eye, is ready to ſee all colours; but to look on ſin as a vile Object, this is the work of a penitential underſtanding, wherein a perſon ſees ſo much intolerable and exceſſive foulneſs in his ſinful wayes, that he now condemns and judgeth thoſe wickedneſſes and abominations ; and himſelf too for higheſt folly and madneſs for love, ſervice and obedience to them.

2. *If it work in him humiliation for ſin*; we read of *Peter* that he conſidered, or thought on the words of Jeſus (and through them, of his great ſin in the denial of maſter) but how did he conſider of them? What, only by his ſimple reflection, that Chriſt had forewarned him, and that he had done evil in denying him? Surely thus he thought, but the matter went further then his thoughts ; he conſidered it in an affecting, or rather, in an afflicting way ; for the Text ſaith, That when he had thought thereon, *he went out and wept bitterly*. There is a fourfold conſideration of ſin : One is only *a conſideration of ſin*; when a man thinks of ſin as he hears a Sermon, hear it only: ſo, think of it only, and that's all ; this is an empty conſideration. Another is, *a ſinful conſideration only*; when a man conſiders of ſin in a ſinful way, either to boaſt of it, or to excite his heart to more delight and propenſion to ſin ; this is a guilty conſideration. A *third* is a *Judicial conſideration*, which ariſeth from the promptings and ſuggeſtions of a conſcience awakened, now accuſing, and condemning, and purſuing the ſinner, both with the remembrance of former ſins, and with the evidence of Gods preſent and future indignation. A *fourth* is, a *Penitential conſideration*; wherein, upon the evidence of ſinning, the ſoul is ſenſible, not to deſpair, which breeds hopeleſs terror, yet to repentance, wherein it is exceedingly grieved, and troubled, and diſpleaſed for the ſins, committed. If the conſideration of ſin be a dry act, ſuch an act as ſets where it riſeth (only in the mind) and hath no influence upon the affections ; if it be not a ſympathizing act, (*i.*) ſuch an act as works

If it work in him Humiliation for ſin.

grief

grief in the foul, as well as difcovery of evil in the mind, it is but a vain thing and never conduceth to repentance; for as it is with mercies received, unlefs the apprehenfion of their kindnefs and goodnefs defcends to the affections, they never ftir up thankfulnefs; and as it is with the promifes, unlefs their excellency and futablenefs come down from the mind to the will, they never excite faith: fo is it with fin; unlefs, befides the confideration of it, there be not an operation and influence upon the heart to grieve and mourn, it will never prove right and penitential.

Thou fayeft, thou knoweft thy fins as well as any man can tell thee: Be it fo, but if thy heart remain hard, not humbled, abafed, broken, grieved for thefe fins, alas! as their unworking faith, *Jam.* 2. fo thy unaffected fpeculation of fin, is vain: but findeft thou this, that upon the ferious confideration of thy fins, thy heart is humbled and abafed in thee? that thou art caft down in the fenfe of thy exceeding vilenefs? *O wretched man that I am! O Lord to me belongs nothing but fhame and confufion!* and that thy heart is grieved within thee and afflicted? that bitter mournings arife becaufe of bitter finnings? *my foul hath them in remembrance and is humbled within me*; *Lam.* 3. Thy heart melts before the Lord; I affure thee, this is a right and bleffed confideration of fin.

If it work Deteftation of fin
3. *If it work in him Deteftation of fin.* Griefe feemes to be more paffionate, but hatred is a more fixed quality, as I may fo phrafe it, *Ezek.* 36. 31. *Ye fhall remember your own evil wayes and your doings that were not good* (here is the confideration we fpeak of) *and ye fhall loath your felves in your own fight for your Iniquities and your abominations* (here is deteftation, the proper effect of true confideration;) for in a right confideration, the fingular caufes or reafons of hatred do arife: *v. g.* Excefs of evil, abfolute repugnancy to our beft good, effectual prejudice, and greateft injury. *Repugnans & Offendens*, the Schoolmen make the two chief grounds of hatred. *Vide Summiftas in* 1. 2*da. q.* 29. But I will not profecute that. Now then perufe thy felf, Haft thou confidered of thy finnes aright? if thou doeft not hate them, thou haft not; Seeft thou finne, and art thou brought to hate it? Let me but propound a few things unto thee, that thou mayeft fee whether

thou

thou loathest and hatest sin, or no. "*Is it peace, or is it war?* If sin lies quietly in the soul, it is peace, it is not hatred; hatred breeds variance, enmity, opposition, conflict. *Paul* hated sin, *Rom.* 7. 15. and wars with it, *v.* 23. "*Is it a deadly war?* is it for life? Will this suffice thee, that sin doth not terrifie thy conscience; or wilt thou not be satisfied, till sin be mortified and crucified in the lusts and affections thereof? "*Is it like* Davids *war*, wherein he left not one *Amalekite* to escape and carry tidings; and not like *Sauls*, to kill some, and spare the rest? Canst thou say, *Lord, I hate the thing that is evil?* Psal. 97. 10. and *I hate every false way?* Oh, if there be raised in thee, upon the consideration of sin, a deadly enmity and defiance with it, an implacable, general dislike, abomination, resistance, and desire to root it out; happy art thou; thy consideration of sin is rightly and effectually penitential.

4. If it *work in him, Reformation of sin:* Do you not read in *Psal.* 119. 59. that *David considered and thought on his wayes? I thought on my ways,* saith *David,* (so do many, many indeed do so, but not as *David* did; for after he had said, I thought on my ways, he addeth,) *and turned my feet unto thy testimonies.* He so thought of his ill ways, that he left them, and betook himself unto good ways. If thinking on sin doth not produce leaving of sin, it is nothing; if thinking of sin doth not breed leaving of sin, then going on in sin will make you leave thinking of sin: And though we think of an ill way, yet if we do not enter into, and walk in a good way, it is nothing. There is a two-fold leaving of sin, one which is proper to the condition of Glory; another which is proper to the condition of Grace. I speak not of the former, which is the absolute dissolution of sin; but of the latter, which is an imperfect (though true) separation from sin; consisting, in *Affection,* wherein the Will is alienated from sin; the *evil which I would not do,* saith the Apostle: In *Mourning; O wretched man! who shall deliver me from this body of death?* In *Endeavour; willing,* or endeavouring *to live honestly,* Heb. 13. 18. There is a purpose to walk in new obedience, and an hearty desire so to do, and not to serve sin any longer; and also an active endeavour to put off the former conversation, and to crucifie the flesh, with the affections and lusts thereof.

If it work in thee, Reformation.

M To

To confider of fin, and yet ſtill to love it, and ſtill to live in it, to ſtudy to fulfil the luſts of it, to give up our ſelves to the ſervice of it, to walk in darkneſs, to be the ſame in our affections to it, and in our obedience unto it, this is not onely a vain, but a fearfull conſideration: But if, when we have throughly conſidered of fin in the vileneſs of it, we are effectually wrought upon to ariſe from our ſinfull courſe; O Lord! I have ſinned exceedingly, and done very fooliſhly; I am reſolved to leave this ſinfull way; Lord! help thou me, give me thy grace; turn thou me, and I ſhall be turned; turn away my heart and eyes, cauſe me to put off my old converſation; enable me to walk and live in newneſs of life. This is an happy Fruit, eſpecially if it hath two other Effects accompanying it, viz.

1. *Fervent Supplication*; if it carries the ſoul to God in Chriſt for mercy, for grace, for ſtrength. The reſolution to reform, if it goes no further than the ſtrength of the ſoul, it will eaſily cool, and quickly fail us; if ever it prove right, it muſt carry us to Chriſt, for as much as it is by his ſtrength, and by his grace, that we get our hearts turned from ſin, or that we are able to forſake our ſins. Haſt thou conſidered of thy ſins? why and doeſt thou not diſcern ſuch infinite guilt in them, as makes thee for ever accurſed, if thou haſt not mercy in Chriſt? and doeſt thou hereupon apply thy ſelf, in all humbleneſs of heart, to the Throne of mercy? *O Lord be mercifull to me a ſinner; according the multitude of thy tender mercies, blot out my tranſgreſſions*: Behold me through the bloud of Chriſt, yea, O Lord! heal my ſinfull ſoul; O Lord! change my heart; O Lord! diſſolve the powers of ſin in me, by thy mighty power ſubdue my iniquities; turn me from all ſin, make me a ſervant of righteouſneſs.

2. *Diligent application of our ſelves to the Means*, private and publick, ordinary and extraordinary; through the right uſe of which, we may expect ſufficient grace from God to work Repentance never to be repented of. Haſt thou rightly conſidered of ſin, why! what art thou now doing? where mayeſt thou now be found? what courſe doeſt thou take to leave ſin? what helps doeſt thou apply thy ſelf unto? what occaſions of ſin doeſt thou decline? what furtherances of a new life doſt thou regard and uſe?

use? If there be no watchfulness over thy spirit, no restraint to thy flesh, no stoutness of resolution, no separation from the occasions of sin, no humble study and respect to the Word, no fruitfull converse with holy society, how is it that thou sayest thou hast considered thy sins?

Whether *the consideration of sin may be right, and available to Repentance, when yet there are some sins which a man thinks not on?* To this, I conjecture it may be thus answered. 1. That *actual or particular inconsideration, if it be voluntary and affected, doth prejudice Repentance:* For it is to be supposed, that he who will not take the pains to think of his sins, hath not yet found an heart or a will to leave his sins. Therefore consider, that actual inconsideration may arise, either, *From want of light or evidence*; the eyes of the mind are not yet so fully opened, they are not so perfectly acquainted with the Law, which discovers sin; much sin they see, but not all; not that they would not, but because they cannot; so a weak eye hath not such clear and full sight: Or, *From hypocrisie of will*; when means of evidence are present, and commands of consideration are urged; but either from a secret love of sin, or from a lazinesse of spirit, the person will not take pains to consider throughly of his manifold sins, this kind of inconsideration being wilfull and affected will be interpreted for Impenitency, because the person will not endeavour faithfully the wayes of Repentance. 2. *That the latitude of the Object considered, doth not so immediately discover and decide, as the efficacy and influence flowing from consideration it self.* Though I am not able to find out every particular wherein I do offend; yet if by the consideration of those sins, which I do consider of, my heart doth melt and mourn, and strives to loath and forsake them, because they are sinfull: If these drive me out of my self unto Christ; if these occasion me earnestly to acquaint my self with God, to beg for Reconciliation, for Grace, for Mercy, for Strength, &c. though there be many sins which I have not actually thought on, yet this may be a right and penitential consideration.

Another Case may be this; Whether the Consideration of sin, tending to Repentance, must be frequent? or, Whether *a single Consideration may be sufficient?* For the resolution of this

II. *Case.* Whether Consideration of sin may be right, when there are some sins that a man thinks not of? Particular inconsideration, if it be voluntary, doth prejudice Repentance.

III. *Case.* Whether a single Consideration of sin be sufficient to repentance?

Distinctions premised. Repentance is either Initial, or Gradual.

There is a two-fold consideration of sin. Solemn.

Ordinary.

Distinguish twixt the Grace of Repentance, and the Act of it.

Solemn consideration necessary to Initial Repentance.

Ordinary consideration necessary to Gradual Repentance.

this Case, thus. 1. Divines distinguish of Repentance, that it is either Initial, or Gradual: The *Initial* Repentance is, the first turning from sin, nay, the very first will and desire so to do, with a purpose and endeavour to effect it: The *Gradual* Repentance is, the ripening and perfecting of Repentance in the degrees of all the parts of it. 2. Again, There is a two-fold consideration of sin: One is *solemn*, wherein the soul sequesters it self, earnestly searcheth into the Law of God, and into its own spirit, and into the ways of Life; perusing and reviewing the sinfull condition all over, in the parts and kinds, in the hainous circumstances and agravations; and hereupon solemnly indites it self before the Lord, by confessing, judging, &c. Another is *ordinary*; which is a daily looking over the Book, and perusing of the sinfull Accounts from time to time. 3. You must distinguish twixt the *Grace* or *quality* of *Repentance*, and twixt the *Act* or *exercise* of *Repentance*; the Grace is wrought onely by Gods Spirit; the Exercise or operation is wrought and occasioned by consideration. These things being premised, I conjecture thus much.

1. That *solemn Consideration is necessary to initial Repentance.* The Heart is not effectually excited to the actual leaving of sin, until it doth first seriously examine and try it self, find out and ponder the vileness of its sinning and transgression; slight thoughts work no more then slight confessions, That we are all sinners, and there's an end; but the heart must look on sin in the kinds, circumstances, hellish vileness of its thoughts, if ever it will repent indeed. 2. That *ordinary consideration is necessary to gradual Repentance.* If ever you would perfect your Repentance, you must ever think of your sins, those that are past, those that are present. By ordinary consideration, I do not mean, a slight and perfunctory view of them; but a daily view, though not in length of time, yet having the same disposition of heart to condemn and abhor them, and quickning us more fervently to seek God for strength, and to decline the occasions of sin, and to grow more watchfull and tender, &c. If you do not ordinarily consider of the vileness of sin, you will be ordinarily insnared by the deceitfulness of sin; if you would enjoy constant victory and deliverance,

verance, you muſt admit of frequent conſideration. As for the *ſolemn Conſideration,* that I conjecture *is not neceſſary at all times,* but upon ſpecial occaſions: Either 1. Before we enter into ſome weighty buſineſs: 2. When we lie under ſome weighty afflictions: 3. When we are to die, and make ſtraight our weighty accounts: 4. When we are more ſolemnly to meet the Lord and renew our Covenants with him; as in the day of Humiliation, or when we are to come unto the Sacrament. Now are we more ſolemnly and ſeriouſly to conſider of our ſins, partly, 1. Becauſe now the Lord conſiders them who come into his ſpecial preſence, how you come. 2. Becauſe you are ſeriouſly to renew your Repentance, which you cannot ſeriouſly do, without ſerious conſideration. 3. Becauſe you are to renew your Covenants with God, to keep a more ſerious watch, &c. Therefore now let us ſearch our hearts, try, and conſider of our ways, renew our Repentance, turn with all our ſtrength unto the Lord, put away iniquity far from us, humble our ſelves low before the Lord, confeſs our ſins, judge our ſelves; thus if we do, we ſhall find more ſtrength in our Repentance, more peace in our Conſciences, more ſweetneſs in the Sacrament, more confidence towards Chriſt, and may comfortably expect the pardon of our ſins, and ſalvation by his bloud.

ſolemn corſideration not neceſſary at all times. The times when it is neceſſary.

Reaſons of it.

The third and laſt Uſe ſhall be for Exhortation, to ſet upon theſe two works of Conſideration and Compariſon. Here let me propound two things unto you, reſpecting the practical exerciſe of them. Qu. 1. *What is required to enable a perſon rightly to conſider, and to compare?* &c. I conceive thus. 1. *There muſt be knowledge:* Right Conſideration and Compariſon, are works of an illightened mind; to underſtand the proper nature and diſtinction of things, neceſſarily requires knowledge: For Ignorance can neither conſider nor diſtinguiſh; therefore ſtudy the Word, and other Books, to underſtand what objects are, of which you are to conſider. 2. There muſt be *ſome Wiſdome:* For every Underſtanding cannot find out things, nor is able to make their differences of vileneſs or excellency; as *David* ſaid of the Works of God, that *a brutiſh man underſtands them not,* &c. *Pſal.* 92. 5, 6. that we ſay

Uſe 3.
Exhortation to conſideration and compariſon.
What is required to enable us thereto.
Knowledge.

Wiſdome.

of

of persons onely enlightened, That if they have not spiritual Wisdome, to compare things, or to consider of them, they will never, by the evidence of the vileness of Sin, or excellency of Grace, be drawn to Repentance. 3. There must be *Retiredness*, or Sequestration: You must separate your selves, as *Solomon* speaks. Tumults of business, or violence of noise, distract the thoughts, and alienate them, utterly disabling to consider. 4. You must *gather your selves together:* You must strive against division in mind; be carefull to unite and to center your thoughts, not suffering your selves to be scattered, or blown away from your self. 5. You must *pray* unto God to open your eyes to see, and to give a judgment to discern, and to unite your hearts, and enable them to go through the work; for verily you shall find much reluctancy and opposition of spirit, to such a work.

Quest. 2. In what manner we are to consider, and to compare, *&c.* I Answer, 1. *The Rules for a right consideration,* so as to occasion Repentance, are these. 1. Do it *in a free time*; there are times, wherein a man is most unapt for such a work as this, as when very sick in body, or under some passion of grief, or fear, or loss: Now the soul is in a Tumult, it cannot see things aright, nor judge aright. Take a calm time for all works of moment, either to know, or to judge thy Estate. 2. Do it *with a full time:* The matter is weighty, not the work of a day, as they spake concerning the separation in *Ezra,* it *was not a work to be done in one day.* Nor is this of sound Consideration, a business which can be hastily done, and well done; you must do it deliberately and seriously; for there are many sins, and many circumstances to be considered of, and to be weighed and judged, *&c.* 3. Do *it throughly:* Do not begin a little, and then give over; leave not till you come to the bottome; see the worst of it, and the utmost of it, if ever you will see the good of it: You are never a jot the worse, by seeing how bad you are; but you may be the better all the dayes of your life for it. You must be faithfull to your own soul, not to pass over any sin that you can well conceive your self guilty of. 4. You must do it *orderly:* Consider not of all sins in a Lump, but break your thoughts: And as they in Judgment consider of one Cause, and then of another; so do you of your sins; what are your chief sins,

in

The Sinners Conversion to God.

in affection, or practice, or inclination, and so go to other, &c. in their order, time, place, &c.   5. You must *do it so long,* ⟶ Do it till your *until your heart begin to relent,* and grows tender and soft: Ah! heart begin to how vile, and abominable, and wretched, &c. and then strike Relent. in with God by Prayer and Confession, &c. And this is a way to bring you to Repentance.

Secondly, the *Rules for Comparison.* If you would so com- ⟶ Rules for compare the miserableness of the sinfull, with the happiness of a con- parison of the verted condition, so as to be brought to Repentance, then 1. verted state. *You must compare them in their proper natures and effects*; not by ⟶ Compare them that which is accidental, but by that which is natural; there in their proper may be some trouble to a converted estate, and some delight up- nature and efon an unconverted estate; these then are preternatural, they fects. arise not from the things themselves, but are contingent accidents: But compare the real natures and fruits of the one with the other, and then you shall see reason to leave the one, and to choose the other.   2. You must *compare them by a pro-* ⟶ Compare them *per Rule:* not standing, in point of definitive sentence, what by a proper your own heart, or what the World approves; but onely what Rule. God in his Word doth sentence to be most vile and miserable, and what he pronounceth to be most good and comfortable. The Rule of Comparison must ever be pure, impartial and perfect. 3. You must *have so much faith also, as to believe what God saith* ⟶ Believe what *of either estate:* For though you should refer the decision unto God saith of him, yet if upon his resolving, you are resolved to quarrel against either state. it, and dispute the truth and validity, and say yet, It is otherwise, we will not believe that our sinfull course is so bad and so dangerous; alas! you will never repent while you live: But you must resolve of this, that the Word shall captivate your thoughts, and shall discover, and set the differences of estates; and so you may be occasioned to repent.   4. You must take an *humble* ⟶ Resolve to fol*and firm resolution to take, and follow that way which God disco-* low that way *vers unto you for the best*; and to decline that way which God God discovers discovers to be bad and damnable: (i.) You will betake your to be best. selves industriously and stedfastly unto all the ways and means by which you may be strengthened to leave your sins, and to walk with God in newness of obedience.

Luke

Luke 15. 18. *I will arise, and go to my Father.*

<small>The Resolution of the Prodigal,</small>

These words contain in them, the other fundamental part of Repentance appearing in the Prodigal, *viz. The Resolution of his Will.* To apprehend evil, is somthing; but to leave it, is the safest thing; to see a better condition, shews that the eye is opened, but to go to our Father, this shews that the heart is changed.

<small>Set forth by The Matter of it.</small>

This Resolution of the Prodigal, is set forth, partly by the 1. *Matter of it*, which is very compleat; it contains as much as Repentance requires, (*Surgam & ibo,*) *I will arise, I will go.* St. *Austin* is something facetious upon the words; *Surgam*, I will arise, *quia jacebat,* for the Prodigal was down before: Sin is a fall, and Repentance is a rising: and *ibo*, I will go to my Father, *quia longe aberat*, for the Prodigal was far from home: Sin is a long travel, a wandring rather; and Repentance is a sweet returning: We go abroad when we sin, we come home when we repent. And *Chrysostome* upon *Ibo ad patrem*, I will go home to my Father, wittily compares the motions of Repentance to those of a journey. That though which I do most conjecture at in the words, is, The Prodigals compleat Resolution for the matter of Repentance. Repentance is a motion twixt two terms, and is made of *Aversio* and *Conversio*; Aversion from a sinfull course, and that is in *Surgam*, I will arise; Conversion to God, and this is in *Ibo ad patrem*, I will go to my Father. 2. The *Manner or Form of it:* It is not *votum*, a wish, nor yet *velleitas*, a woulding, nor yet *volitia de futuro*, I will hereafter: But his Resolution to arise and to go home, is as compleat as the Matter on which he doth resolve; *I will arise, I will go*: It was a strong and peremptory and present Resolution. 3. *The Motive or Inducement to it*, and that is in the word [*my Father.*] The apprehensions of a Father, work most to the return of a sinner. That I shall find a Father of God, prevails much to make a penitent Child of men. There are many excellent Propositions observable out of the words; some I will onely point at, the rest I will insist upon. Thus then.

<small>The Manner of it.</small>

<small>The Motive to it.</small>

<small>General Propositions.</small>

<small>Repentance is a Gradual thing in working.</small>

1. *That Repentance is a Gradual thing in working.* Though the habitual implantation of it be instantaneous, (for it is a Grace infused, and therefore admits not of space and leisure,) yet the actual operation of it is successive, and by degrees; as here in the

the Prodigal, 1. *He came to himself.* 2. *He confiders of his perishing condition.* 3. Then *compares it with the happy condition of those in his fathers houfe.* And then 4. *Refolves* to leave his fins, and go home to his fathers houfe.

2. *That Repentance is an Active thing*; it will make a finner to leave his place and to find his feet: rifing and going are active motions. He who repents indeed, is doing, indeed; it is not an an indifferent, cold, grave, dull nothing, but the foul ftirs indeed againft fin, and ftrives indeed to enjoy and pleafe God. *Ephraim* defiles his graven Images, and *will no more have to do with them*; and readily come unto the Lord, *Behold we come unto thee, for thou art the Lord our God.* And therefore S. *John* faith, *Bring forth fruits meet for repentance.* Repentance is a working Grace, it fets the judgment, the will, the affections, the whole man on work. *Repentance is an active thing*

3. *That found refolution is requifite to found Reformation.* The Prodigal here is peremptory, *I will arife, I will go to my Father*: This is a point of great confequence, and very proper to the Text, and therefore I will infift upon it, by inquiring, 1. What this found refolution is? 2. Why it is requifite to a found Reformation? 3. Then what ufeful Application of this to our felves? Sound Refolution is requifite to found Reformation.

Queft. 1. *What folid Refolution is?*

Sol. *It is a well grounded, ftrong, conftant and active purpofe of the Will of a penitent finner, wherein he is peremptorily bent to forfake a finful courfe, and to lead a holy and a better life.* What Solid Refolution is.

1. *It is a purpofe or bent of the Will*: So it is called, *Act.* 11. 23. *A purpofe of heart*: when matters of faith or fact are only difcovered unto us, the work of the mind about them is called Apprehenfion; when they are debated and difputed there, this is called Deliberation: and when the will is fully inclined and wrought upon, that it is with it as with the body carried to the Center, the natural Inclinations poyfe and bend it thither; So the very Spirits, as it were, of the will, the *Pondus* of it, is carryed about the work, it is fet upon it; this is called *Refolution.* It is a purpofe or bent of the will.

2. *To forfake a finful courfe*: You muft diftinguifh twixt Intermiffions, and Excifions; twixt paufing and forfaking. In folid refolution the will is purpofed not to make only a ftop, or to admit of fome interruption, but alfo to make a divorce, an utter feparation, To forfake a finful courfe.

tion: *What have I to do with idols any more?* said *Ephraim*; and this separation is not only in respect of a particular or personal act; as thus, I will do this evil this time, or for so long a time; but also in respect of course, I am purposed to relinquish it, both in part, and in whole, both now and for ever: there is difference betwixt 1. Abstaining. 2. Forsaking. 3. Stopping. *Non propono peccare, sed propono non peccare.* *Isai.* 30. 22. *Thou shalt cast them away as a menstruous cloath, and say, get thee hence.* In the extent and latitude, though they have been *Mala utilia, jucunda & chara.*

To lead a Godly life.
3. And *to lead a Holy or Godly Life*: And in this respect, this resolution is called sometimes, a choosing of the way of God, sometimes a cleaving to the Lord, sometimes a serving of the Lord, sometimes a Covenant to serve the Lord, and to walk with him, and somtimes a readiness to hear what the Lord will speak; *I and my house will serve the Lord.* Psal. 119. 106. *I have sworn and will,* &c. The sum of all is this, Then is it a resolution of the will, when a person attains thus far; " This is an evil " way, I am heartily purposed never to walk in it more; this is " an holy and good way, I am heartily purposed to walk therein for " ever; these sins I will follow and serve no longer; but this " God shall be my God, his Lawes shall be my rule, and guide, " and his wayes shall be my wayes in the which I will walk.

The properties of this Resolution.
A well grounded purpose.
4. In the discription consider *the properties of this Resolution,* which are four. 1. It is *a well grounded purpose* of the will; it is not a house without a foundation, nor a ship without a bottom, nor yet with a weak bottom; It is not raised, I know not how, or on a sudden, in an irrational and humorous way, or in all haft: Ordinarily, he who will leave an ill course in haft, comes off from it (indeed) with too much leisure; but it is such a purpose, as is throughly bottomed upon such grounds as can give life, and maintain the bent and inclination of the will. It doth arise from, and depend upon mature consideration, and upon deep conviction: The sinner doth first look into, and seriously peruse and weigh an impenitent and sinful course, and seeth the strongest, and forciblest, and justest causes to renounce it for ever; and also upon due trial, and searching, and weighing in the ballance of the Sanctuary, he doth find the wayes of new obedience to be the true and only wayes of life; to which if he doth not turn, he cannot

cannot pleafe God, nor be faved; and unto which if he doth turn, then he is under the beft God, and in the moft excellent and faving condition: and hereupon begs of God for grace and ftrength; and fo refolves, &c. In a Word, the Refolution is well grounded; when it followes ferious deliberation, and is raifed upon divine affiftance, and entred into with earneft fupplication; for our ftrength cannot bring forth, nor maintain fo great a work as reformation.

2. It is a *ftrong purpofe of the will*: The operations of the will are reputed ftrong, when either they are not divided, but united; or when they are rooted in an habit or principle, and not only in an occafion and accident; or when they are abfolute, and not conditional: If the operations be divided, they are weak as Rivers, &c. fo when a man partly wills this, and partly that; he is inclined fomewhat to leave his fin, and yet he is inclined to keep it; this divifion hinders right refolution, which is not fo indifferent, fo indeterminate, fo divided, but centers the inclination of the will, only one way, *viz.* to a peremptory rejection of evil, and a peremptory election of good; the fcale goes down, and it is not a grain which will turn it: Again, if the operations of the will arife only from occafions which is bufied in alterable circumftances, they can never be ftrong; as the colour in the face, which arifeth from violent exercife only, goes off prefently; fo that refolution (if it may be fo called) which arifeth from changeable impreffions, is alwayes weak and fading; a deceitful bow, unftedfaft: *In their afflictions they will feek me* early, but, &c. Hof. 6. 4. But to the production of a penitential refolution (which makes a ftrong purpofe in the will) there muft be an habit which will fet the heart, and incline it fo, that it will not be taken off; as in *Ruth* to *Naomi*, *Intreat me not*, &c. there was a ftrong principle of love, which made up this ftrong purpofe to cleave unto her. Again, if the operations of the will be conditional, they can never be fo ftrong, as when they are abfolute; for a fuppofition and cafe, where the will may put off and difpence with it felf, cannot make the act of the will fo firm as where the cafe is abfolute.(for now the whole bent of the will is carried without any check or diminution.) If a man faith, I will leave fuch a finful courfe, in cafe I may have the countenance of fuch friends, or the benefit of fuch an eftate; and I will lead a godly life, in

A ftrong purpofe of the will.

case I may hold correspondence and esteem in the world, &c. purposes upon variable conditions are variable. These conditions do diminish the strength of Resolution; but when a person is carryed in an absolute way, come what will come, friendship or enmity, greatness or poverty, life or death, I will change my course; this is a strong purpose of will, and a right Resolution.

It is a constant purpose. 3. *It is a constant purpose, or continued:* The Philosophers do well distinguish twixt *Passions*, which are but the soul in a mood, and a fit, and twixt *Qualities*, which are setled tempers and Constitutions, as it were. Resolution is not a transient passion, but it is a fixed quality. Not that it is not interrupted, but that it is not renounced and given over, but is still maintained. Nor that it is not assaulted, but that it is not changed. A twisted Cord, *Propositi tenax*, that is a resolute man, *& sibi constans*, but a double minded man, an unstable spirit, a will, though strong as Passion, yet if unstable as water (hot in the first assault, as if we would be stronger then Men, and flat in the succeeding assaults, as if we were weaker then Women) these humours are rather some complements, which still shrink at the acting, then resolutions for change of Life: Passions are violent, but not constant, as the *Galathians* to *Paul*.

It is an active Purpose. 4. Lastly, It is an active purpose: for as it is a vain thing to deliberate much, and to resolve on little at length, so it is a vain Resolution which purposeth great things, but doth nothing. If I resolve to take Physick for my health, and never take any, what avails that Resolution? Like *Antigones*, *I will give*, but never gave. So, if a man resolve to leave his sins, but the day is still to morrow; he sets not upon it indeed, but yet a little slumber, yet a little sleep, as S. *Austin* spake of himself, *cras*, *cras*, this is vain. But true resolution is stirring and striving; it puts a man upon the work, as the Prodigal, *I will arise and goe to my Father*, who indeed did thereupon arise and go. I am resolved to confess my sins, to judge my self, to seek unto God by prayer; and I do indeed do so, I do confess, judge, pray, use the means, &c.

Why Resolution is Requisite. *Quest.* 2. Why this Resolution is requisite to a sound Reformation?

1. Be-

The Sinners Conversion to God. 93

1. Because *Reformation of our wayes cannot be performed without much Opposition:* As when *Nehemiah* began to repair the walls, was with much opposition. If you will not serve *sin* as a Lord, you must expect to hear of *sin* as an Enemy; if you will not serve its Lusts, you shall be hindred and molested with its Lusts. Stronger rowing is requisite against a strong Tide: So for Satan, he will not easily be dispossest; if you will not follow his Counsels, you shall feel his Darts; and the world will wonder at you, and reproach you, and vilifie you; temptations on the right hand, and on the left. Now, all these shocks and brunts, will not be sustained without a firm Resolution. It must be an house strongly built, upon an unmoveable Rock, which will stand against all winds and waves.

There can be no Reformation with out much opposition.

2. Because *sin hath been very dear unto us, and is beyond measure subtile to perswade and entice us.* It is not an easie thing (though death otherwise be threatned) to make a man willing to have his Arm or Leg cut off. Sin is as our members to us, it is called our self, born and bred with us. The separation is not easie where the Conjunction is Natural, and hath been more familiar: It will not be done by reasoning or intreaty, but Resolution is necessary. Again, *Sin is most subtile to alure us, to entice us,* to put out our thoughts of Reformation. How often doth it untwist the Cord and propound delights and pleasures (some sweet baits or other) which take us quite away from our private intentions? How extremely doth it fill the heart with Unbelief, that the Reformation of such a sin can never be? and if we set upon it, how strangely doth it amaze us, that there is no hope of mercy, and therefore we were better enjoy some pleasure a while, then bitternes and anguish for ever.

Sin is very subtile to Intice us.

3. *The heart is naturally deceitful, and apt to turn or be turned:* A small thing will make the eye to shut, and the very imagination of danger is enough to discourage many a man, and to make him to recoyl: A cunning man must be tyed in firm bonds. We think that we will do much, and suffer any thing; but this we find, that if the way be good, we do not easily like it; if it be long, we are quickly weary of it; if it be harsh, we are ready to forsake it. Now occurrents and accidents do ordinarily put on us new Intentions and Byasses.

The heart is naturally Deceitful.

4. If you consider the *frame and disposition of that new course of Godly walking,* you will confess that a resolution is necessary; for,

The frame of the new course of Godly walking.

1. It

The Returning Prodigal, or

It is spiritual. Strict. 1. It is spiritual, and wholly heavenly. 2. It is strict, and must be ordered by rule: no room for any one sinful lust or way, strait is the gate. 3. It is opposite and contrary to that nature and will which is corrupt in us, it is *supra & contra*. 4. It is difficult and very high; grace and supernatural works are hard, to deny our selves, our own righteousness, &c. 5. It is *capable of such dangers, which will not easily be digested*, even loss of life it self. 6. *It is very laborious*, it must cost a man much study and search, much care and watchfulness, much prayers, and many tears, much self-denial, and mortification; much going out of himself, and adventuring upon pure promises. 7. Of *necessity, the soul must undergoe much, if it will lead a godly life*; many violent temptations from Satan, inward conflicts with the love of sin, outward persecutions from the world, *They that will live godly* must suffer persecution. Now tell me whether a firm resolution be not necessary, when a man changeth to a course which is very spiritual and holy, whereas before he lived in a course that was sensual and impure; again, into a course very strict and contrary to him in great part, and very difficult, and very dangerous, and wherein he must be very industrious, and go through many a sharp trial and brunt.

Opposite to corrupt nature.
Difficult.
Capable of great dangers.
Very laborious.
The Soul must undergoe much for it.

Use All the use which I shall make of this assertion shall be reduced unto two heads. 1. Of Exhortation. 2. Direction.

Exhortation to bring our hearts to this Solid Resolution.
Motives.
Six dangers of Irresolution.
You will not be free from strong temptation.

1. The *Exhortation* is, that as we do desire a real reformation of our sinful wayes, so we *strive to bring our hearts to a solid resolution against them*. Two things I will propound as motives to edge this exhortation. 1. The *folly and inconvenience* of an irresolute and tottering and hovering spirit viz. 1. Till you attain to a firm resolution, you will *never be free from strong temptations*: Faint denials are interpretative Encouragements; as it is with the ill humours of the body, they flock and resort to a crazy part; So it is with Satans temptations, they will ever be frequent where the heart is ready to embrace, or not resolved to resist: why shouldest thou expect that Satan should fall off, when thou art yet irresolved to resist him? that he should not be backward to tempt, when thou art not resolved not to yield? 2. Till you attain to a firm resolution, *you will never come to a firm peace*; Conscience cannot be clear in its testimony, when we are indifferent in our purpose against sin. *Paul* could say, *the evil that I would not doe*;
thou

You will never come to a firm Peace.

thou canst not say so: The decision of that estate will be under a cloud, and you will be struck with more suspicions of hypocrisie and wrath, while you come to be plain-hearted and resolute, I wi'l serve no sin any longer. 3. Till you attain to a firm resolution, *you will be subject to the frequent intanglings of sin*; weak resolutions are like a weak child, or a feather, or like weak walls, through which any bullet will flye: Thou hast no armour on, till thou be resolved; any sinful occasion or opportunity is too hard for him, whose heart is not clad with a peremptory denial: How can he be stedfast, who is not sound? a lame Legg is apt to fall; or what shock can a weak body sustein? it cannot be, but thou shouldest be under the guilt of much corruption, who art not determinately fixed in thy resolves against all sinful suggestions: Thou wondredst at it, that perhaps after many Prayers, and much hearing, yet some sin or other still prevails: but can it well be expected, that Sin should not be thy Conqueror, when as yet, thou art not resolved to be its enemy? 4. Till you attain to a firm resolution *you will but shuffle in a good course*, off and on, sometimes much, sometimes little, sometimes nothing: *A doubleminded man is unstable in all his wayes*, saith St. *James* 1. 8. every businefs will withdraw you, and any occasion will excuse you from Gods service, while you are indifferent unto it; every wind drives through thy Boat, and every frost will nip thy Bud. 5. Nay, Irresolution will prove *a bitter root of apostacy*: if dangers surprize thee on the left hand, or temptations on the right hand; it is a thousand to one, but thou wilt deny the faith, and make Shipwrack of conscience. There lies much of our hopeful constancy in Religion as we set forth; if we begin with faint and irresolved hearts, we shall fall back with wounded and broken Souls; he cannot be long good, who is not resolvedly good. 6. *Flat and poor communion with God*: You will make no prayer, or but cold indifferent Prayer: *Austin* was affraid that God would hear him.

2. The *benefits and comforts of a firm Resolution*, which are many. 1. *It will be a great Testimony unto you*, *that your hearts are upright*. He who will not resolve against a sinful courfe, either his heart hath a flaw of hypocrisie, or a sink of impiety; he loves sin, or would not yet leave it: the greatest part of our integrity lies in the hearts frame and purpose: that man who is resolved

You will be subject to the entanglings of Sin.

You will but shuffle in a Good Course.

It will prove a bitter Root of Apostacy.

There will be flat and poor Communion with God.

The Benefits of a full Resolution.

It will be a testimony, our hearts are upright.

ed to part with all sin, hath an heart who loves all good; it is only found grace which breeds sound resolution. 2. *It will be a great apology, in case of falling*, that yet it is not *presumptuous*, but of *Infirmity*. (*The evil that I would not do, that do I*, &c. Rom. 7.) and rather an affect of a strong temptation, then of any secret affection of the heart to sin; for where the purpose and resolution of the heart is set against a sin, and makes its resistence; though the sinning may be great, yet it is not presumptuous. Four effects this firm Resolution worketh about sin; either it doth, 1. *Cease the motions of it*; or 2. *Abates and lessens them*; or 3. *Disappoints and frustrates them*; as Joseph about his mistress: or else, 4. *It mitigates and corrects them* in the degree of guilt; either it keeps me sound, or else causeth that the wound is less. 3. *Such a man may confidently go to God for help and assistance*. *If I regard iniquity in my heart, the Lord will not hear my prayer* (said David) *but verily, God hath heard me, he hath attended to the voice of my Prayer*, Psal. 69. 18, 19. Thou shalt not struggle with sin in vain, nor cry unto God in vain; if once thou couldst be firmly resolved against sin, thou shouldst more confidently repair to Christ, and shouldst assuredly find more Victory over it, as *Paul*, Rom. 7. 24, 25. *What have I to do any more with idols? I have heard him, and observed him; I am like a green Fir-Tree, from me is thy fruit found*. Hos. 14. 8. 4. And more *confidently, expect the remission of sins past*; with what face can a man embolden himself before the Lord? "O Lord I beseech thee to pardon such or such a sin, "and I trust thou wilt do it, but I am not yet resolved to leave "it. And when a person can come before the Lord, and say, "Search and tell me, O Lord, if there be any way of wicked-"ness, which I know and allow against, which I am not resolved "and strive. Now O Lord, thou art a gracious God, I beseech "thee for thy mercies sake, forgive my sins, blot them out, I "hate them with an unfeigned hatred, do thou for thine own "sake pardon and subdue them. 5. You shall much *free your selves from the ancient suggestions of Satan, about particular Sins*: *Resist the Divel and he will flee from you*, Jam. 4. 7. Where there is no hope of Victory, there will be little encouragement to fight; firm resolutions are like rocks, against which the waves may beat and strike, but cannot move nor alter; Satan may indeed

The Sinners Converſion to God.

deed ſomewhat moleſt, but the heart is in a ſort impregnable, which is ſtedfaſtly reſolved. *Chriſtiana ſum,* ſaid ſhe, I am a Chriſtian, who was much aſſaulted to deny the Faith; and ſo ſilenced all threats and allurements for the abnegation of Chriſt. When they ſaw *Paul's reſolution fixed for Jeruſalem,* they gave off their importuniy: ſo Temptations will ſlack when our Reſolutions are ſettled. It is in vain, I will not hearken; thou mayeſt moleſt me, Satan, but I will never yield unto thee. *Luther in Gen.*

6. *You will be leſs interrupted in your holy ſervices.* Whileſt the heart is any thing indifferent and flexible, ſinfull motions, like the Birds, will return and flock about the Corn, if the Watchman be now there, and anon removed. When the Miniſter is ſpeaking to your ear, Sin will be ſpeaking to your heart; and when your tongues are ſpeaking to God, your thoughts will be buſied in giving Sin an anſwer, or the World: But if the heart were more reſolved againſt ſin, it would be more united in duty; the thoughts, and mind, and affections would be more collected and center'd upon the τὸ ἐργὸν, the work in hand; it would not ſcatter ſo much, it would not follow that which it cares not for, but peremptorily abhors. We ſhall be leſs interrupted in our holy ſervices.

The next Uſe ſhall be for *Direction,* and that in two particulars: 1. How to raiſe a ſolid Reſolution: 2. How to keep and maintain it. *Uſe 2. Direction.*

Firſt, *The Means to raiſe it.* There are ſome things of which you muſt take heed and ſtrive againſt, as being vigorous impediments to the rearing of this frame, and twiſting of this firm cord. *How to raiſe a ſolid Reſolution. Take heed of*

1. *A ſecret favouring of ſin.* As long as your hearts cunningly connive at, and harbour your luſts (thoſe evil Inmates) you will never throughly come to a Reſolution to caſt them off. For love will untwiſt many arguments, and prevail againſt ſtrong Motives; it will let down your mind, as faſt as reaſons do raiſe it up. It is the beſt Friend, and ſtrongeſt Advocate that ſin hath. You ſee a Parent (perhaps *David* againſt *Abſalom*) reſolved to exile his Child from his preſence; but natural affection turned him, and wrought ſo, after a while, that *David* longs for *Abſalom* again. As a Spring will work out that which is caſt in; ſo will a ſecret affection to ſin, work off the impreſſion of all Arguments, *A ſecret favouring of ſin.*

and

and any such preposterous Resolves against sin.

Delicacy of spirit.

2. A *tenderness or delicacy of spirit:* I mean, an inordinate self-love: Love of sin, and so also the love of our selves, both of them are adversaries to a penitential Resolution: If a man will go to Heaven asleep, have his ease, and his friends, and his liberty, and his safeties, and his quiet, and his pleasures, and great matters, he will never come to a through Resolution. God likes no such bargain, no condition ; as, I am willing to serve thee, but I am resolved never to suffer for thee ; I will be good, if I may be safe ; I will go to sea, but on condition I shall meet with no storms ; I will enter into the war, but on condition that I will have no blows. We must be at a point for all things except what is good, if we be resolved to be good indeed ; no, not Life it self must be dearer to us, than that which is far better than Life.

A perversness of spirit.

3. A *perversness of spirit*, or self-wilfulness ; if you do resolve to be your own Master, you can never resolve to be Gods Servant ; if your hearts be not disposable to his will, they will never be flexible and fixed on his work. You must in many things be contented to deny your own thoughts, and to captivate your own judgments and reasonings, and to submit both your judgment and will to a Divine Rule, and there take forth directions for your lives, how contrary soever to your own conceits and delights.

A faintness of spirit.

4. A *faintness of spirit.* If you make the work absolutely impossible, you do but cool and quash resolutions. There is a need of bellows, not waters, for tender sparks ; for no man will attempt a hopeless work, or that which he knows will certainly prove fruitless. Do not side with such thoughts as these ; I shall never be able to get victory over such strong sins, and long corruptions : Or, I shall never be able to do what the Lord requires, so much, and with such affections ; nor shall I ever bear such reproaches, losses, disgraces, indignities. Never consult with flesh and blood in a case of holy Resolution, nor credit Satan about the leaving of sin : but if thou wilt consult with what may fear and dishearten thee, consult also with what may encourage and quicken thee. Though thy sins be strong, yet they are conquerable, (onely true Grace is invincible.) It is possible for a sinfull nature

ture to be altered and renewed, and therefore it is not impoſſible for any ſin to be ſubdued: Though thy own ſtrength be inſufficient, yet Chriſt's is not; He who hath commanded thee to combat with Sin, hath likewiſe promiſed to conquer ſin; if thy duty be active, he is able to work in thee both to will and to do; if thy duty be paſſive, he can give thee not onely to do, but to ſuffer for his ſake; if thou muſt not be leſs then a Sufferer, he can make thee more than a Conqueror: Thy helps are far greater than thy diſcouragements, there are more with thee than againſt thee: Therefore fear not to reſolve; 'tis a vanity to talk of another, or fitter ſeaſon; you will be more unwilling to leave ſin, the more time you take to commit ſin.

II. There are ſome things which you muſt, in ſome meaſure poſſeſs, if ever you would be brought to a penitential Reſolution. *Labour for*

1. Get *as diſtinct a knowledge of ſin, as clear conviction as you can.* It is our blindneſs which keeps us in ſervice; and the Will is uſually perverſe, becauſe the Judgment is greatly dark: Did we know ſin aright, (truly, fully, experimentally,) you have attained to Reaſons enough, why you ſhould reſolve againſt it. Sin carries its own condemnation with it: Sometimes the particular effects of ſin do half perſwade us to be Chriſtians, to leave the ſervice of ſin; a ſtroke or two upon the Conſcience, do thus far prevail, as to pauſe and ſtop; ' If then we knew ſin ' in the latitude of its bitter effects, and in the intenſiveneſs of ' them (beyond all thoughts) for bitterneſs and perpetuity, ' as alſo that extreme vileneſs in the formal nature of it, which ' is the vaſt womb and Ocean, out of which theſe bitter waters do ' flow; if we did know ſin as the darkeſt blot, and loath-' ſome blur, oppoſite to the trueſt Glory of pureſt Holineſs; ' and as the moſt deformed and higheſt Rebellion to the moſt ' equal Laws and Rules of Divine Soveraignty; and as the very ' Eclipſe, and utter Inconſiſtence with all real Happineſs; and ' as the infallible and unavoidable Precipice of our intollerable ' and eternal Damnation: At leaſt, this would be an occaſional excitation, if not a ſtrong foundation, upon which to raiſe a Reſolution to quit and forſake it. Sure I am, the defect of this, that men know not ſin, makes them bold and venturous, obſtinate, and tenacious; they will not deſiſt from the *Clear Conviction.*

practiſe

practice of sin, because they know not the evil of sin.

Cordial detestation. 2. You must get *an hatred of sin*, else you will never truly and effectually resolve against it: All the actions of our lives are fed by the affections of the will; these are (in morals) *principia immediata & vincentia*; and of all the affections (as the Anatomists observe in the body, two master-Veins, *Vena cava*, & *vena aorta*;) so in the soul, there are two which are Soveraign, and bear sway; one is Love, and the other is Hatred; that bears sway in matters eligible and practicable, this in matters sinfull and declinable. Resolutions against sin, not rooted in hatred, will slack like a deceitfull Bow; and Resolutions to a better course, not raised from love, will be but as the morning dew: It is hatred which makes us bent and peremptory against evil, and it is love which makes us resolute and stedfast for good. Hatred hath three properties in it against an evil Object, Enmity, Flight, and Irreconcileablenefs: And Love hath two properties in it, Union, and Adhæsion; *Ruth* clave in love to *Naomi*, and was setled in it, never to leave her: And *Ephraim* was strong in detestation, and therefore peremptorily in resolution, *What have I to do any more with Idols?*

Faith. 3. There must be *Faith*, and then there will be Resolution. Faith, 1. *To believe the Word of God*, discovering and threatning an evil condition and course; 2. *To believe the excellency of a good Condition*, and Life, and Rewards. If thou didst indeed believe that sin would damn thee, wouldst not thou resolve against it? if thou didst indeed believe that the holy life were the happy life, couldst thou by Faith see him that is invisible, and the beauties of holiness, which are hid from the World, and those great consolations and rewards reserved for a pious heart and conversation, thou wouldst quickly turn the Scale, make the choice, and resolve, 'Tis true, I must leave my sins, but I shall gain my God; their pleasures, but I shall gain his delights; I may forfeit the love of Friends, but I shall find kindness of God; I quit Earth, but I shall get Heaven; I leave but filthiness, but guilt, but misery, but Hell; I shall get holiness, and peace, and Christ, and Comfort, and Heaven; I am insufficient, but God is sufficient.

Vehement prayer. 4. *Vehement Prayer*, that the Lord would give a heart willing to forsake sin, and willing to choose him and his ways: For the purposes

purposes of our hearts are from him. Resolution should be a Posie of Prayers, steept in prayer, blown up by the breath of Heaven; *Psal.*119.5. *O that my ways were directed to keep thy statutes.* v. 8. *I will keep thy statutes; O forsake me not utterly.* What you undertake without prayer, you will forsake without comfort: All resolutions are best made, which are made upon the knee of prayer.

Secondly, The means to maintain and keep up this Resolution. *The means to maintain this resolution.*

1. Let *your Resolution not be presumptuous, but humble:* If you raise your Resolutions upon your own strength, you will shortly quit them by your own weaknefs. No spiritual frame or work is safe or strong, which is reared upon it self alone; it must not be less than a rock higher than our selves, upon which we must build. The wings bear the body of the flying Fowl, but this they cannot do without air to spread and bear up those wings. *I can do all things through Christ that strengthens me.* Philip.4. There must be some strength in us to advance a Resolution, but then there must be another Strength, upon which both that Resolution and that Strength must depend: And therefore as a Warrant is of no force, if it goes not out in the Kings name; so a Resolution is too recoiling, which begins not in Christs power: As *David* encountred *Goliah*, not with his own Sword, but *in Gods Name*; so we must resolve against our sins, with Gods strength assisting of us; otherwise, our sins may reply to us, as the Devils to the sons of *Sceva*, *Jesus I know, and Paul I know, but who are ye?* A ship, though well built, must have wind to drive it, and set it forward; and a Christian needs more strength than his own, to forsake a bad, or to follow a good course. It is a wise course, in lending of Money, to joyn another party in the Bond, who is more able and sure than the borrower: Doest thou resolve against such a sinfull way, or for a holy life? take not single Bond; (thy own heart, though to thy thinking well furnisht and stockt with resolution, is yet but a creature, and may deceive thee, and make thee to break:) but take double Bond, beseech the Lord to be bound for thee, to give thee his strength, which is indeed sufficient to preserve, and to perpetuate thy resolutions. *Let it not be presumptuous, but humble.*

2. You must be sure that you *get a mournfull heart for what is past*, or else you will never get a resolute heart for the future: *Get a mournfull heart for what is past.*

future: if the heart be not broken for sin, the resolution of the heart; He who will w be joyously good, I fear, least after a while, bad. We seldome observe, that an unb fast; that his foot stands sure, whose ey who can leap into a good way, yet never a bad. *Peter*'s Resolution to confess his M after his tears, than after his confidence membrance of a bad life, wherein God dishonoured, and his spirit so often grieved, ens, and doubles our hatred, and fears, an Should I any longer continue thus? shoulc *Paul* doth frequently remember his sinfull p and then is inflamed, with a more zealous re to preach and advance him: Nothing daur ing of that good Lord and Christ, whom l wronged.

Be active against sin.

3. *Be active against sin*, and that is th Resolutions against it: My meaning is this to mortifie an evil heart, if you would hol against an evil course: The heart is all in for a good, or for a bad way; kill the r will soon wither; diminish the Spring, and weaken the Spirits, and the Limbs will be us thing to say, *I will not have the fit of t* you receive something to alter the evil hun *I will never sin thus again!* thus how oft yet break out again! why? because we v without surprizing their causes. Be more a sober heart, and for a chast heart, and for a heavenly heart, and a meek and quiet heart onely resolve, but prevail against evil acts mently strive with God, to season the Spr ture, to better and strengthen the heart, these arise and flow; for all things are Hre and the strength of the cause is the strength casion may be vigorous to produce a res required to make it firm and effectual; it i strength.

4. Let *it be watchfull, and not careless:* They are not the ma- *Be watchfull,*
ny Souldiers which keep the City, but the watchfull Souldiers; *and not care-*
the City which is got by strength, may be lost by carelesness. To *less.*
be active and inquisitive how to make resolutions against sin, and
afterwards to be negligent of our hearts, this is to make a strong
door, but not to mind whether it be lockt or no. Our hearts
(take them at the best) are very untrusty and deceitfull (at least
in part) and are quickly weary of spirituall bonds; and as an
untoward Servant, after all warnings and threatnings, is hanker-
ing to whisk out after his old companions; so our hearts, after all
resolutions, are yet inclining to evil. Therefore let us not onely enjoyn our spirit to take heed of sinfull courses, but guard them,
set a guard upon them, as *David*, Psal. 39. 1. A man may quickly stumble, who hath an able foot, if yet he hath a careless eye; the eye and the foot must go together to keep us upright.

5. If you would still keep up your Resolutions, then *often re-* *Often review*
view and renew them. Our resolutions come to be strengthened *and renew re-*
by frequent enquiry, how they are performed. Daily account- *solutions.*
ings with the servant, may be the means to keep him faithfull.
If we did daily sequester our selves, and commune with our spirits,
and take an account of them; ' O my soul, thou hast seen the vile-
' ness of such sinfull courses, and hast felt the bitterness of them,
' and hast solemnly protested against them before the Lord, and
' resolved to prosecute them no more; thou hast given thy Word
' and Bond for this unto the great God: Well! how hast thou
' performed this purpose? art thou still willing? hast thou been
' faithfull to thy self, and to thy God? wast thou no way surpri-
' zed this day? though thou didst not break, yet didst not thou
' bow to day? though thou didst not fall, didst not thou trip? did
' nothing come from thee to undo, or else to weaken thy resoluti-
' on? Such evil motions sprang from thy heart to sin again, didst
' thou abhor them, and cry unto God against them? such tempta-
' tions presented themselves unto thee, didst thou reject and stout-
' ly resist them? or hast thou not found an heart somewhat heark-
' ning, somewhat yielding, somewhat venturing? If so, then
humble thy self, and as *David* to *Joab*, 2 Sam. 11. 25. *Make thy*
battel more strong against the City; so do thou, bewail thy failings, and renew thy resolution again more strongly and carefully.

6. If

When resolutions are impaired, let them be presently repaired.

6. If your *Resolutions be any thing impaired, let them be presently repaired.* It is possible, notwithstanding our Resolutions against evil courses, to be surprized with evil acts, and now we are apt to give up the Resolutions themselves; but do not so: Though the winds drive back the Mariner, yet he holds fast his resolution still for such a Cape; and if a man falls in his journey, yet he will rise and be going again: So let us do; if we have not answered our Resolutions, let us not end them, but mend them: Above all, search the causes of impairing thy Resolutions, and then thou mayest see thy reparations. Say seriously, 1. Didst not thou relie too much upon thy Resolution, as if therefore thou wert safe, because resolved? 2. Didst not thou grow weaker in Prayer, when thou grewest strong in Resolution? or, 3. Hast thou not been more venturous upon occasions? hast thou not been tampering with sinfull occasions, such acts, ways, objects, as thou knowest have powder to irritate and inflame Lust? Consider seriously how thou camest to violate thy purpose and intention, and penitently confess it before the Lord, and take up thy Resolution again upon right grounds.

Let resolutions be accompanied with the use of holy means.

7. Let *your Resolutions be accompanied with the use of all holy means which will strengthen and perfect them.* Doth not the strong man grow weak by fasting, as well as by sickness? How is it possible but that thy Bow should slack, (i.) thy Resolution, should start aside, when thou art a negligent Hearer, and an inconstant Petitioner? why! where lies thy strength to perform? why doest thou put off thy helps? what! art thou alone? He who hath not strength to fight, how shall he have power to conquer? wouldst thou stand? wouldst thou resolve? wouldst thou resolve so as to reform? Be much in Prayer; Keep thy servant, O Lord, uphold me by thy Word, preserve me by thy Spirit; work in me the will and the deed, work thine own works in me, finish what thou hast wrought; shew thy power in my weakness, let thy Grace be sufficient for me; leave me not, nor forsake me; incline my heart to thy testimonies, turn away mine eyes from vanity. And so for the Ordinances, attend them; they are the Strength of God for thee; they work holy qualities, holy motions, holy convictions, holy excitations, holy affections, desires, a fear lest we depart, and fall from our stedfastness; and they kindle

more

more and more our purposes to walk with God, and to shun iniquity. Oh, how admirably the heart under them is caused to burn with ardent love of God! with desires and resolutions to keep closer to him, how is it stirr'd up with more detestation of sin? how often do they melt the heart? recover the heart, restore the heart, and send it away with this resolution, Well! by the grace of God I will never go on in such a sinful course, &c.

The last Use shall be for *Exhortation* unto us, though we have taken ill courses formerly, yet now *to resolve against them*, to arise and go home to our Father; What shall I say to move and perswade us here to consider. 1. Either you *must resolve to leave your sins*, or be *damned for them*, why wil thou lose thy pretious soul for ever. 2. Whether *is better to come back and find God a Father*, or to *depart still from him, and feel him a Judge*. If mercy be better then wrath, if heaven be better then hell, resolve to arise and leave thy sinful waies, and return unto a God and Father. 3. *Hast thou not found thy sinful courses to be evil and bitter unto thee already*: why wilt thou serve an evil master for evil wages, the which also will still be more fearful and heavie, by how much the longer thou continues sinful and wicked; thy terrours will not shorten, while thou dost lengthen thy sins, nor maiest thou expect that thy latter daies will be peace, when all thy daies have been wickedness; if thou livest in sin, thou must lie down in sorrow. 4. *Sin is an hateful object, and a conquerable enemy*, therefore resolve against it. It onely hath the most absolute reasons of the *strongest hatred*, as being completely evil and vile; it is the basest of all objects, and is thine highest enemy, there is nothing which can undo thee but sin; and yet *i is a conquerable enemy*, it is very possible that a sinner may be changed. 5. If thou *once couldst but get an heart to resolve against sin, thou shouldst find the work more easie*. Saint *Austin* professeth, that though the thoughts of leaving his sins were once a great burthen to him, yet at length being peremptorily resolved he found it a most easie and delightful thing to live without hem. 6. *A new course of obedience*; O this is *life indeed*. No art thou alive from the dead, if thy heart be truly resolved, I may say to thee as *Christ* to *Zacheus*, *This day is salvation come to thine house*; an holy life and

3. *Use*.

For Exhortation, to resolve against sin.

Motives.

and courſe is the moſt excellent, is the moſt eaſie, is the moſt peaceable, is the moſt gainful, it is the beſt, it is the ſweeteſt, it is the happieſt life; it begins in Grace, it will end in Glory.

LUKE 15. V. 18, 19.

And will ſay unto him, Father, I have ſinned againſt Heaven, and before thee, and am no more worthy to be called thy Son; make me as one of thy hired ſervants.

You have heard of the Prodigals *penitential conſideration of his ſinful eſtate*, and of his *penitential reſolution*, to forſake that condition and courſe, *I will ariſe and go to my father*: now you are to hear his *penitential confeſſion*, *And will ſay unto him, Father, I have ſinned againſt Heaven*, &c. In which words you have conſiderable. 1. *Who doth confeſs*; I. 2. *What he doth confeſs, I have ſinned.* 3. *To whom he doth confeſs, Father, I have ſinned,* 4. *How he doth confeſs, Againſt Heaven and before thee; In te & coram te:* There is no difficulty in the word; and therefore I will proceed to the intent of it, which is this: *That true Repentance for ſin againſt God, will bring forth true Confeſſion of Sin unto God.* This is evident almoſt in all perſons, whether ſingle or conjoyned, who are ſet out for penitents in Scripture. *David*, his heart bleeds, and his tongue acknowledgeth, *I have ſinned,* 2 Sam. 12. upon *Nathans* conviction. *The Publican, Lord be merciful to me a ſinner*; he ſtood afar off, ſmiting his breſt, and inditing himſelf for his ſins: A whole Church in *Ezra*, in *Nehemiah*, in *Daniel*, all at once confeſsing, We have ſinned, we have done wickedly, our ſins are gone over our heads. For the better explication of the aſſertion; know,

That there is a *threefold confeſſion of ſin*;

1. *Auricular*, or Sacramental, which the Church of *Rome* doth injoyn, but not the Scripture. *Confiteri ora & ſingula peccata mortalia*, to confeſs all, and every mortal Sin, *quorum memoria cum debita & diligenti præmeditatione habeatur*; which a diligent, and induſtrious memory can recal *etiam occulta*, even your ſecret ſins, *& quæ ſunt contra duo ultima decalogi præcepta*; Nay, thoſe which are committed againſt the two laſt commandments, *& circumſtancias*, yea, and all the circumſtances of your ſins; this is the confeſſion which the Church of *Rome* in

(marginal notes: True Repentance for ſin, will bring forth true confeſſion of ſin to God. A threefold confeſſion of ſin. Auricular.*)*

the

The Sinners Conversion to God.

the *Trent* Council doth injoin upon pain of Anathema to be made unto the Priest. *Seff. 14. Can. 7.* but without any warrant from the Scripture, or averment from true Antiquity; for Scripture assures us, that confession of sin made to God alone, obtained remission of sins and favour, *Psal. 32. 5. I said, I will confess my sins unto the Lord, and thou forgavest the iniquity of my sin.* Lo! here confession to God alone, not to a Priest, and upon it remission of sins by God himself; dares any Popish Priest reverse this absolution or confession, because not made to man, which yet is accepted with God. Saint *Chrysostome* speaks strange words; Let God onely see thee confessing. And again upon *Heb. 12. Hom. 31. ἀποκαλυψον πρὸς κύριον τὴν ὁδόν σου,* Reveal thy way unto the Lord, *ἐπὶ τῷ Θεῷ ταῦτα ὁμολόγησον,* Confess them before God: and again, *ἐπὶ τῷ δικαστῇ ὁμολόγει ἁμαρτήματα,* Confess thy sins before thy Judge; and Saint *Austins* tongue needs to be clipped; *Quid mihi cum hominibus, ut audiant confessiones nostras quasi ipsi sanaturi sint omnes languores meas?* What have I to do with men, that they should hear my confessions, as though they could heal all my diseases? Saint *Basil* saith, that the groans of his heart did suffice for a Confession. Surely here was no absolute necessity to confess all to the Priest: but yet again observe, there is a use of Confession in case of 1. Injury. 2. Anxiety. 3. Scandal to the Church, as in the next particular.

Tom. 5. Hom. de pænit. & confess Lat. ed.

Baf. an. 1558.

Conf. lib 10. cap. 13.

In Psal. 37.

2. *Christian and prudential* Confession; and this is the acknowledging of sins to men, either in case of *notorious scandal*, which the primitive Churches much urged and used; or else in case *of trouble*; and thus we deny not but any person may lawfully, and warrantably go unto a faithful, godly, skilful, compassionate Minister, and confess his sins, either to obtain counsel out of the Word of God for the remedy of sins, to recover or prevent them; or to be informed aright concerning his present estate, or to have his conscience quieted and settled.

Christian and prudential.

3. *Penitential*, which is made onely to God: this the Scripture doth command, and this wee hold as absolutely necessary; when wee do repent, then to make confession of our sins to God.

Penitential to God.

Secondly, This *penitential confession* may be considered, either in respect of the *material* part onely, and so it consists of words where-

Penitential confession considered, In respect of the material part onely, or,

The Returning Prodigal, or

Of the formal also:

whereby we acknowledge wherein we have transgressed, *Hos.* 4. *ver.* 1, 2. Out *of the formal part also,* and thus it conteins those ingredients which specifie and distinguish it from all superstitious, or hypocritical, or false confessions.

And so it is

An hearty acknowledgment:

1. It is *an hearty acknowledgment,* not *nuda confessio* ; feigned or meerly verbal confession : It is affectionate, the lips do utter the mind of the heart in it, *cum sensu peccati & miseriæ,* as a sick man opens his disease, here I feel it, &c. *The publican smote upon his breast, and confessed.* True confession is the language of the very soul, being very sensible of sin. 2. It *is voluntary,* not

And voluntary,

coacta confessio; the Thief may confess upon the rack : though there were no wrath in God, no rack in conscience, no flames in hell, yet the true penitent will confess : When there is no other cause of confession of sin but that which is penal, it is not then truly penitential. *Pharaoh* confessed under the plagues, and *Judas* under the stings of conscience, it was an extorted confession, but penitential confession is voluntary, it is an act that ariseth from an inward displicence with, and detestation of sin, though there be no apprehension of hell, no sense of wrath, yet the penitent confesseth even to a Father, *I have sinned. Many of the Saints did I shut up in prison, and when they were put to death I gave my voice against them. I punished them oft in every Synagogue,* Acts 26. 10, 11. 3. It is *distinct,* and not confused : the

And distinct,

penitent hath special bills of inditement : he knows his sins, and wherein he hath exceeded and failed : such sins as he hath most delighted in, such as he hath most walked in, such as he hath most dishonoured God by, such as cleave most unto his nature, such as conscience may be most clogged with; these he doth more especially confess unto God, and indite and condemn himself for small sins as well as great ; *Sauls lap,* as well as *Uriahs murther,* antient sins as well as present, secret sins as well as open. But must our confession of sins be particular ? *Sol.* Either *explicitly* so, or *virtually* so ; the heart hath a particular intention or affection ; the more particular, the better, to humble our hearts, to obtein mercies, to make us fervent. As *David,* though hee did give a touch at all his sins in the beginning of the 51 *Psalm,* yet at length

brancheth

brancheth his confeſſion into particulars, into that of *Adultery*, and the other of *Blood*. So doth *Paul* often uncover his ſpecial ſins of Perſecuting the Church, and Blaſpheming, and of Injuriouſneſs: *Judas* cryed out of Blood, but not of Covetouſneſs and Hypocriſie. 4. *It is Humble*, and not proud (as *Benhadads* ſervants, with ropes, &c.) done with Contrition of Heart, not with Oſtentation of Spirit. Like a flaſh of Lightning, breaks out of a cloud rented; and *Joſephs* garment was ſhewed to his father rent and dipt in blood. Anciently, when they did confeſs their ſins to God, they did it with *Sackcloth and Aſhes*; and the opening of their ſins is termed, *The pouring out of water before the Lord* (*I am vile*, Job 40. 4. *Not worthy*, &c. Luke 15.) becauſe when they poured out their ſins in confeſſion of Tongue, they likewiſe poured out contrition of Heart; their tears of Grief, ſpake as much as the words of their Lips: *I will declare mine Iniquities, and be ſorry for my ſin*, Pſal. 38. The Papiſts indeed have as courſe a Garment, and as ſevere a Garb in penitential confeſſion as any, but underneath they have dainty Linnen; there lies great pride under all this pretended Humiliation, as if all this did merit at the hands of God; the Voice is humble *Jacob's*, but the pride upon the act is proud *Eſau's*. If they ſaw the wrong which they did by ſinning, how could they ſo proudly challenge God upon their confeſſing (what doth the murtherer deſerve becauſe he confeſſeth?) But truly Penitential Confeſſion is accompanied with grief in the heart, and with ſhame in the face, and with acknowledgment, That by reaſon of our ſins there belongs nothing to us but ſhame and confuſion, *Daniel* 9. 5. *It is mixt with ſome Faith*, not overcome with Deſpair: If the confeſſion of ſin be not mixed with ſome hope of pardon, it is not penitential but deſperate: *Cain*, in ſome meaſure confeſſed, but *fled into the Land of Nod*, and reputes his offence Unpardonable, beyond the power or intention of Mercy to pardon him. *Judas* likewiſe utters his ſin in particular, *I have ſinned in betraying innocent Blood*; But then he *goes out and hangs himſelf*:

And Humble.

And mixt with ſome Faith.

But.

The Returning Prodigal, or

But if the confeſſion be truly penitential, it acknowledgeth ſin fully, yet believingly; not to a meer Judge, who out of the mouth of the Confeſſor condemneth, but to a father (*Father, I have ſinned*, ſaith our *Prodigal*)who knows how to abſolve and forgive him, that knows how to accuſe and condemn himſelf. As you muſt in Confeſſions acknowledg, O Lord my ſins are very great; ſo likewiſe muſt you relieve your ſelves, O Lord, thy mercies are exceeding many; thus have I ſinned, but thou canſt pardon; I deſerve wrath, but thou canſt freely ſhew me mercy; I am a ſinner, yet, Lord, be merciful to me a ſinner. 6. It is

And Sincere. *Sincere* and not fraudulent.: then is the Confeſſion ſincere, not only when the heart acts in it, but when alſo it acts plainly and plenarily in it. We are but Fleſh and Blood, it is my nature, I cannot help it; I am not the firſt that did ſo; it was company that drew me. I did eat, ſaid *Adam*, but the *woman gave it me to eat.* I did eat, ſaid the woman, but the Devil tempted me. I did offer Sacrifice, ſaid *Saul*, but *I was afraid of the Philiſtims.* Theſe are fraudulent Confeſſions, when either a part is knowingly and willingly kept back; or if all comes forth, it is extenuated as much as may be. Not that any perſon is to accuſe himſelf of more then he is guilty, but that he is not to extenuate and mince any thing wherein he is faulty, but therein to ſet out himſelf to the full; *Of whom, I am chief,* ſaid *Paul*: And the *Prodigal* here, *I have ſinned againſt heaven, and before*

And joyned *thee.* 7. *It muſt be joyned with deſire and endeavour of Refor-*
with deſire and *mation*: Therefore forſaking of ſin (at leaſt in *Voto & conatu*)
endeavour of is annext to confeſſion, *Prov.* 28. 13. *Saul* confeſſed his ſinful
Reformation. injuries to *David* his Son in Law, 2 *Sam.* 24. 16. Ch. 26. 2. and wept, but then he purſued him again: So did *Pharaoh, Exod.* 9. 27, 34. but then he hardned his heart, and ſinned yet more. They loved eaſe, but not cure; but *David* deſires medicine as much as quiet; Grace to heal, as well as Mercy to quiet: he did not open his wounds, and then make more, but deſires thoſe which are made, that they might be bound up and healed. So did *Shecaniah*, not only confeſs their treſpaſſe, in taking of ſtrange wives, *Ezra* 10. 2, 3. but intends reformation: *Now therefore let us make a Covenant with God to put them all away.*

Theſe ingredients I do conjecture that they make up the very

The Sinners Conversion to God.

ry form and vitals of a penitential Confession. But why should
true penitents make confession of their sins to God? *Reasons of it.*
1. There is a necessity so to do: *Necessitas ex parte Dei, &* There is a ne-
ex parte rei. 1. *Ex parte Dei,* God requireth you so to do: cessity so to do.
Acknowledge thine Iniquity, that thou hast transgressed against Ex parte Dei.
*the Lord thy God, and hast scattered thy wayes to the Strangers
under every green tree,* Jer. 3.13. So Hos. 14. 1. *Return to the
Lord thy God.* Ver. 2. *Take with you words, and turn to the
Lord, and say unto him, Take away all Iniquity, and receive
us graciously.* 2. *Ex parte Rei:* When the heart is peniten- Ex parte Rei.
tially changed, it cannot but confess sin will lye so heavy; as
when health comes in, pain is felt: There is such an abundant
sense of sin, that the heart cannot contain it self. If the affection be full, it must vent it self, *Joseph* could not refrain: So is
the heart of a penitent overcharged with the iniquities of
his Life, and Indignity by him cast on God, a gracious
God.

2. There is *Utility in so doing*: Though true confession of There is a Utili-
sin doth not at all merit, yet it is a way or means to obtain three ty in so do-
singular things; viz. 1. *Remission of Sins:* This is a most sweet ing.
and surpassing mercy; *David* accounts him *Blessed whose iniqui-* It is a means
ties are covered: but Confession is the means for Remission, to obtaine,
which may evidently appear, 1. *By Gods direction of his people* sin.
to take this course, that so they might be pardoned, *Jer.*3.12,13.
2. *By his special Promise,* upon their true confession, for to pardon them their sins, *Prov.*28.13. *He that confesseth and forsaketh his sins, shall find mercy.* 1 Joh. 1. 9. *If we confess our
sins, God is faithful and just to forgive us our sins.* 3. *By frequent experience:* David said, *I will confess my Transgressions,
and thou forgavest the Iniquity of my sin,* Psal. 32. 5. The *Publican* penitentially confessed, and went home Justified, *Luk.*18.
13, 14. 2. *Power against sins*: By hearty confession to uncover Power against
sins, is a way not only to get God to cover them by Justificati- sin.
on, but also to cure them by Sanctification. You must take off
Vulnerati tegumentum, if you will obtain *Medici Emplastrum,* *Austin.*
as S. *Austin* alludes upon the *Psa.* 32. When you open the
wound, then you make way for the healing Plaister; and therefore S. *John* doth not only say, *If we confess our sins God is
faithful to forgive us our sins*; but also addeth, *and to cleanse*
us

The Returning Prodigal, or

Peace of Conscience. *us from all unrighteousness.* 3. *Peace of Conscience*: You may see this manifestly in *David*, who being distressed in spirit for sin, is much disquieted, and roars, and his moisture is turned into the drought in Summer, *Psal.* 32. 3, 4. His silence raised his Impatience and Trouble, but as soon as he confessed his sins, he recovered his peace, ver. 5. *I acknowledg my sin unto thee, and mine iniquity have I not hid: I said I will confess my transgressions unto the Lord, and thou forgavest the iniquity of my sin.* Selah. So Job 33. 27. *If any say, I have sinned, and perverted that which is right, and it profited me not;* Ver. 28. *His life shall see the light:* It is one of the Windows to let in the beams of heavenly comfort.

God is much Glorified by it. 3. Lastly, *God is much Glorified* when the penitent doth humbly and truly confess his sins: *David* acknowledgeth his sins, *That thou mightst be justified when thou speakest, and be clear when thou judgest,* so Psal. 51. 4. *q. d.* Lord, thus have I sinned; and whatsoever punishment thou hast inflicted, or mayest inflict, I must quit thy Justice in all thy proceedings; thou canst not but be Righteous, for I confess my self to be sinful: Nay, his Justice only is not glorified, but his Wisdom, that he knows all our sins and wayes; and his Power, that he is able to Judge and condemn us; yea, and his Mercy too, that we hope yet he will pardon and forgive the sins which we confess unto him.

Use 1. *Then there are very few true Penitents.* If true Repentance brings forth true Confession, then by this it will appear, *That there are very few true penitents,* because very few who do truly and aright confess their sins.

1. Some may say of sin, what *Pilate* did of truth, *What's Truth?* So they, *What's Sin?* They are so ignorant, that they know not what is evil, or when they do evil. Now, how can any confess or acknowledg that sin to God, which is not known at all to himself.

2. Others are so far from confessing themselves to be sinful, that they (like the proud Pharisee) *justifie themselves to be righteous;* talk of their good meanings, purposes, just dealings, &c. *Sana membra ostendebat* (saith S. *Austin* of that Pharisee) *vulnera tegebat;* *I am no Extortioner, no Adulterer,* &c. Ask some persons, Do you acknowledg One only God, who is most Merciful, Just, Holy, Omnipotent, Faithful, Long-suffering, full of
Goodness

Goodnefs and Truth, &c. Yes, that do they, God forbid elfe, &c. Ask them again, Are you Idolaters? make you no Idols? or did you ever worſhip them? Who they! nay, they defie them, and all ſuch trumpery. But do you not uſe to ſwear, and take the Name of God in vain? Nay, for ſwearing, of all ſins they cannot away with that; a man gets no good by ſwearing. But do you remember to keep holy the Sabbath? Yea, all their neighbours can bear witneſs, that they keep to the Church conſtantly. Ask them again, Did you never injure your Parents? O, they were always dutifull Children. But did you never play the whore, or the adulterer, or the thief? Nay, now they will talk no longer with you, if you be ſo uncharitable as to imagine ſuch guilt. Why, O thou ignorant ſinner! why doeſt thou deceive thy ſoul? if thou art thus righteous, thou needeſt not to repent; and if thou art free from all ſin, how canſt thou confeſs thy ſins (as a true penitent ought to do) to God?

3. But ſome others there are, who do both know and acknowledge their ſin; but how? *onely in a formal, cold, indifferent manner*. True, we are all ſinners, God help us, and there is no man but he ſins, yea, the beſt of them all; Never conſidering, That great Juſtice of God which is provoked by their ſins; nor that vile and abominable nature in their ſins; nor that infinite wrath unto which their guilt doth oblige them; nor the excellency and neceſſity of pardoning mercy, which we ſhould earneſtly ſue out when we confeſs our ſins.

4. There is another ſort, who do more diſtinctly, and perhaps ſomewhat feelingly and freely, confeſs their ſins; but then they *keep Benjamin back*: And as *Rachel hid the images under her*, ſo they *reſerve ſome one ſpecial luſt*; they do not bring all the Priſoners forth unto the Bar: There is a *ſin* which *they hide cloſe* becauſe it is *ſweet*, as *Zophar* ſpeaks, *Job* 20.12. Now this argues, 1. *Hypocriſie* and guile of heart, a ſecret love to ſin; it is made, in *Job* 20.12. the guiſe of an Hypocrite, *to hide his ſin*. 2. *Extreme folly* and vanity of ſpirit; for, canſt thou conceal any ſin from that God, who is acquainted with all thy paths, and knows thy thoughts afar off, and to whoſe eyes all things are naked? will not the Lord diſcover the ſin (which thou doeſt cover) before Men and Angels, to thy eternal infamy and condemnation? aſſuredly, though thou wilt not ſet thy ſins in order before him, yet he
will

will *set thy sins in order before thee, and will reprove thee for them,* *Psal.* 50. (1.) he will publish them, and he will everlastingly punish thee for them.

5. Others do confess all their sins, but this onely *in times of wrath, and judgment, and death;* not like Penitents, but as Malefactors, (as men make their Wills upon a death-bed;) not out of an hatred of sin, but out of meer sense or fear of punishment; it is not filial, ingenuous, free, but onely extorted, involuntary, and servile, and therefore not truly penitential: They do not go and confess their sins, as they to *John the Baptist,* but cry out and confess their sins; it is that, not which they would do, but which they cannot avoid: Conscience, like an over-charged stomack, doth so over-press and pain them, that they cannot hold, but out it comes, what oppression, injustice, usurious, injurious, beastly, filthy, swinish sins they have lived in.

6. Others seem to be more ingenuous and voluntary, or ready to confess their sins; but then this is with *such pretences, colours, shiftings, shuffling,* as if they were, like Lawyers, to mitigate and colour a bad cause. S. *Austin* complains of some, who would impute their sins to Fate, to Fortune, to the Devil, nay, to God himself: The complaint may well suit with us; generally, we have some device or other, either to deny, or to extenuate our sinfull facts; rather to plead for our selves, than to plead against our iniquities. It was company, and we are but flesh and bloud, and it is not usual, or (which is contrary) it is my nature, and the Devil was strong with me, others do worse, &c.

7. But of all men, they are most contrary to penitential Confession, who *call evil good,* and darkness light, and that make a a mock, and a sport of sin; whereas they should, with grief of heart, and shame of face, mournfully, penitently, humble themselves before the Lord, and acknowledge their iniquities, instead thereof. They boast themselves of their iniquites, and make but a jest of that which cost the bloud of Christ; It is but a trick of Youth, and good Fellowship, and Handsomness, and Complement, and discreet Thrift; thus do they phrase their Uncleanness, their Drunkenness, their Pride, their Lying, their Covetousness.

8. Lastly, to mention no more, They are defective too about the true penitential confession, who are *assiduous to confess,* but

desiduous

The Sinners Converſion to God.

defiduous to forſake; frequent to acknowledge and declare their ſins, but negligent in forſaking and leaving of them: D'ſcovery ſufficeth, but Recovery they mind not. This is moſt ordinary with us, that we make our confeſſion of ſins to God, rather an act of our Memory, than a work of our Conſcience: it ſufficeth us to deliver in the tale, to number our tranſgreſſions; but then we wreſtle not with the Lord in Prayer, for his Spirit of Grace to heal our hearts, and to turn us from the ſinfull ways unto which we find our hearts ſo apt and forward. But I will no longer inſiſt upon the Convicting part, I proceed to another Uſe.

Which ſhall be, *Not to hide our ſins, but to declare and acknowledge them in a right penitential manner before the Lord*, that ſo we may declare our ſelves true Penitents. This exhortation you ſee conſiſts of two parts; Not to Cover, To Diſcover.

I. *Not to hide and cover our ſins.* There is a two-fold Covering of our ſin; One is *natural*, which is that Vail of Ignorance and blindneſs drawn over the ſoul by Original ſin, keeping the mind in ſpiritual darkneſs, not able to ſee it ſelf, nor acts, nor wayes aright: This is ſuch a Cover, wherein we our ſelves are hid from our ſelves. There is another Covering, which is *voluntary* and *artificial*; wherein we dig deep to hide our counſels, intentions, delights, actions from the Lord, cunningly contriving and feigning a ſecrecy, as if we could put a curtain or a cloud twixt Gods eyes, and our actions; doing evil, and ſaying, None ſhall ſee it: And when it is done, never bringing that forth by a penitential confeſſion, which we did bring out by a ſinfull commiſſion. Oh take heed of this, though we be forward to ſin, beware leſt we be artificial to conceal it. If we cannot have eyes to foreſee, and ſtrength to prevent evil; yet let us have hearts to bewail, and tongues to confeſs it. Conſider ſeriouſly

1. This *hiding quality is a very ill quality*; it is an embleme of an heart, that will not yet be rid of ſin: As Beggars, that will not be cured of their ſores; for if thou wouldſt be cleanſed, why concealeſt thou thy diſeaſe?

2. *It adds much to your ſin:* To commit a ſin may be an act of infirmity, but to hide and conceal it argues either ſtrong Atheiſm, that the ſinner thinks God regards it not though it be vile; or elſe perverſe wilfulneſs, he will not humble, he will not turn unto the Lord.

Uſe 2. Exhortation, To confeſs our ſins in a penitential manner. Not to cover our ſins.

This is a very ill quality.

It adds much to your ſin.

3. It

The Returning Prodigal, or

It adds nothing to our safety.

3. *It adds nothing to our safety: Adam hid himself in the thicket,* what got he by it? what if you keep the fire close in the thatch? You may put gold in a secret place, and perhaps it may be under a safer custody; but he who will hide his sin, doth but put a fair cloth upon a dangerous wound, which now rankles, gangrenes, kills. Of all sins, those do most endanger the soul, for which we are not truly humbled, or do not seriously confess them unto God. Why should God shew thee mercy, who wilt not acknowledge thy self guilty? and how can sin but be fiercely reigning, where it is most willingly harboured and concealed?

Nor doth it add to our secrecy.

4. *Nor doth it add to our secrecy:* For *all things are naked and bare before God,* &c. God can easily discover thy sin. 1. He sees it, he has an all-seeing eye. 2. He can make thy conscience the rack of torment at confession. 3. And will at the last day; *Nothing is hid that shall not be made manifest.* In two things doth the inconfitent sinner much prejudice himself by hiding of his sins: One, that he contrives himself for a sore punishment; another, that he reprieves himself for an open shame. It is Gods disposition, this, that when we discover our sin, and condemn our selves, then will he cover those sins, and not judge our persons. 1 Cor. 11. 31. *If we would judge our selves, we should not be judged.* But when we with wile and guile contrive to keep them close, God then will publish and manifest them; for there is nothing (in this kind) secret, which shall not be made manifest: Nay, simply, manifestation is not all; judiciary is it; he will so discover them, as to question, as to arraign, as to convict, as to sentence, as to condemn your sins.

Object. But sinners are ready to object; Who is able to confess his sins? Doth not *David* say, *Who knoweth how oft he offendeth?* Psal. 19.

Sol. It is true, every particular, numerical thought and act of sin, is not possible to be cited and confessed; but who urgeth that? This belongs to thee; 1. To study thy heart and life; 2. To observe what the Lord forbids and commands; 3. To hear what thy Conscience will speak for kinds and acts; 4. To give diligence to find out as many of thy sins as thou canst, and by no means to omit thy special sins; and so to spread all of them, with humble, hearty, and mournfull acknowledgment before the Lord.

Object.

The Sinners Conversion to God.

Object. This is the way to breed despair, to see an Army of sins on a sudden raised up in the soul.

Sol. 1. See them you must, first, or last; either now to your humiliation, or hereafter to your confusion; better see them now, when you have time to get God to pardon them, then after life, when it is Gods time onely to condemn you for them. And 2. He who bids thee to see thy sins, bids thee to confess them; and he who bids thee to confess them, hath promised also to pardon them.

Object. But I shall be ashamed to confess them, so many, so foul transgressions.

Sol. 1. If it were to Man, then thou mightst blush and fear; he might wonder at thee, and perhaps incompassionately censure and blab. 2. But it is to a God onely; One who is very mercifull and will keep counsel, he is very ready to pity and to spare thee. 3. The commission of sin should be a shame, but the confession of it is an honour; it is an honourable thing that a sinner will glorifie God, and confess and forsake his sins. Let the disease be what it will, thou wilt discover it to the Physitian; why then this sinfull modesty to reveal thy sins to God? And 4. especially, if thou considerest thus much, that thy confession is not to give him knowledge of any fact with which he is not acquainted, but to yield a testimony of thy obedience, and repentance, and grief, and to get thy acquittance and discharge:

II. But *discover and confess them:* and to move you to this, consider 1. Though it *be a shame to commit sin, yet it is an honour to confess it. My son, give glory to the God of Israel, and confess unto him,* said *Joshua,* cap. 7. 19. to *Achan.* But discover and confess them. Motives.

2. Though *the commission of sin brings heavy guilt,* yet the *confession of it brings peace and ease:* It is the letting out of corrupt & ulcerous matter, which rages, and swelleth, and boils in the conscience.

3. *Is it so great a matter, being greatly guilty, freely and humbly to confess?* If the Prophet had bid thee to have done some great thing, &c. so if the Lord had required of thee some great matter, proper and high satisfaction for the wrongs thou hast done unto him, thousands of rams, or ten thousand rivers of oyl, &c. But when he saith, Be grieved for what thou hast done, do so no more, *onely acknowledge thine iniquity, that thou hast transgressed against the Lord thy God,* Jer. 3. 13. Is it so great a matter for the guilty person freely to confess.

4. It

It shall surely find mercy.

4. *It shall surely find mercy.* O pardoning mercy! how necessary, how sweet for a sinner! But who shall have it? *He that confesseth and forsaketh his sins, shall find mercy,* Prov. 28. *I said, I will confess my sins unto the Lord, and thou forgavest the iniquity of my sin,* Selah, Psal. 32. 5. *Nondum pronuntiat, sed promittit se pronuntiaturum, & ille dimittit,* saith Saint *Austin, ibid.* And again; *Vox nondum in ore erat, sed auris Dei in corde erat:* So was it with the Prodigal; he purposeth to confess, and his Father seeth him a far off.

LUKE 15. 19.
And am no more worthy to be called thy Son; make me as one of thy hired Servants.

He confesseth his unworthiness.

These words contain in them, a continuation of the Prodigals humble Confession; he had in the former Verse acknowledged his sinfulness, and in this *he confesseth his unworthiness,* [*And am no more worthy to be called thy Son.*] 2. A modest supplication, [*Make me as one of thy hired Servants.*] There are three Propositions which these two parts do afford us, *viz.* 1. *That penitent persons are humble and lowly persons.* [I am no more worthy.] 2. *That unworthiness is no just prejudice to supplication.* [I am not worthy, yet make me, &c.] 3. *That penitent persons earnestly desire some relation to God.* [Make me as one of thy hired Servants.]

Doct. 1. Penitent persons are humble persons.

That penitent persons are humble and lowly persons. [*I am no more worthy.*] Look on every word almost in the Text, and you shall see in it the blush of humility; *I am not worthy.*] The language of Pride is, I am not as other men; the voice of Humility is, I am not worthy; what I have is of meer mercy, what I crave is not of my merit; God may give what he pleaseth, and I may receive what he giveth, but I am unworthy of both; I dare not expostulate nor challenge, I have sinned, and what mercy can I then deserve. *No more worthy.*] Was he ever worthy? No. Why then no more worthy? *q. d.* O Lord, I deserve nothing, no, nothing at all; so vile a wretch have I been, that it's singular mercy if thou look at all upon me. *To be thy Son.*] A Son, thy Son, O it is a high Relation, an high Dignity! for a Vassal of Wrath to be made a Vessel of Glory! for a

Slave

Slave to Sin, to be tranflated to a Son of God! Who am I? it is that which I want, it is that though which is too great for me to ask; I am not worthy to be thy Son, nay, not worthy to be *called thy fon,*] the very title and name is too good for me: that fo debauched and luxurious a finner as I, fhould have that honour from thee, to be mentioned or fpoken of, to be in any fort reputed among thofe of fo fingular Relation unto thee; I who have finned fo much againft thee, that I fhould in any kind be owned as a Son by thee, this is an eminency; I am not worthy to be called thy Son. Thus you fee his humblenefs in confeffion; Not worthy, utterly unworthy to be a Son, nay, to be called thy Son: See fome fteps of it in his Petition; *Make me as one of thy hired fervants.*] A low requeft, but it is the modeft breath of a lowly fpirit. If *I* may be *thy fervant, I* fhall be glad of that; not thy onely fervant, but *one* of thy fervants; not the chiefeft of thy fervants, but any one of thy fervants, *thy hired fervant:* And perhaps even that is too good for me, to be a fervant, to be an hired fervant, to be one of them; *I* fhall count my felf happy, if *I* may be *as one* of the meaneft fervants, if *I* may be but a fervant to the meaneft of thy fervants that ferve thee. And Father, I beg for this too, *make me* as one of thy hired fervants; *I* am not worthy of the leaft place, nor of the meaneft Relation; *I* challenge it not, onely be thou pleafed to beftow it upon me. He is not worthy to defire the greateft, and he doth modeftly intreat for the loweft Relation; both which fhew the humblenefs of his penitential fpirit. Thus was it with *Paul* after his converfion; how he finks his thoughts and eftimation of himfelf! When he is to fpeak of his fins, 1 *Tim.* 1. 15. then *Primus peccatorum,* I am the chief of finners; *Nemo prior,* none exceeded me, *nemo pejor,* I was worfe then any: And when he fpake of God's mercy to him, then, *minimus Apoftolorum, I* am the leaft of the Apoftles, 1 *Cor.* 15. 8. *& indignifimus,* not worthy to be called an Apoftle. Nay, he falls lower than this, *Ephef.* 3. 3. *Minimus fanctorum minor minimo,* lefs than the leaft of all Saints, is this grace given, *&c*, Do you not fee this alfo in the *penitential Publican? He ftood afar off,* and *would not* fo much as *lift up his eyes to heaven,* but *fmote upon his breft, faying, God be mercifull to me a finner.* He judges thofe feet unworthy to carry him unto God, which fo often carried him

Paul.

Publican.

from

from God; and those eyes unworthy to look on his holiness, which had been so frequently cast upon sinfulness; and whereas the Pharisee spreads his hands abroad, he turns them upon his breast, his contrite breast, and doth not boast of his righteousness, but cries out of his sins; and justifies not himself, but humbly begs, Lord, be mercifull to me a sinner. Thus was it with *Mary Magdalene* upon her repentance, *Luc.* 7. 38. *She stood at the feet of Jesus, behind him, weeping, and began to wash his feet with tears, and wiped them with the hairs of her head, and kissed his feet, and anointed them with ointment.* Mark it; all her service is lowly; she stood, she did not sit; sitting was a posture of familiarity, standing of humility: and she stood behind; to look after Christ was enough, to look upon him she was unworthy: And then she stood at his feet, the humblest posture, and there all her work is acted: Stood at his feet, wept at his feet, washed his feet, wiped his feet, kissed his feet, anointed his feet.

But now for the opening of this Proposition, I will briefly discuss, 1. What this lowly humbleness is, which accompanies true Repentance? 2. The Causes why true Penitents are so humbly lowly? 3. Some usefull Application of this.

What this lowly humbleness is.

Quest. 1. *What that humble lowliness is, which is to be found in the true penitent?*

Sol. It is not *a promiscuous familiarity* with every body; such an humbleness becomes *Solomon*'s fool; nor is it an affected garb of *complemental dissimulation,* that was *Absalom*'s treacherous stirrup to mount up himself into the Throne; nor is it a slavingly abasing of a mans self to acts incongruous with the dignity of his place and calling; this were to be the *Tom* of a Parish; nor is it a *denial of those gifts and graces that God hath bestowed upon us,* this is a modest lie, it is not lowliness; nor is it *passive humiliation,* wherein the spirit may be crackt as low as Hell, and yet be still as proud as Hell; nor is it a *rejecting of Gods promises, because we can bring no worth unto them:* But Humbleness which accompanies Repentance, *It is a Grace of Gods Spirit, whereby the penitential person, from right knowledge, becomes low in his own eyes, and judgeth himself most unworthy in his addresses unto God.*

Humbleness described.

It is a Grace of Gods Spirit.

1. *It is a Grace of Gods Spirit.*] It is one of the Pearls in the Chain which the Apostle would have us to put on, *Col.* 3. 12. an humble spirit is a spiritual ornament. Some Graces are more visible

The Sinners Conversion to God.

ble and stirring, as Faith and Charity; others are more reserved and hidden (like *Saul* among the stuff) as Patience and Humility. But a Grace it is, being a supernatural Quality, not born with us, but added unto us. In our first Birth, we come out with very high and stout Spirits; in our second Births, with very lowly and humble Spirits; in our low Birth, with high Spirits; in our high and excellent Birth, with lowly Spirits.

2. *Making us low in our own eyes:*] Behold, saith Job, 40. 4. *I am vile*, (.i.) nothing worth, base, *What shall I answer thee?* *I am as a weaned child*, said *David*, Psa. 131. 2. *I have not the Understanding of a man*, said *Agur*, Pro. 30. 2. *Not as if I had yet attained*, saith the Apostle, *Phil.* 3. Hence is it that in Scripture humble persons are called *Little*, (one of *these little ones*, saith Christ) little, not only in the proud contempt of the World, but little in their own humble estimation of themselves. As *David* is said to be little in his own eyes; one who set a very low rate and value on himself. And they are said to be poor, *poor in spirit*; they have indeed very rich Graces, but very poor opinions and conceits of themselves; *I, who am but dust and ashes*, saith *Abraham*: *a worm and no man*, said *David*. Excellencies they have, but they are not puffed up by them. God doth raise them, but they raise not themselves; they are precous and honorable in his sight, but vile and nothing in their own; they have an high Calling, and high Graces, and high Priviledges, but still low hearts: when they look on their Natural frame, that's as low as Earth; when they look on their sinful frame, that's as low as Hell; when they look on their Spiritual frame, then how little; it is but some faith, Oh, that God would help my Unbelief! that sorrow is but a drop, that love but a spark, that knowledge but a dawning light, their strength but weakness; others have more, they have but little; still they complain of defects, infirmities, failings; what they have is nothing to the much they want: No Vines so unfruitful, no servants so unprofitable as they.

Judging themselves unworthy in their addresses to God:] *Thy Saints*, said *Moses*, *humble themselves at thy feet*; unworthy to come before God, unworthy to obtain any thing from God: the Publican dares not lift up his eyes to heaven; *Ezra* is ashamed and confounded to look up: the very Majesty and Purity of God do dazle, and sometimes silence their thoughts; and when they do worship towards his holy place, then mark how their Petitions run, Not for my sake, O Lord, not in my own name, not for my righteousness, shame and confusion belong to me; but do it for thine Own sake, for thy Mercies sake, for thy Truths sake, for thy Chrifts sake, O Lord: If thou shewest me no Mercy, I deserve none; if thou givest me any Mercy, it is only of thy abundant Mercy.

Arising from a Right knowledge,

Arising from a right knowledg:] As Pride is rooted in Ignorance and Error (it is but the corrupting of our Text, a foolish blast and mistake) so Humbleness is grounded in right Knowledg and true Judgment.

Of God.

1. *Of God:* Humble persons do more exactly apprehend him (what He is, what his Will is) in his perfections of Holiness, and Mercy, and Justice, and thereupon are abased in their own sense. To compare our selves with our selves may be dangerous, and to compare our selves with others inferior to us in gifts, and graces, and services, it may be a speedy way to puff us up. But a comparison of our selves with God, O how short are we? how nothing are we in comparison of that infinite fulness of excellency in him? The Stars make a twinkling in the night, but when the Sun appears they hide their faces and Veile themselves. Our Graces may seem to cast their Rayes, their Beams, and to have some Lustre in our eyes, whilst we compare them with others, or our selves in darkness; but when we look on God, that Sun, that fulness of all Holiness, then we are ashamed, may hang down our heads, and, with the Angels, cover our Faces: Our Features are but as Deformities, and our Fulness but Poverty, in comparison of him: And therefore when *Job* had a while conferred with God, he then confesseth his folly and ignorance, and *abhors himself, and will speak no more.*

Of our Selves.

For Evil.

2. *Of our selves,* both in *Evil* and in *Good.* For *Evil:* It is discerned in the proper nature, forms, colours, deserts of it. Oh, how much hath God already been dishonoured by me? How often? how highly? Any one Transgression, rightly apprehended, may serve to abase us all our dayes. But then I still feel a corrupt nature, apt to rebel, to step aside, to break out. Oh, how wonderfully do unbelief, hardness, security, dulness,

nefs, diftraction, hypocrifie, vain-glory, unthankfulnefs, folly, indifpofitions, evil thoughts, corrupt affections cleave unto me, though under many mercies, opportunities, helps, affiftances; what am I worthy of? It is pure mercy that I am not almoft every hour thrown into Hell, by reafon of continual finnings? For *Good*; look on it in all refpects, and know it aright: you may fee caufe of humblenefs: 1. Look on it in the *Qualities or Habits:* at the beft very weak, things rather of defire, then of poffeffion; we know but in part, believe with fear, truft with doubtings, fee but as in a glafs; we rather imitate then apprehend. As *Profper* fpake of the joyes of Grace, *Ipfa & virtutum gaudia vulnus habent*, that is true of the very Graces, even our wine is mixt with water; and like *Jacobs* fpeckled Sheep, fo is it with our fouls, fome of all graces, yet but alittle, and accompanied with the reliques of all, and too much finfulnefs. 2. Look on it in the *Acts and Fruits:* We cannot go without a Staff, and, too like *Jacob*, halting to our dying day; either we want minds to good, or wills or power, not able of our felves to hatch one good thought, and when the will is prefent, yet we find not power to perform; and though fometimes we do good, yet evil is prefent with us: like Beer which runs low with the liquor, there runs out much muddy grounds; or like *Abrahams* Sacrifice, many Birds lighting on it; or like *Solomons Ointment*, in which is fome *dead Flie*; or like a Candle, which burns with a Snuff; or like the fire, which afcends with much fmoke. Our actions are like the Arrows which are fhot, one is too far, another is too fhort, another is too wide, not one of an hundred that hits the mark; fo is it with us, many Duties and Services are performed by us, but which amongft them all is performed with that reverence of Spirit, faith on Chrift, integrity of Affection, unitednefs of Soul, and fole fidelity of intention to Divine Glory. Our excellencies are weak, and the Lord be merciful unto us, how often do we weaken them? our work is but little that we do, very little; take afide the averfnefs, the indifpofitions, the formalities, the coldnefs, the diftractions, the unbelief, the wearinefs, the inconftancy, the infinite infirmities which accompany them, what poor things will they then appear? may we not fall down and fay, having done our beft, We are
but

but unprofitable servants. Nay, and that which being known may likewise abase us, is this, we may justly say of all our poor excellencies, as the Widow of her Vessels, They are but borrowed ware; What have we which we have not received? Every Gift and Grace which we have, is but a Beam born of the Sun, a drop coming from another Fountain then our Natures: all our good is but free Gift; take the borrowed feathers from the Crow, it is then a most black creature alone. So that consider our good aright, either in the initial cause of it, *viz.* Divine and free Grace; or in the upholding cause of it, Divine assistance; or in the qualities of it, how weak and imperfect; or in the acts of it, how rare and uneven; all these are the springs as it were, which feed humbleness of heart in the true Penitent.

Why true penitents are humble persons.

Quest. 2. Now I proceed to the next inquiry, *Why true Penitents are such humble and lowly persons? I am not worthy to be called thy Son.*

Sol. The reasons are most of them insinuated already; I will either express them again, or add more to them: thus then. 1. *Conversion necessarily infers an alteration in the whole man*: Though it doth not destroy Substances, yet it changeth Qualities; of unholy, it makes us holy; of ignorant, knowing; of filthy, clean; of obstinate, flexible; of unquiet, meek; of proud and lofty, humble and lowly; therefore penitent persons, who are converted persons, must needs be lowly, *ex natura rei*; this is forcible. 2. They never did experimentally know themselves till they began to repent: Sin was but a delight, or a mock, or a meer discourse unto them before; the vileness of it, the contagious pollution of it, the stinging guilt of it, the terrible effects of it, both in respect of God and themselves, they never saw it till now; they see that of sin which they saw not before, both for the filth and the guilt of it; and they see it with other eyes then they saw it before; no marvel then that they become low in their own eyes. Should they not be very vile in their own eyes, who perceive themselves guilty of that which is most and only vile in Gods? *I have sinned what shall I say unto thee, O thou preserver of men?* 3. They never saw till now how short they came in that good of duty which they owe to God, and how unanswerable they are to the many bonds of obedience: I have done nothing for God all my dayes, nor to him in any Service and Honour.

Conversion infers an Alteration in the whole man.

They now experimentally know themselves.

Job 7.10.

They now see how short they come in duty.

4. They

The Sinners Conversion to God. 125

They never knew till now *how injurious they have been unto God*, to the kindness of his Love, to the counsel of his Spirit, to the righteousness of his Will; how unworthily and stubbornly they have resisted, despised him, abused all his mercies: Thus for the Explication of the point. Now for the Application of it to our selves; Doth true Repentance produce humble lowliness of Spirit, *then let us reflect on our own hearts*, and judge what *solidity of Repentance* is wrought in us by that *lowliness and sense of unworthiness* which is to be found in true penitents. Consider Pride, and loftiness, and *self-worthiness are very natural to us*: though we be born wholly naked, not any external ornament is upon us, no inward excellency, yet our natures are puft with wind and a haughtiness; and could we be rifled and stript of every sin, we should find this of pride (so opposite to lowliness) most intimately cleaving to us: Paradise was not free of it: What do I speak of it? nay, Heaven it self was troubled with it; the Divels, who are cast into the lowest darkness, fell thither by reason of their proud loftiness. Look over all sorts of persons, it s a wonder almost to find one truly humble-hearted sinner. If a man hath parts, the Apostle tells us that knowledge puffeth up; the the wind gets into the bladder: as it was with *Diotrephes*, &c. *Who is the Lord*, said *Pharaoh*? if a man have dignities, how rare is it to see greatness stooping, and lowliness of heart with highness of honor. If a man have riches, he needs an Apostles charge, *Not to be high-minded*. If a man be poor, he is like *Diogenes*, trampling upon the Philosophers chair with greater pride. Generally the scum is most light, and vulgar spirits most censorious and insolent. If a man be ignorant, yet *Laodicea* thinks her self *rich, and increased, and to have need of nothing*; though indeed she be *poor, and blind, and miserable, and naked*.

2. *If habitually and predominantly proud, thou art as yet impenitent*; 'tis true that Conversion doth not give an absolute cessation to sin, yet it do h take off dominion, and causeth diminution. It cannot be, that a man should have an heart rightly sensible of sin, and set against it, and yet be high in the opinion of his own excellencies and worth. The mountains are cast down into a valley, and the high imaginations brought into captivity; the swellings of our corrupt spirits are in great measure abated and let out, when once Grace enters our hearts, and Repentance hath opened.

And how injurious they have been to God.

Use.
Let us judge of our Repentance by our lowliness.

Pride and self-worthiness are very natural to us.

If Habitually Proud, thou art impenitent.

opened our eies. Though you may be free from many other actual and gross exorbitancies, if yet the spirit of pride (be it in Spirituals, or Naturals, or Civils, or Morals) dwell within you, and rule over you, it may be said of you what the Prophet spake of the stout-hearted, *They were far from righteousness.*

Few men use the means to make them humble.

3. *Few men use the means to make them humble,* they seldom are at home, they are so studious of other mens sins, that they neglect their own. This is a most ordinary truth, that they who are so prying after the faults of others, seldom search themselvs, and hereby onely enable their own pride, but disable themselvs for humbleness. It is not forreign, but experimental knowledge which makes us lowly. But you may reply, How may it bee

How it may be known that our hearts are not lofty, but lowly.

known that our hearts are not lofty, but lowly, that so we may judge our repentance not to be be formal, but sound. *Sol.* Premise a word or two and then I have done, that I speak onely of *Lowliness,* as it is to be found in Christians *in this life,* which is not a state of perfection, but imperfection. Secondly, as it is *in conflict and combate,* not as absolute and free. Now then 1. *If*

You then live upon meer mercy.

you be truly lowly, then you live altogether upon free and meer mercy. Every mercy is an alms unto you, and is sued out not upon desert, but upon promise: you can find no mony to buy corn, but all must be free gift: you will be content to buy without mony, and to receive without price. 2. *You will then be more patient*

You will be patient under delayes.

under delays: it is but a proud beggar who will be served at first knock, or else will be gone. It is a very ill sign when we are so quick with God, that he shall lose our service if he doth not presently send out his answers. Were we indeed sensible of our own unworthiness, we would hold it no disparagement to wait at heaven gates; he will patiently wait for some mercy, who humbly knows that he deservs none. Even an humble heart may urge God to make haste, but it is our proud heart which accuseth and quarrels with him for delay. 3. *You will be silent in denials and withdrawments.* Doth

You will be silent in denials.

not God answer me? Why! I deserv no look nor answer. Doth he not give what I ask, but take away what he hath given? Why! it is the Lord, let him do with his own what he pleaseth. It is mercy that I have yet any mercy: I am unworthy to enjoy any good, who am most worthy to enjoy all evil. When we are our selves, this will be our temper, if we be humble, God shall use his own authority and pleasure to dispose of the mercies which we crave, and of the

mercies

mercies also which we have; we will be more patient in denials, and silent in losses; What can we say who are unworthy of all? 4. *You will be very thankful for any answer, or the least mercy.* You will be very If nothing will content us but great mercies, assuredly we are not ry thankful for humble, but have too great spirits. He who indeed judgeth him- the least merself not worthy of the least of all the mercies and truth which cy. God shews unto him, will take up a great misery with quietness, and a little mercy with thankfulness. The body of man if it bee found, can stoop for a pin, as well as for a piece; and the heart, if it be humble, can bless for little mercies, as well as for great. The touch of the little finger, as well as of the great, will make a well-tuned stringed instrument speak, and even the whisperings of the voice are ecchoed back in an exact concave. The least drops of mercy affect the lowly heart, which can awake upon the least noise. The proud heart like the mountain yields a poor crop after a shower of mercies, but the humble heart, like the Gardens, yields plenty of sweet smelling sacrifices, after the least dews or drops of merciful blessings and answers from God. Now say, How do you plead with God when you approach unto him? what can you shew for the mercies that you ask? onely his own mercie, no worth in you to move him: And how are you when God delaies, or denies, or removes his mercies? can you then be in dust and ashes, and not in fire and flames? can you yet quietly serve him, wait on him, depend on him, submit to him upon this ground? Ah! I am a sinner; I have wronged the Father of mercies; abused all his mercies; am not worthy of the least of mercies: It is mercy that ever I had mercy, that now I have any, that which is oft and denied, I am not worthy of them; that which I have, I am not worthy of. And when God answers you either in spirituals, to your souls; or in temporals, to your outward man, How do you look upon his answers? Do you look a squint on them as he upon *Solomons* Cities? Are you able to abuse great mercies, and slight the least? 5. If you bee The more mer- truly humble, then the *more mercies and answers from God, will* cies from God, *still add and make you more humble and lowly*. Not onely the will make you sense of your iniquities, but the experience of Gods mercies will more humble. make you low in your eies. Mercies have two effects upon humble hearts, they make them more humble, and more fruitful. *David* in 2 *Sam*. 7. when God gave him the advouzon, and, as it were,

con-

confirmed and added to his former Charter, an intention of greater mercy to his posterity, Why! this casts *David* down, *ver. 1?*. *Then went King David in, and sate before the Lord,* and he said, *Who am I, O Lord God, and what is my house, that thou hast brought me hitherto.* The more corn is in the ear, the more it hangs down the head; and the tree bends most, when laden with fruit. But if mercies make us forget God, as afflictions make us forget our selves; if it be with us as with the Arrow, which when the Bow is most bent and drawn, it flies farthest from us; Or as with the Dial which casts the shortest shadow, when the Sun is highest; or as with some grounds, which yields the rankest corn after the fullest tillage: we grow carelefs of God, of his Ordinances in publick, of his worship in private, scornful of heavenly reproof, admonition, obedience; alas! this shews we are not humble.

2. Use.
We should be humbled for the want of this humblenefs.

If upon due search we find our hearts lifted up with an opinion of our own worth and excellencies, and far from penitential humblings, *We should be humbled for want of this humblenefs*: as *Hezekiah,* though his heart was lifted up, yet the text faith, *He humbled himself for the pride of his heart,* 2 Chron. 32. 25, 26, 27. And *use the means by which we may become humbly fenfible of our own great unworthinefs. v. g.* 1. *Study our selves more.*

And use the means to become humble.
Study our selves more.

Alas! what are we? but dust and ashes; nay, but sin and corruption: We cannot say of our sins, as the Prophet spake of the fore-running calamities, *Gray hairs are here and there upon him.* No, no, but as *David*, *Who can tell how oft he offends?* if we knew our selves, we would abhor our selves. 2. *Study the Law more,* the perfection and excellency of it, and bring thy many blots to that purity, thy many crookednefles to that plainnefs. *Paul* was *alive before the Law came*, but *when the Commandement came, fin revived, and he died.* 3. *Study your own performances better.* 'Tis true, something is done, but there is more undone, then done: thy best services have more in them to humble, then to puff thee; thou canst not do at all, unless God aids thee (but art like a Mill without water, or a Dial without the Sun) and when thou dost go, it is like *Mephibofheth,* lame on both feet. When thou hast made the best praier, thou maiest well bow the knee, and pray again, that God would forgive thee the much dullnefs, the many distractions, the infinite unbelief in thy prayer.

Study the Law more.

Study your own performances better.

4. *Study*

The Sinners Conversion to God. 129

4. *Study the creatures better*, which are the bellowes to blow up your self-conceits and high thoughts. What is thy *beauty* but a fading dye, a changeable tincture, which one blow or one disease may dash! if it escape both, yet time will unvarnish the house newly painted? What are *riches* but a labour, an heap of vanity, and a vexation of spirit; they are a Tree long in growing, and quick in fading: *Solomon* compares them to a *Bird ready to flye*; *Paul* reputes them *uncertain*, and *David* wonders *who shall enjoy them*. What are *cloathes* but a few Garments of Trees, of Beasts, somewhat trimmed up? And our *Honours*, but the breath of the People, a vain aire and wind at the best, quickly stirred, easily turned about and allayed? And our *bodies*, but a piece of clay, a wall of earth? Our heads are but earthly Globes, and our eyes but walling Candles, and our feet but decaying Pillars, &c. 5. *Study God more*, in his excellencies of holiness, of justice, of mercy, and then you will abhor your selves in dust and ashes.

Study the creatures better.

Study God more.

Now I proceed to the second Proposition, *viz.*

That personal unworthiness is not prejudicial to spiritual supplication; [*I am not worthy, yet make me as.*] Of this Proposition, I will give you 1. The sense. 2. Arguments to confirm it. 3. Some useful Applications.

Doct. 2. Personal unworthiness is not prejudicial to spiritual supplication.

Touching the *sense* or *Explication* of it, premise these particulars. 1. There is a twofold *unworthiness*; *Privative*; when there is no quality or act which the person can shew to God, as a meritorious cause, why he should accept of him or his services. *Negative*; when there is no meetness or fitness of capacity in the subject, enabling of him to receive any thing from God: for as there is a double dignity or worthiness; One of Causality to deserve good, another of Receptivity to obtain good; so answerably there is a double unworthiness, one which consists in the defect of merit, another which consists in the defect of meetness: I speak only of the former, not of the latter, for a person may not be unworthy, (*.i.*) unfit or uncapable to receive good, who yet is unworthy, (*.i.*) unable to deserve and merit it.

There is a twofold unworthiness.

2. There is an *absolute and plenary unworthiness*, wherein as there is no cause of good, so there is effectual cause to hinder it; this may be called a moral unworthiness; And this a natural, a restrictive and partial unworthiness, when there are qualities

There is an absolute and plenary unworthiness.

S

130   *The Returning Prodigal, or*

ties in, or actions by a person, against which strict justice might make exceptions, yet through a gracious indulgence they avail not to the prejudice of the person. David saith in *Psal.* 66. 18. *If I regard iniquity in my heart, the Lord will not hear me*; and the blind man cured, said well, *Joh.* 9. 31. *We know that God heareth not sinners.* When people have not onely sin living in them, but themselvs living in sin; when they know and affect their sins, have means to leave them, but will not have hearts to forsake them; this now imprints an absolute unworthiness, (i) such an unworthiness, as doth effectually prejudice their access and confidence to God in praier. Nevertheless there may be the presence of many corruptions for quality and fact (which the sinner knows, and bewails, and judges) and though in strict justice they are a sufficient prejudice.; yet through a divine graciousness, they prove not effectual hinderances to the presenting or accepting of Praier.

The privative unworthiness may be considered two wayes. In respect of the matter of it. Or of the sence of it.

3. The privative and natural or restrictive unworthiness may be considered again two waies: Either in respect *of the matter of it*, which is some kind or kinds of sinfulness, either in nature, or fact: for nothing makes us unworthy but sin, this abaseth us, and keeps us at a distance: Or, *of the sense and apprehension of it*; when the sinfulness which doth make us so unworthy, is discerned by us; and so discerned, that by reason thereof we do judge our selves not worthy of the least of mercies. In neither respect is it prejudicial to spiritual supplication, (i) though there be sinfulness in us, and upon us, and we know it, and that by reason of it wee are neither worthy to speak with God, nor to prevail with God, yet we may present our supplications unto him.

Prayer may be considered in a threefold respect.

Unworthiness should not take us off from Prayer.

4 *Praier may be considered in a threefold respect; Either*, As a Duty to be acted; As a Duty acting; As a Duty acted. The sense of our unworthiness should not be any prejudice to praier in any of those respects. 1. *Not to take us off from performing the duty of praier*: We may offer up our sacrifice, though we cannot offer up our worthiness; we may bring our gift, though we cannot bring our merit; though vve cannot buy heaven, yet vve may beg it. Poverty doth not hinder, but a man may be a fit beggar; and sin doth not hinder, but a person may be a fit petitioner to God. David was sensible of his sins, *Psal.* 40. 12. *Innumerable evils have compassed me about, mine iniquities have taken hold upon me, so that I am*

not

The Sinners Converfion to God.

not able to look up; they are more then the hairs of my head, therefore my heart faileth me: Yet he makes his Supplication prefently in the next verfe, v. 13. *Be pleafed, O Lord, to deliver me; O Lord make hafte to help me.* So did *Ezra*, c. 9. 6. and *Daniel*, c. 9. 2. *Nor take off Confidence in the time of Performance:* An Unworthy perfon may lawfully bee an earneft Suiter. He may put up requefts, and alfo believe that God will grant them: See it in the Church; *Ifa.* 64. 6. *We are all as an unclean thing, and all our righteoufneffes as filthy rags, &c.* Ver. 8. *But now, O Lord, thou art our Father.* Ver. 9. *Be not wrath very fore, O Lord, neither remember iniquity for ever; behold, fee, we befeech thee, we are all thy people.* So Pfal. 25. 11. *For thy Names fake, O Lord, pardon mine iniquity, for it is great.* He was fenfible of the greatnefs of his fin, yet puts up a believing Petition for pardon. 3. *Nor yet take off our expectation of the fuccefs and fruit of Prayer:* Though a man hath fown his feed with an hand perhaps foul or lame, yet he expects an Harveft. We may expect a moft gracious, and proper, and feafonable anfwer to our prayers, though we be moft unworthy of the mercy or bleffing which we do defire. Though we know nothing in our felves to commend us to God, yea, though we know enough in our felves to condemn us before God, to non-fuit all our prayers, if the anfwers were to be given according to our deferts, yet we may not only requeft the Lord, but fhould by Faith rely on God; yea, and expect an anfwer what the Lord will anfwer us, and when he will perform his promife to us.

Nor take off Confidence in the time of Performance.

Nor take off our expectation of the Succefs.

2. But you may demand, Why fhould not the fenfe of our unworthinefs prejudice our prayings?

Sol. I will give you divers Reafons for it:

1. *Becaufe though we cannot Sue in our own name, yet we may Sue in the Name of Chrift:* There may be a worthinefs For us though not In us. In the Old Law it was a dangerous prefumption for any man to offer a *Sacrifice* without a *Prieft*, Lev. 17. 3, 4, 5. fuch a perfon was to be cut off: in like manner it is moft dangerous for any man to offer up his prayers to God without Chrift: to come in his own name, it is the way to cut off our prayers. God will not take any petition from us, unlefs it come out of the hands of our Mafter of requefts (.*i.*) Chrift Jefus. And again, in the Old Law, if the Prieft did offer up the Sacrifice,

Arguments to confirm it. Though we cannot Sue in our own name, yet we may in the Name of Chrift.

fice, though it were not a rich sacrifice of a Bullock or a Sheep, if it were but a pair of Turtle Doves; nay, if it were but the tenth part of an Ephah of fine flour, it was available for the person, it was accepted, *Levit.* 5. intimating unto us, That it is not our own names, not any excellencies in us, which make way for the acceptance or the answer of our prayers, they are accepted for his sake in whom our persons are accepted; and therefore you read in *Rev.* 8. 3. of the *Angel that stood at the Altar, having a golden Censer, who had much incense, which he offered with the prayers of all Saints upon the golden Altar which was before the Throne.* The golden Altar, and the golden Censer, and much Incense make all accepted; and ver. 4. *The smoke of the incense, which came with the prayers of the Saints, ascended up before God out of the Angels hand.* It was the Angels Incense which made even the prayers of the Saints to ascend (*.i.*) the meritorious intercession of Christ, which giveth acceptance and audience to our Petitions; as he is a sufficient Redeemer, so is he a sufficient Intercessour, and therefore our own Unworthiness must not prejudice or discourage us, for as much as the name of Jesus Christ is enough to implead God withall.

God is of a most liberal and Gracious nature.

2. Secondly, *When we come to God in Prayer, we come to one who is of a most liberal and gracious Nature*, therefore our unworthiness should not discourage our petitions. That God is of a liberal Nature, is unquestionable, *he is abundant in goodness and truth,* so Moses. *He will give grace and glory,* so David. *He giveth to all men liberally and upbraideth not,* so Jam.1.5. Water comes not from the clouds as from a Pump; a bountiful and noble Nature stands not on desert, it finds principles enough within it self to shew kindness. But which is yet more, the Lord hath not only a nature full of goodness, and most propense to give, but also he hath a gracious Nature which dispenseth all good upon free terms, not for our sake who receive, but for his own sake only who gives. As Gods liberality appears in giving many times before we ask, and sometimes in giving more then we ask, and sometimes in giving a better thing then we ask; so his graciousness appears in not considering how worthy we are, what Causes and Arguments we can bring, but in a a free dispensation of his mercies to us, without all desert or causa-

The Sinners Conversion to God. 133

causality on our parts: The whole cause of the mercy, is only in mercy, as in *Deut. 9. 6. The Lord thy God doth not give thee this good land to possess it, for thy righteousness, for thou art a stiffnecked people :* The gift then was gracious, no desert of it; nay, a desert of the contrary. *Come,* saith the Prophet, *ye that have no mony, come ye, buy and eat ; yea, come buy wine and milk without mony and without price, Isay 55. 1.* If God doth not sell any of his mercies, if he will take none of our coyn; if he doth not stand upon a price, but only upon the asking and on the acceptation of his gifts, then our Unworthines doth not prejudice our prayers.

3. *We do not only advance the name of Christ, and the name of divine Grace by comming with a sense of our Unworthiness, but it is the necessary concomitant of acceptable prayer.* There are two singular Graces which must exercise themselves in prayer; one is *Faith*, by which we go in the name of another; another is *Humility* by which we go out of our selves. When *Abraham* prayes, his form was humble, *I who am but dust and ashes.* When *Jacob* prayes his form was humble, *I who am not worthy of all the goodness and truth,* &c. *He hears the desire of the humble ; This poor man cried unto the Lord and he heard him.* When we pray to God, we are said to fall down at his footstool; not only our bodies but our souls also must fall down at his footstool: And when do our soules fall down? Then when they are fully affected with the sense of their own unworthiness. If we would pray acceptably, we must pray humbly. If we would pray humbly, we must be sensible of our own Unworthiness.

Comming with the sense of unworthiness advanceth the name of Christ, and is a necessary concomitt an accepta Prayer.

4. *God hath rejected the Prayer of such who have rested upon their own worthiness:* The *Pharisee* was rejected upon this account. *Jam. 4. 6. God resisteth the proud* (.*i.*) he regards them not, he rewards them not; the humble he doth, but the proud he doth not: *He hath filled the hungry with good things, and the rich he hath sent empty away,* so *Mary,* Luk. 1. 53. A confidence of our Worthiness makes us uncapable, therefore a sense of our Unworthiness makes us not uncapable. An empty Stomack will receive, but a full Vessel will admit of nothing; you shall never find a rich God, if you come to him with rich Spirits: The Pharisee he goes up to pray; and what doth he discover in

God hath rejected the Prayers of such who have rested on h ir ov n wo thiness.

his

his prayers? *I am not as other men; I am no Extortioner, I am no Adulterer, I fast twice in the week.* He conceales his sins, and difplayes his perfections; he stands upon his worthinefs, but he loseth his acceptance; he justified himself, but God did not justifie him, accept him, acquit him.

None have found more mercy, then they who have been most sensible of unworthinefs.
5. *None ever found more mercy then such who have come unto God in the sense of their own Unworthinefs:* I will give you some instances for this out of Scripture. *Matth.* 8. The *Centurion* was so sensible of his unworthinefs, that he durst not himself presume to invite Christ to the help of his servant; and when he had intreated him, he did not think his house worthy of Christs presence, *I am not worthy that thou shouldst come under the roofe of mine house,* ver. 8. yet he prayes, *Speak the word only, and my servant shall be healed,* and he speeds; his Faith is applauded, and his prayer fully granted; *ver.* 13. *His servant was healed the same hour.* Mar. 5.25. *The poor woman,* who was so sensible of her unworthinefs, *ver.* 33. *she came fearing, and trembling, and fell down;* she durst not either immediately or mediately speak to Christ, only her Faith spake at her fingers ends; for she said, *If I may but touch his cloaths, I shall be whole,* ver. 28. How doth this speed? *ver.* 29. *Straightway the fountain of her blood was dryed up.* What should I speak of the woman of *Canaan,* who confessing her self to be as a *Dog,* and thereupon *craving for crumbs,* was presently fed and answered with a great mercy? Or, what should I speak of the *Publican,* a penitent all in sighs, all in tears, altogether unworthy, and he knew it, and therefore *Stands afar off,* dares not lift up his eyes to heaven, smites on his brest, and cryes out, *Lord, be merciful to me a sinner?* Here was a deep sense of Unworthinefs; here was nevertheless a fervent prayer, and upon it a most gracious answer, *He went home justified.*

Sense of unworthinefs is a strong principle and furtherance of prayer
6. Lastly, *Sense of our unworthinefs, it is a strong principle and furtherance of prayer:* We are most barren and idle in prayer, when we are least sensible of our sins; and we are more diligent to prayer, more spurred on, and are more zealously fervent and importunate when we are most sensible of our own vilenefs and unworthinefs. For indeed the true sense of our unworthinefs, is a special part of our spiritual poverty, and poverty of spirit breeds the strongest desires, even hungring and thirsting after righ-

The Sinners Conversion to God.

righteousness, and both of them have promises of a most full and exceeding great reward, as you may see in *Mat.* 5. 3, 6. And thus briefly for the Explication and Confirmation of the Doctrine. Now I proceed to the useful Application of it:

The Uses which I will make of this point shall be. 1. To try our selves whether we be sensible of our unworthiness in our Addresses unto God. 2. Then to encourage our hearts, notwithstanding our unworthiness to draw near to the Throne of Grace. 1. *For Examination.* Are we sensible of our unworthiness in our approaches unto God? that we deserve nothing at all? that we come not to buy, but to beg? not to deserve, but to receive? There be many reasons why I put you upon this search.

Use 1.

For Examination.

Reasons of our Trial.

1. *Because many pervert this Doctrine of personal unworthiness:* they utterly mistake it; they do profess that nothing that is in them can deserve any thing with God, and therefore trample upon all holiness of heart, and godliness of life, as if there were no use of Grace but to merit; or Gold were of no use but in a Crown. But these are a loathsome people, who would link great mercies and a wicked life together: To be sensible of our unworthiness is not to rest in an evil condition, nor is it to run on in an evil conversation, nor is it to slight holy duties for thy performances, nor is it to disregard habitual or actual Grace: this argues an unsensible and seared conscience: But this it is, to strive against sin, to strive after all holiness, to be careful and watchful to pious performances, yet with all, and after all, to cast those Crowns to the ground, not in their names, but in the name of Christ, and free mercy to expect answer and help. Though imperfect holiness in the habits or acts cannot justifie men, yet they may glorifie God; and though they put not dignity into the hand, yet they put a capacity into the hand; a fitness to receive, though not a worthiness to claim.

Many pervert the Doctrine of personal unworthiness.

2. Because *many tender Christians are not yet rightly sensible of their unworthiness*; they are very apt to insist and adhear unto themselvs. Two things do evidently shew, that, like *Jacob's Sons,* who went *down with money in their Sacks,* and would not go without Benjamin; so these Christians would bring something to buy out their requests with God; One is this, that *all the promises of free Grace and mercy do not satisfie them,* though God hath said he will

Many tender Christians are not yet rightly sensible of their unworthiness.

will love freely, and pardon sin for his own sake, yet they are not contented to accept, to receive; they are most hardly perswaded that the Sun will shine so freely, that God will accept such a vile sinner upon such easie terms, and without any more adoe pass by all transgressions.

2. Another is, that *they are frequent in digging after reasons and causes of good in themselves*; If they could bring Hearts more broken, Graces more strong, Affections more melting, Conversations less tainted; then they could be perswaded that God would hear and grant them the mercy or good which they do desire: I confess that we must strive after perfection in all Grace; enlarged desires, an humble complaint, a fervent endeavour in the use of all sacred means; all of these are commendable practices, yet herein we fail, and exceedingly to, if we pluck back the hand from receiving, because we are not full; that we will not suck the breasts, because we are empty; that we would find any causes of good in our selves, who at our best are unprofitable and unworthy.

It is very dangerous to stand upon personal worthiness.

3. *Because it is a very dangerous thing to stand upon our personal worthiness, when we approach unto the Lord*; For, *Now we come without Christ, we do sacrifice alone*, we take the Office of our high Priest out of his hands; Nay, *we frustrate the worthiness of Christ*, for we cannot joyn our worthiness and his together; if we plead in our own names, we make void his: As it is in the point of Justification, if we stand to our own righteousness, we make void the righteousness of Christ: So is it in the matter of supplication, if we stand to our own worthiness, and will be heard for our own sake, we exclude the merit of Christs intercession; we may as well be our own redeemers, as our own intercessours: *We meet with pure justice*; for if we stand upon personal dignity, then our qualities and actions must necessarily have equality to justice; God must dispence to us according to our own deserts; when we stand upon our own worthiness, then God deals with us in justice; if we renounce it, then room is made for the mercy-seat.

How we may know that we are truly sensible of our unworthiness.

Quest. But then you will demand, how may we know, that we are rightly sensible of our unworthiness, in our approaches unto God?

Sol. I conjecture thus:

1. If

1. If you are sensible of your own Unworthiness, when you pray unto the Lord, *Then Jesus Christ will be your greatest plea*; If Jesus Christ you will begin to move in his Name, and you will urge and pro- be our greatest secute it in his Name, and you will shut it up with an expecta- Plea. tion in his Name: Thou wilt not say, I am now in an excellent soft temper, and for its sake shall I prevail; and I have carried the day through now with more affections, and less distractions, therefore for this shall I prevail; As *Leah* said, *I have born my husband this son, therefore my husband will love me.* But in all thy sacrifices and services, thou wilt fly unto a Mediator, and still plead his Title, his Worth, his Merit; Lord, help me to pray for Christ's sake; Lord, give me mercy and grace for Christ's sake; Lord, hear, accept, answer, do me good, for thy Christ's sake.

2. *Then the Covenant of Grace will put heart into you, and draw* If the Covenant of Grace *you on alone to your performances*; as the wind alone will stir the Mill, or the tide alone will drive the Boat: I assure you, that if put heart into you be rightly sensible of your Unworthiness, you will look af- you. ter a Mercy-Seat, and after a Throne of Grace; you will be inquisitive, upon what terms Grants of Mercy and of Grace are issued out of the Court of Heaven. Nor will it seem a small thing in thine eyes, that the Lord will do good to an unworthy sinner for his own sake, yea, that he hath affirmed as much; and obliged himself thereto in a firm Covenant. This will breed in thee, *Thankfulness*; it will be, not onely a support to thy soul, but a joy to thy heart, thy case is yet hopefull; for, though thou be not worthy, yet God will do thee good readily and freely: And *Usefulness*; thou wilt be readily content to accept of mercy upon the terms of mercy: A beggar ready to starve, will be glad to take an Alms, he will put out his hand to receive it, and thank you too. As the *Servants of Benhadad* catcht the word, *Thy servant*, &c. so will you the word of promise; Respect, Lord, for thy Covenant sake. At this door of free Grace, there you shall have the sinner sensible of his unworthiness, standing night and day expecting when the Scepter shall be held out: Gods own arguments and motives of doing good (which are to be found onely in the Covenant of Grace) they are such as you will accept of with all your hearts, to plead with God.

T The

The Returning Prodigal, or

Use 2.
Encouragement to draw near to the Throne of Grace.

The second Use is for *Encouragement* : That though we be sensible of our Unworthiness, either to approach unto God, or to speak unto God, and much more to deserve any thing from God; yet not to be discouraged, *but humbly and confidently to draw near to the Throne of Grace*, expecting grace and mercy to help in time of need : And to excite you thereto, consider,

It is not our merit, but our duty we must look unto.

1. *It is not our merit, but our duty that we must look unto* : 'Tis not thousands of Rams, or ten thousand Rivers of Oyl; it is not the Pearls of the Sea, or the Treasures of the Earth, or the Excellencies of Angels; alas, God puts us not to that to deserve his mercies, to deserve his graces; if so, what one sinner should ever receive mercy or grace? no flesh righteous can be justified in his sight; and if he should mark what is amiss, who should stand before him. But the Lord puts us upon our duty, *Ask, and you shall receive ; knock, and it shall be opened unto you. Ho, every one that thirsts, come, drink of the water of life freely.*

It is not our worthiness that we must plead, but Gods promise.

2. It is *not our worthiness that we must plead, but Gods promise, when we pray unto him.* *Remember the word upon which thou hast caused thy servant to hope*, said *David*, Psal. 119. *Remember thy Covenant with Abraham, Isaac, and Jacob*, said *Moses*, Exod. 32. *Thou saidst that thou wouldst do me good*, said *Jacob*, Gen. 32. Mercies come to thee, not for thy worthiness sake, but for his promise sake ; not *ex dignitate petentis*, but *ex dignatione donantis*.

You can never be so worthy, but Justice may take exceptions.

3. *You can never be so worthy, but that Justice may take exceptions against you ; nor yet so unworthy, but mercy may fill your mouth with arguments. Though I were righteous, yet would I not answer thee, but I would make supplication to my Judge*, saith *Job*, chap. 9. 15. And, *Though I am poor and needy, yet the Lord thinks upon me*, said *David*, Psal. 40. 17. The proudest *Pharisee* may find enough to stop his mouth, and the humblest *Publican* may find enough to open it. No, not the most righteous can stand at the Bar of Justice, and yet the most dejected sinner may humbly plead at the Throne of Mercy; there are Arguments enough in mercy, for any sinner to plead mercy.

We are not to pray in pride, but in faith.

4. *You are not to pray in pride, but in faith* ; And then what is thy condition, that Faith cannot deliver up to God through Christ? Thou knowest that it is the office of Faith, not to present thy worthiness, but thy wants : It looks on arguments for thee;

not

not how good thou art, but how much good thou needest; not what thou canst deserve, but it looks on what God will bestow. Is it the many sins thou hast committed, which present an utter unworthiness to thy conscience? why Faith will teach thee to confess the debt, and yet to crave for pardon. Is it the hardness or vileness of thy heart which makes thee afraid? Oh! the Lord is of purer eyes than to look on such a dead dog, so vile a wretch as I: Why! Faith will teach thee, that though the Lord be lofty, and high are his habitations; yet of all people he looks after the humble and contrite, and hath respect unto them, and looks on such through the bloud of the Covenant; and that he will give Grace as readily as he will give Mercy; and as freely bestow on thee a new heart, as a gracious pardon.

5. *God onely must have the glory to be the Giver of Good:* and therefore be not thou discouraged, if thou be admitted onely to be the receiver of good. To be King, no way befits the Subject; the King honours the Subject highly, if he make him the Kings Receiver. O Christian, let it suffice thee, let God alone find gifts to bestow, do thou study more for hands to receive them: if ever thou wouldst have mercy, get such an humble and believing heart, as to be willing to receive any mercy, upon any of Gods terms.

Luke 15. 20.
And he arose and came to his Father: But when he was yet a great way off, his Father saw him, and had compassion, and ran and fell on his neck, and kissed him.

These words contain in them two parts.
1. *The very Life of true Repentance:* Which consists not in a bare Resolution, but in an active and real Execution: *I will arise,* said the Prodigal, and here he did arise; *I will go to my Father,* and here did come unto his Father; [*He arose and came unto his Father.*]
2. *The gracious Acceptance of a real Penitent.* The Graciousness of it appears, 1. In *the present observation of him;* (*when he was yet a great way off, his Father saw him:*) the very intentions, much more the present actings of repentance, are quickly eyed and observed by a mercifull God. 2. In *a present affection to him;* (*and had compassion:*) the bowels of mercy will stir, when

The Returning Prodigal, or

when the heart of a sinner is penitentially touched. 3. In *a present Application*: His Father saw him, and his Father pitied him ; but this is not all, [*His Father also ran, and fell on his neck, and kissed him.*] Mercy runs, and Mercy embraceth, and Mercy cheareth the penitent sinner. The first part affordeth us this Proposition, *viz.*

Doct. 5. Penitent Resolutions should be accompanied with present Executions.

That penitent intentions and resolutions should be accompanied with present executions and performances. The Text properly yields this ; for the words of it are but the lively and written copy of the Prodigals private and conceived purpose, to leave his sinfull courses, and to come back to the obedience and service of his Father. It is observed of *Hezekiah,* 2 Chron. 29. 3. *That he opened the doors of the house of the Lord in the first year, and in the first moneth of his reign, and repaired them.* The publick Reformation was the principal work, and it was the prime work too. So must it be with a true Penitent ; as soon as God sets up a Throne of Grace in him, presently to act that Grace, in purging out of sin, and walking in the paths of righteousness. We read this in *Josiah,* as soon as ever he heard the threatnings of God out of the Law, *his heart melted, and humbled it self,* 2 Chron. 34. 19, 27. and *instantly he gathered all the Elders of Judah and Jerusalem,* v. 29. and *made a Covenant,* v. 31. and *they took away all the abominations out of all the Countreys, and turned back to serve the Lord their God,* v. 33. This you see in Practise ; you may see the same likewise in *Precept,* Joel 2. 12. *Therefore, now turn unto me with all your heart, and with fasting, and with weeping, and with mourning.* The Duty is charged upon them for fulness in all the parts of Repentance ; and for quickness, Now, turn, *&c.* For the better opening of this Assertion, premise with me a few particulars.

This is meant of the very practise of Repentance.

1. That the execution of a penitential resolution, is nothing else but *an acting course, or the very practise of Repentance.* When not onely the Judgment approves of the parts and rules of Repentance, and the Will embraceth them with consent and desire, but the Endeavour also doth, as it were, copy them forth in the Conversation. *I exercise my self to have a good conscience,* said the Apostle : So when the sinner doth exercise Repentance, when he doth hate sin indeed, and flies from it, and forsakes it indeed ; and when he doth indeed walk in the ways of new obedience, becomes

comes a very servant of righteousness, and works the work of God, this is the execution, or the performance of a penitential purpose and resolution. As walking is to a journey, or as writing is to a copy, or as fighting is to a war, that is penitential execution to penitential resolution. It is but the Theory (as it were) drawn down and put forth; It is as the tree shooting out into blossoms and fruits: It is repentance in life, which is the life of repentance.

2. That presentness of Execution is *an undelayed acting*. Our actions fall within three spaces of time; either of the which is past (as what we have done;) or of that which is future (as that which shall be done;) or of that which is present (as that which is doing.) Look as true Marriage, it is not a future, but a present acceptation: So true Repentance is not a delayed, but a present reformation. Or as in Writing, the motion of the Pen and the forming of the Letter are simultaneous: Or as in a Clock, the wheel doth move and the finger doth move: So in the business of Repentance; the purpose of amendment, should at the same time drop out into the change of heart and ways. To have repentance onely in our purposes, is onely to have water in a cloud, or physick in a glass, it is not yet to do it. Resolutions may be for the future, but Executions are for the present act; an hearing while it is to day, and not hardning of the heart. As St. *Paul*, being called, went immediately up to *Jerusalem*; so present execution of repentance is, when we do not defer the penitential work; a not allowing of our selves in giving way to our sins, no, not an hour, as the Apostle spake in another case.

And of an unadelayed acting.

3. That there is a two-fold present execution of penitential purposes: One is *immediate*; or when the purpose and the acting (without distance of time) succeed one the other, there being no predominant impediment to the instantaneous execution of that penitential purpose. Another is *seasonable*; where, though twixt the purpose and the acting there may be some distance of time, yet the apprehension of the next occasion may truly make the execution or practise to be present. As in the case of penitential restitution, it may so fall out, either through the inability of the estate, or the subjection of the person, that he cannot immediately restore; yet because the penitent person in such a case layes hold on the next opportunity and occasion, his resolution may be said to be acted presently, (*i.*) upon the next present time,

And of a present execution, either for immediateness, or seasonableness.

time when God enables h'm to act his purpose of restoring: So that penitential Resolution produceth present Execution; either for immediatenefs, as in most cases; or for seasonablenefs, as in some cases.

And in execution, in endeavour, or in victory.   4. That there is again a double penitential Execution of penitential Resolution: One consists in *endeavour* and *application*; when the person, without delays, addresseth or applieth himself to the ways by which sins may be subdued and forsaken: Another consists in *victory* and *assecution*, wherein the Penitent doth in some more eminent degree lead captivity captive. That penitential Execution whereof I speak, properly and naturally consists in the former, though it must aim and strive after the latter also; (*i.*) when a person doth indeed resolve to leave his sins, and to serve the Lord in newnefs of life; this Resolution doth actively excite him to be much in Prayer unto the Lord, and diligently to hearken to, and observe his Word, and to decline the occasions which may give strength to his corruptions: It causeth him to resist evil motions, and to bewail them; it sets him upon all sorts of Duties and Ordinances, so that the person is now really working against sin, and throughly working for God; he is in the ways of God, and according to the measure of grace received, working the works of God.

But why should penitential Intentions be accompanied with present Executions or performances?

Reasons for it. God commands us to repent presently.   *Sol.* Reasons for it are many.   1. *That God who commands us to repent, commands us presently to repent.* The Time is under Precept, as well as the Work. Some Precepts bind us *semper*, but not *ad semper*; other Precepts bind us *semper* & *ad semper* too: When the Lord commands any man to repent, this is a Duty which concerns the whole course of his life; it takes hold of him as soon as ever he lives, and is become a sinner; and concerns him, not onely in his latter days, but all his days.

It is dangerous to delay.   2. *It is very dangerous to defer our penitential Executions* or actings: Whether we consider, 1. *The Resolutions themselves*; they are but accidental, and not natural things; not such qualities (or rather motions) which arise from an in-bred principle, but are forensical to our natures, and being not presently cherished by acting, like little sparks of fire, may easily vanish, languish, and extinguish. We read of the *Israelites*, that they were an unstedfast

stedfast people in Covenant, and like *a deceitfull Bow*. Naked Refolutions will never ripen and abide; if you will not go beyond your Refolutions, you will quickly fall from your Refolutions. 2. *Our own hearts*, ah! how deceitfull are they! how full of rebellion! how averfe to all good! Like the cold hearth to a little fire; how cunning to keep up Sin in the Throne! how willing to break afunder all the bands of Obedience! with much adoe refolving, with little adoe diffolving thofe refolves again. *Volebam* (faith St. *Auftin*) & *nolebam*; I would, and yet I would not; one while I would, and by and by I would not. It is the Genius of our finfull hearts, to apprehend the prefent time for fin, and to crave the future time for repentance: Our worft work we would do inftantly, our beft work we would do negligently: Good motions are like a Bird falling into our hands, which if we prefently catch not, fhe inftantly flees away. Gracious purpofes in our hearts, are like warmth in the water; the impreffion requires fome degrees, and fome blowing; but the receffion is eafie; the natural coldnefs in the water will inftantly rife up and expel that heat: if you be not watchfull, &c. 3. *Extinguifhing occafions*. Repentance, in all the parts of it, hath many enemies and hinderances, fome within us, fome without us: the Refolutions are weak, but the Occafions are ftrong. Let the fhip alone, and if the Pilot hath onely a refolution to fail with, the next tide, or the next wind may carry the fhip away. How ordinary is the experience, That the ftrength of occafions have beaten back, and put to flight many and many a refolution? like a crofs wind, which hath carried back the fhip unto the very harbour whence it came forth. Meer refolutions are but unarmed Souldiers, or as unwalled Cities. You fhall find much of this truth, That meer refolutions are too weak for proper and fudden occafions. 4. *Or the affiftance of Grace* To refolve, and not to act, is one way whereby we quench the Spirit. The Spirit, you know, may be quenched m my ways: *Pofitively*; as when we will walk in paths exprefly contrary to his motions; this is to throw water upon the fire: *Negatively*, when we do not follow nor cherifh his motions; as you quench the fire, if you do not ftir it, or blow it, or add more unto it. So when the Spirit of God fhall deal thus far with us, as to convince us that our courfe is evil, and yet further, to excite a purpofe in our hearts to defift; but then we let the work lie

lie ſtill, we do not ſet againſt that evil way, this may cauſe the Spirit of God to withdraw, to deſert the ſinner who doth deſert his counſel; who will be a Counſellour to him, who will walk in no counſel but his own.

Preſent execution will be More eaſie.

3. *Penitential Executions, if preſent, will be more eaſie, and more comfortable.* 1. *They will be more eaſie.* St. *Auſtin* had almoſt waſted his ſpirits with reſolutions and conflicts; *Quamdiu, cras, cras, &c.* and he thought it many times impoſſible for him ever to be rid of ſuch an inmate as ſin: But when his reſolution brake out into practiſe, then *Facile & ſuave*, the work grew eaſie and ſweet. When we come to the acting part, then the Lord will exert and put forth his power in our weakneſs: the acting and doing Chriſtian partakes of moſt aſſiſtance. Do we not find it thus in Prayer, and in many other Duties, which perhaps we look upon with much fear and ſuſpition? But when we are acting of them, how ſingularly doth the Lord enlarge our thoughts and affections? Why! this holds in the very Duty of Repentance; ſet againſt thy ſins in good earneſt, ſet upon a holy courſe in good earneſt, thou ſhalt experimentally find, that it was thy own deceitfull heart which repreſented the work with more difficulty; but now having taken upon thee the yoke of Chriſt, thou ſhalt find it eaſie, and that God can as well work in thee to do, as to will.

More Comfortable.

2. They will *be more comfortable.* Meer purpoſes cannot ſpring up ſuch comforts as actings; nay, even weak actings yield a thouſand times more comfort than ſtrong reſolutions: All the ſap in the root doth not make the flower to ſmell ſweet, unleſs that ſap comes to a bloſſome. We cannot ſay our reſolutions are ſolid, if unactive. If they do not alter the courſe, for ought as we know yet, they may be but falſe flaſhes, occaſional impreſſions, not ſpringing from renewing Grace, (which will break out into practiſe,) but from ſervile cauſes, which may be ſufficient to ſtop a ſinner, and with *Saul*, to profeſs he will perſecute *David* no more: But when Execution attends Reſolution, now the heart may be confident, that there is a renewing Principle implanted, which carries the ſoul from one degree to another; from convictions to reſolutions, from reſolutions to actions, from actions to courſes with ſtedfaſtneſs and fruitfulneſs.

4. *The*

The Sinners Conversion to God. 145

4. *The Soul gets no ground by meer Resolutions*: It doth neither alter the inward frame, nor mend the outward life; that which is of no influence, is of no furtherance: if the resolution be on y a resolution, it is but a dead thing. *(The soul gets no ground by meer resolutions.)*

Now I come to the Application of all this to our selves: You have seen that penitent resolutions should fall into present executions; good purposes should be turned into quick practices. The great enquiry will hence be, *What do we?* it is observed of some Nations, that they are too soon in the Field, and of others, too long on the bench; too quick in action, and too long in consultation. I confess, that Repentance should begin in deliberation, and it should descend to resolution; but there is more required to building then a preparation of wood and stone. Thou hast resolved to leave such and such a sin (Oh! in thy last sickness, in thy last cross, in thy last distress of conscience; at the last Sermon, didst thou not resolve upon it, I will never serve such a lust more, I will walk more conscienciously before the Lord ?) But what is done ? shew me thy Repentance in the acting part, as well as in the contriving part; thou art still held fast with the Cords of the same lusts, and art wallowing still in the same mire, and art lingering yet, and hastes not to come out of thy sinful wayes. *Zacheus made haste*, and came down at once; do we do so ? David *thought on his wayes, and turned his feet unto Gods Testimonies; he made haste and delayed not to keep his Commandments*; But may not the Lord say of us, as he did of the *Israelites*, How long will it be ere they believe me ? so, how long will it be ere we turn indeed from our sins to God ? 'Tis true, some resolutions there are working in us, oftentimes, but like the *goodness of* Ephraim *and* Judah: *Oh*, Ephraim *what shall I do unto thee? Oh*, Judah *what shall I do unto thee ? for your goodness is as a Morning Cloud, and as the early Dew it goeth away:* So is it with many of us, we purpose and profess, but we fall back to our sins still; what we were, that we are; *The time is not yet come* (said they) *to build the house of God, Hag.* 1. Our purposes are past, but our executions are still, still to come: Consider of a few things. 1. *Why do you resolve at all, when yet you execute and act nothing at all. Resolutio est opus imperfectum & Ordinabile*; doth not resolution tend to action ? will God be mocked with meer purposes ? or think you to charm and satisfie your consciences alwayes upon frequent sinnings, to

Use

Inquire whether it be so with us.

Luke. 19. 5.
Psal. 119. 59.

Hos. 6. 4.

Why do you resolve at all without execution.

to multiply refolutions only? Alas! if Repentance be not now done, it is not yet begun; fo much as thou doft, thou repent'ft; if fin be yet to be left, as yet it is not left; and then where art thou as yet,

Is not Repentance a great work, why not then thy prefent work?

but in an impetitent condition? 2. *Is not Repentance a great work? Why, then is it not thy prefent work?* Thy Soul is embarked in that Veffel; eternity depends upon a moment: That which muft be done, why is it not quickly done? and if it be not prefently done, we may be eternally undone; why do we defer the doing of that? the beft work fhould have the beft time and place. 3. *Is not thy life a fhorteft breath?* a thinneft vapour? a flying Poft? a gleaning fhadow? every moment we are dying; eat and dye, fleep and dye: Should not our laft work be our prefent work, when our laft work may be our next work? 4. *It cannot be lefs then prefumption, to put off the practical part of Repentance:* Either you muft prefume upon future life (which yet is a Cord that thou canft not lengthen;) or you muft prefume on future ftrength (which is a marrow ftill wafted by a lingring difeafe;) or you muft prefume on Divine Grace, which may be an hand juftly withdrawn, becaufe it was a mercy unjuftly referred and delayed. 5. *You will but harden your hearts the more*, and skill the way of hypocrifie the more; for thus to unwift your Cords, wherewith you have fo often bound your felves, makes you to venture, and venture yet a little further; yet once more, till a little and a little inflames your Souls to much evil, and the cuftome of finning wears out both the fenfe of fin, and refolutions againft it. 6. Laftly, *You do but aggravate your fins the more, by naked and empty refolutions againft them;* you do not hinder the courfe of it, and you do intenfively raife the guilt of it; for finning againft refolution is a finning againft exprefs light, and againft a condemning light: A perfon who hath refolved to leave fuch a courfe, it is fuppofed that he not only knows it to be evil, but likewife condemns it as evil: Now it is a great aggravation of fin to continue in it, with light revealing, and accufing, and cutting.

Thy life is very fhort.

It is prefumption to put off the practical part of Repentance.

Delay hardens the heart the more.

And aggravates our fins by empty refolutions againft them.

Obj. But fome may fay, We hope, that though our Executions are not fo full, yet they are real; the quality is there, though the equality be not; fomething we do, though not fo much. *Sol.* To this I anfwer. 1. That it is moft evident, that *many perfons do not by practife and execution anfwer their refolutions at all;*

all; their refolutions arife from fuch grounds as will not hold out to an execution and practice: If one fhould demand, what are become of the many fick-bed refolutions? of thofe that you made, when the hand of God was upon you? you vowed much unto God (as he did in a ftorm, &c.) but as the King faid of *Mordecai*, *What hath been done to* Mordecai *for this*? fo what have you done to make good your refolutions? I believe your hearts are fpeechlefs, your confciences do condemn you, that health hath been the time of more finning, though ficknefs was the time of more refolving. The fame may be faid for others, whofe confciences have been more actively and fiercely ftirring; Oh! if the Lord would abate that wrath, and cool that inflamed fpirit, &c. yet what are the fruits of many fuch refolutions. As the Divel faid of *Job*, *But now ftretch forth thy hand, and he will curfe thee to thy face*; fo here on the contrary, as foon as the Lord takes off his hand, thefe are as ready to continue and proceed on in their fins, as the *Ifraelites* were, when they were delivered out of the Land of Egypt, from the fiery furnace: Yea, and of others; is it not manifeft that they are far enough from prefent executions, when they voluntarily defer the acting part of Repentance to old age? Hereafter is time enough, &c.

2. Others *perhaps do all and execute prefently, yet they are exceedingly out*: For 1. Though it be *prefently*, yet it is *partially*; they act refolutions, as *Saul* did his Sword, upon the meaneft and pooreft, not upon the greateft; they do not anfwer their refolutions to the full. *Deal kindly with the young man for my fake* (faid *David*) So when many perfons come to execute their Refolutions againft fin, they fail, they falter, they do not execute *Agag*; fome pleafant corruption (which will mar all) finds favour. 2. Though it be *prefently*, yet it is *but prefently*; the prefent execution of the purpofe is but a prefent, a tranfient execution, an hanging down the head for a day or for a week; a bufie and earneft reformation for a while, but this Affize (like ours here) is but for a few dayes, it breathes away; the heart turns again to fin, and the next convenient occafion is too prevalent, it carries away the Soul.

2. But to draw nearer to our felves; however we have been defective to anfwer our manifold refolutions by prefent executions and practices; yet now let us for the time to come, as he faid of words,

Ufe 2.
Let us fet upon a prefent execution.

148 *The Returning Prodigal,* or

words, fo I of purpofes, *vertere propofita in Opera*; Not be like Clouds, feeming to be full of Water, but to pour down: Let us act the parts of Penitents, as the Prophet faid to the hovering *Ifraelites, if God be God, ferve him*; fo here, if Repentance be a neceffary duty to be performed, let us *then act it, act it prefently.* For this, I will only propound two things. 1. The *Motives.* 2. The *Means* for a prefent Execution. 1. The *Motives.*

Motives.
A prefent execution is the trueft part of Repentance.

1. *A prefent Execution is the trueft part of Repentance:* At the beft, you are but in a preparation, in a meer difpofition towards Repentance, until you act it; it is not fo much what you would be, as what you are; what you intend, as what you practife, that will give the moft real teftimony of your Repentance. 2. *A*

And the fafeft part of Repentance.

prefent execution, it is the fafeft part of repentance: Of the two, he is in the more fure condition, who refolves to leave a wicked life, and doth indeed forfake it; and refolves to lead a holy life, and doth indeed enterprize it; than he who refolves on both, but practifeth neither. The doer of good is a thoufand times more fure then the refolver: fomething in fome cafes may be faid to ftay a perfon from his refolutions; yet if nothing comes of the refolutions, I affure you the fcales will hang trembling: but action doth more fully determine the eftate, and the Scripture is more clear for the fpiritual eftate, as it lies in practife, then as it lies in purpofe. 3. *A prefent execution, it is the comfortableft part;*

And the comfortableft part of Repentance.

While repentance lies only in refolution, it is but as a Tree in the Winter, perhaps well rooted, but it lives dry; but when repentance breaks out into action, it is as a Tree in the Spring, well rooted, well flowered, and well fmelling too. There is more comfort to do, then to intend to do; indeed to ceafe a finful courfe, and indeed to walk an holy life, this opens all the comforts of the promifes, draws down the favour of God, affures us more of intereft in Chrift, excufeth more in the confcience, reviveth

And the wifeft part.

more in all occurrences. 4. *A prefent execution, it is the wifeft part;* we cannot fay what we fhall do to morrow, when we cannot affure our felves, what, and where we fhall be to morrow: He is wifeft for Divine Glory, and for his own happinefs, who acts an immediate duty of falvation, upon prefent terms. There are four things which declare wifdome; One to fow in feafon; Another, to fail in feafon; A third, to accept and receive the Word of Grace in feafon; A fourth to act repentance in feafon, even now while it is called to day.

2. *The*

The Sinners Conversion to God.

2. *The means*: If we would execute our penitential resolu- Meanes.
tions, then we muft 1. Take heed of the impediments of this
prefent Execution. 2. Make ufe of the helps and furtherances
of it.

1. The impediments of a prefent execution are many.

1. *Imbecility of refolution*: *Debile fundamentum fallit opus*; if the foundation be weak, how can the building be ftrong? the houfe which was built on a Rock, did ftand; but that which was erected on the Sands, fell down: Where refolutions are either weakly raifed on ftrong grounds, or fuddenly raifed on weak and mutable occafions, there is either no execution, or uncertain; for no effect doth exceed the virtue of his caufe: *Thou haft almoft perfwaded me to be a Chriftian*; this left King *Agrippa* ftill in Heathenifme. You will never go through with the work, if you attain not to a thorow refolution; when you have an heart that goes and comes, you will have only fits of repentance, which will come and go: Of two things be fure, if ever you would penitentially act to purpofe; One that you fee ftrong and prevalent reafons to change your courfe of life, fuch as may not be overtopped by any arguments that fin may fuggeft hereafter; they are the fpirits in the brain, which confer to motion in the Hands and Legs: Another, that you refolve not on deceitful and fallible grounds. If your refolutions be upon Motives, either mutable, or conditional; you may be troubled with much temptation, but you will never advance in much penitential actions.

Take heed of the Impediments. Imbecillity of Refolution.

2. *Servile fear*: When we fo exalt the opinions of men, and their Tongues, and their Power; what will they think of me? how will they nick-name, and difgrace me? what may befall me? who can tell what mifchief they may do unto me? Thefe are the Frofts which nip the buds, and the Winds which bind the Ship, and the Remora's which hold the Children ftill in the birth. We love the opinions of men, to be well thought on; and the Tongues of men to be well fpoken of; and the refpects of men to be countenanced, and encouraged: A crofs way makes us ftart; *Zedekiah* would not obey the Lord, leaft the Princes fhould laugh at him; and many of the Jews durft not confefs Chrift, for fear of the Scribes and Pharifees. For a man who enjoyes friends, and eafe, and eftate, and abundance in all forts, to thruft out into a Sea, to enter

Servile fear.

enter into a holy and strict course of Life, wherein he shall be sure to be scorned as the off-scouring of the world, be trampled upon as the mire in the streets, be torne in his name by the teeth of wild beasts, suffer ship-wrack in his liberty, in his plenty, in his body; Why? these apprehensions are enough to quell and to keep in all forwardness, all action; as *Spira* confesseth, That they wrought on him when he denyed the profession of the Truth of Christ. Therefore if you would descend into the present execution of penitential purposes, you must not be slavishly affected unto man; you must not fear the power of man, nor be ashamed of the Cross of Christ; you must put your shoulder under the Cross, and the contempts of men under your feet: *I am ready* (saith Paul, Acts 21.13) *not to be bound only, but also to dye at Jerusalem for the Name of the Lord Jesus. If ye be reproached for the Name of Christ, happy are ye, for the Spirit of glory and of God resteth upon you,* saith S. *Peter*, 1 Pet. 4.14. *I will not fear what man can do unto me,* said *David. Who art thou, that thou shouldst be afraid of a man that shall die, and of the son of man who shall be made as grass? and forgettest the Lord thy Maker, and hast feared continually because of the fury of the oppressor, as if he were ready to destroy? and where is the fury of the oppressor?* Isa. 51. 12, 13.

Despair of performance.

3. *Despair of performance*: Why, say we, as good never a whit as never the better. It is not possible that ever we should get hands to conquer all these sins, or feet to walk in all these wayes which are so holy, so many, so strict, so difficult. We cannot find words to pray, nay, God knows, sometimes not hearts; the motions of sin are thick and strong, and able every moment to lead us captive; we have made some assay, but alas, the work proves so harsh, so uncomfortable, so unprosperous; we are without all strength, we shall never break these bonds of sin, nor tread through all these pathes of holy duties. Thus as death closeth up our eyes, so doth despair shut up all our actions; where there is no hope to finish, there will be no heart to begin: But let us reject such despairing delusions; what hath been done may be done; what God commands to do, he can enable to do; and what he promiseth that we shall do, that he will make and cause us do: But God hath commanded us to leave all our sinful courses, and to lead a life of holiness; God hath promised grace suffici-

sufficient to forsake an evill way and to walk in a good way, *I will put my Spirit within you, and cause you to walk in my statutes, and you shall keep my judgments and d<i>o</i> them,* Ezek.36.27. If God gives strength to work, why should we with-hold hearts to work? *Da Domine quod jubes, & jube quod vis*, said S. Austin: Lord, give what thou commandest, and then command what thou wilt. Seriously consider any one penitential work, for which God hath not promised grace and strength to perform. Many have travelled in this penitential Work, and have found it very feisable and passable: How many are this day in heaven? and how many are walking towards heaven? all of them prove, that it is not impossible to execute penitenial resolutions.

4. *Hypocrisie and guile of heart:* Where the heart is false, Hypocrisie. there the performance is faint; if the work be not done in the heart, it will never be done in the life; the work is best done in the life, which is first done in the heart. They in *Jeremiah* had rotten hearts, they did not cordially intend to leave their own wayes, and therefore when they were put to it indeed,they would not yield to walk in the wayes which God prescribed. Where an holy way is not throughly approved, and where an evill way is not throughly hated, there may be many flashes, but there will never be solid performances or courses: *Yet a little sleep, yet a little slumber, yet a little folding of the hands,* said the Sluggard, who loved sleep and idleness, *Prov.* 6. 10. So where our affections are hankring about a sin, there is ever, at the least, a slowness to leave that sin: *Modo, modo,* said S. Austin, when motions came into him to forsake his uncleanLusts, they answered, Shortly, shortly; Hereafter, hereafter; and this *modo, modo,* was *sine modo*; this putting off from day to day, would have continued so all the dayes of his life. Therefore if you vvould execute your penitential resolutions; take heed of corrupt affections; if they again prevail upon you, they vvill assuredly intangle and hinder you, they mar the judgment, and close vvith temptations, and hinder actions. Oh how suddenly vvill they quench your spirits, alter your judgments, put aside your duties, extenuate your purposes, bring you into further bondage, confirm your unwillingness, excite your fears, raise up discouragements, and all to frustrate the present executions of

of your former resolutions. Corrupt affections are the very gates of sin, the Bane of holiness, the Quenchers of resolutions, and the Impediments of all good performances.

Worldly cares. 5. *Worldly cares*: Our Saviour saith, *That the seed which fell among thornes was choaked*, Luke 8.7. And what was it which did choak it? see verf. 14. *The cares, and riches, and pleasures of this Life*, There are two things which worldly cares do choak viz. Heavenly directions of the word, and Heavenly resolutions of the heart; so that neither the one nor the other do come unto perfection, Holy performance or action, it is the end or perfection of all knowledg and resolution, and worldly cares stifle both. You have many a man who comes to the word, and hears the terrours of God and his wrath revealed against his unrighteousness, insomuch that his soul (with *Felix*) trembles under the strokes of divine justice; Or he hears how happy and blessed the condition and life of holiness is; what heavens of mercies, what rivers of comforts, what excusations and peace of Conscience, what blessings in life, what supports in death, what rewards after death it shall procure to persons; upon the one and the other he is stirred up to the sense of his sins, to the admiration of Holiness; to a condemnation of his evil course, to a resolution for a better. But then it is with him as with some ship, sometimes as soon as it is putting out of the Harbor, it strikes upon a rock, or falls into the sands, and loseth all the precious lading: Or as with Corn sown and let fall in an open and solid place, where the Birds come down and instantly pick it up; so is it here with this man, the world meets him again at the Church door, or at his own door, and all these impressions and resolutions are spilt and gone; Worldly engagements take present possession of his thoughts, and all the service of his affections, so that he hath no time to consider what God did speak or work in him; no time secretly to beg of God to write those truths in his heart, to keep all this in the purpose of his heart, to give him the Spirit of Grace and strength to walk in the wayes of God revealed now unto him. When you turn the course of the water another way, the Mill cannot stir; so when men turn the course of their thoughts and affections to secular and vain imployments, all resolutions stand still, they have nothing now to elicit or draw them on and out into any holy or careful diligence of obedience

The Sinners Converſion to God.

ence and performance: *The Oxen and the Farm*, &c. took them quite off, and they *made excuſes* (.i.) for the preſent they had other engagements: therefore take heed of worldly cares. It is impoſſible that you ſhould be much in the actings of any Grace, if you be very much in the ſervice of worldly cares.

6. Laſtly, *Preſumptuous Confidence* is alſo an Impediment to the preſent executions of good reſolutions; whether it be of *future time*, hereafter ſhall ſerve the turn; it is not wiſdom to be ſo forward; ſoft and fair will go far; we have day enough yet before us; a year, two or ten hence; after ſuch a buſineſs is effected, or (which is worſe) after the pleaſures of ſuch a ſin is a little more taſted. Or of *Future ability*: This is a work which we will do at pleaſure and at leiſure: when we ſee the ſcouts, the forerunners of the army, then we will buckle on our armor: when we eſpy the harbingers of death approaching, old age, ſickneſs, weakneſs, diſeaſes, then we will think of heaven, and forſake hell: what need we be troubling our ſelves to be doing of that a long time, which we can diſpatch at any time?. if we have but time to ſay, Lord have mercy upon me, what would ye more? Or of *Future Mercy*: Wherefore hath God Mercy but for ſinners? and he hath ſaid, That if at any time a ſinner convert he will have mercy: We have found him kind unto us all our dayes, and doubt not of his fatherly compaſſion at the laſt. Thus do men poſt off all penitential executions, and for ever endanger their ſouls. Alas! for future time, whoſe is it? *Seneca* the Heathen could ſee more truth then this: *Solum tempus preſens noſtrum*: No time is ours but the preſent. Thou carrieſt thy life in thy hands, thy breath in thy noſtrils, and ſeeſt more Graves made for the young then for the aged. And as for thy future ability, why doſt thou ſo groſly befool thy ſelf? knoweſt thou not that preſent Neglects cauſe ſtronger Indiſpoſitions? *Qui non eſt hodie, cras minus aptus erit*, the School-boy will teach thee. Every man by more ſinning grows more ſinful, and therefore moſt unapt and averſe to good. And then *Future Mercy*, it is of all things the moſt uncertain to pardon ſin, where preſent mercy leaves us not to repentance from ſin: it is all one as if thou ſhouldſt thus argue, God will hereafter pardon me, and therefore for the preſent I will ſin againſt him, diſobey, diſhonour, vex, and grieve, and abuſe him. Theſe are the principal impediments to a preſent

Preſumptuous confidence.

X exe-

expectation of penitential refolutions, and are to be declined
Helps. by us. I now proceed to the *helps* and *furtherances to a prefent execution of penitential refolutions*, which are thefe, amongft many.

Solid convi- 1. *Solid Conviction of a finful eftate*: This will put us upon
ction of a fin- a prefent Execution. When the Soul is brought to an experi-
ful ftate. mental fenfe of the vilenefs and bitternefs of fin, it will not then lye hovering; Were I beft to give up this courfe, or fhall I go on in it ftill? No, but when the Soul is indeed wounded, the wayes fhall without delay be reformed; take a perfon in fome judicial, and clofe conviction of fin, upon a fick and dying bed, how forward is a perfon then to change and better his courfes; much more do folid and evangelical convictions fweetly difpofe, and incline the heart to the forfaking of an evil, and walking in a good way. They in *Acts* 2. 37. were pricked in their hearts, and what did this work in them? they cry out prefently, *Men and brethren what fhall we do*? So *Saul* was ftruck to the ground, and was aftonifhed, and trembled, and then prefently cries out, *Lord, what wilt thou have me to do? Act. 9. 4, 6*. Outward afflictions you fee many times do put on men to alter and reform their wayes; of much greater force are inward afflictions of fpirit. Go on yet in fin! God forbid! fhall I continue in fin any longer, who, if I make not hafte, may lofe all mercy, and drop into Hell it felf? what I feel is much, what I deferve, I cannot bear.

Holy wifdome. 2. *Holy Wifdome*: To know times and feafons, is an high part of Wifdome; *Walk not as fools, but as wife, redeeming the time*, (faith the Apoftle) *Eph.* 5. 15, 16. There are four things which folid Wifdome teacheth a man; One is, to look to the beft part; Another, to make choice of the beft good; A third; to walk in the beft wayes; A fourth is to do all this in the firft place, and fureft time: Have I any thing more near to me, then my foul? more concerning my foul then God? more concerning God, then walking before him? Where am I, if I lofe my Soul? what am I, if I enjoy not God? whether run I, if I continue in fin? if my foul be neareft, and God choiceft, and his wayes fafeft, why do I demur? what, fhould I take time, or put off the doing of that which is ever beft done, when it is done? If I will live yet in fin, for ought I know, I may then dye in fin; and if I

dye

dye in sin, I must for ever perish for sin; Why should I not? Do I not admit the present loss of that, which else may be the eternal loss of my Soul? But if I set into an holy life, this is the very path of God, the image of Glory, the Ark of safety, and the pledg of an happy eternity. Why should I be so foolish, to be miserably bad, who in a moment may be assuredly blessed? any wisdome will teach me to leave a wicked life, for an holy and good; which hath made me to know, that mercy is better then misery; and that Heaven is better then Hell.

3. *Christian Courage*: If we will not act the wayes of Heaven, till we see all difficulties removed, and all dangers secured, we shall never enter into those wayes: but when the love of Christ hath inflamed our hearts with a right zeal of his Glory, assuredly, we will be doing: *Modo magnificetur Christus*, I must bring some Glory to my God, &c. *Luther* feared not to go to the Diet at *Worms*, had there been as many divels, as tiles on the houses: What do you tell S. *Paul* of bonds, or speak to the couragious Christian of discouragements; *I have sworn, and will perform it* (saith David) *that I will keep thy righteous statutes.* S. *Jerem* would not only renounce, but throw off, and trample upon father and mother for Christ: What do you speak of poverty, of disgraces, of losses, of want, of self-denials in ease, in pleasures? &c. He who will be good, can lose nothing but that which will loose him; and get that which he should never have gotten, had he not been good indeed.

Christian courage.

4. *A precious estimation and affection after Gods honour*: Ah! did we in any holy measure comprehend the height, and brēdth, and depth of his favour in Christ; would we not strive to enter in at the strait Gate? should not the Kingdome of Heaven suffer violence? What to stand upon a sinful pleasure, or profit, or way, and to lose a good, gracious, bountiful God: What sinful lust, pleasure, way would we stand upon? What holy course or way would we set upon? would we be slow to see the face of God, and live? Would we not speedily set our selves in the wayes of his countenance? *Zacheus* being desirous to *see Christ*, upon his call, *made haste and came down.* Luke 19.6.

A precious estimation of Gods honour.

5. *A tender fear of God*: This also causeth a present execution of our purposes. You read what it wrought in *Josiah*, in *Noah*, in others. When the heart apprehends its way to be evil, and the displeasure of God to hang over it, and his threatnings all in armour, &c. Oh, I dare not go on to offend any longer!

A tender fear of God.

6. *A right belief in God*: Whether you take it in the *threats*, as they of *Niniveh* believed the preaching of *Jonah*, and presently humbled and reformed themselves and wayes, chap. 3. 5. *Promises* of sweetest mercy made unto real penitents, that full, free, soon mercy shall be had: Why? if those be believed, they will draw off the soul from a sinful course unto a good course. The Apostle therefore *beseecheth* the Romans, *by the mercies of God to be transformed*, Rom. 12. 1. O this, that God offers and assures me of mercy, and now I may have it if I will now reform, puts the soul to the present work; To day I will hear his voice, for to day is the day of mercy, this is an acceptable season, now I may be made happy for ever.

A right Belief in God.

LUKE 15. 20.
And he arose and came to his father. But when he was yet a great way off, his father saw him, and had compassion, and ran and fell on his neck, and kissed him.

These words contein in them two parts,

1. *The real practice of Repentance*; which consists not in a bare Resolution, but in a sincere Execution (*I will arise*, said the Prodigal)this was *Motus volentis*; (and he did arise,)this was *opus penitentis. I will go to my father*; and here [*He arose and came to his father.*]

2. *The comfortable issue of real Repentance* [*But when he was yet a great way off, &c.*] Wherein you have considerable, 1. *The quick observation of this penitents Father*,[*His father saw him*, yea, when he was yet a great way off:] Even in this sense God sees our thoughts afar off; God many times is unwilling to see the sinner, but he is at all times very willing to espy the penitent. 2. *His present commiseration*,[*His father saw him, and had compassion on him.*] Wicked men look on a penitent with derision; penitent persons

look

of the Returning Prodigal.

look on themselves with abomination, but God looks on them with compassion: he looks on the sinner with indignation, he looks on the penitent sinner with a pitiful affection: When *Ephraim* repented, and turned, *My Bowels* (saith God) *are troubled for him, I will surely have mercy on him:* As soon as ever the Prodigal looks back, mercy looks out. *q.d.* Ah! is he returned indeed? I pity him, I will receive him, I will forgive him. 3. *His gracious acceptation* expressed in three particulars;

1. One of *speedy readiness:* [*The Father ran*] The Son doth go, the Father ran. Mercy hath not only a quick eye, but foot also; it posts, it speeds, it runs to embrace a penitent: God is very slow to punish a sinner, but he is very ready to relieve and accept of a returning sinner.

2. A second, Of *wonderful tenderness:* [*The Father fell on his neck*] To have looked on him, was it not enough? to have given order for his usage, had it not been well? to have taken him by the hand, had it not been too much? but the Father did more then all this [*He fell on his neck.*] Divine mercy will not only meet a penitent, but embrace him. That sinner whom the hands of justice would have everlastingly confounded, if he be penitent, the arms of mercy will lovingly clasp, *&c.*

A third, Of *strong affectionateness:* [*And kissed him*] Here are eyes to behold the returning Son, and an heart to pity him, and feet to meet him, and armes to embrace him, and lips also to kiss him: Naked mercies are not enough (in Gods account) for a true penitent, he must have sealed mercies too. God doth not think it enough that he is reconciled unto him, unless also he doth testifie and make it known that he is so.

There are many excellent Propositions observable out of these words. *v. g.*

That *the very Initials of true Repentance are seen by God:* The penitent Prodigal was in the way, but yet it was a great way off; and his Father saw him, and had compassion, *I said, I will confess my trangressions unto the Lord, and thou forgavest the iniquity of my sin,* Psal. 32. 5. *Vox nondum in ora erat & Auris Dei in corda erat,* So S. *Austin* in Locum. Isai. 66. 2. *To this man will I look, even to him that is poor and of a contrite spirit, and trembles at my word.* Repentance may be considered in three degrees. 1. In the *Impression of it:* And this is when so much grace

Doct. 1.
The very Initials of true Repentance are seen by God.

158   *Gods Gracious Acceptance*

is implanted, as to turn the heart. 2. *In the expression of it:* and this is, when so much Grace appears, as to enter into a new path, and do new works. 3. *In the progression of it:* And this is, when a greater Victory is obtained over our sins, and appears in our course of new obedience. Now the Initials of true Repentance, I conjecture, to consist partly in the Conversion of the heart; when the mind, and will, and affections are healed, and turned: and partly, in the reformation of the life; when the person out of an hatred of sin, and love of God, sets upon another course of obedience, and service. It is just like a Ship, that is going out, or like a Shop that is newly set up; things are very raw, there is much dross with the little Silver; a little health, and much lameness; a great journey, and but a few steps; the work is rather in desire, and much in complaints; and though perhaps little be done, yet all is heartily endeavoured to be done; this I call the Initials of Repentance.

Six things shew Repentance is begun in truth.
Condemnation.
Aversation.
Weariness.
Lamentation.
Resistance.
An active Inclination.

There are six things shew that Repentance is begun in truth. 1. One is *Condemnation*: When the judgment looks upon all sin after another manner then formerly, sentencing it as the most vile, and accursed of all evils, and no sin (knowingly) finds favour. 2. Another is *Aversation*: When the will flies, and shuns it, as that, which is most contrary to all goodness, and happiness. 3. A third is *Weariness*: When the Soul is as weary of Sin, as any Porter can be of his Burthen, or as a sick-man is of his Bed. Psal. 51. 17. *The sacrifices of God, are a broken spirit; a broken and a contrite heart, O God, thou wilt not despise.* 4. A fourth is *Lamentation*: That the Soul cannot yet be rid of the unruly motions, and insolencies of sin; It is grieved, that Life and Death, Hell and Heaven, Grace and Sin should thus be together. 5. A fifth is *Resistance*, or conflict: The Soul doth use the best means it can, to separate more from sin, and all sinful wayes, and to walk only in all holy pathes, in the pathes of righteousness. And the sixth is *an active Inclination*, to obey God in all things; a thirsting and striving, an aiming, a writing after the Copy.

Four things shew that Repentance is but begun.
Impotency.

And there are four things, which do shew that Repentance is but begun, it is only initial. 1. One is *Impotency*, or weakness of operation: When the penitential parts do move and stir, yet like a child, who begins to go very feebly. There is as much

appears

Of the Returning Prodigal. 159

appears in the courſe, as declares another ſpring or principle, and rule, by which the Soul ſtrives to walk, but the performance is very tender and feeble; like a young Tree that hath but tender branches, and ſmall fruit: The perſon doth mourn, and confeſs, and pray, and live, and obey, but with much weakneſs. 2. A ſecond is *efficacy of Temptation*: When Temptations do eaſily beſet and diſcourage the Soul; as when the Tree is but a young plant, the Winds do toſs it, and make it reel; ſo when Temptations do, as it were, drive the Soul, and are apt to raiſe quick fears, and diſcouragements: Oh! I ſhall be overcome again, I ſhall hardly hold on, I cannot well ſee how I ſhall be able to perform, and perſevere in theſe wayes which I have choſen. A third is the *Validity of preſent Corruption*; which though it be truly hated, and bewailed, yet it is very apt upon occaſions to aſſault and prevail; when every little ſtone is apt to make one ſtumble, it argues that the ſtrength is weak. 4. *Neceſſary preſence of many helps*: When a Man cannot go, but with two Crutches; and a Child muſt lean upon many props, and a penitent upon many ſenſible encouragements.

Efficacy of Temptation.

Validity of preſent Corruption.

Neceſſary preſence of many helps.

Now that theſe Initials of Repentance are gracioufly accepted of God, may be thus manifeſted. 1. *The Lord doth reſpect the truth of Grace, as well as the degrees of it*, every quality as well as the quantity. *Are not thine eyes upon the truth?* The Goldſmith hath his eye on the very thin raies of Gold, as well as on the great knobs and pieces; Grace is excellent and amiable at the loweſt, though then admirable when at higheſt. 2. *The main thing that God looks upon, is to the heart*; (*My Son, give me thy heart*:) All that is done, if the heart be not in it, it is of little or no eſtimation with God; but if the heart be right, this the Lord prizeth exceedingly, and ſo much, that for its ſake, he paſſeth by many infirmities. *The good Lord pardon every one that prepareth his heart*, &c. 2 *Chro*. 30. 19. Now in the Initials of Repentance, the heart is ſet right; it is ſet on God, and towards God in truth. 3. *Even the Initials of Repentance are his own Gifts* (ſpecial gifts of his bleſſed Spirit) it is he that *worketh in us to will and to do*, *Phil*. 2. 13. The ſpiritual will, and the ſpiritual deed (though both be imperfect) yet are they the genuine effect of Gods own ſpirit; ſparks out of his fire, works of his own hands: Now as in the Creation, God looked upon all that

The Doctrine proved. God reſpects the truth as well as the degrees of Grace.

God looks moſt at the Heart.

The Initials of Repentance are his Gift.

that he made, and saw that it was good, he liked it well. So is it in our Renovation; all that good which God works in us, he doth accept and approve, he doth not despise his own image, which though it shine more fairly in progressive Repentance, yet is it truly stampt in our initial Conversion. 4. That *which comes not only from a person, having faith, but from faith it self, that the Lord will graciously accept:* For as our actions do not please him without faith (it is *impossible without faith to please God*:) So on the contrary, when the actions do come from faith, they do please the Lord. *Abels Sacrifice* presented in Faith, did please him, when *Cains* presented without faith, was not regarded; faith puts a value and acceptance on our actions. But even initial Repentance comes from faith; the person is by faith united to Jesus Christ, from whom he hath received strength and grace to forsake his sins, and to become a servant of righteousness. 5. *The Lord hath said, that he will not despise the day of small things; nor quench the smoaking flax, nor break the bruised reed:* What Husbandman doth despise the little plant which he hath set? Or what father doth despise the little child he hath begotten? Why! that God who hath appointed all the meanes and ordinances, to cherish, and prop, and comfort, and nourish, and perfect the initials of Repentance; doth not he graciously accept of it? have we not reason to believe that he doth countenance these beginnings, who presently makes all provision for the nursing and supplies of it?

To make some Application of this. 1. It *convinceth* the common obloquies and aspersions cast upon religion and religious courses to be meer injuries and falsities. *viz.* that *if once you begin to be religious and penitential, then farwel all comfort*; as if the grave of sin were the Resurrection of Griefe; or of necessity, men must be everlastingly pensive, if once truly, and seriously penitential: But this is false, no course so good, so comfortable, as the penitential; mercy to invite you, mercy to receive you, mercy to pardon you, and mercy to save you. As soon as ever we begin to be good, and to be penitent, and are entred into the way of new obedience, presently the merciful eye and favour of God is upon us; mercy looks after us; and though we have been foul Transgressours, and have now but the very seeds and implantations of repentance (mixt

with

Of the Returning Prodigal.

with exceeding imperfections) yet the Lord will benignly and graciously accept of us, and love us.

And as it doth convince that errour, of the *sadneß* of entring into a good courſe; ſo alſo another errour, of *the auſterity and harſhneß of God towards poor Penitents*, as if nothing would pleaſe the Lord but quantity, and great meaſures of Grace. Oh, if I had ſo much ſorrow for ſin! if I had ſo much hatred! if I had ſo much power over my corruptions! Why! it were well if thou hadſt, and thou doeſt not well, if thou ſtriveſt not beyond all the meaſure of grace which thou doeſt attain: But then to think, that onely great grace is in grace with God, and not little grace; Repentance grown, and not Repentance begun; that God will not look on drops, but rivers; not on weakneſs, but ſtrength onely; that a poor, contrite, broken, troubled ſoul, which prizeth grace above heaven, and hates ſin above hell, but yet is troubled with the preſence of much corruption, and is apprehenſive of manifold wants in all kinds of grace, that the Lord will never look upon ſuch a thin, new, weak Chriſtian, unleſs with auſterity and diſtance: Why do we thus belie the Lord? and falſifie the gracioufneſs of the Almighty? who doth ſo love holineſs, and delight in the converſion of a ſinner, that as ſoon as ever the ſinner begins truly to repent, the Lord hath thoughts of mercy and peace for him, he is obſerved and accepted, (*Ananias is preſently ſent to Paul*,) meſſengers of peace are preſently diſpatched, Patents of mercy are ſealed for him.

Uſe 2. And of that errour of the auſterity of God towards Penitents.

And thirdly, It doth juſtly abaſe that *unworthy, proud, and cenſorious harſhneß and ſtrangeneß*, which many (who would take it ill, if they be not in your opinion ſet up in the higheſt form of Piety,) do ſinfully or fooliſhly expreſs, either *in condemning, or in contemning ſuch as fall very ſhort* (in the penitential work) *of others, or of themſelves* ; yea, and will ſhun tender ſociety with them, till they ſee ſome further perfections and ripeneſſes. Alas, what do we! by what rule do we walk? whoſe example do we look upon? We muſt be wife, it's true; and what wiſdome is it to leave tender buds to the froſt, which we might have covered and enlarged with heat and warmth? I beſeech you, let us pauſe a while: 1. *Are all in our Family Men?* Are there not ſome Children, perhaps new-born Babes? Are all in the Flock ſtrong Sheep? are there not ſome Lambs (perhaps) newly

Uſe 3. It diſcovers the proud harſhneſs of men towards ſuch as come ſhort of themſelves or others.

Y

newly yeaned? Are all the Stars in the Heaven of the same magnitude? some are greater, others are less, yet all in the Heavens. Do you despise Children? reject the Lambs? or slight the Moon, because of her spots, and lesser light than that of the Sun? Why! we read of the like disparity in the heavenly course: St. *John* tells us of *Fathers*, and of *Young-men*, and of *Chidren* too, yea, and of *Babes*; and Christ advised *Peter's* respects, as well unto the *Lambs*, as unto the *Sheep*.   2. *Were not we Beginners once our selves?* Was our Sun at the top? our Gold so exquisitely pure? did not we then need compassions and helps in times of infancy, weakness, conflicts, temptations? What is our present strength, but some help to former weakness? Time was, we could hardly go or stand, although now we can walk and run: What a childishness is it, for the Artist in Grammar to slight the Youth who is now spelling his Letters, when this was the first Line of his own Learning, the first step whereby he went to his height?   3. And *did God despise us in our beginnings?* Did not he *gently lead those that were with young*, and carried the Lambs in his arms? as the Prophet speaks. How often hath he laid our fainting and weak souls to the brests of consolation? comforted us in our fears? strengthened our feeble hands? answered our doubts?   4. *Nor doth he now slight them,* whom he tenderly owns upon the very entrances into a new and holy course, sees them afar off, and hath compassion: Why then do we so slight and neglect them, and put them from us, who have as good a God as our selves, (and if we be good,) the same, the same Christ, and also the same truth and reality of Repentance? And is not *Minimum Christi amabile?* But they are indiscreet? Surely, they are no true penitents that are very fools: No man so wise as he who is wise for his soul. But they have many failings? And not one of them approved, all bewailed. But they come short in Duties, alas they are very short? In expressions, which the vilest hypocrite may excel in; not in affections, which the true penitent onely abounds in.   Therefore repent of your pride and state: Seest thou a penitent higher than thy self, honour him, and imitate; seest thou a penitent lower than thy self, honour and cherish him: God will meet him with much mercy, do thou meet him with much love and pity. And take these *Ten Evidences*, that a *mans Repentance is true*, though

Ten Evidences of True Repentance, though Initial.

Of the Returning Prodigal.

though weak; and *real*, though but *initial*. 1. *He is much in Grief, though little in Strength*: He will grieve for finning, though he should never be damned for sin; and sin is his daily grief, as it is his daily temptation. 2. *He hates sin, though he cannot be rid of it*: His soul loaths not onely the actions, but nature also of sin. 3. *He conflicts with sin, though he cannot conquer it*; is an Enemy to it, though not a Conquerour over it, though much affaulted by it; fears Sin more than Hell. 4. *He will not be a Servant, though sometimes he is forced to be a Captive*: His Will and Love are unconquerable. 5. *He cries out for help, though he be not yet delivered*; O Lord, help: Laments his condition, becaufe so peftered with finfull motions. 6. *He muft have God reconciled, though he much queftions it*: He muft have Chrift, and Mercy, &c. 7. *He would obey God in all things, though he falls very short of it*. 8. *He prizes more Grace, and ftrives after it, though he enjoyes very little of it*. 9. *He holds up his purpose to walk with God, though he be not able, in every thing, and at all times, to make it good*. 10. *What he wants in the heights of Repentance, is made up in the depths of Humblenefs and Mournfulnefs*.

A fourth Ufe of this Point shall be *for Comfort and Support*, to such as have though *but the initials of Repentance in them*: The fountain of Godly forrow drops, though but a little, and the journey of an holy life is but begun; they have newly (within thefe few dayes) fet the firft foot in the paths of God. What shall I fay to fuch perfons? Surely,

1. *Let them not be difcouraged at all*: Though it be but a little grace, Repentance newly planted and begun; yet *if it be true Grace*, 1. *It is worth a whoe world*: One mans Soul is worth the World, much more is Grace; Grace (even in the leaft degree of it) is of an invaluable allay: The Lord hath shewn thee mercy indeed, if he has beftowed any grace on thee; it is more worth than if he had given thee all the Kingdomes of the World; more, in refpect of Excellency, and in refpect of Confequence. 2. *As little as it is, it is as much as ever any Penitent had at the firft*. 'Tis true, our improvements of Grace are very different in the courfe of our lives, but the habitual implantations of grace are alike and equal: Thou haft as much now as ever any had at firft, who are now gone to heaven. 3. *As little*

Y 2

little as it is, it shall pull down, and work out the strongest sin that ever did cleave unto thee; though not at once, yet by degrees; a beam of Light which appears in the morning seems no great matter to deal with all the darkness in the ayr, yet depending upon such a strong principle and fountain as the Sun, it doth by degrees chase away, *&c.* 4. *As little and as weak as it is, it shall never cease, till it hath brought thee to heaven:* The Ark had many tossings, and thy weak Grace shall have many assaults; but thy weak Grace is in the sure hands of a strong God, who by it will make thee more than Conquerour, through him that loved thee. 5. *As weak as it is now, it shall be stronger and stronger:* God hath but begun his work in thee, the which he will finish; the Foundation is laid, but the Covering is to come: The seed is but sown, which will arise and spread; the fire kindled, which will be blown and flaming: God doth not leave any gracious work, until he hath made it glorious; and having given truth, will also enlarge it to a just measure, sufficient for thy soul, and place, and salvation.

2. Nay, let *them be encouraged and rejoice:* Even a little Grace may be just cause of great joy. The Mother rejoyceth much if the Child be born: Though your Repentance wants much, in respect of gradual perfection; yet being real and true, 1. *All the sins that you have committed, are pardoned:* The promise of pardon or remission of sins, presently and assuredly opens to every true Penitent; as soon as the *wicked forsakes his ways, and the unrighteous man his thoughts, and turns to the Lord, he will have mercy, and abundantly pardon.* He who doth more perfect and polish his repentance, it is confessed, that he hath the more assurance and comfort of his pardon; but the right unto, and grant of pardon, immediately appertains to a person upon the very entrance of his repentance. Now pardon of sins is a testimony of Gods highest Love, and therefore a cause of most exceeding joy. 2. *If you should now die, you should be saved.* The first fruits you know were a pledge of the full harvest; though you have but as it were the first fruits of Repentance, yet these are sure pawns of fullest glory. *Godly sorrow worketh repentance to salvation.* Christ saith, *Blessed are the poor in spirit; for theirs is the Kingdome of Heaven,* Matth. 5. 3. Though you have but some lower, weaker stock of Graces, so that you

[marginal notes:]
This little will be victorious.

It shall not cease till it bring thee to heaven.

It shall grow stronger and stronger.

They have matter of rejoycing.

Their sins are pardoned.

If he should now die, he should be saved.

Of the Returning Prodigal. 165

you are in your own opinion poor, scarce worth any thing, or enjoying of any thing, yet the weakest Christian shall have an Heavenly Kingdome. 3. *Your persons are dear unto God.* Jer. 31.18. *I have surely heard Ephraim bemoaning himself; Is Ephraim my dear son? is he my pleasant child?* &c. So *Isa.*66. *To this man will I look, even to him that is poor, and of a contrite spirit.* 4. *Your weak services are accepted:* God hears your groans, considers your sighs, puts your tears into his bottel. 5. *By reason of that reality in your repentance, the Lord will pass by many infirmities and imperfections:* Infirmities shall not hinder, where a reality of Grace and Repentance is begun. They in the time of *Hezekiah* did truly repent and prepare before the Passover; and though they were very defective, yet the defects did not prevail to hinder the effects and acceptance of their service. *I will spare them, as a man spareth his own son that serveth him,* Mal. 3.17. How indulgent is the tender father to the obedient child, though he can do but very little, and very weakly? Where the Lord seeth that the heart is rightly set; O Lord, I would not offend thee; O Lord, I would obey thee; then he is very mercifull to pass by our failings, and to accept of our weak beginnings, and very weak endeavours.

Their persons are dear to God.

Their weak services are accepted.

God will pass by many infirmities.

Now I come to a second Proposition, which is, *That God is very ready and quick to shew all kinds of mercy to the true Penitent. I said I will confess, and thou forgavest me.*

Doct. 5. God is very ready to shew all kinds of mercy to the truly penitent.

You see here in the Text, what tender, what affectionate, what speedy, what free mercy is shewed to the returning Prodigal (*His Father saw him afar off, and had compassion, and ran, and fell on his neck, and kissed him.*) What could he do more? There is a great difference twixt Gods coming to punish a sinner, and his coming to shew mercy to a Penitent: (*Tardus ad vindictam,*) when he is to inflict punishment, then he walks and deliberates, as it were, there is a kind of strife within him; *How shall I give thee up, O Ephraim? how shall I deliver thee up, O Israel? how shall I make thee as Admah? how shall I set thee as Zeboim? Mine heart is turned within me, my repentings are kindled together,* Hos. 11.8. *He is slow to wrath,* Nah. 1.3. but then he is *velox ad misericordiam,* swift, quick and ready to shew mercy. He runs here in the Text to accept of the penitent Prodigal. As soon as ever *Ephraim* said, *I repented,* Jer. 31.19. instantly it follows, *I will surely have mercy upon him saith the Lord,* v. 20. *I have sinned,* saith faith *David*; *Nathan* hath it in Commiſſion preſently, 2 *Sam.* 12. 13. *The Lord hath done away thy ſin.* The Prophet *Eſay*, c. 30. 18. hath a ſingular phraſe; *The Lord will wait that he may be gracious unto you.* He doth even watch, and liſten, and hearken for the firſt hint and occaſion to ſhew mercy; *I hearkened and heard*, Jer. 8. *Why will ye die, O houſe of Iſrael!* Ezek. 18. 31. What an expreſſion is that? *q. d.* Lo here's mercy for you, if you will but leave your ſins: I pray you draw not confuſion on your ſelves; mercy is better than wrath, turn you and live; do not refuſe mercy: I ſtand not upon what is paſt, ſo that you will repent, I had rather ſhew you mercy.

For the opening of this excellent Aſſertion, premiſe theſe particulars. 1. What it is to ſhew mercy. 2. What it is to be ready and quick, *&c.*

What it is to ſhew mercy.

1. To ſhew mercy to a Penitent, imports many things, *v. g. Pitifull Compaſſion, Acceptance into Grace and Favour, abundant Pardon, withdrawment of Wrath and Evil, collation of any Good*; all this is ſhewing of mercy; when God doth pity a man, bring him into favour, remit offences, take off judgments, pour down bleſſings; thus is the Lord ready to do to the true Penitent, if a man repents (indeed) of his ſins. The Lord, 1. *Will pity him*:

God will pity him.

He will have compaſſion on us, faith the Church, *Mic.* 7. 19. and will pity him as a Father doth the Child, *Pſal.* 103.

Accept him into favour.

13. 2. *Will accept him into favour*: (*i.*) He will be reconciled unto him, and will be highly well pleaſed with him; *He ſhall pray unto God, and he will be favourable unto him, and he ſhall ſee his face with joy*; ſaid *Elihu, Job* 33. 26. When they in *Iſa.* 1. did *ceaſe to do evil, and learn to do well, Come now, faith the Lord, and let us reaſon together: q. d.* We are now very good friends, all is well, I love you, I am pacified towards you. 3. *Will pardon him*: (*i.*)

Pardon him.

diſcharge him of all the guilt, that it ſhall not be redundant; he

Jer. 31. 34.

will *blot out his iniquities, and remember them no more*; and *though they be ſought for, yet they ſhall not be found*, Jer. 50. 20. *If the wicked forſake his ways, and his thoughts, God will abundantly pardon him*, Iſa. 55. 7. 4. *Will withdraw his wrath*: And

Withdraw his wrath.

therefore it is ſaid, that he *reſerves not wrath for ever*, and it is but for a moment: He breaks off the ſhackles and bolts, *Mic.* 7. 18. *Mine anger is turned away from him*, faith God of penitent

tent *Israel*, Hof. 14. 4. Lastly, *Will bestow any Covenant blessings upon him:* If you consent and obey, you shall eat the good of the Land, Esa. 1. 19. And Hof. 2. 21. *The Lord will hear the heavens, and the heavens shall hear the earth, and the earth shall hear the corn and the wine, and all these shall hear Jezreel.*

2. To be ready to shew mercy, is *opposite to dulness and slowness*, and imports a speedy aptness, and quickness, and chearfulness. There is a four-fold readiness in this kind. 1. One is of *apprehension*, which consists in a quick observation of the misery and need that a sinner lies under: Such a readiness to mercy there is in God to a penitent sinner. *I have heard Ephraim bemoaning himself*, Jer. 31. 18. *Ephraim* did grieve for sin, was much troubled, and ashamed, and confounded, (Alas, I have sinned, I have offended the Lord:) Well, saith God, I have heard *Ephraim* bemoaning himself ; *q. d.* I take special notice of him. Or as he expresseth it in *Hof.* 14. 8. *I have heard him, and observed him.* 2. Another is of *Commiseration*, (that is) God takes the condition of the Penitent to heart. He doth look on him with tender affections, (*my bowels are troubled for him*, Jer. 31. 20.) As when a Parent beholds a Child falling down and begging for acceptance with flouds of tears, this goes to the very heart of him, it stirs his affections, *&c.* 3. A third is of *Resolution : I will surely have mercy upon him.* The nature of God doth presently incline him to pass by offences, and to accept of the Penitent, to think thoughts of peace and mercy towards him. 4. A fourth is, of *Expression :* (i.) the Lord is very ready, not onely to intend mercy, but to manifest it unto the penitent person ; and therefore as soon as ever any soul doth repent, God doth send unto him by the Ministry of the Gospel, and assures him by all his loving promises, that there is mercy for him. *Isa.* 40. 1. *Comfort ye my people.* Act. 2. 39. *The promise is to you, and to your children.* 'Tis thus spoken presently upon their Repentance. The Promises of Pardon are Letters Patents of Graciousness, and are sealed by the very Truth of God, and left open for any penitent person to behold Gods abundant mercy to forgive him, and to accept of him.

3. God is not *onely ready to shew mercy to the Penitent, but all kinds of mercy.* You may read in Scripture of several qualifications

168　　　　　*Gods Gracious Acceptance*

Free mercy. tions (as it were) of mercy; 1. There is *Free mercy*; which is an acceptance of, and a remission or discharge, without any desert in the party receiving; though he hath nothing to deserve mercy, nay, though he hath enough to deserve wrath, yet the Lord will freely forgive him; such a kind of mercy hath God for the Penitent; and therefore he saith of such, *I will love them freely*, Hos. 14. 4. and *that he forgives them for his own sake*, Esa. 43. 2. There is *Abundant mercy*: God is

Abundant mercy. said to be *rich in mercy*, to be plentifull in compassion, to have manifold mercies, even multitudes of mercy, and to pardon abundantly. Though the penitent hath many sins to be pardoned, and many necessities to be supplied, yet the Lord is very ready to multiply pardons unto him; not to forgive some sins onely, but all the sins committed: It is not the quantity of sins for number, nor the quality of sins for kind, nor the aggravations of sins by circumstances, which hinders mercy, if a man be penitent; but though the sins were *as red as Scarlet, they shall be as white as Snow; and though they have been like*

Tender mercy. *Crimson, they shall be as Wool*, Esa. 1. 18. 3. There is *Tender mercy*: Tendernefs confifts in an easinefs of Compassion, and forward willingnefs to help. The tender Mother easily draws out the breasts. Such a tendernefs of mercy is there in God to the Penitent; he is most willing to forgive, he rejoyceth to shew mercy, and doth it with his whole heart. Nor doth he upbraid and grieve the sinner when he sheweth mercy; but in the shewing of mercy, onely shews mercy; he will forgive sins, and never mention them any more to the forgiven Peni-

Sure mercy. tent. 4. There is *Sure mercy*: A penitent person may be unsure of many things of his earthly comforts, of his worldly friends, of his own life; but of two things he may be sure, of Heaven hereafter, and of Mercy prefently; as soon as ever his heart is taken off from sin, his faith may look on mercy: Though he hath reason to be grieved for sins, yet he hath no reason to doubt the pardon of his sins; for that God who hath promised to pardon abundantly, hath also said, *I will surely*

Reviving mercy. *have mercy on him*, Jer. 31. 20. 5. There is *Loving and reviving mercy*, such as takes off the turbulency of the Confcience, settles, and compofeth, and speaks peace unto it, and admirably refresheth it by the impreffion of Divine consolations.

Even

The Sinners Converſion to God.

even ſuch mercy is God ready alſo to give to the penitent, even to bind up their bruiſed ſpirits, and to *give them beauty for aſhes, the oyle of joy for mourning, and the garment of praiſe for the ſpirit of heavineſs.* Iſa. 61. 1, 2. He will create lips of peace, and words of comfort, *Speak comfortable to Jeruſalem, ſay unto her, that her ſins are pardoned.* Iſa. 40.

But why is God ſo ready to ſhew mercy to the penitent perſon? *Sol.* There are reaſons, partly reſpecting God, and the penitent. 1. In reſpect of God. 1. *It is his nature* to be the *Lord, the Lord God, gracious, merciful, abundant in goodneſs and truth, forgiving iniquity, tranſgreſſion, and ſin*; therefore called a Father, and the *Father of mercies*, a Husband, Friend, Phyſician: Every nature is apt to produce, or ſend out ſuch acts as lye within it, and are ſuitable unto it: The Fire is apt to heat, and the Sun to ſhine, and the Water to moiſten: The liberal man, it is his nature to be apt to give, and the courteous man to ſpeak kindly; the nature of the Lord is merciful, and therefore no wonder, that he is ready to ſhew mercy. 2. *It is his promiſe* to ſhew mercy to the penitent; his nature is ready to pity any man in miſery, and to offer him mercy and help; but beſides this, he is ready to make good his promiſes, he hath paſſed his holy word of truth, that he will have mercy on the penitent; the promiſes are ſo many that I cannot mention them, See *Iſai.* 55. *Ezek.* 18. &c. 3. *It is his delight* to ſhew them mercy; *he delighteth in mercy.* Mic. 7. 18. What any delights in, that he is ready to do; there is nothing more facile to action, or more abundant in action, or more unweariable in action, then delight; delight is no burden: when God ſhews mercy, he is doing that, wherein he delights. Two things God delights in, One is, a penitent ſoul (there *is joy in heaven for his converſion*,) and another is, to ſhew mercy to that Soul. *Jer.* 33. 8. *I will pardon all their iniquities, whereby they have ſinned againſt me.* v. 9. *And it ſhall be to me a name of joy.* 4. *It is his glory*: is it the glory of a man to paſs by an offence, and is it not the glory of a God mercifully to paſs over tranſgreſſions? you get by it, and God gets by it. *Iſai.* 30. 18. *Therefore will he be exalted, that he may have mercy upon you*; there be many things which do exalt God, (ſet his glory on high;) our humility doth it, our faith doth it, and his own mercies do it. *Jer.* 33. 9. *This ſhall be to me a name of joy and praiſe, and an honour before all the nations of the earth*;

Reaſons of it.
In reſpect of God.
It is his nature.
It is his Promiſe.
It is his Delight.
It is his glory.

Z who

who shall hear all the good that I do unto you. When he pardons a sinner and shews him mercy, why now he gets him a Name; *Who is a God like unto thee, forgiving iniquity, transgression and sin?* God gets him a name three wayes; sometimes by *Omnipotent* acts, as when he works wonders: never was the like seen in Israel. Sometimes by *Vindictive* acts, as when he over rules and confounds the great enemies of his people; so he got him a name upon *Pharaoh*. Sometimes by his *Gracious* acts, as when he pardons a sinner. *Paul* sets it down for all posterity to look on that mercy which was shewed unto him. The Lord gives the Penitent mercy, and hereby he gets unto himself much Glory.

His love is great to Penitents.

5. *His love is great to Penitents*, and therefore his mercy is ready for penitents: his general Love, his Philanthropie inclines him thus far as to reveale mercy, and to offer mercy, and to beseech by mercy, even the unkindest Impenitents, *Why will ye dy? turn and live: When shall it once be?* O then what must his special love produce? if he be ready to shew mercy to enemies, is he not ready to shew it to sons? If to Rebels, surely then to friends? if to them that disobey him, how much to them who do humble themselves at his footstool? who repent, for whose souls he gave the blood of his Son?

In respect of the Penitent.

Secondly in *respect of the penitent* themselves, God is very ready to shew them mercy. 1. There is nothing in the World that

They need nothing like mercy.

they need like mercy: It is the only Plaister for their wound, and Anchor for their Ship; if they have not mercy, they are undone. Usually there is in every condition some one thing, which the heart of man doth most need; if he be sick, then health; if poor, then sufficiency; if dejected, then comfort; *Christ* tells *Martha* of *one thing that was necessary:* and *David* he hath *one thing to desire of the Lord;* and the penitent person he hath one needful request too, *O that God would be merciful to me a*

Else he might be swallowed up with Despaire.

sinner, so the Publicane. 2. *If God were not ready to shew mercy to the penitent, he might be swallowed up with despaire.* Isa. 57. 16. *I will not contend for ever, neither will I be alwaies wroth, lest the spirit should fail before me*: Do you know what belongs to a wounded Conscience, to the fence of sin and the wrath of God? how great, how sharp, how bitter? Is it a small thing, think you, to dwell with everlasting burnings? to see nothing but sin, and Hell? No, No, the Lord knows what the severity of his wrath

is,

is, and he knows what the Impotency of the foul is, and he knows what the terrour of a troubled confcience is, how it finks, and cracks if no hope of mercy appears; and therefore he is very ready to fhew mercy to the penitent, left defpair fhould overwhelm them: defpair is ready to rife in two cafes; One is when there is exceeding tendernefs and fenfiblenefs of fin; Another is, when there is a long abfence and improbability of mercy; for what hath the foul now to reft on, and to fupport it? Now of all perfons living there are none fo fenfible of fin, as true penitents; (we may fay of other people, as the Apoftle did, *the reft are hardned*) and of all penitent people, they are moft tender in confcience, and apprehenfive of fin, and fearfull about mercy, who are newly converted from a finful way: O how hard is it to keep them above water, to perfwade them that any mercy belongs to them? and therefore the Lord is ready to fhew them mercy, that their fpirits might not fail before him, nor be overwhelmed with defpair.

Is the Lord fo ready to fhew all kind of mercy to the penitent? Thence may we be inftructed unto two things. 1. To the approbation. 2. To the application of our felves to a penitentiall Courfe.

Ufe 1.
Inftruction.

1. To *the Approbation of a penitential Courfe :* Why are ye fo averfe, and accufe, and condemn it? They have a faying, that *Finis dat amabilitatem Mediis :* the end doth make the means lovely, it doth give fpirit and encouragement to the ufe of means. Repentance is in it felf a moft excellent and peculiar grace, a fingular gift of God, and therefore defirable; But befides that (*Behold thy fon liveth,* &c.) it brings the foul to partake of mercy (of the choiceft mercy in God) pardoning mercy, which is of moft immediate concernment and influence to the everlafting falvation of man: nay, it brings mercy and falvation prefently, *This day is falvation come unto thy houfe :* 'Tis granted, many perfons do accufe a penitential courfe of much vexation, and fadnefs, and grief, as if it were the grave of all delight (whereas indeed it is only the fepulchre of our Lufts, and of luftful pleafures.) And others cry out upon the difficulty of it, as if it were an heavy yoke, and an intolerable burden. But judge not of duties by the opinion of ignorant and gracelefs men; nor by the folly and error of your own finful and inexperienced hearts. No, but

To approve.
of a penitentiall courfe.

Gods gracious Acceptance

but judge of them by what the Word pronounceth of them, in themselves, and by their ends. Is Salvation a desireable thing? is mercy an excellent thing? Why, then Repentance must be an excellent thing, which brings us unto mercy, and unto Salvation.

Object. But there must be brokenness of heart for sin, and there must be a diligent endeavour to leave all sin, and there must be strict care to walk with God.

Sol. And what of all this, It is as if thou shouldest say, O but I must not be wicked, I must become a new man, I must leave that which will damn me, I must think well of such a course as will bring me to find saving mercy with God; there cannot be a worse estate and more fearful end then Impenitency, and there cannot be a better and more soul-saving estate then Repentance.

Apply your selves to a Penitential course.

2. *To the quick application of our selves to a Penitential course:* I beseech you at length, if there be any understanding in you, any sense in you, any credence of a hell and heaven, any belief of a God or happiness, seriously consider with me that, 1. *You must perish for ever, if you have not mercy*: If Mercy does not save you, Justice must damn thee; what shall become of thy soul, if thy sins be not pardoned? they cannot but be condemnation unto thee, without gracious and merciful Remission. *Therefore now, saith the Lord, turn unto me, &c.* Joel 3.12. & Heb. 3.15. Whiles it is said to day, harden not your hearts. Repentance is a present duty, *Now God commands every one to repent*, Act. 17.30. 2. Are you sinners, or are you not? if you be not sinners, then I confess you need no pardoning mercy; but if you be sinners, *then mercy must be your plea and anchor: Save me for thy mercies sake, and blot out my transgressions, according to the multitude of thy mercies,* saith David, Psal. 6.51. Ah wretches that we are! we are sinners by Nature, and sinners by Life; who can say, My heart is clean? We lie down in our sins every moment; so that we need mercy, much mercy, all mercy. 3. *Unless you do practically repent*, (*i.*) indeed forsake your sinful wayes, and walk in newness of obedience, *you shall never have mercy; Except you repent, ye shall all likewise perish,* said Jesus Christ. It is the unchangeable Decree of God, and the revealed pleasure of God, that no man shall have his mercy but the Penitent: It were an

un-

of the Returning Prodigal.

unreasonable thing, that he should have mercy to pardon sin, who will not have an heart to leave sin. I know very well, that the Lord is very rich in measure, and delights in mercy, and is ready to shew mercy, and is able to pardon abundantly; God forbid that any should straighten the Mercy Seat at all. But O thou vainly presumptious soul, look over all the Bible, read it often, and tell me, where doest thou find, that God will be thus merciful to any one sinner, but him who is truly penitent? It is not to him who is civil, but penitent; it is not to him that saith he is a sinner, but who doth forsake his sins; this is he that shall find mercy.

4. Yea, and consider one thing more; *how utterly inexcusable you are before God and men, if you doe not repent*: ah! what a sad and shameful appearance wilt thou make before the Lord, when he shall at the last day judg thee for all thy sinfulness? When thou shalt be set in the presence of Christ, and Angels, and men, and devils; And the Lord shall say, This is the person to whom I have offered the saving blood of my son, and all my pardoning mercies, if that he would but have left his sinful wayes. Thy own conscience will condemn thee for ever, that ever thou shouldst exalt the lust of thy sin before the mercy of God; yea, the very Devils will cry shame of thee; they may say, If we had had such mercy offered, we could not have been worse then have refused it; thou hadst mercy offered to pardon thee, and yet thou wouldest go on in thy sins. Know, O man, thou art inexcusable before God, thou canst make no apology at all. Two things let them be for ever ingraven in your brests; One is, that if mercy will not bring in your souls to repentance, nothing will do it; I affirm it, that if you were in hell it self, the torments of it would not incline you to repent, if the mercies of God now upon earth will not prevail with you: Another, if mercy do not lead you to repentance, there remains nothing but a fearfull expectation of the fiery indignation of God; thou art as sure to be damned as thou now livest, if thou doest not repent thee of thy sins.

Thou art Inexcusable if thou do not Repent.

A second Use shall be of Caution: Since the Lord is so ready to shew all mercy to the penitent, therefore *take heed that you keep not off from repentance by despairing of mercy*. There are three sorts of sinners: Some whose hearts are hardned as the Adamant, through an habitual iteration by sin, and in a mad affection unto sin: who like that *unjust Judg fearing neither God nor man*, so they are sensible

Use 2. Caution, Keep not off from Repentance by despairing of Mercy.

neither

neither of the vileness of sin, nor of the goodness of mercy: Some whose hearts are mollifyed, graciously altered, have seen the evil of their wayes, and forsaken them, and are turned unto the Lord, seeking him with mourning, and with supplication, to whom the Scepter of Mercy hath been gracioufly stretched forth, and they have effectually touched that Scepter with believing hearts, and are returned with much peace and joy unspeakable: Others there are twixt both these; they are not so low as the first, for their consciences are awaked and troubled; nor yet so high as the last, for they cannot believe any mercy will reach unto them; their souls cannot discern any intention of mercy towards them, and all the promises of mercy seem to them as restrictive, nay, as exclusive proclamations, denying unto them (though granting unto others) the priviledg of their Books, and the Psalm of mercy, and so are apt to despair; mercy seems to them a far off, and slow, and long a coming. Therefore now, to such persons who are awakned in their consciences, to see the vileness of their sinful ways, and their lost condition; my advice is, by no means to despair of mercy.

Reasons against despair. Despair is a very heinous Sin.

Reasons why I thus advise are these. 1. *Despair is a very heinous sin*; It is one of the highest impeachments of Gods greatest glory and delight: there is nothing wherein God doth more magnifie himself in the eyes of the world, or more glory in, then to sit upon his mercy-seat: Now despair is not every diminution, and eclipse of mercy, but it is (in its kind) a very extinction of all the love, and kindness, and mercifulness in God; it gives, 1. The lye to the promises. 2. Reproach to Gods nature; and particularly to the attribute of mercy, that it is not, 1. Kind enough. 2. Willing enough. 3. Full enough. 4. Free enough. 2. It is a sore enemy to Repentance; if no hope of mercy, then no care to repent, I can but be damned. 2. And then it is *the most uncomfortable sin*: Other sins afford some (though ungrounded and poor) contentment either in profit or pleasure: But despair being the grave of mercy, it is also the very night, and funeral of all comfort; and, as S. *Austin* spake of an evil conscience, that is true of despair, It is *its own torment*; for taking the soul off from all remedy, it must necessarily afflict it with the most exquisite sense of fear and horrour. 3. *Satan is very apt to fall in with an awakened conscience*, and there to aggravate sin above all measure, thereby *to incline it to despair of mercy*;

The most uncomfortable sin.

Satan is very apt to draw us to despair.

if

Of the Returning Prodigal.

if he cannot make us dye in a senseless Calm, his next aim is to make us perish in an unquiet and despairing storm; either to undervalue our sins, and so to slay us with security; or else to undervalue mercy, and so to sink us with distrust. 4. Yea, and no *conscience is more propense to suspect divine favour, and to credit false suggestions, then a newly awakened conscience:* Indeed while our hearts are totally seared, and past feeling (much sin being not at all felt) here is an easie ground to delude our selves, that mercy will quickly bend unto us, who do take our selves to be good enough, and not much to need it; but when many sins shall be laid to our charge, and great ones too, with that wrath which a just and holy God hath threatned, and we feel the burnings of the wrath begun within us; I assure you, it will be most difficult to withhold that Soul from despairing of mercy, which at once sees much guilt, and feels much wrath. 5. *There is infinite mercy in God:* It is his nature, and he can forgive iniquity, transgression, and sin; *Est in misericordia divina, divina Omnipotentia*; Therefore this I say unto you, any of you, whose consciences God has awakned to the sight and sense of your sins (whether by the Ministry of his Word, or of his rod) as you desire not utterly to cast dishonour, extreemest dishonour to God, and to draw the saddest, and yet most fruitless anguish, on your own spirits; and yet again, as you tender the welfare of your Souls, your everlasting safety, by repentance and faith; do not despair of finding mercy with God, but come in unto him by solid repentance, and you shall find him, even unto you a God ready *to forgive iniquity, transgression, and sin.*

A newly awakned conscience is apt to it.

There is Infinite mercy in God.

Obj. Yea, but *though the Lord be merciful, yet is he just, he will by no means clear the guilty,* Exod. 34. 7. I have refused mercy; I cannot pray; I cannot be heard or answered! How then can I? I, who have sinned so much, now expect any mercy! *Sol.* To this I answer briefly: There are two kinds of sinners, whom God will not clear. One is, *Who do not see their sins, yet love them.* Another, *Who do not see their sins, and yet go on in them.* Psal. 11. 5. The *wicked, and him that loveth violence, his soul doth hate.* And Psal. 68. 21. *He will wound the head of such as still go on in their wickedness.* If you be such sinners, who do see your sins, and will love them, and not forsake them, be confident, that remaining thus, there remains nothing for you, but an expectation

I, but God will not clear the guilty.

Answered.

tion of wrath and just judgment from the righteous God: But if you see your sins, and desire to repent, to bewail them, to forsake them with all your heart, to turn from your evil wayes; why! the Lord hath mercy for you, he is very ready to pardon and accept of you: *If we confess our sins,* 1 Joh.1.9. *he is faithful to forgive us our sins.*

Ob. But do ye *not read the threatnings of God?* as Jonah 1.3. *Yet fourty dayes, and* Ninive *shall be destroyed. Sol.* Remember one thing as a Preservative, that *all Gods threatnings* against our sins, are to be understood *in sensu composito,* as the schools speak, *viz.* thus, if we continue impenitent, and not otherwise; not *in sensu diviso,* if we return from them: like a Kings proclamation of death, if the Traitors do not lay down their Weapons, but if they do, he offers and assures them of his pardon.

I did not yield when mercy was tendered.

Obj. I, this is it! *I had mercy offered in the Kings Proclamation,* if I would lay down my Weapons; but *I did not yield when mercy was tendered*: If I had repented, when God formerly offered me mercy, there had been hope; but I continued in sin, where grace abounded, and since mercy was offered; therefore now too late, in vain. *Sol.* To this also, let me give answer. 1. Indeed it *was thy duty to have repented, upon the very first proposal of grace and mercy;* and it was thy sin (at all) to stand out, yea, and thy sinnings contract a deep guilt by commission after the tender of divine mercy, (sin is more sinful, where the offer of mercy is more plentiful.) But secondly, Though *the precedent refusals of mercy make the course of sin more guilty, yet they do not make the condition of the sinner to be hopeless, and utterly uncapable of mercy:* For 1. *Mercy is able to pardon, even sins against mercy;* as it is the antidote for sins against the Law, so likewise the salve for sins against the Gospel: There is so much mercy in God, as can rejoice against judgment, yea, and that can rejoice over sins against mercy too; my meaning is, that Gods goodness is so natural to him, and great, that it can pass by the evils, against his goodness, and kindness. 2. And that, *God is willing and ready so to do,* it may appear by this, that he continues his invitations, and offers of mercy, though formerly neglected; *How often would I have gathered thee?* faith Christ of *Jerusalem:* and *let it yet alone one year,* of the Tree. And then know that this is certain; as long as God continues a suit of mercy unto thee, neither is the date of thy mercy expired,

Answered.

nor

nor doth thy former refufal juftly prejudice thy prefent right to or acceptance of mercy. If the King renews his Proclamation of favour to thofe who have formerly defpifed it, it is now lawfull and fafe for them to come in and accept of it: But fince thy former refufal, God hath, as it were, renewed the Embaſſage; He hath fent other fervants unto thee, to proclaim unto thee Mercy, if thou wilt return; yea, and hath affured thee, that he will pardon all former rebellions in all kinds; if now thou wilt hear his voice, thou fhalt live, and not die: Therefore now turn unto the Lord; this day doth Mercy befeech thee to leave thy fins, and faith, If thou wilt forfake them, I am thine.

Object. But furely the Lord hates me, and hath no delight towards me; I have been a vaffal of fin, and now muft be a veffel of deftruction. *Sol.* Ah foolifh and fenflefs finner, who pleafeft thy felf with the arguings of an unbelieving fpirit; Doth God hate thee! or doth he delight in thy deftruction! Had this been fo, what wants there that thou hadft not been irrecoverably fent to the place of the damned long ere this? How eafily could he, (if he had delighted in thy confufion and deftruction) ftruck thee at once? Doeft thou not fee, that when thou waft mad in renewing thy fins, then did his repentings kindle within him? When he had juft, and many, and ftrong occafions and provocations, yet he hath fpared thee to this day; would he have done fo, had he defired to have deftroyed thee? 2. *And what is the end of all this patience and forbearance?* Doeft thou fo ill interpret it an intention of revenge, which is altogether a fruit of his great mercy? No, no, it is not thy deftruction, but thy repentance and converfion which he delights in: See *Ezek.* 33. 11. Not the ruine of thy perfon, but corruptions: *He delights not in the death of a finner, but rather that he fhould turn from his wickedneſs and live.*

Object. But I cannot repent, and I cannot turn mine own heart. *Sol.* Pray unto him, *Turn me, and I fhall be turned.* *Object.* But I cannot pray. *Sol.* Sigh then, and grieve; pray that you may pray, and mourn becaufe you cannot mourn. And therefore leave thefe falfe furmizes of God, and finfull, foolifh, unworthy reafonings; fet upon the work of repentance indeed, and thou fhalt quickly find, that God is fo far from hating thee, that he will meet thee with loving kindnefs, and great mercies.

God hates me, and will deftroy me. Anfwered.

I cannot repent. Anfwered.

I cannot pray Anfwered.

A a. *Object.*

Never such a sinner as I have been.

Answered.

Object. O no, never such a sinner as I have been; a sinner above measure sinfull, so wholly sinfull, so onely sinfull, so continually sinfull. To this also a word. 1. *Greatnesse of sinning is not an absolute impediment to Gods readinesse in pardoning;* for as much as great sinners are called upon to repent, as well as lesser sinners; and if the duty of Repentance concerns them, then there is a capacity of mercy for them. 2. *God doth upon repentance promise to pardon great sinners. Cease to do evil, learn to do well,* Isa.1.16. *Come now, and let us reason together, saith the Lord.* V.18. *Though your sins be as scarlet, they shall be as white as snow; though they be red like crimson, they shall be as wooll. Isti duo colores sunt valde tenaces & mansivi quibus intelligitur peccata quantumque sint gravia ex genere & habituata ex consuetudine, divina gratia purgabuntur,* saith *Lyra* well upon that place: Yea, though they have been *peccata sanguinea,* so S. *Jerome* upon the same place. 3. *Great sinnings, upon repentance, have found greater mercies:* Adam's sin, very great, (whether you consider it formally or causally,) yet upon repentance, mercy pardoned it. *David's* sin of *murther,* (it was a crying sin,) and of *adultery,* (it was a wounding sin;) yet, upon his repentance, both pardoned by mercy. What should I speak of *Manasses* in the Old Testament, or of *Paul* in the New? 4. *The greater sinnings should ever prove the quicker reasons of repentantance,* and not be made *the causes of despair,* or *more sinning:* If thy sinnings had not been so high, it had been better; but being so, thy remedy is not an addition of a worse sin, or a continuance in the same sins, but to pray unto the Lord to turn thee, and to forgive thee.

I have prayed, and yet can get no mercy.

Answered.

Object. Why, I have prayed, and yet I can get no mercy, nor see any hopes or appearance of mercy; therefore, surely God will not be so ready to shew me mercy. *Sol.* This is a sore Objection, and usually troubled Consciences are enthralled with it, and many times receive great discouragement because of the silence of mercy to their tears and prayers: But let us see how we may instruct and support persons in this case. 1. *God is ready to hear prayer.* Psal.65.2. *O thou that hearest prayer. Before they call, I will answer; and while they are speaking, I will hear,* Isa.65.

God is ready to hear prayer.

Most ready to hear the prayer of the afflicted.

2. *Of all mens prayers, he is most ready to hear the prayer of afflicted persons.* Psal.18.27. *Thou wilt save the afflicted.* Psal.22.24. *He hath not despised nor abhorred the afflictions of the afflicted, neither*

neither hath he hid his face from them; but when he cried unto him, he heard him: Of all the Prayers which he is ready to hear, there are none which he doth more feelingly and compassionately tender, than the Prayers of afflicted people, especially such as are inwardly afflicted in their souls and consciences for their sins. No people are more apt to fear that the Lord doth not hear their Prayers, and yet no Prayers doth God sooner hear than theirs; for as much as the Lord doth exceedingly delight in the sacrifices of a broken spirit, and he is full of pitifulness and bowels towards them; *I have surely heard Ephraim bemoaning himself,* Jer. 31. 18. *When Ephraim smote upon the thigh, and was confounded and ashamed,* why! you know the Lord could not contain his affections; *Is Ephraim my dear son? is he a pleasant child? for since I spake against him, I do earnestly remember him still: therefore my bowels are troubled for him; I will surely have mercy upon him,* saith the Lord. *David,* you find him much afflicted and distressed in his soul, *Psal.* 32. 3,4. he did no sooner acknowledge his sin, but God did express his mercy, *v.* 5. The like you may see of him, in *Psal.* 6. 1, 2. compared with *v.* 8, 9. *The Lord hath heard the voice of my weeping, the Lord hath heard my supplication, the Lord hath received my Prayer.* So true is that of the Prophet, *Isa.* 30. 19. *He will be very gracious unto thee at the voice of thy cry; when he shall hear it, he will answer thee.* But then know we, that there may be sometimes some special Reasons, why the Lord doth not presently make known his mercy to the troubled and seeking soul. The Reasons may be either on their part, or on Gods part.

God doth not presently make known his Mercy. Reasons of it on our parts.

1. *Quick mercy must first see quickned fervency:* Though God be ready to hear their Prayers, yet there may be some reasons, why he doth not presently give them sensible tokens that they are heard. If you pray for pardoning mercy, as *Austin* did for repentance; if you pray with a careless, dull, flat, formal, neglecting spirit, not esteeming of Gods mercy and favour as your lives, nay, above your lives; if you seek not the Lord in this with all your hearts. Pardoning mercy is the greatest mercy for the soul, and must be desired with the greatest affections of the soul, with cries, with importunities: If you do not mightily wrestle with him, as *David* in *Psal.*6. and as *Daniel* in *c.* 9.

Quickned fervency may be wanting.

No marvel that cold Suits have slow Answers; though you be afflicted in your consciences, yet if those inward afflictions cannot raise the price of mercy, and set a stronger edge upon your affections, if the burnings of your consciences do not kindle flames of affections for mercy, you may wait for your answer.

Or a pure affection.

2. As it must be a quickned affection which must find quick mercy, *so it must be a pure affection. I will that men pray every where, lifting up pure hands,* 1 Tim. 2. 8. Art thou sure that no iniquity cleaves unto thee, and is an impedit to thy suit for mercy? Thou art troubled with the grossness of some one of thy sins, but doest not thou connive at the shreds of the same sin? the limbs of it afflict thee, but do not the leaves and the twigs hang on still? If we do not purely and entirely put off our sins, why should we complain, that God doth not let down his mercy? *If I regard iniquity in my heart, the Lord will not hear me,* Psal. 66. 18. If you favour your known sin, in any part, or the least degree of it, where now hath God promised to shew thee favour or mercy? Or suppose thou shakest off one crying sin, and yet retain some other sin; put off one servant, and take another; be troubled for one transgression, and yet live in another; is this repentance? Thou doest not change thy course, but thy sin, and how then canst thou expect mercy? *But if thou prepare thine heart, and stretch out thine hands towards God, and putst iniquity far from thee, then shalt thou lift up thy face without spot,* said Zophar, Job 11. 13, 14. *If thou thus return to the Almighty, and putst away iniquity,* Job 22. 23. *thou shalt make thy prayer unto him, and he shall hear thee,* v. 27. As your prayers must be fervent, so they must be the *fervent prayers of a righteous man, which do prevail much:* Not that he who prays must have no sin, but that he must love and connive at none.

Doest thou mourn for the vileness and filthiness of thy sin.

3. Thy heart is troubled with the guilt of sin, but *doth it mourn for the vileness and filth of thy sin?* Thou seekest for a Cordial, but doest thou pray for Salve too? Vehement thou art for Mercy, but what for Grace? Where guilt onely troubles, it may make me earnest for mercy to ease me, that is involuntary; would not be troubled but is troubled because he is troubled: But where the filthiness of sin troubles me, now I do not onely importune in prayer, but mourn also, and am as desirous of healing, as I am of pardoning, this is voluntary; he would mourn, and

Of the Returning Prodigal.

and mourns becaufe he can mourn no more : If thou feekeft the Lord with a mourning heart, as well as with a troubled heart, the *fountain is fet open for tranfgreffions and fins,* Zach. 13.1. and if the fountain be opened for thee, it cannot be long ere mercies will fwim unto thee.

4. *And with what faith haft thou prayed ?* Thy troubled Confcience would trouble thee if thou didft not pray, and therefore haft thou prayed to give it a little quiet, as we do a crying child the breft to ftill it: What things foever ye defire, when ye pray, believe that you receive them, and ye fhall have them : Haft thou, and doeft thou confider and ponder the promifes of Gods mercy made over to penitent perfons ? Haft thou confidered of his mercifull nature, tender love in and through Chrift ? of his commands to broken and afflicted fouls to come unto him for Balm and Oyl ? Haft thou found how proper his mercifull promifes are to thy condition ? (every way good and convenient ;) and doeft confefs this word of promife a gracious and a good word? and judgeft him to be faithfull who hath promifed, and thy felf unworthy of mercy ? and thereupon, in the Name of the Lord Jefus, haft bended thy heart and knees to the God of mercy, trufting through him to find grace and mercy to help in time of need, and thofe his promifes to be Yea and Amen to thy foul through Chrift ? *Joh.* 14. 13. *Whatfoever ye ask in my Name, that will I do. According to your faith* (faid Chrift to the blind men, *Matt.* 9.29.) *fo be it unto you.* Alas! thy prayers have not found the way to Gods Mercy-feat all this while, becaufe they have not had faith for their Guide ; if our Meffengers lofe their way, no marvel if we ftay long for an anfwer.

Laftly ; *Why haft thou called home the Embaffadors, thofe prayers of thine* which were Leigers at Heaven ? In a fit of proud impatience, and fruitlefs vexation, and bold prefumption, thou haft limited the holy One of Ifrael to a day : And if at fuch another prayer God did not fenfibly anfwer thee, thou wouldeft and haft reftrained feeking of him. What doeft thou mean to beg, and yet to prefcribe ? Alas ! that there fhould be fo much pride yet in an heart, which we would think humbled as low as Hell ! That it fhould profefs it felf to deferve a thoufand damnations, and yet quarrel with God, for not being quick in a prefent expedition of mercy ! Thou art too

With what faith haft thou prayed ?

Haft thou not called home thy prayers ?

quick

quick with God. Judge how these answer one the other: O Lord, I do not deserve the least mercy, I deserve never to find mercy; and yet if the Lord doth not presently shew me mercy, I will not seek unto him any more. As you must get humbled hearts, so you must get humble hearts; *He hears the desires of the humble.* Your Prayers must be patient, as well as fervent: Mercy, pardoning mercy, is worth the waiting for: It is the most excellent of mercies, and most sure to the patient Petitioner; *Psal.* 40. 1. *I waited patiently for the Lord, and he inclined unto me, and heard my cry. Blessed are all that wait for it,* *Isa.* 30. 18.

Reasons on Gods part.
God suspends mercy.
To give us some taste what it is to provoke him.

Or there may be *Reasons on Gods part*, why he doth a while suspend or hold up the demonstration of his mercy to a troubled soul and seeking. 1. *To give us some taste, what it is to provoke him, and sin against him.* Jer. 2. 19. *Thine own wickedness shall correct thee, and thy back-slidings shall reprove thee: know therefore, and see, that it is an evil and a bitter thing, that thou hast forsaken the Lord thy God.* As we have had years to bath our selves in the delights of sin, so we must have some minutes to taste the proper fruits, the bitterness of sin: *Thou wouldst not believe the Gall and the Wormwood,* &c. *Lam.* 3.

To alienate our affections from sin.

2. *To alienate or work off our affections wholly from sin;* which now is so deadly a sting, so smart a wound, so noisome a prison, which fills us with such horrible terrours, and costs us almost our lives to obtain pardon and mercy: Thou wouldst not easily part with sin. Who would love sin any more, which 1. raiseth so great terrours, 2. utterly depriveth of mercy, 3. or hinders it, and makes it flow to answer. 3. *To abase us more in our own eyes,*

To abase us the more in our own eyes, that we may exalt his mercy.

that so his mercy may exalt us, and we may exalt his mercy; to value the excellency of mercy, to confess our unworthiness of mercy, to enlarge our desires of mercy. 4. *Nay, not onely*

That we may retain his mercy.

to exalt his mercy, but retain his mercy; not easily forfeit the excellency and sweetness of mercy, by any future sinning. The Church which had much adoe to find Christ, she then caught him, and would not let him go. The pardoning mercies of God ordinarily yield us most sweetness, and abide in their strength with us, after deepest humiliations, and difficultest fruitions of them. 5. *Perhaps the Lord will make thee a great Instance of mercy, and a great Instrument to comfort others;* and therefore

To make us an Instance of mercy, and Instrument of comfort.

suffereth

suffereth thee to lie a long time in darknefs and filence, and at length will relieve thee.

Ob, ect. Yea, but how shall *a troubled foul be supported in the interims, until mercy,* pardoning mercy *doth come,* and prayers therein be anfwered fully. *Sol* I anfwer to this alfo; 1. *If thou canft not have comfort to feed on, yet thou haft duty to work on:* Every Chriftian may either find it an Autumn to gather fruit, or elfe a Spring to fet it. It is a great mercy that thou art at the gates of Mercy; it is a great mercy, 1. to enjoy, 2. to beg, 3. to wait for mercy; a comfort, to have fuch an heart to come fo near to mercy; thou haft a time to fearch thy heart more, and to review thy eftate, and to perufe thy prayers, to mend and continue all. All which are but thy improvements in grace, and will eventually prove the enlargements of thy mercy and peace. No man can make a better progrefs in his repentance, but he doth thereby prepare for the greater, for the fweeter, for the longer mercies. 2. *Though you have not experience to fupport you, yet you have faith.* It is written, and fealed, though not delivered as yet, Whofoever doth truly repent, (mourn for fin, forfake it, endeavour to walk with God, &c.) though he have not the joy of his pardon in his confcience, yet he hath the affurance of his pardon in the promife. Now Gods Word fhould fupport us as much as Gods Teftimony; his Word fhould be as good to our faith, as his Teftimony is fweet to our fenfe and feeling. 3. *The dawnings of pardoning mercy* (which are rifing upon you) *may alfo fupport you :* Though you cannot read your Pardon under the Broad Seal, yet you may find it paffing the Privy Seal. For 1. Upon your humble praying for pardoning mercy, you do feel your confciences more quieted and fetled and revived with better confidence and expectation of mercy. 2. You find your hearts more enflamingly refolved, that you will never give over; you will now follow on to know the Lord and his mercies. It was a fign (anciently) that *God regarded prayers, when fire came down upon the facrifice,* as 1 *Kin.* 18. 24. 2 *Chro.* 7.1. fo is it a fingular argument that God accepts of your prayers for mercy or grace, when upon your prayers he doth enlarge and enliven you more earneftly to feek him in thofe kinds. If God doth himfelf hold up thy fuit, he will not long hold off his anfwer; when we will have no Nay, then, *Be it unto thee as thou wilt. If he prepare thine heart, he will at length incline his ear.*

And

[Side notes:] How shall one be supported in the interim? If thou haft not comfort, look to duty. Though thou haft not experience, yet thou haft faith. The dawnings of pardoning mercy may support.

And fell on his neck, and kissed him.] You have seen already, the *Eyes* of Mercy to espie a returning Penitent, and the *Feet* of Mercy, its speedy pace to meet a returning Penitent, *the Father ran*; and of the *Bowels* of Mercy, *He had compassion on him.* In all which, we have discovered that singular readiness which is in God to shew mercy to a true Penitent. Now there yet remain, 1. The *Arms of Mercy*, Amplexus misericordiarum, [*And he fell on his neck.*] 2. The *Sealings of all this mercy*, though not verbally, yet most significantly expressed towards the returning Prodigal, [*and kissed him.*] What they say of *Scire*, that though we do know, yet this satisfies us not, unless another doth know that we do know; the same is true of Love and Mercy; though we have loving affections and mercifull intentions towards any, yet this is not enough to the party, unless he be made to know the same. Therefore here are singular expressions, as well as admirable intentions; the Box of Ointment is opened; *Joseph* cannot contain himself, but cries out, *I am Joseph:* The Father of the Prodigal doth forgive and accept of him, and testifies all this, by falling on his neck and kissing of him. There be divers Kisses: Not to speak of the *Kiss of Subjection and Reverence*, which *David* calls for, *Psal.*2.12. Nor of the Kiss of *Incivility and Filthiness*, the *whorish kiss*, of which *Salomon* speaks, *Prov.*17.13. Nor of the Kiss of *Falshood and Treachery*, *Judas-kiss*, Matth. 26. 49. Nor of the Kiss of *Courtesie*, common to all friends, the Heathens used it, as *Xenophon* and *Herodotus* relate: Nor of the Kiss of *Charity*, used among the primitive Christians, especially before the Lords Supper. The Kiss in the Text is a Kiss of *Mercifull Affection*; and it is given unto the Prodigal by his Father, *in signum Reconciliationis*, that He and his Father were now friends, and in a state of love and kindnefs: *In signum Pacis*, to take off all fears and doubts, all was exceeding well; and *in signum Latitiæ*, to intimate unto him, what a welcome child he now was. His Father was not more grieved at his sinfull departure, but he is now much more gladded at his penitential return.

Nisi te scire hoc sciat alter.

Doct. God is not onely reconciled, but manifests himself so to be unto the Penitent.

The proper Observation from this I conjecture is, *That God is pleased, not onely to be reconciled, but also to manifest and declare himself as one reconciled to penitent people.* Joh.14.21. *I will love him, and manifest my self unto him.* Rev. 3.20. *If any man hear my voice, and open the door, I will come in to him, and will sup with him,*

and

and he with me. Rev. 2.17. *To him that overcometh will I give to eat of the hidden Manna: and I will give him a white Stone, and in the Stone a new name written, which no man knoweth, saving he that receiveth it.* Rom. 5. 5. *The love of God is shed abroad in our hearts by the holy Ghost which is given unto us.* This is a Proposition of deep consequence, and also of some difficulty, and therefore must be the more warily opened and attended. For the sense and meaning of it premise these particulars:

Something premised.

1. *That Gods reconciled favour is a thing demonstrable to a fitted soul*; (.i.) it is not besides the nature of Divine favour, to open it self so that it may be apprehended, no more then it is against the nature of Light, to reveal it self. Nor is it beyond the capacity and proportion of a penitential soul to be cognoscitive, (i.) to be able to look on, and know Divine favour. In *Universali*, the Papists and others do grant, as, That God was in Christ reconciling the world to himself: but more then this, I affirm in particulars, There is not only a Notional knowledge in the general, but there may be an Experimental knowledg in particular of Divine favour. *By this*, saith David, *I know thou favourest me.* And S. *Paul* of Christ, *Who loved me.* God hath actually manifested his love and favour to his people of old; *Son, be of good comfort, thy sins are forgiven thee*, Mat. 9. And Rom. 8. *Paul* had it, and all the Saints had it: And he doth manifest it, and will manifest it to all true penitents. But then,

Gods R. conciled favour is demonstrable to a fitted soul.

2. There is a double manifestation of his favour; One is *Natural*, and this is when God doth imprint such qualities on the soul, which are the sole fruits of a reconciled Love, as when he bestowes on it the sanctifying graces of his Spirit; Another is *Formal*, wherein he doth evidently make over the goodness of his Love, (i.) make us directly to know that he doth love us, and is reconciled unto us: which is done two wayes, either, 1. *By the Testimony of the Word* apprehended by faith; 2. *By the Testimony of his Spirit*, causing in us an express evidence and sense of Gods love, as a witness, and as a seal. Now one of these wayes God is pleased to manifest his reconciled favour, or to evidence it unto the penitential soul, and sometimes both.

A double Manifestation of his favour. Naturall. Formall.

3. *The time which God taketh to declare or make known* (in a more formal way of evidence) *his reconciled love unto the penitential soul*, is not *necessary* and *determinate*, but *arbitrary* and

The time of this manifestation is arbitrary

and *free*. It is not reſtrained to the very birth or hour of our Converſion, nor limitted to any one part of time after it more then an other. But God is pleaſed differently to make himſelf known, and his loving favour known. *Lydia* partaked of Joy as ſoon as ſhe partaked of Grace; but with other Chriſtians it may be, perhaps, as with *Simeon*, that their eyes do not ſee their Salvation till near their death in the latter end.

The meaſure of Gods Diſ-penſation of it is very different.
4. The *meaſure of Gods diſpenſation in this particular, is alſo very different and various:* Every Penitent hath not one and the ſame degree that another hath; and he who hath moſt of it in evidence, hath it but mixt and imperfect. A Declaration there is to every penitent ſoul that God loves it, but not equall, nor abſolute.

This Declaration is ſeparable at leaſt in the ſence of it.
5. *This Declaration of Divine Love, though it be very-comfortable, yet it is very ſeparable, eſpecially in the ſenſe and feeling of it:* For it is (for the duration of it) an effect of meer favour, which is let out *ad Bene placitum* only, and it is not an eſſential to the Chriſtian condition, therefore it may go off. So that this is the ſum of the Propoſition, That Gods reconciled favour is a thing which may be known, and God is pleaſed to make it known to all penitents either Naturally or Formally, at ſome time or other, in ſome meaſure or other, ſo long as he himſelf ſhall judge beſt.

Reaſons of it. Gods Promiſe is to make known his love to them.
The Reaſons whereof are theſe: 1. *His promiſe is not only to love his people, but likewiſe to make known his love to them*; not only the affection, but the declaration of it is in promiſe, *Ezek*. 34. 30. *They ſhall know that I the Lord their God am with them, and that they, even the houſe of Iſrael, are my people, ſaith the Lord God.*

It is the thing which Gods people deſire.
2. *It is the thing which the penitential people of God do exceedingly crave and deſire.* Pſal. 4. 6. *Lord lift up the light of thy Countenance upon me.* Pſal. 17. 7. *Shew thy marvellous loving kindneſs.* Pſal. 106. 4. *Remember me, O Lord, with the favour thou beareſt unto thy people, O viſit me with thy ſalvation.* Pſal. 119. 132. *Look upon me, and be merciful unto me, as thou uſeſt to do unto thoſe that love thy Name.* Cant. 1. 2. *Let him kiſs me with the kiſſes of his mouth, for thy love is better then Wine.* Now I pray conſider two things, that, 1. The prayers which God commands his people to make. 2. The things which God promiſes to grant: where promiſes are

of the Returning Prodigal.

are made, and commands are made, there if prayers be made, God will fulfil them. The manifestation of Gods favour is that which the people of God are commanded to seek; (*Seek ye my face*, Pſal. 27. 8.) and God hath promiſed to declare his loving favour to them, and therefore if they ſeek it, he will.   3. *It is the thing which they do exceedingly need:* Though not ſimply to their *eſſe*, yet reſpectively to their *Bene eſſe*. *The loving kindneſs of God it is their life*, and it is the *Joy of their ſalvation*, and it is their reviving, it is the binding up of their wounds, the ſetling of their fears, the ſtrength of their ſoul, the peace of their conſcience, the anchor of their ſhip, the Ark of reſt. *It is the thing which they Need.*

4. *The Lord will grant unto his people, even in this life, the firſt fruits of their glorious life*: though hereafter they ſhall ſee him *face to face*, yet here they ſhall *know him as through a Glaſs*; here they ſhall taſt how good he is, that they may more earneſtly look after a full and Beatifical fruition of him. *God will give his people here the firſt fruits of a Glorious life.*

5. And likewiſe *to let them know the difference twixt a ſinful and penitent courſe;* in the one they ſhall know how juſt he is in wrath, to hate, and puniſh ſin; in the other how gracious, and merciful he is, to comfort, and revive a penitent.   6. Yea, yet more, he doth declare his reconciled favour to them that they likewiſe *may diſtinguiſh twixt theſe poor, falſe, miſerable jollities, and pleaſures, which they had by ſin;* and twixt *thoſe ſoul reviving tranſcendently affecting comforts, unſpeakeable joies, unconceivable peace which ariſe to them, upon the knowledg of God reconciled to them in and through Chriſt*: That there is not that juice, that ſupport, that delight, that ſingularity of contentment in any way, as in a good way; nor the like life and ſpirit to be drawn from any ſinful or earthly ſprings, as from the goodneſs and kindneſs of his loving favour: that a God reconciled is the only happineſs of the ſoul. *To let them know the difference twixt a ſinful and penitential courſe. To diſtinguiſh twixt the pleaſures of ſin and the joy of the Holy Ghoſt.*

Doth the Lord manifeſt unto penitential perſons his reconciled favour? Then you who take your ſelves to be converts and penitents, *ſatisfie not your ſelves, be not contented until you find the Seals and tokens of Gods favour*. You have (I know) his Word and Bond for your reconciliation, and your condition really is the ſtate of reconciliation; you do love the Lord, and the Lord doth love you: But yet advance ſomwhat farther, ſtrive to find the kiſſes, the gracious expreſſions and evidences from God, that he is reconciled unto you.   *Uſe. Satisfy not your ſelves without the ſeales of Gods favour.*

B b 2   The

Motives.

The differences twixt God and you have been very great.

The Motives to excite you hereto, are many and forcible. 1. *The differences twixt God and you have been very great and high,* such as have much provoked the Lord; and they have been of long continuance, such as have deserved ten thousand Hells: Now why will you not strive to make it out of doubt that God hath pardoned you, and is in Christ graciously reconciled unto you? If there have been differences betwixt us and a man of place, we will use all the means to take up the controversie, and get a releafe of all things; how much more having to do with God?

Reconciled love is worth the suing out.

2. *This Reconciled Love is worth the suing out*: No love like it; partly, *because it doth so immediately concern the soul of a Christian.* It is a love which accepts of a sinner, and makes the sinner accepted; it is more to him then the Princes pardon to a Traitor: Indeed, it is his passing from death to eternal Life. What should become of a sinner, if the Lord were not reconciled to him? If the Lord be his enemy and holds distance, the soul can never stand before him in Judgment: Farewel Peace, farewel Heaven without it. Partly, because it is *the choicest & chiefest Love* that God doth bestow: There is no one whom he doth imbrace with the love of friendship and reconciliation, but Elect persons, and such as he intends for Glory. Therefore this Love is called, *the ancient Love, great Love, Eph.* 2. and the *free Love,* and the *Love of his chosen,* and a *Love* which is sure, and a *Love* which *neither Powers, nor principalities, nor world, nor life, nor death, nor things present, nor things to come, can extirpate or abolish.* You may partake of his common Love, and the common effects of that Love, yet you may be his very enemies, and vessels of wrath. Partly, because *it frees you from the sorest fears, and sharpest torments.* You know that there are no troubles like those in Conscience, nor fears like those concerning our eternal Conditions. What! if I be one whom the Lord hates? what if I should dye, and then be damned? what if I be not in favour with the Lord? what if such or such a sin be not yet pardoned? Now the evidence that God is reconciled to you, doth silence these fears, and eases the conscience of these tormenting suspicions: *The Lord is my light* (said David, Psal. 27. 1.) *whom shall I fear?* And, *I will lay me down in peace,* Psa. 4. 8.

It comforts the soul in any condition.

3. *It is one of the most admirable comforters of the soul in any condition. If your condition be prosperous,* why, the assurance that God is reconciled unto you, makes all your outward comforts the more

com-

of the Returning Prodigal.

comfortable unto you: It is like health to a good complexion, which sprinkles it over, and inamels the face with a fair beauty; or like the light to colour, which unveils and difclofeth all their art ; or like the dew to the herbs, which makes them the more fragrant ; when a man can fay, I have all things, and God is reconciled to me too ; I have fuch a Lordſhip, and the King is my friend too; fuch honours, friends, eſtate, and the Lord hath accepted of me too, and I know that all is pardoned ; is not this a comfort, when all is pleaſant on earth, and all is right in heaven : whereas, if the Lord be not reconciled to a man, what avails all the world ? *If your conditions be calamitous,* yet the aſſurance that God is reconciled to you, is an admirable cordial. You read in *Mat.9.2. Of a man ſick with a dead Palſey,* (a difeafe which exceedingly dejects the fpirits;)Chriſt comes unto him, and gives him a Cordial ; what was it, think you ? why this, *Son be of good comfort, thy ſins are forgiven thee.* You will think this an improper comfort to a man in fuch a difeafe, but it was not ; the aſſurance that our fins are pardoned, and that God is reconciled, revives, and cheers up the heart, nothing more. So S. *Paul* ſpeaks of *Tribulation, Diſtreſs, Perſecution, Famine, Nakedneſs, Peril, Sword,* Yea, *of Death it ſelf,* Rom. 8. 35, 36. and addeth. *v.* 37. *In all theſe things we are more then conquerours* : he made light of them all, they were as nothing. How ſo? whence came this? why! from aſſurance of Gods love; for (faith he, *v.* 38, 39.) *I am perſwaded, that neither death nor life, nor any Creature ſhall be able to ſeparate us from the love of God, which is in Chriſt Jeſus our Lord. If your condition be pious,* this evidence is the main thing which makes it moſt comfortable ; all the habits of graces are no actual comforts, unleſs they become evident ; and fo far do they comfort you, as they are true and real evidences of Gods reconciled love and favour unto you.

4. *It will be an unſpeakable ſtay unto you in death* ; you know the day of death will ſhortly overtake every one of us: Here is no abiding City ; and what temptations may befall us then, we cannot aſſure our felves ; we know not what Satan or confcience may raiſe up againſt us : When our fouls are ready to depart, then either to be determinate ; God is not yet reconciled to me , (that juſt God , before whom I muſt immediately appear to anſwer, and make accounts ;) or to be indeterminate ; It may be, I am

It will be a ſtay in Death.

am reconciled, it may be I am not, I never had any solid evidence of it; how distracting a thing is this, that the soul, one minute hopes the best, and presently, it doubts the worst? Now I think I shall go to Heaven; and by and by, I fear left I shall be cast into Hell: But if you had obtained to an evidence of Gods reconciled favour unto you, that the Lord had pardoned all the sins of your life, and had graciously accepted of you in Christ, though death itself appears, you would not much be moved. *I know that my redeemer lives,* said *Job* c. 19. And *we know, that if our earthly house be dissolved, we have a building of God, an house eternal in the heavens,* (saith the Apostle) 2 *Cor.* 5. 1.

1: Is the most Quickning in duty.

5. It *is of all the most quickning and forwarding thing to the heart, for the performance of all sorts of holy duties*: We oftentimes complain, what dull and slow hearts we have *to Prayer*; were we more assured that God is reconciled to us, we should quickly find hearts more affected, and more enlarged for Prayer; though we be afraid, and flye from an angry and just God, yet we would hye in, and speed unto a reconciled, and gracious God. Psal. 63. 1. *Thou art my God*; (here he discerns that whereof we speak. *sc.* God reconciled;) and then it followes, *early will I seek unto thee*. Again, we wonder at our liftnesses of our spirits *to the word*, that we do not mind it, long after it, affect it more; were you more assured of Gods love, being more affected with him, we should certainly grow more affected with his word. They, in 1 Pet. 2. 2. must *desire the sincere Milk of the Word, as new born Babes* (.i.) with much eagerness, and delightfulness; but how might this apprehension be wrought in them. Why! v. 3. *If so be, that you have tasted, that the Lord is gracious,* q. d. a taft (an experience, an assurance) that God is your gracious God, that is it which will whet an edge and appetite after the word; I say no more but this, you will serve the Lord with more willing hearts, and cheerful, then ever you did in all your lives, if so be you could get assurance that God is reconciled.

It makes us Confident in evill times.

6. *It makes your hearts most confident on God in evil times*; when afflictions are upon you, when dangers arise, when distractions are in the world, when any near calamity breaks in; these are like Land-floods, which carry away all, or like the deluge in *Noah*'s time, which exceeded all the mountains, so do these drown all the vain hopes, and confidences of evil men, that are not reconciled

Of the Returning Prodigal.

conciled to God; they know not in the world what to do, they have no heart to go in unto God, for their consciences now tell them plainly, that they are in the estate of enmity, and wrath. But even now, though the foundations of the earth be shaken, the assured person, who knows God is reconciled to him, knows also that his foundation of love stands sure and firm, and through all, does he make his addrefs unto the God of his mercies, and shall find acceptance with him.

7. Lastly, *It is that which will wonderfully inlarge your gra-* | It will wonderfully inlarge our Graces.
ces; the Apostle delivers it in the general, that the *knowledge of the love of Christ*, is a means by which we come to be *filled with all the fulness of God.* Eph. 3. 19. See but *Luke* 7. 38. You shall find *that much was there forgiven*; the woman, though a great sinner, was gracioufly reconciled; what follows on this, *she loved much, she wept much*, she humbled her self much, her affections to Christ; her tears for her sins, her humility of spirit, all of them are set down as exemplary copies; this is it, which will make the *light of our Moon, to be as the light of the Sun; and our light of the Sun, as the light of seven dayes.*

You may perhaps reply unto me, this evidence that God is reconciled to us (which is so excellent in it self, and produces such effects) were a very heaven upon earth, if we could attain unto it. But, *what means should we use, that we may at length enjoy it*: | Means to attain it.
I conjecture thus, that the means of obtaining it, are twofold, Internal, External. The Internal means are three, *viz.* Conscience, the Spirit of God, and Faith; for all these have in them a reflexive, and an evidencing virtue or power. | Internal means

1. *Then, you must get your consciences renewed*: Conscience, | Get your Consciences renewed.
absolutely considered, hath a reflexing power, it can look on our natural acts and conditions; but it must be conscience renewed, which must testifie of the spiritual estate, and that God is reconciled to you. The testimony or evidence of conscience renewed, is (you know) syllogistical, and nothing else but the eccho of the word, *v.g.* whosoever truly repents of sin, the Lord is reconciled to him; this is the proposition of the word, as you may read in *Hos.* 14. 1, 2, 3. They are described, as acting the parts of true penitents; and then v. 4. *I will love them freely*: So Jer. 21. 19. Ephraim *is turned*, and repents, and then v. 20. Ephraim *is a dear child, and a pleasant Son*; he is earnestly remembred, and sure mercy is his;

(.i.) *Ephraim*

(.i.) *Ephraim* is reconciled, and dearly loved of God. Here renewed conscience assumes, But I do unfainedly repent, I do truly mourn, and forsake sin; and now with assurance, it concludes by way of evidence and testimony, Therefore the Lord is reconciled unto me, he doth freely and surely love me. *Obj.* But it is objected, Conscience may be deceived; it may assume without ground, and so deludingly conclude the matter. *Sol.* I grant that conscience may be erronious in its grounds, but conscience as renewed, and concluding as a renewed conscience, will not delude you, nor err; for conscience renewed, concludes not upon an empty imagination, but upon a solid examination of the heart and life. It finds that integrity in the heart, and that uprightnes in ordering the life, which doth answer the word of God; And reading that the *Lord loves the upright, and that he will shew his salvation to him that orders his conversation aright* : Now upon search, finding this habitual and actual uprightnes, it concludes, Surely I am the person whom the Lord loves, and to whom he is reconciled.

Get the spirit of God.

2. *You must get the spirit of God :* The Apostle in *Rom.* 5.5. saith, that the *love of God is shed abroad in our hearts by the holy Ghost* ; so that if ever you would know the love of God unto you, you must have the spirit of God : the spirit of God hath many operations given unto him, as that he *inlightens* the mind, *humbles* the heart, *sanctifies* it, and then that he *sealeth* and *comforteth* it; and as these effects, so the order of them is observable ; he doth not first of all seal or assure, and then inlighten, and then sanctifie, and then humble ; but he first inlightens, humbles, sanctifies and converts the soul, and then assures and comforts it: Peruse *Rom.* 8. you shall find, that *the witnefs of the spirit that we are the children of God,* v. 16. *followes the spirit of bondage, and of adoption, and of supplication,* v. 15. *and the quickning of the spirit,* v. 11. *and a leading of the spirit,* v. 14. So that if ever you would be assured that the Lord is reconciled to you, you must get his spirit convincing, humbling, renewing, and leading you ; so much evidence as you have of holines, so much assurance you may build on of Gods reconciled favour unto you. *Obj.* But here also it is objected, we may *thus be cozened with Enthusiasms*, taking a fond dream and delusion, for a witnessing or testimony of Gods spirit. *Sol.* I answer, this is a fond and ridiculous exception ; for the spirit of God (as S. *Ambrose* speaks) can neither deceive, nor be deceived.

The

of the Returning Prodigal.

The sealing or assuring testimony of Gods Spirit, is never *Nudum* nor *Nudati m testimonium*; but as it is a seal to a deed drawn, (I mean an heart first written over with renewing graces;) so in the sealing, it alwayes produceth more tender and lively operations of holiness, in all good works.

3. Lastly, If you would get assurance of Gods love reconciled unto your souls, *you must get Faith*. Faith is the eye, by which we look on God, and it is that light, by which we see God looking on us: How did Simeon *see Christ* to be his *Saviour?* Or *Paul know that Christ loved him*, but by *Faith?* There are two wayes by which Faith can and will bring the soul to see or know God reconciled unto it: One is, *by and in Christ*; there is no seeing of a reconciled God, but in a Mediator, and therefore Christ is called so often our Peace, our Atonement, our Reconciler: The other is, *by and through the Promises*, which is therefore called the Covenant of Grace; *q.d.* sets forth, and presents God unto us, as graciously reconciled. If you have so much faith as will bring you to Christ, to know him, to embrace and accept of him, to rely on him, you may with safest confidence conclude and be perswaded, that God is your reconciled God: *For God was in Christ reconciling the world to himself.* {Get Faith.}

2. The *external means* of obtaining assurance are: 1. *Conscionable and diligent application of our selves to the Word.* The word of God is both the instrument of our *Regeneration*, and of our *Consolation*; and is not only productive of faith, as it is an adherence, but able also to produce it, as it is an evidence: and therefore, as you read that faith in acceptance depends on the word, *Rom.* 10. 17. so we read that faith in assurance flowes likewise from it. 1 Joh. 5. 13. *These things have I written unto you that believe on the Name of the Son of God, that ye may know that ye have eternal life.* And as the Word is oftentimes called a Word of Faith, so it is sometimes called a Lip of Peace. *Isa.* 57. 19. *q.* it produceth an assurance from which that peace doth flow. {External means. Diligent Application of our selves to the Word.}

2. *And to the Sacrament.* The Sacrament hath, I confess, many ends; and it is (as the Word of God is) an Organ or Instrument of the Divine spirit, for much good unto believing souls. Among the rest, it hath a singular virtue to breed assurance of Gods love, and therefore it is called, a *Seal* in *Ro.* 4. 11. In it Christ Jesus (in whom God is reconciled) is most distinctly represented in his Passion, as making peace by his blood for our souls: In it the same Christ Jesus is {To the Sacrament.}

particularly offered and applyed unto us, with all the benefits and efficacies of his person: *Take, eat, this is my body which was given for you,* 1 Cor. 11.24. As if God should say, As surely as I give thee this bread and wine, so I give thee my Son, and the purchase of his death, even reconciliation, and pardon, and mercy. A believing celebration of the Sacrament is a most admirable means to remove our doubts, and to establish our hearts with an assurance that God is reconciled unto us. 3. *Fervent and patient Prayer*; prizing the favour of God, as *David* did, Psal.63.3. Hungring and thirsting after it, as he hid, *Psal.*106.4,5. And thus continuing to seek with diligence, being withall tenderly careful in our hearts and wayes to please the Lord; we shall have the desires of our Souls crowned with the testimonies of his love here, and with the full glory of his face, and favour hereafter.

Fervent and patient Prayer.

LUKE 15. 21, 22, 23.

21. *And the Son said unto him, Father, I have sinned against heaven, and in thy sight, and am no more worthy to be called thy Son.*

22. *But the Father said to his servants, Bring forth the best Robe, and put it on him, and put a Ring on his hand, and Shoes on his feet.*

23. *And bring hither the fatted calf, and kill it, and let us eat, and be merry.*

These words contain in them. 1. *The real acting of a penitential intention:* The matter whereof, in his humble and sad confession, I have insisted on already, when I touched on *v.*18,19. Now I shall observe a little more from the circumstance and manner of it. 2. *The strange alteration of his condition:* The heart of man never alters from sin to its prejudice; the best courses ever draw after them, the best comforts. While he was a prodigal, he had neither bread to eat, nor Rags to cloath him, nor house to lodg him, much less Jewels to adorn him, and feasts to entertain him: But now he becomes a penitent, here is a Father to admit him into a house, to put the best Robe on his back, and the Ring on his finger, and Shoes on his feet, and likewise to provide meat, even the choicest for his belly. Before I touch on these, distinctly and particularly, there are some Propositions, which I will briefly touch on, *v.g.* Doct. *That*

of the Returning Prodigal.

Doct. *That, no not the kindest expressions of mercy do silence a truly penitential heart, from an humble confession of sin* ; Kindest mercies draw out humblest confessions : The Father pities, meets, embraces, kisseth this penitential Prodigal. What doth he ? rise up and slight all that hath been evil ? Oh no ! mercy melts him down, and he confesseth with tears, *Father I have sinned,*&c. *q.d.* What is this, that thou shouldst so easily, so freely, so mercifully behold so sinful, so unworthy a wretch as I have been ? As *David*, when God declared unto him the intentions of his further mercies, for him and his posterity : He sate before the Lord and said, *Who am I, O Lord God ? and what is my house that thou hast brought me hitherto ?* So is it with the true penitent, upon the Declaration of pardoning and accepting mercy. Now, O Lord God, who am I ? I, who have done so wickedly, yet to be remembred so graciously ? The same you find in *Paul*, who, though he received a testimony of his pardon and acceptance, by a messenger graciously dispatched from Jesus Christ himself, *Acts* 9.17. Yet he doth most frequently, and humbly acknowledg and confess the kinds and greatness of his former transgressions.

The kindest expressions of mercy, do not hinder an humble confession of sin.

There is (for the time) a twofold Confession. 1. *Antecedent*, which is that humbling way, which God designs for the assecution of mercy. See *Prov.* 28.13. & 1 *Jo.* 1.9. To make us indite, and condemn our selves, that he may acquit and pardon us. 2. *Consequent*; which is that judging, and self-condemning way, after mercy is obtained : The sight of mercy breeds four notable effects in a true penitent ; 1. *Much Admiration,* (Oh, that God should look on me!) 2. *Much Detestation,* (Oh, that God should ever pardon me !) 3. *More contrition,* (Oh, that I should sin against such a God;) 4. *More Confession*; (I have sinned, and done very foolishly to sin against a God much in mercy.)

There is a twofold Confession. Antecedent. Consequent.

2. *This consequent confession*, which followes the expressions or testimonies of pardoning mercy *hath these qualities.* 1. *It is an acknowledging of sin, with more compunction of spirit* : Sight of pardon doth not only open our lips, but our eyes, and fetcheth forth not only words but tears ; the heart doth break out , when mercy breaks forth : The heart never confesseth sin with more filial grief, then when it apprehends sin, much sin discharged with a paternal love : the wind breaks the clouds, but the Sun melts them most into showers, so &c. 2. It is an acknowledging of sin,

Consequent confession hath these qualities. It is an acknowledgment of sin, with more compunction.

C c 2

With more indignation. sin, *with more indignation* : The greater mercy makes a penitent to be the sharper Judg; the more God is now pleased with him, the more is he displeased with himself, for sinning against him. When *God remembred his Covenant,* Ezek. 16. 60. then did the penitential Israelites *remember their wayes with shame.* v.61. And when he made it known to them, *that he was pacifyed towards them, then were they confounded, and never opened their mouths more,* v. 63. 3. It is an acknowledging of sin *with more* *With more aggravation.* *aggravation*: Servile confessions are usually more deceitful and partial; as *Adam* did acknowledg his sin, but puts it on *Eve*; no confessions are so free and full, as such which arise from the apprehension of mercies. *David* got his pardon for a great transgression; but then how exact is he in the distinct accusation of himself, and humble acknowledgment of his sin, in all the articles and circumstances of it? *Psal.* 51. 4. It is an acknowledgment of *With more detestation.* sin, *with more detestation.* Evidence of pardon produceth two effects: One is, *more ardent affection of love to God*; Another is (which necessarily followes) *a deeper hatred of sin,* which opposed so gracious a goodness. All that good which God mentions in the Covenant, *Ezek.* 36. 25. to the end of *v.* 30. produced a better remembrance of former evils, and also a deeper loathing of themselves for their iniquities, *v.* 31. As *Job* upon Gods appearing to him, and conferring with him, *now abhors himself in dust and ashes:* So the penitent upon the manifestation of divine favour, doth more acknowledg his vileness, judg his follies, and abhor his iniquities; it is ever true, that the greatest mercies set the heart at greatest distance with sin.

But now it is demanded; Why should the expressions of mercy elicite confession of sin, if it be pardoned? why any more con-
Reasons of it. Piety in man is not opposite, but subordinate to pity in God. fession? Reasons though hereof be many. 1. *Piety in man is not opposite, but only subordinate to Pity in God.* Divine love doth not destroy, but increase duty: Assurance followes the habits, and alwayes advances the acts of grace: As it is our duty to seek our pardon by confession, so also to carry away the same with continued confessions; confession of sin is not a transient, but a constant duty; As the Mathematicians speak of a Line, That it is not *punctum,* but *fluxus punctorum*; so I say of any duty, It is not one indivisible act only, but an act repeated: to believe is a duty, in which one act only is not enough, for I must still keep my
eye

eye upon Chrift. So to confefs fin, is a duty not done altogether, becaufe once done; but ftill to be done, becaufe a duty to be done: though God be pleafed to forget, yet it is our duty to remember. But fecondly, *By confeffion of fin, after remiffion and teftimony,* [margin: Mercy is now acknowledged to be mercy.] *mercy is now acknowledged to be mercy:* What a man may fpeak in ftraights is one thing, what in free circumftances, when *extra aleam,* is another. Many a man cryes out for mercy, who perhaps fcarce will give mercy all the glory afterward. But when we are pardoned, and yet confefs fin, we do really profefs, That it was not Worthinefs in us, but only Goodnefs in God, that pardoned. No man can more fully give the glory of his pardon to fole mercy, then he who doth confefs his fins after mercy: What is this confeffion of fin, but as if the perfon fhould fay, O Lord, to me, indeed, nothing did belong but fhame and confufion; for I, for my part, have thus and thus finned againft thee, and deferved thy wrath, but it was meer mercy that faved and pardoned me? 3. The more pardoning mercy God fhews, *The more humility is thereby wrought in the heart;* [margin: The more pardoning mercy, the more Humility] for who can behold much pardon, but withal muft know, it was much fin that hath that much pardon? He hath greater caufe of fhame, becaufe all this while a God of fuch mercy hath been offended: So that here is more caufe for the heart to abafe it felf and to confefs its own vilenefs. 4. *Upon gracious remiffion, more, and new grounds of Confeffion do arife:* [margin: New, and more grounds of confeffion do arife] Before I am pardoned, I confefs my fins, becaufe God requires confeffion, and alfo becaufe he doth upon a right confeffion promife Remiffion. When I am pardoned, more reafons of Confeffion are upon mercy, namely, mercy granted, and mercy fealed. O then! have I not more caufe to confefs my finful vilenefs, having tafted of moft unfpeakable goodnefs in the pardon of it?

Doth the penitent perfon humbly confefs his fins after the pardon of them? Why, *let us (if any of us think that we are pardoned) do fo too:* [margin: *Ufe* Upon fenfe of pardon let us do fo.] Tis a truth, that of all things we are moft willing to forget our fins; we have much adoe to keep our thoughts on them in a penitential way (its death almoft to fome men to think on their fins thus) and in cafe if by a little duty we have got the leaft hope of pardon, we ordinarily put thofe fins off from any future folemn Confeffions. This I conceive

ceive ariseth from two causes; the one is the *sensible influence which sin* (often to be thought on) *imprints on the conscience.* After considerations of sin, we have usually most bitterness and trouble, which we willingly would not feel. Another is *an ignorance of the power and use of pardoning mercy*; which as it brings Rest, Peace, so most hearty grief and confession: I will say to men presuming on pardon, and yet failing in an after confession of their sins, 1. *It is suspicious whether ever they had any pardon at all*, or real assurance thereof; forasmuch as they fail in this after effect of confession, which is alwayes the more increased by the greater evidence of divine mercy. 2. *It is suspicious whether they ever truly repented or no*; for as much as true repentance doth incline us to go over and perfect all the acts and branches of Repentance, whereof confession, in a right manner performed, is not the least.

Such as fail in after confession. It is suspicious whether ever they had any Pardon at all. Or whether they ever truly repanted or no.

But for our parts, if any of us upon a penitential course have been so far blessed as to see the face of God with peace, and have found any testimony of his pardoning mercy, let us never cease to bless that mercy, and with mournful and self-judging hearts to iterate and continue our confession of the sins for which we have found mercy.

Motives to it. We shall hereby the better increase our assurance of mercy.

Motives hereunto are these, 1. *We shall hereby the better prolong and increase our assurance of divine mercy:* I conjecture that you shall in your experience find this truth, *viz.* That assurance lives longest in a believing Eye, an humble Spirit, and in a Soul accustomed to the strict exercise of Repentance: the way to get assurance of pardon, is ever the best way to preserve and inlarge it. 2. *Hereby our Consciences shall most acquit us for the sincerity of our confession:* Antecedent acts do not alwayes yield unto us that solid ground as subsequent acts: As about our outward mercies, after prayers do more denominate the celestial frame then former prayers, because those may be depending on self-love and necessity, but the other springs out of spiritual love and piety, and respects to divine glory. So is it in the business of confession of sin; to confess under the beams of mercy is a better temper then to confess under the strokes of Justice; it argues a more holy Ingenuity to acknowledg and bewail our vileness, being discharged of wrath and punishment, then only to exclaim either upon the Rack, or upon hopes to be taken off.

Our Conscience will hereby acquit us for the sincerity of our Confession.

3. *Hereby*

Of the Returning Prodigal. 199

3. Hereby the frame of the heart is kept more tender against sin, as *Ezra* 9.14. *Should we again break thy Commandments?* Continued sense of sin produceth four singular effects, and with much addition too; *Most cordial Thankfulness, Most tender Fearfulness, Most diligent Fruitfulness, Most careful Tenderness.* The daily judger of his former sins by a penitential confession, he is the man who abounds most with the thankful Lip, the watchful Heart, the fruitful Hand and tender Conscience. Two things make us hardned and careless; *Forgetfulness of Mercies from God, and of Sins against God.* But no more of this Assertion.

The frame of the heart is hereby kept more tender against sin.

There is another implicit Observation from the carriage of the Father to this penitential Prodigal upon his Confession. It is this, As there is nothing in the Sons thoughts and expressions but his Sins, so there is nothing in the Fathers Intentions and expressions but Kindness. The Son he thinks of his sins, intends to leave his sins, and to confess them, and so he doth; The Father he thinks of mercies and compassions, intends to accept and pardon him; and when he comes, he doth not speak a word of his sins, but every expression is mercy, and peace, and kindness; *Fetch the best Robe, put on the Ring, &c.* Whence I conjecture this Proposition is observable;

That God takes no notice of our sins upon our true Repentance, but wholly expresseth himself in love and kindness. There are two Branches of this Assertion; 1. One, *that God takes no notice of former sins upon our true Repentance.* There is a threefold notice of sin in respect of God; 1. *Notitia Intuitiva*; which is his all observing eye of Omniscience, from which nothing can be hid; but every Creature, and operation of the Creature, whether open or secret, is visible and manifest unto God: that distinction of known and unknown, secret and open, hath no place in God, to whose eye all things are naked. In this respect the former sins of a penitent fall within Gods notice; for the goodness of Divine Mercy doth not blind-fold the eye of Divine Omniscience. 2. *Notitia Charitativa*; which is a notice of sins, as a kind Creditor takes notice of Debts owing unto him, and set down in his book, his eye is on them, and his Pen also to cross and dash them out. And in this respect also God takes notice of former sins, namely, so as out of rich love, and

Doct. 2.
God takes no notice of our sins upon Repentance, but expresseth himself wholly in love and kindness.

God takes no notice of former sins.
There is, *Notitia Intuitiva.*

Notitia Charitativa.

and gracious favour to crofs and forgive them: unlefs we will fondly imagine that God forgives fins by hap-chance, at an adventure, never feeing and confidering what he doth. 3. *Notitia Vindictiva*; which is a Judiciary notice, as a Judge takes notice of the evil facts of a Malefactor to Condemn him, or to trouble and vex him. In this refpect, upon true Repentance, God takes no notice of former fins, (.i.) either *to condemn the penitent perfon for them*, or, *to upbraid him* and difhearten him by cafting them into his difh, or hitting of him in the teeth, as we fpeak Proverbially. Hence thofe phrafes in the Scripture upon fuppofition of Repentance, Jer. 31. 34. *I will forgive their iniquity, and I will remember their fin no more*. Not that Repentance makes God forgetful (for he is not capable of fuch a defect as Oblivion) but that when men ceafe to fin, God will ceafe to argue and fpeak with them after a Judicial manner for their fins. So Ezek. 18. 21. *If the wicked will turn from all his fins that he hath committed*; ver. 22. *All his tranfgreffions which he hath committed, they fhall not be mentioned unto him*; he means, in any harfh, judicial, and cutting way: More fuch phrafes there are, as, that he will cover our fins, caft them into the depths of the fea, and caft them behind his back; and though they be fought for, yet they fhall not be found.

Notitia Vindictiva.

He expreffeth himfelf wholly in love and kindnefs.

The fecond Branch is, that he expreffeth *himfelf wholly in love and kindnefs*; the which is moft evident in *Jer.* 31. 19. when *Ephraim* repented and confeffed his fin, all the expreffions now from God are full of tender Love, *Is Ephraim my dear fon? is he a pleafant child? I do earneftly remember him ftill*, (Ephraim thinks that I have forgotten him, that I regard him not, but there is no fuch matter;) *my bowels are troubled for him, I will furely have mercy on him*. Hof. 14. 2, 3. Ifrael is repenting, and confeffing, and praying, and how doth God anfwer him? See *v.* 4. *I will heal their back-flidings, I will love them freely, for mine anger is turned away from him*. Ver. 5. *I will be as the dew unto Ifrael.*

Diftinguifh Twixt Gods expreffions. And the Penitents Apprehenfions.

Yet here we muft diftinguifh, 1. Twixt *Gods expreffions*, which are alwayes very gracious, gentle, clofing up, comforting and reviving of the penitent. And the *penitents apprehenfions*, which by reafon of feveral principles in him, are fometimes mifplaced and miftaken: God is juft, and he is a finner; he is a penitent

finner,

sinner, and God is merciful: Now whiles the penitent apprehends his Sins only, and not his Repentance; or Gods Justice only, and not his Mercy, that tender gracioufness and loving kindness, is not so acquitted by him in his apprehensions. Not that God is not really tender to him, but that he, through mistake and error, apprehends it not so.

2. Again, you must distinguish *Gods tender love* and kindness as it is confiderable, *in Divine promise, and in Humane sense and feeling*: You can no sooner repent, but God is wholly in termes of tender love, if you will behold his *behaviour towards you in his Promises*: In them indeed you have the Idea, as it were, of his mind and affection; they are the right glasse to behold the face of his mercifulness in; through which, if you look, you shall not find any one harsh word, or look, or intention towards a penitent, but all his thoughts in them are thoughts of peace, and all his words in them are lips of peace. Though the *Samamaritan* poured both *Oile* and *Vinegar* into the wound, yet God, through his promises, pours out only the Oile of gladness. But if you consult with *his sense and feeling* (which is out of the roade of Faith) then indeed this gracious tenderness is not so evident, but we are apt, through incredulous hastiness, and ungrounded mis-judgings, to exclaime with *Zion*, *But my God hath forgotten me*; or with *David*, *He hides away his face from me*: or with *Job*, (it was in the fits of impatience) *He writes bitter things against me*.

Distinguish of Gods love, as it is confiderable in Divine Promises and Humane sense.

3. Thirdly, *You must distinguish of the penitent behaving himself*, either, *ad modum penitentis*, as a penitent, *ad modum peccantis*, as a delinquent. Let him repent and keep on in the wayes of repentance, he shall meet with nothing from God but sweetness of love and mercy; every *step of righteousness is a path of peace and joy*; but if he step aside, if he goes to a by-Lane, he may quickly lose the sight of the City; if the arm or foot slip out of joynt, then indeed there is ache and pain, instead of ease and quiet; so, if a penitent person do what is sinful, he must not think that God will appear in that amiableness; for as God will frown on no man which is in a good way, so will he smile on no man, if found in an evil path.

Distinguish of the behaviour, as a Penitent, or as a Delinquent.

4. Lastly, *You must distinguish of Gods expression of himself*, *and either Satans or our own unbelieving hearts representations*

Distinguish of Gods expressions of himself, and Satans representations of him.

ons of God : Before we repent our own hearts and Satan represent God all in mercy to us, and when we do repent, so far as our hearts are sinful, they are still guileful, and conjoyn with Satan to represent God unto us all in Justice and terror. But a natural and proper representation is one thing, and a preternatural and corrupt representation is another thing. How the dispositions and actions of men may present me in their due and real Entity to a man, is one thing; and how the cunning lies, and artificial devices of an envious enemy may report me, this is another thing. This then is the sense of the assertion, That when any person doth truly repent, God will not only not upbraid, and object unto him his sins, but will graciously pass them over; and for his part, the penitent behaving himself like a penitent, and judging of him aright, according to his nature and promises, shall find all in love, graciousness, and kindness to him and for him.

<small>Reasons of it. Upon true Repentance sin is pardoned.</small> Reasons whereof are these; 1. *Upon true repentance sin is pardoned :* Repent, saith S. *Peter, that your sins may be blotted out,* Acts 3. *And he that forsakes his sin shall find mercy,*Prov. 28. And *Isa.*55.7. *Let the wicked forsake his way, and I will abundantly pardon :* Whence I infer, If sin be pardoned, then there is no voice from heaven to be heard but that of Love and kindness. Indeed while we continue in sin, like *Adam, we hear the voice of God and are afraid ;* for then it is the voice of his wrath and threatnings : but sin being pardoned, wrath is removed, God is reconciled, and his voice now is only the sweet voice of the Gospel ; not the thunders of *Sinai,* but the glad tydings of *Sion :* Therefore, 2. *God hath said, That he will not break the bruised reed,* and takes it ill from any to add afflictions to the afflicted. Now there is no expression more observed by a penitent then Gods. Gods expressions are bruising or raising ; all is for comfort or discomfort, as it comes from God ; the least harshness from him would set back the penitent into an overwhelming multitude of terrors, fears, and distractions, and discouragements ; the which the Lord likes not, having made the soul fit for his mercies. 3. *Comfort is the proper expression for the penitent* : As threatnings are the most proper for an impenitent person, so comfort for a penitent. It were a dangerous mistake to give a Vomit when a Cordial is or ; binding up is proper for the broken

<small>God will not break the bruised Reed.</small>

<small>Comfort is the proper expression for the Penitent.</small>

of the Returning Prodigal.

broken in heart, and comfort for mourners, and reviving for the contrite. Gracious expressions from God, are the very thing which the penitent needs, his spirit cannot else live and uphold it self. There are two things under which the spirit of man cannot well bear up and sustain it self; One is, near and strong afflictions without Divine strength; Another is, the quick sense of sin without the gracious sight of mercies. As they are needful, so are they seasonable, for as much as 1. Satan is most ready to fall foul upon the Soul, upon its Repentance, with strongest accusations, falsest suggestions and oppressions, to overwhelm it with despair, as on him in the *Corinthians*. 2. The *Heart* at such a time is most apt to fear the worst, to suspect its own soundness and Gods kindness. 3. Nothing would settle and quiet the Spirit of the penitent person more then Gods gracious expressions: This is light in darkness, life in death, the only Restorative to a sensible sinner, and a languishing soul. Therefore,

The first Use of this Point, shall be to *imitate God in this kindness of expression, and goodness of oblivion:* When we see persons truly penitential for former sins, as we must not call *Evil, Good,* so neither must we call *Good, Evil*; if God will not mention former sins to a penitent, how dare we to do it? It is an usual way of a sly and malicious person in his detractations; Yea, he is so and so now indeed, but what was he heretofore? And thus he digs up those old rotten corruptions with his malicious tongue, which the penitent hath long buryed with many tears, and God hath covered with much mercy. It is an argument that thou art of a beastly nature, who art still in the wounds and not on the sound parts. Speak against sin, and condemn it as well in thy self as in others, with all fit zeal, but spare at least the converted and penitent sinner: Never open a wound which God hath healed, nor shamefully blaze the sin which God hath mercifully pardoned. 2. *You see the way to have your sins covered and hid:* Men upon sinful commissions devise many shifts, and colours, and arts to keep their sins close and hid, as if the Sun could be muffled, or the Fire stifled, or the Wound not cured, would not break out; No, truly repent of sins, and that is the best way for to get sins concealed as well as pardoned. Now the Lord will not mention them; but if we

Use
Imitate God in this kindness and goodness.

You see the way to have our sins covered and hid.

D d 2 con-

continue impenitent, the Lord will set our sins in order, they shall break out to our shame as they have broken out to his dishonour.

But the Father said to his servants, Bring forth the best Robe, and put it on him, and put a Ring on his hand, and Shoes on his feet.

The special favours conferred upon the Penitential Prodigal.

These words are a List of the special favours which were conferred upon the penitential Prodigal; where you have, 1. The *Number of them*, 1. The *Robe*, 2. The *Ring*, 3. The *Shoes*; a suit large enough from top to toe. We need a compleate furniture, and God here bestows it. 2. The *Quality of them*; 1. The Robe is the best; and 2. The Ring is precious; and 3. The Shoes are proper, and fit, and the best. God gives unto his people what is most excellent, and what is most useful. 3. *The Order of them*; first the Robe, and then the Ring; because if the Allusion be to a Marriage, the Wedding Garment is ever put on before the Wedding Ring. Or else because the Garment (which is the Robe) is alwayes more necessary then the Ornament (which is the Ring.) Or which is choicest, because Interest in Christ, precedeth our Benefits by Christ. Again, as the Robe before the Ring, so the Ring before the Shoes; not because the Hands are more estimable then the Feet, but because our Feet can never tread well with Shoes of Patience, untill we first finger the Ring of Faith; we can never go well, nor bear well, unless first we believe well.

The prime favour bestowed upon the Prodigal.
The matter of it.
The Author of it.

I begin with the first of these, the prime Favour bestowed on the Prodigal; in which you have observable, 1. *The matter of that favour*, called a *Robe*, and the *Best Robe*. What this Robe is, and why called the Best, whether for Order, or for Dignity, or for Necessity, or all, we shall presently discuss. 2. *The Author of this favour*; *The Father said.* Why that phrase, the Father? why not, God said? Surely because our mercies, choicer mercies, come out of the hand of a reconciled God; they come from the Father of mercies, who is also the God of all grace. And why no more then, *The Father said*? &c. because saying from God is enough, it is as good as doing: his Imperative saying, is a Causative saying; if he speaks the word, we are made whole; and we, though naked, are cloathed.

The manner of conferring it.

3. *The manner of conferring it*, [*He said to his servants, Bring it forth,*

forth, and put it on:] Some think the servants here are the Angels; Others rather think them to be the Ministers of the Gospel. But why, saith he, to his servants, bring it forth, and put it on? is he not able to do it himself? True, God alone is able; but he who for power is able alone to confer any grace, being Lord of all, in wisdome thinks fit to confer and dispence Grace by the Ministry of servants, that so the use of means should alwayes accompany the dependance on his power: But why, saith he not, let the Prodigal put it on himself? I conjecture, because, as God only hath Grace, so he only can invest us with it; we can no more dress our selves with spiritual abilities, then the child that is newly born: God finds the Garment, and he also finds the hands to put it on; gives Christ, and an hand of Faith to put him on; gives grace, and a will also to receive it. If the Prodigal had been naturally able, as the Pelagians clamour it, it had been enough that the Garment had been brought forth, and shewed unto him as the best, and then he could have of himself put it on, but there is no such matter; the Prodigal wanted not only a Robe to wear, but strength also to put it on, and therefore the Robe is by his Fathers will, both represented to him, and he invested with it by a Forinsecal Induition. So that you have at this time, 1. The *gift* and the *excellency of it.* 2. The *Author, or cause of it.* 3. The *means*, or *manner of Application of it.* Touching the first, two questions crave our resolution:

1. *What this Robe or Garment is*, which is here bestowed on the returning Prodigal? *Sol.* There is, you know, a forefold Garment. 1. *Natural*: Our Skin is the Garment that swathes our flesh and body. *Job* seemeth to insinuate this, to be as a motheaten Garment, c.13.28. and a *changeable suit*, c.30.18. The Text speaks not of it. 2. *Civil*: Such as we, wear for use and distinction; nor of this doth the Text speak. 3. *Evil*: The Apostle calls it a *Garment spotted with the flesh, Jude v.23.* and the Prophet stiles it a *menstruous cloath*, and S. *Paul* adviseth us to put it wholly off, *Eph.4.* 4. *Spiritual*: Which is of that regard and concernment to the Soul, as a civil Garment is to the body; this is the garment of which the Text doth speak. This again is twofold, either 1. *Imputed righteousness*. 2. *Or Inherent righteousness*, both of these are in Scripture expressed as Garments, and we are often called to

What this Robe or Garment is.

The Spiritual Robe.

to put them on, as *Rom.* 13. *Eph.* 4. and the *Woman* in the Revelation is said to be *cloathed with the Sun.*

The Robe, though as I conjecture in this place, is, *that of imputed righteousness,* namely, the active and passive obedience of Jesus Christ, which we then put on, when by faith we receive Jesus Christ; and it is well compared to a Robe or Garment.

Of imputed Righteousness Put on by Faith. Compared to a Robe. For Necessity.

1. For *necessity*; though all sorts of Garments be not necessary, yet some are, partly, *to cover our shame and nakedness,* and defects, that they appear not: before the fall of *Adam,* nakedness was a badg of innocency, but after it, a reproach and shame; and therefore God made our first parents Garments to cover their shame: In like manner, if we would have our sinful, naked Souls, which are shameful in the eyes of God and man, covered from the revenging eye of his justice, *that our nakedness appear not, Rev.* 3. 18. Of necessity, we must be cloathed with the Robe of Christs righteousness: Partly, *To protect us from injuries of extreme cold in the Winter, and violent heat in the Summer,* &c. Of the same virtue, is the Robe of Christs righteousness to secure the Soul from the scorching flames of divine wrath, and the piercing terrours of a guilty and accusing conscience; by the shadow of it, we enjoy peace unspeakable, and most delightful tranquillity: *To preserve and cherish natural heat and life;* our Garments are the warm Bed we walk in, and somewhat answerable to food for preservation: Such is Jesus Christ, in respect of justifying righteousness, a very quickning spirit, our life, and the stay thereof, and the spring of our sweetest comforts, and refreshings in conscience; for what is justification but life from the dead, mercy at the bar, pardon to a condemned person, God at one with us, and we estated into his favour and happiness? 2. For Ornament, Therefore you read of costly Apparel, of Purple, and soft Raiment, of Cloathing of wrought Gold, and Raiment of needle work, all which are beautiful adornings, and set us out in a kind of Majesty and State. Doth not the righteousness of Christ do so? it is our comely and glorious Ornament, which for the glory of it, is called the *cloathing of the Sun, and beautiful Ornaments;* such as make us altogether comely, and lovely, without spot or wrinkle, and very pleasant and precious: It is the choicest Jewel which the Christian can wear. 3. For *distinction*: Nations you know, are distinguished by their habits; and so amongst

For Ornament.

For Distinction.

Of the Returning Prodigal.

amongst us, the orders of Callings are, or should be differenced by variety of Garments. Thus our profession of, and reliance only on the righteousness of Christ, doth distinguish us from all Infidels, Jews, Papists, who either deny the thing, or else rely on something else.

2. But why is this *Garment* called the *best Robe*? Some think it is called Best, by reason of its *antiquity*; and therefore they expound ἢ ϲολὴν ἢ πρώτην, *Stolam primum*, the first Robe, as if *Adam* had wore this Garment before his Fall; but how he should get Christs Garment (who in that estate neither had, nor did need his person) I cannot yet conceive: Others interpret the Betness of this Robe, not so much by the antiquity, as by *the excellency*; for it is a garment more excellent then any other in all the world: To shew its precedency, in respect of our ordinary Garments, is a meer idle and vain labour; for indeed there is no comparison twixt them, because of different kinds, and of vast disproportion. But frame the comparison with Garments, which have some excellency in them, yet, as *Solomon* spake of the daughter, *she surmounted* them all; so here, &c. *To the best Robe. For excellency.*

First, Compare *it with that Garment which* Adam *had in Innocency*, yet this of Christs is better: Better if you consider the *subjects*, Christ and *Adam*; or the *duration*, for stability, or vigour, for our benefit: The *first Adam* was a perfect man, but the *second Adam* was perfect God as well as man; the righteousness in the one, though it was perfect *pro statu*, yet it was both mutable, and incommunicable: *Adam* might, and did lose it, nor did he derive it in the virtue and benefit of it to another, or in the matter it self: But Christs righteousness is immutable, and also communicable; it is a Garment for the head, and for the members, and not in our keeping, but in his own; and therefore not a changeable Suit, but a Garment which shall never wax old. *Compared with that of Adam in innocency.*

Secondly, Compare it *with the Garments which the high Priest did wear*, it is far more excellent then any of them. The *Ephod*, which the high Priest was to wear, was made of white Linnen, and it was large, and set with many precious stones; and so also was the *Brest-plate* of judgment very precious, and the *Robe* of the Ephod, which had the Pomgranats, and the Bells of Gold; as also the *Embroidered Coat* which was curiously wrought of most precious matter, and cunning workmanship. But far inferiour *Compared with the Garments of the high Priest.*

to

to this Garment of Chrifts righteoufnefs, of which all thofe Garments were but types and fhadowes, but a Ceremonial adumbration of his fubftantial perfection, fuggefting that more admirable perfection, and excellency which was to be believed, and found in Chrift and his righteoufnefs. Or thirdly, *Compare it with that holinefs which we call inherent*, becaufe exifting in us; though this be a rare and diftinguifhing, and excellent Garment, yet it is not comparable to that of Chrifts righteoufnefs: Becaufe 1. *It wants much of perfection:* It is not the Sun, but a twinkling Star; there be many holes to be pickt in this Coat, it falls fhort for length and breadth; much corruption clings about it; we know, and believe, and love, and obey, but in part. 2. *It wants exceedingly in refpect of dignity and merit*; we cannot get the bleffing for its fake; though it be *via* yet it is not *caufa*. But the righteoufnefs of Chrift, it is a moft abfolute and compleat thing, and alfo eminently meritorious; it is a full price, and deferves Heaven it felf for us; we ftand perfect, *recti in curia*, before God in it; it covers all our defects, and reprefents us altogether acceptable before the judgment-feat. In a word, to fum up all concerning this Garment: It is the beft in refpect, *Of Divine Defignation*; the wifdome of God appoints it as the choiceft and chiefeft: *Of Divine acceptation*; He looks upon it with more favour then any other righteoufnefs: *Of Comparifon*, with all others, as I have fhewed: And *of our Condition*, there is not fo proper, and fo ufeful, and fo meritorious a Garment for any Chriftian to put on, as this.

Thus briefly of the excellency of the Gift. Now I proceed to the fecond Branch, which contains the *Author* or *Giver* thereof, [*The Father faid, Bring forth*] as alfo the manner of Application of it. [*He faid to his fervants, Put on.*]

1. The *Author of this Righteoufnefs* (which is the beft Robe) is God, and therefore it is frequently called the *Gift of righteoufnefs, Rom.* 5.17. and *the righteoufnefs of God, Phil.* 3.9. Becaufe it is a righteoufnefs of his giving. God is the caufe of it, By giving of Chrift to be our righteoufnefs, who is exprefly faid, *of God to be made unto us wifedome and righteoufnefs*, 1 Cor. 1. 30. By giving unto us the means by which that righteoufnefs is communicated, *viz.* Word and Sacraments: By bleffing thefe means to work in us Faith to receive Jefus Chrift, and fo become partakers

of the Returning Prodigal.

takers of his righteousnefs; by imputing that righteousnefs of Chrift unto us, upon our believing, and so accepting of us to eternal life.

2. *The manner of Application*: *Put it on him*, faith the Text. There is a threefold Application of this Robe of righteousnefs unto sinners: One, *ex parte donantis*, which is God, the prime caufe, who applies it to us *by Imputation*, as you may evidently see in *Ro.4. R*), 5. A second, *ex parte miniftrantis*, which are the means, through which the righteousnefs of God is revealed, and likewife (*by the effectual concomitancy of the Spirit*) applied unto us: The *Ordinances of God* are the Orb which carry the Sun of righteousnefs. A third is, *ex parte recipientis*: and the Application, or putting on of this robe of righteousnefs on our part, is partly *Sacramental*, when we are baptized into Chrift, and profefs publickly to receive him: partly *Spiritual*, which belongs to that faith (which God alone implants) inabling us to put on Chrift, as the Scripture often expresseth it.

The manner of Application.

I will now bring down all this to our felves, in some useful Applications: All that I will infift on at this time, shall be reduced unto two heads. 1. *For Examination*; whether this beft Robe be put upon us, yea or no. 2. *For Direction*. 1. How to get it, 2. How to use and wear it. Examine your felves what Wardrobe you have? You have, I perceive, many faffions, many habits; we know not how to call them, whether civil, or uncivil, you shift so often: there is such a vanity in man, that difpofeth his fancy to alterations; and befides that, there is an extream pride in perfons, they muft be in brave cloathing, and miftake their conditions, and abilities: though they lofe their Reputation and their Eftate for it, They will wear after the beft. Wel, if you have fuch a mind to rich Garments, what say you to the beft Robe that ever any finful perfon did wear? what fay you to the righteousnefs of Chrift? have you put it on, yea or no? Confider

Ufe.

For Examination.

Have you put on this Robe or no?

1. *It is fuch a Garment, that of all other thou needeft moft*: Our beft Garments are many times fuperfluous, we need them not, we can attire our felves, well enough without them; but this beft Robe is the moft needful; thou canft not live without it, nor mayft thou dye without it: How naked art thou with thy filthinefs, before the eyes of a pure God? And how at once may his wrath pour out it felf like fire, and confume thee, having no covering at all to fhelter thee? *Friend* (said he) to that intruder in the Gofpel, *How cameft thou in here without thy*

It is a Garment that of all others we need moft.

E e

thy *Wedding Garment*? When thou goest to Prayer, or steps to the Sacrament, or art giving up thy Soul into the hands of God, and hast no covering for any of thy sins; may not God in the same way of judgment say unto thee, and bespeak thee: How dost thou present thy self before me with all this sinfulness? thou knowest that I am a God of purer eyes then to behold sin, and there is no communion twixt light and darkness: I tell thee, that there is, No acceptance of thy person without this Robe; the Lord cannot abide the sight of thee without it, for thou canst not but provoke him, as oft as thou appears before him in thy nakedness and vileness: No respect unto thy services; not that the Lord do h dislike any duty, but that the person must be first covered with the righteousness of Christ, if he would have his offering to be ac-

By nature we are born naked. cepted. 2. *By nature we are born naked*, utterly destitute of this precious Robe. *As for the nativity* (said God to Jerusalem) *in the day that thou wast born, thy Navel was not cut, neither wast thou washed in Water to supple thee, neither wast thou salted at all, nor swadled at all.* Ezek. 16. 4. Or as *Christ* to the Church of *Laodicea, Thou art wretched, and miserable, and poor, and blind, and naked*: So we by nature, cloathed only with raggs of corruption (with *filthy raggs*, Isa. 64. 6.) and, as *Joshua* in *Zach*. 3. 3. *Cloathed with filthy Garments*, destitute of God, of Christ, of all righteousness: as if you should see a naked child, born with Sores, and Boils, and Plagues,

We are of no excellency without this Robe. and Leprosies, running and spreading from top to toe. 3. *You are of no excellency without this Robe*: Then only we come to excellent Ornaments when this is put on. All the Robes you get on you, are but the shrouds of dead men, or like Velvet cast over an Herse. As *Solomon* said of beauty in a foolish woman, it is but as *a Jewel in a swines snout*: So we say of all other Garments, they are Or-

There is none like it. naments put on a base dead and loathsome soul. 4. The Robe of *Christs righteousness, there is none like it, for thy good and benefit*:

It is an Ornament as well as a Garment. For 1. *It is an Ornament as well as a Garment:* All our acceptance before God is as we are cloathed with it, then are we cloathed with the Sun, now are we precious in his eyes; it makes us beautiful and

An Armor as well as an Ornament. lovely, and accepted in the eyes of God. 2. *It is armour as well as Ornament:* For the preciousness of it, it is a vesture of pure Gold; and for the strength of it, it is as a Coat of Mail: *Let us put on the Armor of Light*, Rom. 13. 12. We may by it, keep off the strongest accusations of Satan, and stand even before the judgment-seat.

of the Returning Prodigal.

feat. *I am black but comely*, faith the Church, *Cant.* 1. 5. though in her felf black, yet in this righteoufnefs comely. It can anfwer all our own imperfections, and all that Satan can object againft us, or the Law, or our own fearful hearts : Sins and imperfections, and defects, cannot anfwer God; but a perfect righteoufnefs can.

3. *It is a Garment for warmth as well as for fight* : When we look on our felves and our own righteoufnefs, our fpirits may dye within us; but peace and comfort flow from the righteoufnefs of Chrift, it was perfect, and meritorious, and accepted; and this will chear the heart above all, if we be *found in Chrift having his righteoufnefs*. There goes wonderful virtue from the hem of this Garment, both to fatisfie God, and to pacifie the confcience; as *Jacob* got the *bleffing with the elder Sons Garment*, fo do we get all our mercies, and comforts, and bleffings, by being cloathed with the Robe of Chrifts righteoufnefs.

It is a Garment for warmth as for fight.

But how may we know that we have put on this beft Robe ?
Sol. I will inftance but in three particulars to difcover this. 1. *If we have put on Chrifts Robe, we have put off our own Rags*; (we have put them off, 1. *Affectu.* 2. *Conatu.*) As it was with *Joshua*, Zach. 3. 4. *His filthy Rags were taken away, and then he was cloathed with change of Raiment* : So here, no man can affure himfelf that he is cloathed with Chrifts righteoufnefs, unlefs he doth difmantle himfelf of his own unrighteoufnefs. Eph. 4. 21. *If ye have been taught as the truth is in Jefus*; v. 22. *Put off concerning the former converfation, the old man which is corrupt according to the deceitful lufts.* v. 23. *And put on that new man*, &c. Rom. 13. 12. *Caft off the Works of Darknefs, and put on the Armor of light* : For a man to imagine that he hath the Robe of Chrifts righteoufnefs, and yet to walk in the paths of unrighteoufnefs, *in chambering and wantonnefs, in ftrife and envying*, in all voluptuoufnefs, and beaftlinefs, &c. *No man*, faith Chrift, *foweth a piece of new Cloath to an old Garment*, Mark 2. 21. 'Tis true, that none but finners are cloathed with this Robe; but then it is as true, that no finners are cloathed with it, but ftrive with all their might, to put off their finful rags by hearty contrition, and confeffion, and converfion. 2. *Only faith puts on this Robe*; And therefore, as this Robe is called *the righteoufnefs of God*, both for defignation, imputation, and acceptation; So it is alfo called the *righteoufnefs of Faith* : Not that Faith in a formal

How may we know that we have put it on. Have we put off our own Rags.

Only faith puts on this Robe.

E e 2 fenfe

sense is our righteousness: For Faith did not dye for us, nor can Faith of it self merit for us; nor is Faith of it self compleat, but imperfect: but because it is *the instrument* which apprehends Christ and his righteousness, and by which we put on Christ with his righteousness. Have you Faith, or have you not? Nay, but deceive not your selves, The Faith which puts on this righteousness, must be able, 1. *To deny our own righteousness*, to take off all confidence in the flesh; Faith cannot put on Christs righteousness, until it hath put off your own. 2. *To see a need of this righteousness*; and to prize and desire to be found in it, above and before all other; the *Laodiceans* must *see that they are naked, and then buy Raiment*, Rev. 3. 3. *To unite us to Jesus Christ*: It must work in us, both estimation (for our judgments) and acceptation (for our wills;) so that it must make us one with Christ, and so we come to be cloathed with the Garment of Christ: But perhaps you can rest upon your own good meanings, works, innocency. You are *rich*, and *need* not to borrow any Garment; you are united to your lusts, and will not part with them for Christ, nor for all his Ornament. 3. *This Robe of righteousness, and that other of holiness are inseparable:* It is granted, that inherent holiness is not formally the same with imputed righteousness; it is granted, that the one is in Christ, the other is in us; that the one is perfect, the other is imperfect; that the one is meritorious, the other though it be precious, yet it is not meritorious: Yet as the light, and heat of the Sun, though the one be not the other, yet they go together; so the Robe of righteousness, and the Robe of holiness go together; the new Garment is only to be seen upon the new man. Therefore you read, that *Christ is made* not only *Righteousness*, but also *Sanctification*: Righteousness, this is a grace without us, whereby we are advanced; Sanctification, this is a grace wrought within us, by which we advance and glorifie God; that respects the State, this the nature of the person: *As Grace must reign through righteousness to eternal life*, Ro. 5. 21. *So also holiness must reign to everlasting life*, Ro. 6. 22. The one as a cause, the other as a means. Now then, as if thou canst discern any light in the morning, thou concludest that the Sun is risen, so if thou canst discover any true holiness in thy heart, thou maist conclude that the Sun of righteousness is risen: the appearing of holiness is a sign of the rising of righteousness.

Yea,

This Robe, and that of holiness are inseparable.

of the Returning Prodigal.

Yea, the Prophet speaking of the Sun of Righteousness, saith, *He shall arise with healing in his wings*, *Mal.*4. 2. to intimate, That where righteousness comes, there holiness comes. Ah! dost thou find no change in thy Nature, in thy Judgment, in thy Mind, in thy Will, in thy Affections? why (as sure as the Lord lives) thou hast not yet put on this Robe of righteousness. Doth Christ present thy person unspotted before God? and doth he (thinkst thou) leave thy heart with all its spots and filthiness?

[*And put a Ring on his Hand.*]

This is the second favour conferred on the penitent Prodigal by his Father. A Ring is such a piece of substance which is put on the finger, partly for Ornament, and partly to testifie Nuptial union and conjunction. S. *Chrysostom* doth conjecture, that the Ring in this place is, *Nuptiarum insigne quibus Christus Ecclesiam Sponsat*, an embleme of the Espousals twixt Christ and his Church. So that then we have this Proposition to insist on:

That God gives unto the penitent person a precious Faith, by which he is Espoused or Married unto Christ. There are three things, which being explained, will give up unto us the full sense of this Assertion: 1. What it is to be married unto Christ. 2. That Faith doth Espouse and Marry a person unto Christ; and what faith that is, and in what respect. 3. That the penitent person hath this faith.

Doct. 2. God gives the penitent person Faith by which he is married to Christ.

Quest. 1. For the first of these; *What it is to be Espoused or Married unto Christ?* (which is here signified by putting on the Ring.) *Sol.* They who write of Marriage do conjecture that these six things concur unto it, 1. *Mutuus Consensus*, a mutual Consenting. 2. *Mutuus Contractus*, a mutual Contracting; 3. *Mutua Obligatio*, a mutual Obliging; 4. *Mutua Conjunctio*, a mutual Union and Conjunction; 5. *Mutua Potestas*, a mutual faculty or Right; 6. *Mutua Societas*, a mutual use or Society. Translate this from a Civil to a Spiritual consideration, and then to be married to Christ implyes, 1. *A Consent* to take or accept of Christ: Though knowledg of persons be necessary and fit, yet it is not sufficient to marriage without consent; for marriage ought to be a voluntary transaction of persons, and in it we do, in a sort, give away our selves; but then this is not without our selves; yea, and therein we do elect & make choice for our selves, and therefore consent is a necessary concurrence

What it is to be married unto Christ. It implyes, A Consent.

rence to marriage. Now this consent is nothing else but a free and plain act of the will, accepting of Jesus Christ, before all other, to be its Head and Lord. Christ offers himself in the Gospel unto a person, I am the only Saviour of sinners, and Lord of all, designed to be Priest, Prophet and King; art thou willing to accept of me? canst thou like of me before all others? dost thou so? dost thou make choice of me for thy Saviour and Lord?

A mutual Contract.
2. *A Contracting of the Soul with Christ: Contractus* is nothing else but *consensus explicatus*, a contract is a consent expressed in words; but then they must be words proper to make Marriage. They must not be *verba dubia*, dubious words; as, I will marry none but you; but *verba clara & affirmativa*, affirmative, I will marry you: for the Rule of the Casuists is good, *Consensus non datur per meram negationem.* And as they must not be *verba dubia*, but *affirmativa*, so they must not be *verba futura & conditionata*, hereafter, or upon such a condition, but *verba de presenti*, I now accept or take, &c. Then a man is Married unto Christ, when he doth freely, and absolutely, and presently receive the Lord Jesus. Not, I would have Christ if it did not prejudice my worldly estate, ease, friends, &c. Or, hereafter I will accept of him, when I come to dye, and be in distress; but now when Salvation is offered, now while Christ tenders himself, I now yield up my heart and life unto him. 3. *An ob-*

A mutual Obligation.
liging of the Soul to Christ; for, *ex contractu oritur vinculum*; some call this *traditio*, or, *resignatio*: and therefore Marriage is a Knot or Tye, wherein persons are mutually limited and bound each to other in a way of Conjugal separation from all others; and this in Scripture is called a Covenant. So when any one Marries Christ, he doth therein discharge himself in affection and subjection from all that is contrary to Christ; and solemnly Covenants and binds himself to Christ alone: He will have no Saviour and no Lord but Christ, and to him will he cleave for ever; *Simpliciter & indissolubiliter, & persona, & statu, & tempore:* It is not every apprehension, nor every transcient approbation, but the Will must come to an obligation, binding it self

A Mutual Conjunction
in a perpetual Covenant to Christ alone. 4. *An Union or Conjunction with Christ:* Before Marriage the persons were distinct, and had no other relation but what was common to Nature; but upon Marriage *two are made one flesh*, 1 Cor. 6. 16. This is

Of the Returning Prodigal.

is bone of my bone, and flesh of my flesh, said *Adam* of his Wife, *Gen.* 2. So when the soul is married unto Christ, not only in respect of affection (for love unites) but likewise in respect of nature; he that *is joyned to the Lord is one Spirit,* faith the Apostle, 1 *Cor.*6.17. That Nature which is in Christ, it is participated of by him that is married unto Christ; so that there doth arise, upon this marriage, the nearest and dearest relation of union that is in all the world. 5. *A faculty of right or interest*: Indeed Christs faculty over us is, *facultas Dominii, & facultas Influentia*; a faculty of *Dominion* (he hath a right to rule and guide us) and a faculty of *Influence*, he hath a right to teach and heal us: Such a faculty of Soveraignty we have not over Christ; yet we have *facultatem Juris,* a faculty of Right or Interest, which they call *Jus in re,* or as others, a faculty of propriety. Though the Wife hath not a power of authority over her Husband, yet she hath a power of propriety in her Husband; that as he can say, This is my Wife, so she can say, This is my Husband. In like manner, whosoever is marryed unto Christ, he hath an interest in the person, in the condition of Christ; there hath passed such an intire, and proper, and peculiar, and mutual resignation, that he may say as the Church in the Canticles, *My Beloved is mine, and I am his*: The married unto Christ gives up the right, of his soul and body unto Christ; O Lord Jesus, all that I am, all that I have, all that I can do, is thine and for thee. 6. Lastly, There is *Society and Use*: As marriage infers with it Co-habitation and Co-interest, they dwell together, and make use of either, both persons and estates. Thus is it when any person is married unto Christ, there is a holy society and fellowship of him with Christ; Christ dwels in him, and he dwels in Christ; Christ delights in him, and he delights in Christ; Christ makes use of him, and he makes use of Christ: If he wants grace, or mercy, or strength, or peace, or comfort, why, faith Christ, I am thine, I have them for thee, make use of me: And if Christ would use him in any service, Lord, faith the soul that is married to Christ, If thou wilt have me to speak for thee, I will speak for thee; If thou wilt have me to do for thee, I will do for thee; if thou wilt have me to suffer for thee, I will suffer for thee; if thou wilt have me to dye for thee; I will dye for the Name of Christ, said *Paul.* So that you see

A mutual Right.

A mutual Society.

what

what the Ring in the Text may import, namely, the marriage of the foul unto Chrift, and what that is.

What it is which marrieth us unto Chrift, viz. Faith.

Queft. 2. The next thing to be difcuffed is, *What that is which marryeth us unto Chrift?* and that I told you was Faith: The principal caufe of this match is the Spirit of Jefus Chrift, but the internally inftrumental caufe is Faith. I know you know the feveral acceptations of the word Faith; I take it in the Habitual fenfe, not in the Doctrinal, and there too in the choice and eminent part; I mean, as reftrained to Juftifying and Saving: of all other Graces in man, this is it which makes the match and draws up the marriage twixt the Soul and Chrift. And the manner how it doth effect it, I conceive may be thus:

How Faith doth it.

By Difcovering the excellencies of Chrift.

1. *By difcovering the preheminent excellencies of Chrift*: For till the foul can difcern a better excellency in Chrift then in any other thing, it will never yield to match it felf unto him. Now Faith hath two Virtues; One is, to *make the mind rightly to judge all finful and worldly things as bafe and vile, drofs and dung* (Phil. 3.) *in comparifon of Chrift*. Another is, *to reprefent unto the foul the real and furpaffing excellencies of Chrift*. It is the *Jacobs* Staff which makes us to take the heigth, and depth, and breadth of the excellency of Chrift; that there is no Beloved like Chrift; he is the Choiceft of ten thoufand; fuch a one in whom the God-Head dwels bodily; full of Grace; the holy One of God; the brightnefs of the Fathers Image; the Lord of Life; the Prince of Glory; the moft excellent in himfelf, and moft complete and abfolute for the Redemption and Salvation of a finner.

By fubjecting the Judgment to the Approbation of his excellency.

2. *By fubjecting the Judgment to the affent and approbation of this excellent truth, That none is like Chrift for a finner*; That he is the only Saviour and Redeemer; and that fuch an offer of Jefus Chrift unto a finner, is worthy of all acceptation; the finner is made for ever if he can get Chrift, and he perifhes for ever if he enjoyes him not. As a woman in a difpofition to Marriage, fhe confiders of the perfon, and his qualities, and condition, and thinks often, This man hath choice parts in him, a good eftate, I cannot better my felf if I refufe him, I fee I may do very well if I match unto him. Anfwerable effects doth Faith work in the foul, it doth make the minde of a man

to

Of the Returning Prodigal.

to see the superlative excellency of Jesus Christ, and to fall in liking of him and them. Come, I need a Saviour ; Christ is he, and none else ; he is the Prince of my peace, the Lord of my life ; his Nature is excellent, Redemption sufficient and proper, Laws righteous and good ; it is my wisdome, it is my safety, it is my salvation to accept of him, and to bestow my soul on him.

3. *By inclining the will to consent and embrace the Lord Jesus :* For true Faith is not a meer notion, but an operating grace ; it is as light in the mind, and as heat in the will ; there it is a singular representation, and here it is an effectual inclination. It is granted, that to embrace, or to be willing, or to consent, are the acts of the will ; but to embrace Christ with a conjugal consent, to be willing to bestow our selves on him, this comes from faith enabling the Will so to will. Not by way of coaction, for the Will cannot be compelled ; nor doth Faith work in a violent way, though it works in an effectual way, enabling the Will to a free election of Christ before all others, (*i.*) predominant causes in Christ, to accept of him, and to resign up to him, rather than to sin, or world, or any thing else ; and when the Will is wrought upon, so as to accept of Christ in his Person, and Offices, and Estates, the soul is now matched or married to Christ by Faith. It bestows it self, and gives Christ all the right, and cleaves unto him in an indissoluble bond of affection and service.

By inclining the will to embrace him.

Quest. 3. The third resolveable is, concerning *the Subject of this faith*, who hath it ? The Text resolves that, by telling us, that the *Ring* was put on the returning Prodigals finger, so that the *penitent person is he who wears the Ring*, (*i.*) who is an espoused or married person by Faith unto Christ : You may be married to your Lusts, and to the World, though you be impenitent ; yet none but Penitents are married unto Christ by Faith. Not that Repentance goes before Faith in Christ, (for no Grace habitually considered, is in time before another, though in operation it be:) Nor that Repentance is the cause of Faith ; for it is a most improper Assertion, to make one Grace to be the cause of another Grace, when as every Grace doth come onely from the Spirit of Christ as the cause. But because, 1. *The penitent person is only the subject of Faith which doth marry us to Christ* ; no person is a believer, who is not a penitent person : The Prodigal, while onely a Prodigal, he hath neither Garment nor Ring; but when he is a returning

The subject of this faith.

The penitent person is onely married unto Christ.

Reasons.

The penitent person onely hath faith.

Ff

Onely penitent persons can evidence their faith.

...ning Prodigal, then he hath both, and not till then. 2. *Onely penitent persons can evidence their faith* and espousal unto Christ: Another, who is impenitent, can no more evidence his interest or title to Christ, then an Alien that never heard of this Land, can evidence or conclude his title and right to any Goods or Chattels of yours. The title to Christ is proper onely to the Penitent; for them he lived, and for them onely he died.

Why will the Lord give this to penitent persons.

Now if any should yet further demand, *Why the Lord should give unto penitent persons a precious faith to espouse them to Christ?* I conjecture, briefly, that these may be the Grounds or Reasons.

To convince the world, there is no loss in leaving sin.

1. *To convince all the world, that there is no loss in leaving of sin.* *Abjice tectum & tolle coelum*, said one. The repentant person forsakes his sins, but presently finds a Saviour; he is divorced from that which would damn him, and by faith is espoused unto one that will save him.

To support the soul of the heavy laden.

2. *To support the soul of the penitent, which of all other is most sick and heavy laden:* It is most sensible of sin, and guilt, and Gods displeasure, on all which it cannot long look alone. If the penitent person had not faith to see a Mediatour, he would not long have an eye to look upon his transgressions. It is a truth, that Repentance could never act it self, unless the penitent person had faith to act it self too. The sorrow in Repentance would infinitely sink into despair, and the forsaking of sin would turn into a forsaking of God, if Faith saw not a Mediatour for Transgressions, and a mercifull God through him.

God intends singular mercies to the Penitent.

3. Lastly; *The Lord intends singular mercy to the penitent persons*; to perform many precious promises of pardon and grace and comfort unto them, and therefore gives them Faith, unto which all the Promises are made. The promises may be considered two ways; either in respect, 1. of *Intention*, so they look unto the Penitent; of *Application*, so onely Faith is the Hand in the Penitent which actively applies the Promises. Again, you know that the Promises of God are *Yea*, and *Amen in Christ*, (*i*.) they are all sealed by him, and made good unto us by him; so that first we must have Christ, before the Promises made good unto us by Christ: And therefore God gives unto the penitent person the Grace of Faith to espouse him unto Christ, that so he may settle upon him all the Dowry (upon the Marriage) of the rich mercy and good in his precious Promises.

Of the Returning Prodigal.

The main Use which I will make of this assertion, is, *To try our selves, whether we have this precious Ring of Faith,* (a Ring more precious than that of Gold,) put on our fingers, yea, or no. It is as necessary a demur as ever you were put unto all your dayes, whether you consider, 1. *The paucity of true believers.* *All men have not faith,* saith the Apostle : All men ? nay, very few ; *Who hath believed our report ?* said the Prophet : We preach, we offer Christ unto you, we beseech you to accept of the Lord of Life, to give up your hearts and lives unto him ; but who believes our report? We tell you that Christ is better than all the world, his bloud is better than sin, it's better to love and serve him than world or sin; but who believes our report ? Men care not to know the excellencies of Christ, they prize him not, they care not to hear him speak in his Ordinances, they will in no wise consent and yield to his terms and conditions. 2. *The Uti-lity of it.* To the Sacrament of the Lords Supper, if we come without our Wedding-Ring, it will be as sad a day to us, as to him *who came without his Wedding Garment.* We do not onely receive no good at the Sacrament; for we have neither hand nor mouth to take and eat, if we have not Faith ; not title at all to the intrinsecal benefits by Christ, if we have not faith in him. Nay, we occasion much evil and Judgment upon our selves, we adventure to *eat and drink our own damnation, not discerning the Lords body* : And righteously may the Lord judge us for coming to his Sacrament without Faith, for as much as in so doing, we do not onely presume against an express prohibition that we should hold off, but also we do (at the least interpretatively) assay to make God a Liar, and a favourer of all villany, as if he would put his Seal of Pardon and mercy, and for all the good of his Covenant in Christ, to a wicked, impenitent, and unbelieving sinner. 3. *The Hypocrisie of our hearts,* so apt to deceive themselves with shadows in stead of substances, not considering, that Satan can delude a man with the shew of any grace. Every Ring is not a Ring of Gold; nor is every Faith a precious and unfeigned Faith : There is a thing called Presumption, which is bold enough, but it is not Faith ; and there is Knowledge of Christ, as revealed in the Word, which a man may have, and utter too, and yet not have Faith ; there is Profession of Faith, for the truth against errours, and yet the Grace

Use. Try our selves whether we have this precious faith.

A necessary trial, if we consider, The paucity of true believers.

The utility of it.

1 Cor. 11.

The hypocrisie of our hearts.

Ff 2 of

of Faith is another thing. A man may have so much faith as to believe that there is a Christ, and to confess his excellencies, and in some sort to see his own necessities of Christ, yea, he may begin to article and capitulate as the *Young-man*, and yet break off, and be far enough from a Faith which doth indeed espouse and marry his soul unto Christ.   4. Lastly, *The misery and danger*: Suppose you do deceive your selves, and in the event it appears that you are not espoused to Jesus Christ by Faith, that you never gave your hearts unto him, that there never was any conjugal Union and Bond twixt you; if thou indeed shouldst live Christless, and die Christless, what helpless, hopeless, happyless person art thou?

The misery and danger.

But you will reply, We trust that we are truly penitent persons, and that God hath given unto us such a Faith, whereby we are really married unto Christ.   *Sol.* Well; if that be so, you have great cause to bless the Lord: And that you may not be deceived therein, I will deliver unto you, *some proper effects which that Faith produceth in every soul that is indeed married unto Christ.* There are four Qualities produced by an espousing Faith.   1. *Estimation*: Let the *Wife see that she reverence her Husband*, saith the Apostle, *Ephes.* 5. She must both acknowledg him as a Head, and honour him as a Lord, judge and esteem of him (in a relative consideration) above all other. The like effect doth Faith produce, if it espouseth us to Christ, it sets up Christ above all, accounts of him as most excellent, judgeth of all other things but as dross and dung in comparison of him, will part with all for to get Christ: The beauties of Christ are glorious in the eyes of every believer; Christ doth not seem a mean thing, an ordinary or common thing; but he is the Pearl, the Sun of Righteousness: *My Lord, and my God*, saith *Thomas*. In a word, Faith (if right) exalts the Excellency of Christ, and the Authority of Christ; the Excellencies of his Person, and the Authority of his Will and Laws.   2. *Election*: We make choice of Christ before all other. Though sins, though the pleasures and profits of the world, proffer themselves, yet, as the Martyr at the stake, *None but Christ*: Or as *Paul, I desire to know nothing but Christ crucified*: So the true believer, Give me Christ, I have enough, I have that which is best of all; he is the *Optimum* and the *Unicum* to Faith.   3. *Affection*: Conjugal Faith ever produceth conjugal Love. It were a monstrous evil, for

Qualities produced by an espousing faith.

Estimation.

Election.

Affection.

for a woman to marry a man, and no love him ; and it were an adulterous thing, for her to love any more then her own Husband. Marriage doth, by way of Duty, infer and draw with it two qualities of Love; one is exclusive, and it is an *unity of Love*; the other is intensive, and it is a *redundancy of Love* : Thus is it with us; if Faith hath espoused us unto Christ, it doth kindle in us a love unto Christ; not a divided love, a love to Christ, and a love to sin ; a love to Christ, and a love to the world ; but an *united love* ; none is by us esteemed and loved as our Lord, but Christ: Nor doth it satisfie it self with a remiss and diminutive love, which may serve any inferiour object; but as Christ is in himself the most excellent object, so Faith produceth such a degree of love which bears some proportion with that object, *viz.* a *superlative love*, a love of Christ above all, and more then all; more set on Christ than on any other object, which yet may lawfully be loved more than our father, or mother, or wife, or children. Do we find this love in our hearts to Christ, against all, and above all? Nay again, True conjugal love infers with it a Love, 1.*of Complacency*, to delight in the thing loved; 2.*of Society*, to be with the person loved: Is it so with us? what delght have we in Christ? in his person, in his excellencies, in his works, in his ordinances? Is it our best joy to hear him, to see him, to speak with him. 4. *Subjection* : I confess that marriage doth not make the woman a slave, yet by vertue thereof she is bound to submission or subjection; she doth in a sort give away her self unto the disposal of another in the Lord : *Thy desire*, saith God, *Gen.*3.16.*shall be to thy husband, and he shall rule over thee.* If thou hast a Faith which doth espouse thee unto Christ, that Faith brings thy heart into the obedience and subjection of Christ. It subjects thy will to Christs will, and thy judgment to his truths, and thy desire to his rule, and thy works to his laws. If Christ would have thee be and do one thing, and thou wilt be and do another, that thy will is still contradicting of Christs will, and thy way is still contrary to his way : Though a man may be married to such a stubborn and perverse piece; yet Christ is not ; for all that are married unto him by Faith, have in some measure wrought in them, an obediential spirit, desirous to know the mind of the Lord, and willing to live godly in Christ Jesus. Now this subjection which is the effect of an espousing Faith, hath these properties in it, *viz.* 1. *Vniversality* ; the wife is subject in all things : 2. *Diligence*; we

Subjection.

we must take care to please him : 3. *Delightfulness*; it must be no burthen : 4. *Constancy*; as long as we live, we must be subject to the will of our Lord.

Use 2.
Exhortation.

The last Use shall be for *Exhortation*, That in case you find this Ring of Faith, by which you are espoused unto Christ, given unto you, then be very carefull to wear it, and to bring it along with you to this next Sacrament. We usually put on our Robes and our Rings, when we come to any solemn Feasts : The Sacrament of the Lords Supper is a Feast of good things, there is Christ, and mercy, and redemption, and sanctification, and what not for the soul; but bring your Ring with you; Christ looks that you should come with it, and you can do no good at the Sacrament, if you have not the Ring on your hand : Though you put forth your hand, yet if the Ring be not on it, the hand may take the bread, but the Ring is it which onely can take Christ; therefore bring Faith with you to the Sacrament. *Josephs* Brethren must bring *Benjamin* with them, or else they must not see his face, nor should get food. And let your faith work upon Christ all along; on the love of Christ, on the sufferings of Christ, of the Covenant of God with you in Christ, of the offer of Christ unto you, (now under seal that he is yours;) seal with your Ring, put your Seal to the Covenant and Deed of Christ and God; and feed on him, believe on him, draw from him; This is my Lord, this is my Saviour, this bloud was shed for me, my Christ will do me good, I shall be saved by his bloud, reconciled by his bloud, healed and preserved by his Spirit.

And shoes on his Feet.

What is meant by shoes on his feet.

This is the third Favour which is bestowed upon the repenting Prodigal; his Lips were kissed, his Back was clothed, his Hand was adorned, and now his Feet are shod; the penitent person is onely the compleat person. But what these *Feet* are, and what the *Shoes* which are put on them, is a point differently conjectured of by Interpreters. *Sol.* Not to waste time, both the Words are Metaphorically to be understood for some things which do in some respects answer to Feet, and Shoes. *Feet* are taken sometimes, 1. for the springs of our actions and courses; as for our *Will and Affections*, so *Eccles.* 5. 1. 2. For the actions and courses themselves

themselves, which *Solomon* calls the *path of our feet*, Prov. 4. 26. And in this sense *David* saith, *Wilt thou not keep my feet from falling?* Psal. 56. 13. and God is said to guide the feet of his People, and to preserve the feet of his Saints, 1 *Sam.* 2. 9. And *Shoes on the feet*, are also diversly taken in a metaphorical sense : 1. Sometimes for a *mortified disposition to the world*, as the shoes keep the feet at a distance from the earth, and with them we trample upon the earth. 2. Sometimes for *strength against passive injuries* and evils ; as feet shod can pass upon sharp thorns and stones ; this is called, *Feet shod with the preparation of the Gospel of Christ* , Ephes. 6. 3. Sometimes for a *fit ability in all walking* ; for the shoes do not onely adorn the feet, but strengthen them in and unto motion : From all which we may, I think, observe this Proposition.

That God doth enable a penitent person with grace and strength for a better and singular walking or course of Life and Obedience. The *Prodigal* before his Conversion walked with naked feet, wildly, loosely, disgracefully, dangerously ; but upon his repentance, he hath shoes put on his feet ; not onely his Heart is altered, but his Life ; not onely his disposition, but condition ; not onely his condition, but his conversation : He was another man, and now walks as another man. The same you see in *Paul*, before his Conversion, and after it : *Before his Conversion*, his feet were *swift to shed bloud*, he persecuted the Saints and Members of Christ to the death ; but *after his Conversion*, he exalts Jesus Christ, and is endeared in highest affection unto him and his servants, prizeth Christ above all, loves Christ above all, strives for the propagation and for the obedience of the Gospel above all, and his feet carry him to most places and persons for the service of Christ : And this alteration in the course of life, *Paul* expresseth to be in all that are effectually called and converted, that they *do not now walk as other Gentiles*, Ephes. 4. 17. nor as they themselves once did, in darkness and voluptuousness, but do *put off their old Conversation* , Ephes. 4. 22. and *walk as children of the light*, Ephes. 5. 8. and *become servants of righteousness*, Rom. 6. 18. and *have their fruits unto holiness*. v. 22.

Doct. God doth enable a penitent person with grace and strength for a singular walking.

What this singular walking is.

But the Question may be, *What that singular course of living* or or walking is, unto which God doth enable penitent perfons ? *Sol.* I conjecture of it thus. 1. *It is an heavenly and spiritual walking.* In *Abraham* this is called, a *walking before.* God; and in *Noah*, *a walking with God*; in the Galatians, *a walking in the Spirit*; in others, a *walking in Chrift*; in the *Phillippians*, a *converfation in heaven*. Before our converfion, we mind nothing, and endeavour after nothing, and imploy our felves in nothing but finfull, fenfual, vain things and courfes: But when the foul is truly made penitential, now our hearts mind a God, and his Word, and his Glory; now they meditate on his Will and Laws, now they crave after Grace and heavenly ftrength, now they bufie and endeavour, What fhall we do to be faved? Now our feet can bring us to the Courts of God, and now we can confcionably prize and ufe communion with God; we take more delight a thoufand times to read his Word, than all Play-books, and merry Hiftories; to hear the voice of Chrift, to be reforming of what is evil, to be much in Prayer, and all the works of holy Obedience, than in any wicked or vain way whatfoever.

2. It is a *regular courfe of life* : The feet, when fhoes are on them, are then reftrained, as it were, and confined; they are kept to a fize, and do not fquander and expatiate: So is it with the courfe of a man who is made a true Penitent; it is not now loofe and wild, guided by the feafon of every company, nor by the examples of every man, nor by the courfe of the world, nor by the lufts of his own heart; what others do, is no rule to him; and what others applaud, is no rule to him; and what others decide, is no rule to him; and what his own heart fuggefts, is no rule to him: But he hath a fure rule unto which he takes heed, and according to which he orders his converfation, and walks. If the Word of God faith, Go, he goeth; if that fay, Come, he cometh: If that, like the Cloud before the *Ifraelites*, moves by Precept, he rifeth up, and endeavours to follow it; if that, like the fame Cloud, doth reft and forbid, he fits down, and dares not do it: He doth not do what he will, but what he may; live after an Humour, but after a Law; he would have every action, not bad, but good; and that it may be fo, firft confults with the Word, Is it lawfull? and then refolves to practife it, becaufe it is fo.

3. It

3. *It is an even and upright courſe of life*; as the ſhoes keep the feet up on either ſide. Such feet doth God beſtow upon penitent people, as the living creatures had, *their feet were ſtraight feet*, Ezek. 1. 7. not like the Images feet in *Daniel* 2. 33. which were *part of Iron, and part of Clay*. A converſation that is like the *Prophets cake*, *which was not turned*, Hoſ. 7. 8. Doughbaked bread on the one ſide, and dough on the other; ſo Pious in one part, and Impious in another; publickly Religious, and ſecretly Prophane; in one ſociety Angelical, in another Diabolical; in one place a Doctrine, and in another an Uſe of Confutation: like a Fiſh, to give a friſk into the Aire, and then to plunge into the Ocean of Luſts. Such a Leopard-like life, ſpotted courſe is ignoble; when the Chriſtian runs, like that Beaſt with two feet of different length, with a general unevenneſs in his wayes; but ſtrait feet are thoſe which the Penitent walks withal: as he hath not an heart and an heart, ſo he hath not a foot and a foot: Tis granted, he may be ſometimes lame and trip; frailties and infirmities befal the beſt, but an even, equal tenour is yet to be found in the main bulk of his paths. He hath no Artificial ſhoes, wider and leſſer, made on purpoſe, but in the bent of his heart and endeavours, deſires to have a good conſcience in all things, void of offence to God and man. The Philoſopher doth diſtinguiſh twixt a Complexion which ariſeth from Paſſion, and that which buds out from an Habitual temper; when a perſon occaſionally bluſheth, though he be of a pale Complexion, yet colour ariſeth in his face; but the Sanguine temper is ſtill of a ruddy face: Paſſionate actions are rare and unequal, but natural are frequent and even. The penitent, in the whole courſe of his converſation, is *homo quadratus*, ſquare, and uniform, and beautiful, and comely in the expreſſion of holineſs.

4. It is *Ingenious and ſingle:* His life moves not by ſeveral Rules, nor yet runs by ſeveral Principles, nor yet is carryed unto oppoſite Ends. The Mariner he ſpends his life at Sea for Profit, and the Scholar he ſpends his life in Study for Knowledg, and the Ambitious man he follows the Court for Honour, and the Hypocrite he trades in Duty for applauſe: but the true Penitent, he is careful, and watchful, and diligent over all his wayes, and in all the duties of piety, for Divine glory. *Gregory Nazianzen* diſtinguiſheth of three ſorts of men; ſome are

are *Mercenaries*, who work to get a good reward; others are *Servants*, who work to avoid punishment; others are *Sons*, and these labour for the highest good, to enjoy God, and to set out his Glory: *Whether we live, we live unto the Lord*, saith the Apostle. The Christian lives by the Lord; *By the Grace of God, I am that I am*, said *Paul*. And he lives upon the Lord, *The life that I now live, I live by the Faith of the Son of God*, saith S. *Paul* again. And he lives unto the Lord, both to his approbation and to his honour, *So that Christ may be magnified*, saith *Paul* yet again: his intentions are such as have the glory of God most principally in them; so that if you could unbowel the wayes of a Christian to discern their scope, you should find in them this Inscription, *To the Glory of God*. And the actions themselves (for the course of them) are such as respect the glory of God, they are all of them Holiness to the Lord, God is magnified by them.

A profitable walking.

5. It is *a profitable Walking:* The Impenitent man is a dead man, and his life is a deadly life, like the Plague, which is an infecting disease; like the *Prophets girdle, rotten, and good for nothing*. Either he is a dead letter, barren to any good, or he is a killing letter, doing much evil; either he is a rotten stick, good for nothing, or else he is a fire-brand, causing much wickedness. But when a person becomes penitent, now his heart is made good, and his life becomes profitable. As *Paul* wrote of *Onesimus* to *Philemon*, *That in time past he was unprofitable to him, but now*, saith he, *profitable to thee and me.*
‘ There is good to be got by him that is made good; blood runs
‘ through all the veins of his Conversation; one may get heat at his
‘ fire, and light at his candle, and refreshing at his streams, and
‘ clothing by his fleece; one may melt by his tears, go by his light,
‘ learn to trust by his faith, to fear by his tenderness, to live by
‘ his obedience. Oh how he strives to convert others, with S. *Austin*;
‘ *stin*; to give knowledg to others, with S. *Paul*; to warn and
‘ beseech others, with *Lot*; to profit the souls of others, and help
‘ the bodies of others. In his general calling he is diligent, and in his
‘ particular he is active; his counsels are savoury, and his walkings
‘ are heavenly, such as may save himself and those about him, if
‘ they be so humble and wise as to apprehend and learn.

6. Lastly,

Of the Returning Prodigal. 227

6. Lastly, *It is a comely walking; how beautiful are thy feet with shoes*, saith Christ of the Church, *Cant.*7.1. (Congruous to the condition of his place, of Grace ;) the walkings of a penitent are beautiful walkings, such as adorn his profession, such as become the Gospel of Christ, such as set out the truth of Grace, which he hath received, and the hope of glory which he expects, like so many Stars which are the glory of heaven: so are his particular actions inamelled with that Ornament of *Meekness*, with that Crown of *Wisdome*, with that Tendernefs of *Circumspection*, with that Sweetnefs of *Charity*, with that Gracefulnefs of *Piety*, that not only the mouths of some are stopped, but likewise the mouths of others are opened, by beholding the uniform light of his new Conversation, *to glorifie our father which is in heaven*.

It is a comely walking.

2. *Quest.* Thus you see what that better and singular course of life is, unto which God enables penitent persons: Now let us consider the *Reasons* why God doth enable them thus to walk. It cannot but be thus, if you consider 1. *The principle which is implanted in them*: As things are in being, so they are in working; that nature which is most predominant in any, hath still the command of the actions in him. Doth the penitent now live an heavenly life? Why, God hath given unto him a spiritual, and heavenly nature; *He is made pertaker of the Divine Nature*, which of all others is most holy, and spiritual, and heavenly. Doth he order his life by the rule of the Word? Why, the Word of God is ingraffed in him, and abides in him in the virtues and efficacies of it, so that he was converted by it, and will now be guided by it. Doth he lead an upright life? Why, the Lord hath taken from him the spirit of guile and deceitfulnefs, and hath given unto him an *One heart*, a plain, sincere, perfect, or upright heart; a right heart which cannot abide doubling, and dividing, and hollownefs, but it is of the truth; there is *truth in the inward parts*, and therefore, there is truth in the outward acts. Doth he lead a single life for Divine Glory? Why, he hath received real grace from God, which will work only for God; the Waters which come from the Sea, will run into the Sea again. Doth he live a profitable life? Why, it is the nature of true grace, and true repentance to make us as active in a good way, as we were violent in a bad; the nature of Good is to be

Reasons of it.

From the principle which is implanted in them.

G g 2 diffu-

diffusive, as the nature of fire is to heat, and of the Sun is to give light: *The love of Christ constraineth me* (faith *Paul.*) Doth he adorn his holy profession with an answerable conversation? Why! how can it be otherwise, but that gracious habits, should breed gracious acts; and glorious qualities, should breed glorious effects? It is the nature of a Star to shine, as it is the nature of dirt to defile; and it is the nature of a Diamond to sparkle, as it is of the earth to be black, *&c.*

From the peculiar disposition of Repentance.
   2. *The peculiar disposition of Repentance.* Repentance in the proper nature produceth two effects. 1. One in *newness of life*: It is against the truth of Repentance for a man to live the same life, to keep on the same course, for this is impenitency; not conversion, but continuation; not a regress, but a progress; not a change of life, but a course of the same life: But when Repentance comes, change comes; for what is repentance but the new purpose for a new life? A man must be what he was not, and do that which he never did, and run an other course quite contrary to what he did; *put off the old conversation, and put on a new*; *Cease to do evil, and learn to do well*; put off the service of unrighteousness, and become the servant of holiness: this is to be a penitent. 2. Another is *revenge*: you know the Apostle makes this one of the fruits of godly sorrow and repentance; *yea what revenge?* 2. Cor. 7. Now this revenge, as it consists in many other things, so in this especially; that as we have imployed our soules and bodies in wicked acts to serve against the Lord to his dishonor, so now we imploy and improve them in holy services to the proper glory of God; now we busy them, to know him, to love him, to obey him, to honour him: The penitent person is so sensible of the infinite dishonour which God hath had by his sinful life, that if he had now a thousand souls and bodies, and ten thousand lives, all were little enough in all holiness of Conversation to redeem those dishonours, and repair them.

The peculiar Intentions of God towards Penitent sinners. He intends much Glory by them.
   3. *The peculiar intentions which God hath towards penitent persons.* 1. He doth intend much *glory to himself by them*: for these are the people whom he doth form for his glory, and raise up to declare his praise, as is evident in *Paul*, and all other singular penitents, they have been the great instruments of his glory; but they cannot bring him glory unless they be
enabled

of the Returning Prodigal.

enabled to live better lives then before. If they be alienated from the life of God, they necessarily are alienated from the glory of God. Right believing, and right living, these are our methods to display the glory of God. 2. *He doth intend much peace and joy unto their Consciences*; a peace which passeth all understanding, and a joy which passeth all expression; even that which springs from his gracious favour and reconciliation with them in Christ, which both pacifies the conscience, and also quickens and revives it. But this could not be, unless he enabled them to new and better lives; the life of holiness is the only path of peace, that of wickedness is a way which knows not peace; there is no peace unto wicked men, nor unto wicked wayes. And for Joy, that only breeds joy in conscience, which makes the conscience not to accuse, but excuse; not to torment, but comfort; only the new life is the properly joyful and comfortable life; there are no spirits in the life which is not spiritual. 3. *He doth intend much outward mercy to them*: See how full the field of blessings is to the penitent; but it is upon this condition, If his life be obedient; as it were upon his good behaviour, If ye consent and obey ye shall eat the good of the Land. 4. *He doth intend them Glory before men, and Glory with himself in heaven*: For the penitent he makes to be the excellent on earth; his refined pieces of gold, a choice people whom Nations shall honour, and the people shall call blessed. When a man leaves a sordid and ignominious course of sinning, he then becomes honourable in the eyes of God, and reputable in the eyes of men. Now the spots of Leprosie fall off from *Naoman*, and his flesh grows clear and fair; but how should this Sun break out, if the clouds still remaine? Of necessity the life must alter, if we would have the opinions of men to alter; yea, and to what purpose is it to imagine an eternal life hereafter, unless we here first live an holy life, *without which no man shall see God?*

 Doth God inable the true penitent to a new and better life or walking? *then let us reflect on our wayes and lives.* How do we live? What kind of life is that which we do now live? Is it the life of a penitent or no?. *Never talk that thy heart is as good to God-ward as any mans though thy life be vile*; thou deludest thy self; if thy life be evil, assuredly thy heart is not good: *The Tree*, sayes our Saviour, *is known by his fruits*; for a person to talk of a penitent heart, and what terror he hath had for sin, and in

And much peace and joy unto them.

And much outward mercy to them.

And Glory before men, and with himself in Heaven.

Use 1.

What kind of life doest thou live. Deceive not thy self with the goodness of thy heart; if thy life be bad.

some

some particulars to make a little semblance of godliness, when yet all this while he goes on in a course of drunkenness, or of uncleanness, of riotousness, or of lying, or of pride, or of covetousness, or of injustice, or of scoffing, &c. What a monstrous and wilful deceit is this of a mans soul? Thou a penitent, who art still a servant of Lust! Thou a penitent, who still walkest in darkness! Thou a penitent whose very course of life is nothing but a confutation of repentance, a trade in sin! Knowest thou not, O sinner, that where the heart is changed, the life will change? If thou hast once put off thy corrupt nature, thou wilt easily put off thy corrupt conversation. Who doth as he did, if he be not as he was? No, real repentance turns us, and that is, from the love of sin in the heart, and from the course of sin in the life; as it suffers thee not to be an hypocrite, so it abhors that thou shouldst be profane; if thy life be bad, question it not, thy heart is bad; that filthy speech comes from thy filthy Nature, that haughty look from thy proud Nature, that griping hand from thy cruel Nature, that fraudulent tongue from thy cousening Nature. 2. As much are they deceived who go on gently and gravely in their old, formal, cold, negative way of repentance; deeming themselves no less then Penitentiaries, who have this only to plead, They never in all their lives did wrong or harm, &c. But remember, O self-deceiver, if ever God gives to thee repentance indeed, thou wilt find other sinful courses to be left besides those of Commission; thou wilt find thine Omissions to be a highly guilty course of sin, that thou frequently omits calling upon God, hearing of his Word, reading of his Word, examining of thy heart, humbling of thy soul, walking in an holy, and heavenly, and exact manner, &c. Thou often criest out, What bad course am I in? I demand of thee, what holy course art thou in? what other course of life leadest thou then ever, &c. Well, I will say no more but this; but if other and better lives be the arguments of true Repentance, the Lord be merciful to us, there are then but very few penitents; the same oaths, the same cursings, the same worldliness, the same pride, the same drunkenness, the same uncleanness, the same neglects of God and spiritual duties; we are not others then we were, we live not otherwise then we have done.

But secondly, If any of you take your selves to be penitents, I beseech you then, let us carefully *shew it by our lives and con-*

Not with a cold, formal, negative Repentance.

Use 2. Let us shew our Repentance by our Conversation.

conversations. Consider to this purpose, 1. *If there be truth of Repentance, there will be newness of Conversation:* A monstrous thing to see a man start up and walk with his Coffin and Grave-cloaths. If it be light it will shine, and if it be fire it will heat, and if it be salt it will season; if thy heart be purged indeed, thy life will also be reformed indeed. *If ye have been taught as the truth is in Jesus: put off, concerning the former conversation, the old man.* 2. *The Lord Jesus hath purchased thy Life as well as thy Soul,* and redeemed thy Conversation as well as thy Nature; He did dye not only to recover thy inward Man, but also to cure thy outward Man; that as thy Heart should not be profane, so thy Conversation should not be vain: *Christ hath suffered for us in the flesh, that we should no longer live the rest of our time in the flesh,* 1 Pet. 4. 1, 2. Christ hath dyed for thee, that now thou shouldst live unto him. 3. *The honour of Religion lyes upon thy Life:* Thy heart may be a secret, a closet of much good or evil, we leave it to the Searcher of hearts; but thy life is a publick Letter, an audible Voice, a common Object: The profession of truth and holiness is an honourable thing in it self, but a good and answerable Conversation adds and reflects a greater honour to it. As the Heaven is a beautiful Creature, but it is the more beautified by the shining of the Stars: So is it with Religion, it is an Excellency in it self, and is made the more excellent by an excellent Conversation. But a lewd, rude, foolish, boystrous, incongruous, fowl, uneven, evil life, makes Religion to look like Gold in the dirt, or like a Jewel in a Swines snout, or like Beauty in a Whore. It is the very scandal of Religion, and as a death verse upon an holy profession: What is it, that thou now and then fillest the eyes of men with a little gravity, and the ears of men with a little piety, when still thou, by thy wicked life, armes the hearts of men to scorn, and the tongues of men to blaspheme the Name of God and Professors? The more pretence thou hast to repentance, the more odious art thou, by thy impenitent life, to the profession thereof. The strictest eyes are upon the strictest professors, and no miscarriages take so soon with men, or damp Religion more. 4. *The souls of men lie much upon their life:* What *Greg. Nazianz.* said of the Painter, That he teacheth not by his language, but by his hand; and *Chrysostom* of the Minister, That his first part is to Live well, and then to Teach well; that is true of every penitent Christian,

If there be true Repentance there will be newness of conversation.

Ephes. 4. 21.

Christ hath purchased thy life as well as thy soul.

The honour of Religion lies upon thy life.

The souls of men lie much upon their life.

232   *Gods gracious Acceptance*

Christian, for his inward affections come not so into our scales as his outward actions: We judge of him, and imitate him not by what lies hid in his heart, but by what appears in his life; and of all men we are most confident to imitate the actions of those who pretend most against sin. Now then, if thou who pretendest to repent of all sin, by thy sinful life shouldst multiply sinners amongst men, or strengthen the hearts of sinners from returning, O how bitter, O how dismal, how fearful, how an amazing account, that thou even under a forme of Repentance, shouldst keep men in an estate of impenitency, to damn their souls by thy continual sinnings? Sins in conversation are alwayes of more publick danger then those of disposition, as a Feavor or a Plague.

The comfort and peace of thy Conscience lies much in it.

5. *The comfort and peace of thy Conscience lies much in it*: A good Life is the best Commentary of an upright heart, and uprightness is a comfort: A good Life is the best Star to clear up Gods glory; and to bring him glory, is to bring our selves comfort. Conscience will judge thee more for evil in life, as more perfected, more hurtful, than for that within. A good life is the only Plaister, by which we heal others; the only Pilot by which we direct others; the only Hand, by which we hold up others: We may think good, but this circumscribes it self with our selves; we may desire good, but this also confines it self with our selves. The good life is the life only which doth good to others; and the more good we do, the more comfort still we have.

The Reward will be great to the good life.

6. *The reward will be great to the life that is good:* Its true, that God in his future retribution hath respect to the inward graces and dispositions, but he takes publick notice of the operations of them in our lives, as for acting themselves, and therefore pronounceth the reward to the doer, and the kingdom unto him that cloaths, and feeds, and visits, &c. What! an eternal life for a good life!

All that are truly penitent have been very circumspect of their lives.

7. But lastly, *Look on all who are truly penitent, or have been so, how tender and circumspect they have been of their lives and walkings:* How extremely circumspect was *David* of his tongue, *Psa.* 39. and as exceedingly pensive for any unbeseeming word or fact, much more for any scandalous evil; *such a fool, such a beast was I,* Psa. 51. So the Apostles, both in their wayes and in their directions unto all the Saints, pressing earnestly, and that by the Lord Jesus, that they live and walk as becometh Saints, and as becometh the Gospel, and

tha

Of the Returning Prodigal.

that the Name of Christ be not blasphemed; and as he who hath called them is holy, so should they be holy in all manner of converfation.

Queft. But how should our lives be so led, that it may appear we are Penitents indeed? *Sol.* For the *manner* of life which the truly Penitent should lead, either it respects, 1. God, in duties of Piety. And here these adjuncts of Life are necessary: 1. *Solid*, and *not formal performances of Religious Services*; in the main Duties; not an empty cloud, a naked vizard, a life without life. 2. *Adequate*, and not partial ways of obedience, like and diflike. 3. *Conftant*, and not light and changeable exercifes of holy acts; without wavering and unfetledness. Secondly, *Men*: And here the walking or converfation must be, 1. *Wife*, and not ridiculous; 2. *Meek* and *gentle*, and not turbulent; 3. *Profitable*, and not vain or evil; 4. *Mercifull*, and not cruel; 5. *Humble*, and not cenforious; 6. *Juft*, and not fcandalous and injurious; 7. In all things *circumfpect* without offence. Thirdly, *Thofe in relation to us*: And here the life must be an *Obfervance*, without contempt and flighting of those to whom honour is due; 2. *Affection with love and pity*, without fcorn or rigour; 3. A *Care*, with furtherance of their fouls, without neglect and wearinefs.

The manner of a Penitents life.

As it refpects God in duties of Piety.

As it refpects Men.

For this my fon was dead, and is alive again; he was loft, and is found: And they began to be merry,

These words seem to be an Abridgement of the whole Parable of the Prodigal Child. And they comprehend in them, 1. His *natural*, finfull, or unconverted condition; [*This my fon was dead, and was loft.*] A natural man is a dead man, and a loft man; either of thefe expreffes a fad mifery, but both of them conclude him compleatly miferable. 2. His *fupernatural*, changed, or converted condition; [*and is alive again, and is found.*] No man lives, till he be a converted man. *Fuit* (faid *Seneca*) *non vixit*; *& ab eo tempore cenfemur, ex quo in Chrifto renafcimur*, faith *Hierome*. 3. The *joy*, comfort, and delight of that altered condition; [*And they began to be merry.*] Joy is a drop diftilled from Grace.; the condition is then comfortable, when it is godly. I begin with the firft part, and there with the loft eftate of the Prodigal; where obferve, H h That

That every sinfull or unconverted man is a lost man. [*This*

Doct. 1.
Every sinfull unconverted man is a lost man.

my son was lost.] There are two sorts of sinners in Scripture, who are stiled lost. 1. *Finally impenitent*: These are irrecoverably lost; lost, and never found. Thus *Judas* was lost; *None of them is lost, but the son of perdition,* Joh. 17. 1 *.* And of such the Apostle speaks, *If our Gospel be hid, 'tis hid to them that are lost.* 2 Cor. 4. 3. 2. *Temporary wanderers*; who *quantum ad statum præsentem* are lost, but *quoad decretum de futuro* shall be found: To these that saying seems to refer, in *Luk.* 19. 10. *The Son of Man is come to seek and to save that which was lost.* Again, One may be said to be lost, 1. who is stept out of the way: Every sinning is a straying, and every straying is a kind of lostness; thus even a converted man is many times lost. *I have gone astray* (saith *David,* Psal. 119. 170.) *like a lost sheep.* 2. *Who is not as yet come into the way:* Thus the unconverted man is lost. Psal. 58. 3. *The wicked are estranged from the womb*; they go astray as soon as they be born. And *Psal.* 14. 3. *They are gone aside.* And *Rom.* 9. 12. *They are all gone out of the way.*

And may be so called in eight respects.
He hath lost his God.
Lysimachus.

Now an unconverted man may be called a lost man, in eight respects. Because, 1. *He hath lost his God:* Every man (at the first) had God to be his God; but man sinned, and by sin every man lost God: We never lose our selves, but when we lose our God; and we never lose our God, but by sinning. There was one once, *who lost his Kingdome for a draught of water*; and we, in *Adam,* lost our God for the taste of an *Apple.* This is a great loss, to lose our God. A Child may lose his Father, and yet live; the Mariner may lose his Anchor, and yet sail: But if the World doth lose the Sun, it loseth all; But if Man loseth his God, he loseth him who is better than All. There are four great losses in that one loss of God: There is a loss, 1. of the *Image of God*, that Royal Crown is gone; 2. of the *Favour of God*, that friendly look is gone; 3. of the *Society of God*, that sweet fruition is gone; 4. of the *Happiness of God*, that onely life is gone: A Just God remains still, and a Mighty God remains still; but the Gracious God is lost, but the Blessed God is lost.

Lost his Paradise.

2. *He hath lost his Paradise:* Paradise was the garden of blessings, and of all delights; and some conjecture, that all happiness

Of the Returning Prodigal.

piness consists in delight; but the impenitent, wandring, unconverted sinner, is far from blessing or comfort. The child of disobedience is only an heir of the curse; *Write that man childless*, said God of *Coniah*; so may it be said of an unconverted sinner, Write that man comfortless. Or as *Jeremiah* said of *Pashur*, Thou shalt be called *Magor-missabib, terrour round about*; the same may be affirmed of this sinner, He is exiled from all comfort and blessing, there is no peace unto him, no blessing; he cannot justly expect one crop of mercy, not one good day all his days; the womb is a prison, the world a sea, sin a grave, life a wilderness, death an hell, to a wicked man.

3. *He hath lost his soul:* And what is left when my soul is lost? There are divers kinds of losses; some Losses are Gain to us, (such was *Pauls loss*, Phil. 3.) Some Losses are a Pain to us, a little diminution, an excise onely of this or that comfort; some lose Sin, and get Christ; some lose Earth, and get Heaven; but no loss like the loss of the Soul: Now every unconverted man hath lost this Jewel, this Soul of his: He hath lost his Soul, 1. To *Satan*, who hath the dominion and use of it, he rules, and he works mightily in it, and over it; a wicked mans soul is the Devils slave, he takes it captive at his pleasure: 2. To *a condemning and revenging God*; *The soul that sins shall die*; the Lease is forfeited; sin forfeits the soul into the hands of a condemning God, and there it is stayed for ever, unless a price be paid by the bloud of Christ to ransome and recover it.

Lost his soul.

4. *He hath lost his Excellencies:* His Glory is departed. Sinfull man doth not know what is become of created man; yea, he hath lost these so long, that he knows not whether ever he had any of them, or no; whether he ever had such an eye or Lamp of exquisite knowledge, whether he ever had such a vesture of righteousness, whether he ever had such a stock of ability and sufficiency for Obedience. As he once could not find *Rome* in *Rome*, nor they know *Jezabel* to have been *Jezabel*; just so is it with a poor sinner. He once was a child of Light, a son of Obedience, he was created holy and righteous: But what is become of all his created stock? *But man dieth, and man giveth up the ghost, and where is he?* Job 14. 10. So here, man hath sinned, and man hath lost all his excellencies, and where is he? *Adam, where art thou?* said God: A sad question, Where art thou? An hour since,

Lost his Excellencies.

since, *Adam* was *Adam*; but upon his sinning, *Adam*, where is *Adam* ? Where is righteous *Adam* ? Where is *Adam*, who had power to believe, to love, to obey all my will? Where is he? and where is all this? All is lost.

Lost his way. 5. *He hath lost his way*, his way home: Every sinfull man is a wandring Meteor, a very Planet on earth; he is gone from the fold, as a silly sheep; he is gone from his Fathers house, as a silly Child; he is gone out of the right path, like a silly Traveller in the Wildernets. Sin puts us into a Maze, into a Labyrinth; we go from one sin to another sin, out of one by-path into another by-path; and the further we go in sinfull paths, the more still we go out of the way: But the right path which leads back to our God, O the sinner hath not an eye to see it; and when he hath light to see it, yet he hath not an heart to turn unto it, nor feet to walk in it. *Rom.* 3. 12. *They are all gone out of the way*; v.17. *The way of peace they have not known.* Psal.95.10. *It is a people that do err in their hearts, and they have not known my ways.* The lost sinner hath an erring mind, and an erring heart, and erring affections. There is but one way to come back to God, which is by Christ, (*I am the way*, &c.) but the lost sinner knows not Christ, nor the way unto Christ.

Lost his ability. 6. *He hath lost his Ability:* He who once had power to fall, being fallen, hath now no power to rise any more; a self-deliverance is as impossible as a self-creation: It must be light which finds that which is lost, but sinfull man is darkness; it must be strength which raiseth up one who is fallen, but lost man is less than weakness. He who loseth himself by sin, must come back again by grace; but the natural man hath no grace, no not a desire of it, no not a thought of it, no nothing of all of it. What Sin casts down, Faith must set up; but the unconverted man doth not, nay, cannot believe; of himself he cannot: As all our powers were at first in *Adams* hands, so all our powers now are in Christs hands.

Lost in respect of his liberty. 7. The sinner is also *lost in respect of his Title* and *Plea*, and in respect of his Liberty and Freedome, so that now every sinner is a very slave and bondman. *Obj.* But *how* comes man to be a lost man? I answer, Man came to be a lost sinner, First,

How man comes to be lost.

By temptation. *By Temptation:* The Devil lost his own happiness, and by his cunning seducements, Man lost his happiness too. Four things he used

Of the Returning Prodigal.

used for this : 1. He raised a suspition and jealousie in our hearts of God ; 2. Then a dislike of our present condition ; 3. Then an affectation of an higher condition ; 4. A false perswasion of Gods threatning.   Secondly, *By his own will*. And there were (be- sides our original Liberty *ad utrumlibet*) four principal sins which brought us into our Lostness : 1. *Pride*, 2. *Unbelief*, 3. *Presumption*, 4. *Discontentment*.

By his own will.

Object. But how may a man know that he is as yet in a lost condition ? *Sol.* This may be resolved by these Queries : 1. Where is thy Home ? 2. What is thy way ? 3. When didst thou return? 1. *Every lost man is a man afar off. In longum abiit,* he is gone far from home, from his Father : When the Prodigal was lost, where was he then ? The Text saith, That he *was gone into a far Countrey.* When the *Ephesians* were lost, where were they ? *Afar off,* Ephes. 2. 17. When the *Israelites* were lost, where were they? *They are gone away far from me,* Jer. 2. 5. A natural man is far from God, (take me right,) you can never find God and a wicked man together ; his nature is far from God, and his thoughts are far from God, and his affections are far from God : O, he cannot endure the presence of God, he cannot endure Holiness, he cannot endure holy Ordinances, nor holy Services, nor holy Admonitions, nor holy Reproofs, nor any holy Communion ; the further he is from these, the better doth he think his condition to be. A man is never at home till he hath a God, and till he stands in Gods presence, and till he hath communion with his God : But the natural man, &c.   2. *Every lost man is in a false way,* in a by-way ; his ways are sinfull ways : The lost man, he is out of the common and known Road ; he is in the Woods, in the Ditches, in the Deserts, in the Fields, and he goes from one strange place to another strange place. O man ! whilest thou walkest after thy sins, whilest thou runnest from sin to sin, whiles thy way and course of Life is in the fulfilling and following of thy Lusts, assuredly thou art a lost man.   2. *Didst thou ever yet return to God ?* If not, then as yet thou art in a lost condition. O consider this, consider it seriously, When didst thou return ? How didst thou return ? Wherein didst thou return back unto thy God ? Is not he lost, who is still losing of himself ? who still goes on in his Wilderness ? And this thou doest ; where thou wast twenty years ago, there thou art still.

How a man may know that he is lost.

Every lost man is afar off.

Every lost man is in a false way.

He is lost who doth not return.

That

Gods Gracious Acceptance

Doct. 2.
A loſt ſinner may be found.

That a loſt ſinner may be found. [*This my ſon was loſt, and is found.*] In Scripture there is a two-fold finding. 1. We are ſaid to find God: *Seek the Lord, while he may be found,* Iſa. 55.6. *I found him whom my ſoul loveth,* Cant. 3.4. 2. God is ſaid to find us. Now God finds a ſinner two ways: 1. Judicially, and in wrath, *ad evertendum.*; 2. Gracioufly, and in mercy, *ad convertendum.* Here three Queſtions offer themſelves to be diſcuſſed.

Who finds the loſt ſinner? God onely.

Queſt. 1. *Who is it that finds a loſt ſinner?* Sol. The Anſwer is eaſie; It is God onely. *I will ſeek that which was loſt,* Ezek. 34. 16. It was he who found *Abraham* in *Caldea* amongſt the Idolaters, and *David* among the ſheep-folds, and *Manaſſes* among the thorns and buſhes, and *Paul* in the way to *Damaſcus,* and *Matthew* at the receit of Cuſtome, and the *Iſraelites* in their bloud, and *Mary Magdalene* in her uncleannefs. *The ſinner cannot find himſelf*; he can loſe himſelf, but he cannot find himſelf; he can wander, but he cannot return of himſelf: *Avertere a Deo,* man can do that; but *convertere ad Deum,* man cannot do this. Man loves to wander; but to come back, man hath neither will nor power. *No man can find a loſt ſinner.* He may find a loſt ſinner, by way of diſcovery, but he cannot find him by way of recovery; I may *diſcover,* but not *recover*; 2. *Bewail,* but not *prevail*; 3. *give Counſel,* but not *give Grace*: I may ſee one running from God, but I cannot bring him back to God; I may ſee him wandring to Hell, but I cannot ſet his heart to turn back to Heaven; and I may bewail a loſt ſinner, yet I cannot prevail upon a loſt ſinner; and I can give him counſel to come home, but I cannot give him grace to come home: It is God, God onely, who can find a loſt ſinner. *Quis ovem perdicam requirere debeat, nonne qui perdidit, quis perdidit? nonne qui habuit? Quis habuit, nonne qui fecit.* So *Tertullian* appoſitely, He onely that made man, he onely it is who can find the ſinner.

How God finds a loſt ſinner?
He is moved with compaſſion towards him.

Queſt. 2. *How God finds a loſt ſinner?* Sol. There are ſeven Acts of God, which are converſant about the finding of a loſt ſinner. 1. *He is moved with compaſſion towards him*; the Lord pities ſuch a ſinner: Alas, ſaith God, this poor, ignorant, fooliſh man, is gone from me, the fountain of his life; lo, how his luſts deceive him, how Satan rules him, how he wanders up and down in vanity; he is quite out of the way of his happineſs;

he

Of the Returning Prodigal.

he is running towards hell, but perceives it not; he is undoing and destroying his immortal soul, but observes it not; he knows not whether he goes; he is undone for ever, if I stay him not, if I turn him not. 2. *He intends good to this particular lost* He intends *sinner. I will surely have mercy on him. I have seen his ways,* good to this *and will heal him. I know the thoughts that I think towards him,* lost sinner. *thoughts of good, and not of evil.* I will glorifie all my mercy and goodness in this very sinner; I will not suffer him to run on thus, I will look after him, I will bring him home to my self, and save him. 3. *He sends out after him;* one servant, and another He sends out servant; one Minister, and another Minister: Go, saith God, after him. to such a Parish, and to such a Family, and preach, and make enquiry, Is there not such a miserable sinner here? is there not such a lost man there? one that is gone from his Fathers house? one that hath spent all in riotous living? Is there never a man here, who hath departed from God, lived without God, run all his life in sinfull, loose, base courses of disobedience, and would now be glad of mercy? This is the general seeking of a lost sinner. 4. *He makes a privy search after him;* for (perhaps) He makes a the general Hue and Cry will not find the sinner, and therefore privy search the Lord makes a privy search: As to find out *Achan*, there was after him. Tribe searched by Tribe, and Family by Family, and Person by Person; and thus doth the Lord in finding of a lost sinner; He comes more distinctly, and his Word or Afflictions draw after this sinner more personally; they light at his door, (upon his person) and knock, and enquire, Art not thou the man? doth not the lost sinner abide here? Art not thou, he who hast lived ignorantly, or profanely, and gone astray from thy God? 5. *He* He lights on *lights on him at length:* And then the Lord lights on a lost sinner, him at length. when he actuates and quickens Conscience in him, which now can be silent no longer, but cries out, 'Lord, here he is; Here 'is the Swearer, Drunkard, Whoremonger, Sabbath-breaker, &c. And now out comes the lost sinner, with a trembling heart, and a guilt-smiting spirit, 'Lord, who is it that you look for? 'do you 'look after a sinner, a lost sinner? I am the man you look for: 'Oh I have sinned, I have wandred, I have been lost all my 'days; *what shall I say unto thee, O thou preserver of men?* or 'what shall I do? Oh! if thou takest not pity on me, if thou shewest not mercy unto me; I perish, I die, I am lost for ever.

6. *He*

He deals with him to return.

Four ways.

By Expostulation.

By Conviction.

By Propositions of Mercy.

By directing him into the way of Returning.

6. *He deals with this sinner to return and come back unto him.* Hof. 14. 1. *O Israel, return unto the Lord thy God ; for thou hast fallen by thine iniquity.* And there are four ways which the Lord useth to prevail upon a lost sinner, to turn back unto him : 1. By *Expostulation :* What have I been unto thee, or what have I done unto thee, or what iniquity hast thou found in me, that thou hast all this while departed from me ? Was not I the God that formed thee ? the Father that brought thee forth ? the Master that fed thee, and took care of thee ? Was there not goodness, and kindness, and fulness enough in me ? why hast thou dealt thus unkindly with me ? 2. *By Conviction* of his wandring condition, with the baseness and miserableness thereof. These are thy ways, and these have been thy doings, and what profit hast thou by those things whereof thou art or mayest be now ashamed ? Why! what hast thou got by all thy sinfull wandrings ? See how naked thou art of all spiritual good, how shamefull thy course hath been : Is the Wilderness a place for a Child ? How poor and undone thou art! Thou hast spent all ; and if thou continuest in thy sinfull ways, thou wilt certainly perish with hunger : Sin hath been thy loss ; and if thou return not, it will certainly be thy ruine. Return, O lost Sinner, return, return, why wilt thou die and perish for ever ? 3. *By Propositions of Mercy :* As S. *John* ran after that young lost man of *Jerusalem*, crying unto him, Return, my son, return ; Christ will yet accept of thee, Christ will yet shew thee mercy. So doth the Lord God, when he would bring back a lost sinner ; *Return,* faith he, *and live, return and live.* Ezek. 18. 32. Though thou hast forgot the Duty of a Child, yet I have not put off the Affection of a Father : I am that Father, in *whose house there is bread enough, and to spare* ; Do but come back unto me, and all shall be well : Canst thou live without Bread ? canst thou live without my Mercy ? Mercy shall be thine, if thou wilt return from thy lost and sinfull courses. 4. *By directing him into the way of coming back :* As 1. With *mournfull confession of his sins.* Hof. 14. 2. *Take with you words, and return unto the Lord ; say unto him, Take away iniquity, and receive us graciously.* 2. *With penitential reformation.* Isa. 55. 7. *Let the wicked forsake his way, and the unrighteous man his thoughts, and let him return unto the Lord, and he will have mercy on him, and to our God, for*

Of the Returning Prodigal.

he will abundantly pardon. 3. *With believing application:* Thou must go, faith God, to my Son; for he is the way and the life, and he came to seek and to save that which was lost. Seventhly: Now, notwithstanding all this, the lost sinner is not perfectly found, and therefore the Lord doth one thing more; he doth with this lost sinner, as the shepherd did with the lost sheep, who took him on his shoulders, and brought him home: So the *Lord lays hold on this poor lost soul, by his Almighty Spirit of Grace, and puts into him a returning heart,* an other heart, and makes him willing and glad to leave his sinfull wayes, and to return to himself, and to implore his reconciled favour and acceptance in Jesus Christ: Which being done, now is the lost sinner found indeed; for then, and then onely is a lost sinner found, when he, in truth, turns back to God, and enjoys him as his reconciled God in Christ. *Jer.* 3. 22. *Return, ye back-sliding children: Behold, we come unto thee, for thou art the Lord our God.*

By laying hold upon him by his Almighty Grace, and putting into him a returning heart.

Quest. 3. *Why doth God thus look after and find a lost sinner? Sol.* The Reasons may be these. 1. Although the sinner be not worth the looking after, *yet the soul of a sinner is worth the looking after.* The sinner is the Devils creature, but the soul is Gods creature, (*The soul that I have made,* faith God, *Isa.* 57. 16.) The *lost sheep* was worth the looking after, and so was the *lost groat*; surely then a lost soul is worth the looking after, which is, at least, of as much value as a lost Groat. *Christ* (faith *Theophylact* on *Matth.* 18.) was the man who left the Ninety nine sheep, and lookt after one lost sheep; he left the society of Angels in Heaven, to find one lost Soul on Earth. O, the Soul of Man is a precious, a valuable Substance made only by God, and fit only to match and converse with God. 2. As God knows the worth of a soul, *so God knows the loss of a Soul*: O Sirs! we make little account of losing souls; but verily no loss like the loss of a soul: As Christ spake of the fall of that house, *The fall thereof was great,* that's true of the loss of a soul, the loss thereof is very great. A man, in the event, loseth nothing, though he loseth all the world, if his soul be not lost: But if the soul be lost, all is lost, all is lost to an eternity; and therefore the Lord, out of unspeakable pity, looks after a lost sinner. 3. *Jesus Christ hath laid down a price for some souls,* and Jesus Christ

Why God doth thus find a lost sinner?

The soul is worth the looking after.

God knows the loss of a soul.

Christ hath laid down a price for souls.

I j

Christ *shall see of the travel of his soul*, he shall have his purchase to the full value. 4. *God will have some to magnifie the riches of his glorious Grace*, and Love, and Kindness, and Mercy, yea, and to enjoy eternal Glory with himself; therefore he will find some lost sinners: For no sinner but a found sinner, can either glorifie God, or be glorified with him.

Use 1: The first Use shall be for *Examination* of our selves, Whether our lost souls be found thus of God, or no? I will propound unto you, 1. *Some Arguments* or *Motives* to put you upon this Trial. 2. Then the Trials or Characters of a person whom God in mercy hath found.

The *Arguments* which may move us to a serious Trial, whether we be found persons, or no, are these: 1. *Every man is lost, but every man is not found:* All are lost, but few are found; the way of sin is general, but the way of mercy is special: *Mat.* 7. 13. *Wide is the gate, and broad is the way that leadeth to destruction, and many there be that go in thereat.* v. 14. *But strait is the gate, and narrow is the way that leadeth unto life, and few there be that find it.* You read of a general complaint, *They are all gone out of the way*; but you read not of a general acclamation, They are all returned into the way. Take the way of finding a lost sinner, and bringing him home to God, either 1. *by Repentance*: Why! the number of sinners is exceeding large, but the number of repenting sinners is very scant. As he said once of an Army, Here are many Men, but few Souldiers; so may it be said in this case: Sinners are like the Sands in the sea, very numerous; but Penitent Sinners are like Pearls in the sea, very rare and precious. 2. *By Faith*: All are sinners, but few, very few are true believers: Historical Faith, though it be a common faith, yet it is not very common; *Who hath believed our report?* They are the fewest part of the world, who do *credere Christum*, believe that there is a Christ; but how few, even of these, do *credere in Christum*, believe in Christ? And Men are never found, till Faith be found in them.

2. *It is a very bad, and a very sad condition, not to be found out of, but to be found still in a lost condition:* If it were no more but this, That such a person cannot find himself under the clasp or compass of any saving mercy, this were heavy: To be in a Desert, and not to know that ever he shall come alive out of it;

Of the Returning Prodigal.

to be in the Ocean, and not to know that ever he shall come safe to Land; to be in a sinfull condition, and not to know whether ever Divine Mercy will pull him out of this condition: Yet this is the case of a lost sinner; he cannot tell whether ever Divine Mercy will look after him, or no; perhaps it will, perhaps it will not.

But besides this, let's consider what may find that lost sinner, whom Divine Mercy hath not yet effectually and graciously found. 1. *All external miseries may suddenly find him.* *A-* All external *dam* run away from God, and what did he find? and *Jonah,* and miseries may what did he find? All losses may speedily befal a lost person; suddenly find Safety is at home, and Dangers abroad: In how many dangers is him. the lost sheep upon the mountains? In how many perils is the lost man in the wilderness? they may become an easie prey to all devouring beasts, and are oft times forced to eat up themselves to preserve themselves. A lost, impenitent, unconverted sinner, is sure of no mercy; and he is naked, and exposed to all misery. *In the fulness of his sufficiency* (saith *Zophar,* Job 20. 22.) *he shall be in streights,* every hand of the wicked shall come upon him, *v.* 23. When he is about to fill his belly, God shall cast the fury of his wrath upon him, and shall rain it upon him while he is eating. 2. *A guilty and amazing Conscience* A guilty Con-*may quickly find him*; that inward Hell, as one speaks: The science may glistring Sword cometh out of his Gall, *terrours are upon him,* quickly find *Job* 20. 25. When *Judas* had lost himself, how quickly did he him. find a guilty Conscience? It is an heavy thing, to be found out by that which, as *Bernard* speaks, is Bailiff, and Jailor, and Witness, and Jury, and Sheriffs, and Judge, and Executioner too. *Every man that finds me will kill me,* said *Cain,* Gen 4. 3. *And Death may find thee;* to which thou wilt say, as *Ahab* Death may to the Prophet, *Hast thou found me, O mine enemy?* And find thee. Death may return the Prophets answer unto thee, *Yea, I have found thee, because thou hast sold thy self to work evil in the sight of the Lord,* 1 Kin. 21. 20. 4. *And Gods condemning* Gods condem-*Judgment will find thee.* If thou, O lost sinner, be not now ning Judge-found to thy conversion, God will one day find thee to thy ments will find subversion; if Mercy finds thee not to come back to thee. God, Justice shall find thee to call thee quite away from God.

I j 2 3. It

244   *Gods Gracious Acceptance*

It is unspeakable joy, if God have found thy lost soul.

Here is, Rescuing mercy. Pardoning mercy. Reconciled communion with God.

3. *It is an unspeakable joy, if thou canst find that God hath in mercy found thy lost soul.* O there are many precious mercies which a found soul doth and may find. 1. *Rescuing mercy:* He is delivered from Sin and Satan. Is it not a mercy to be freed of a Disease, of a Prison? O what then to be delivered from Sin, from Satan! 2. *Pardoning mercy.* That of the Prophet is certainly verified of thee, in *Jer.* 50. 20. *In those days, and in that time, saith the Lord, the iniquity of Israel shall be sought for, and there shall be none; and the sins of Judah, and they shall not be found: for I will pardon them,* &c. 3. *Reconciled communion with thy God:* Thou who wast found in Jail before, mayest now be found in thy Fathers house; thou who wast a Vagabond before, art now a Son; God hath accepted of thee, thou hast found favour in his eyes, and mayest find free access unto his presence.

Thy soul shall be found in glory.

4. Nay, *If God hath found thee in mercy, it will not be long ere that soul of thine shall be found in Glory.*

Many men think themselves found, who yet are lost.

4. Many men do reckon upon it, that they are found, when yet they remain in a lost condition. There are three things which discover the mistake of men in this kind. 1. Though they say, that they have found out their sinfull condition, yet still they remain in their sinfull condition. 2. Though they say, that they have found out the true way of life, yet they cannot be found walking in that way of life. 3. Though they say that God hath found them, yet you cannot find them to fear this God, nor to love this. God, nor to honour and exalt this God; all the marks of Lostness are upon them, ignorance, blindness, superstition, profaneness, vile wayes, &c.

How may one know that God hath found his lost soul.

But will some say, *How may one know, that God hath found (in converting mercy) his lost soul?* This leads me to the second thing, which comprehends the *Trials* or Characters of a lost soul truly found: And there are Nine infallible Evidences of a lost person graciously found.

Trials of it.

He finds himself to be utterly lost.

1. When a lost sinner *is found by God, he doth then find himself to be utterly lost.* Unclean, unclean, said the Leper. Undone, undone, *God be mercifull to me a sinner*, said the *Publican. In me there dwels no good,* I am the *greatest of sinners*, said *Paul.* God finds us by making us to find our selves. There is a vast difference twixt 1. A *vulgar confession,* I am a sinner, all men are sinners; 2. An *experimental conviction,* I am the lost sinner, these sins, these my sins

Of the Returning Prodigal.

fins have undone me; I am undone and loft for such a sin, and for such a sin; I perish, I perish, if I get not out of this condition; my God is loft, and my soul will be loft; I am gone from God, I am out of the way of life; if I stay here, I die: *I perish for hunger*, said the found Prodigal. Thou lookest on thy self and state, but how? as sinfull! well; but doest thou look on that thy sinfull estate, as a perishing, as thy perishing condition? as a condition, not a day, not an hour, not a moment more to be stayed in? Doest thou look on it as on the Leak in the Ship, as a sinking Leak, as a splitting Rock, as a soul-destroying, murthering, ruining condition? The Lord never finds any man, but he finds him and brings him back, so as he shall acknowledge who hath found him, (even a God,) and what hath found him, (even his mercy;) and this will never be acknowledged, until God makes us first to see how utterly loft we were; that the found sinner may say, 'Twas mercy that pitied me, 'twas mercy that looked after me, 'twas mercy that lighted on me, 'twas mercy which dealt with me, wooed me, overcame me, brought me back, saved me; meer mercy; for I was utterly loft, I had perished, if mercy had not recovered me, &c.

2. *When God finds a loft sinner, that sinner finds himself without all strength to come back to God.* Though you find your selves to have loft your God, yet if you can find strength of your own to bring you back unto your God, assuredly your loft souls are not found: For (to speak punctually) no man finds himself loft, who as yet can find any thing in himself to set up himself; if I yet possess strength, I am not yet loft: But a truly and experimentally loft soul, feels in it self not onely a loss of God, but also of power to come forth, to come back to God; *Rom. 5. Without strength.* It knows not, by its own light, one foot of the way; and when it is made known, alas, it finds no power to stir; nay, if I might have mercy and heaven upon the freest terms, but for coming home, I am not able to do it. O how a found loft soul complains! It complains as much of an impotent heart, as of a wandring heart: I cannot come, I cannot turn this wandring heart into the right way; come back to my God I should, but come I cannot; go to Christ I should, but go I cannot; if Christ doth not come to me, I shall never be able to come to him; if he doth not seek me, I shall never seek him; if he finds not me with strength, I shall never find him with comfort and safety. 3. If. He finds him self without strength to return.

He will above all things desire to be found in Christ.

3. *If God hath indeed found thee,* Thou wilt, above all things, desire to be found in Christ. The found soul presently finds a need of Christ. *Paul,* as soon as mercy found him, would by no means be found in himself, but by all means be found in Christ; That I may be found in him, saith *Paul,* Phil. 3. 9. There was a Nobleman (one *Elyearius*) who was supposed to be lost, and his Lady sent up and down to find him; One at length meets with him, and tels him how sollicitous his Wife was to find him out; O (answered he) commend me to my Wife, and tell her, That if she desires to find me, she must look for me in the heart of Jesus Christ, for there onely am I to be found. And verily, there is no poor soul, whom God is finding and bringing home to himself, on whom he hath imprinted a true sense of his lostness, but presently the soul cries out, What shall I do? what shall I do to be saved? O that I might have Christ! and O that I might be found in Jesus Christ! Remember two things: 1. *That the Lord will bring back to himself no soul, but by Jesus Christ:* Christ is the sinners *way* to the Father; he is the *door* by which you are admitted: If ever the Lord casts an eye on thee, or take thee by the hand, it is for his Christ's sake. 2. *A lost soul, which is found, finds an absolute need of Jesus Christ:* Nothing out of Christ can make peace, can justifie, can reconcile, can set us straight, can make us accepted. Had I all other things, and had not Christ, I were still a lost person: Had I the righteousness of Angels, yet if I had not Christ, I were lost; could I mourn, could I repent, could I pray, could I live holily, could I walk exactly, yet I am lost; I am still lost, until I get into Christ. *I count all things but loss, for the excellency of the knowledge of Jesus Christ my Lord.* God will look on me as my Judge, he will look on me as his enemy, he will not own me as a Father, as a reconciled Father, but in Christ.

Jesus Christ may be found in that lost soul.

4. *If thy lost soul be truly found, then Jesus Christ may be found in that lost soul of thine.* They report of *Ignatius,* that the *Letters of Jesus were found written in his heart:* This I dare affirm, That the Picture of Christ, the Graces of Christ, the Life of Christ, is to be found in every found man. *Paul, Lydia,* the *Jailor,* Christ was sought by them, and found in them. It cannot be, that a sinner should be found, if Christ be not to be found in him. Why! if thou be a Christless man, who doubts it,

it, but that thou art a lost man? Now do not deceive thy foul; thou canst fay, that Christ once was to be found in the Temple, and Christ once was to be found on the Cross, and Christ is still to be found at the right hand of his Father; but is there not one place more where thou canst find him? hast thou not a heart? Is Christ to be found there, I say, there, in thy heart? I find him in thy Ear when thou hearest, and I find him in thy mouth when thou speakest, and thou findest him in thy mind when thou thinkest; but still I ask, Dost thou find him in thy heart? which loves, which fears, which joys, which delights, which embraceth? O, is Christ in thy heart! what? a found man, and nothing of Christ to be found in thee! I know not, perhaps wilt thou reply. Why this is strange, that Christ should be in thee, and thou never know it! Christ dwels in the broken heart, in the believing heart; Christ lives in him, who onely lives upon Christ. Christ was a crucified Christ, doth he crucifie thy heart? He was a holy Christ, doth he purifie thy heart? He was an humble Christ, doth he abase thy heart? He was a tender Christ, doth he mollifie thy heart? He was a satisfying Christ, doth he pacifie thy heart? He was an obedient Christ, doth he command, doth he lead, doth he rule thy heart? He did for thee, canst thou do for him? He died for thee, canst thou suffer for him? He loved thee, canst thou delight in him?

5. If the Lord hath graciously found thy lost foul, and indeed brought it home unto himself, *Then thou wilt find sufficiency, an enough at least, in thy Fathers house*. There is enough in God, to allure and draw a sinner home, to keep a sinner at home that he needs not wander abroad, mercy and pleasures for evermore: This the Prodigal discover'd afar off, even in the birth of his finding; *There is bread enough, and to spare*. God seems a poor thing, a mean thing, an insufficient thing to a lost man; and therefore he wanders up and down, and serves his lusts, and begs from the Creatures to make him out some delight, some pleasure, some profit, some subsistence, some contentment: But God is a rich thing, a Fulness; He alone is enough; One God is enough for my one soul, if my soul indeed be found of him: O, he hath Mercy enough for me to save me, Love enough for me to delight me, Pleasure enough for me to comfort me, Dignity enough for me to advance me, Help enough for me to preserve

Then thou wilt find sufficiency in thy Fathers house.

preserve me; Happiness enough for me, to save me. If I want Grace, he is the God of Grace; if I want Peace, he is the God of Peace; if I want Mercies, he is the Father of Mercies; if I want for Earth, the Earth is the Lords; if I would have Heaven, he is the God of my Salvation. Now, friend, what say you? hath God found your lost soul? and what hath your soul found in your God? What canst thou say of this God, of his Mercy, Love, Entertainment, Communion? *With thee the fatherless findeth mercy*; *Thy favour is better than life*; *It is good for me to draw near unto God*; canst thou say thus? is there bread enough for thee in thy Fathers house? If so, why doest thou yet run away? run abroad to Sin for delight, to the Creature for satisfaction?

<small>Thou wilt be afraid to lose thy self again.</small>

6. If God hath graciously found thee, and brought thee out of thy lost and wandring condition, *Thou wilt be afraid to lose thy self again*, to wander again, to go astray again from thy God who hath found thee. There are six things which the found and recovered person doth apprehend: 1. *The great iniquity* in his formerly lost and wandring course of life. 2. His *great vanity* all that while, to forsake his own mercies, to sow the wind, and reap the whirlwind. *What profit had ye in those things whereof ye are now ashamed?* Rom. 6. 3. *The great kindness and love* which God hath manifested towards his lost soul, in bringing him back to himself, and now to own him as a Father doth a Son. 4. *The great ingratitude*, to displease that mercy which was pleased to find him. 5. *The madness of folly*, to return to an experimental misery, and to forfeit sweet mercy, which he hath liberally tasted since he was found. 6. *The great hazard*, whether mercy will ever look after him any more, who hath so presumptuously abused mercy received. O no; the found sinner hath found such freeness, fulness, sweetness of entertainment; such rich mercy, such free love, such wonderfull kindness, that as *Peter* in another case, (*it is good for us to be here*;) or as the returning Church, (it is best being with my first Husband;) or as *Paul* about his being with Christ, so he about continuing and complying with his God, *It is best of all*. And therefore he cries out against all temptations, Shall I return to folly, when God hath spoken peace? shall *I* sin again, since God hath given me such a deliverance as this?

Of the Returning Prodigal.

this ? O no, O no ; *Canaan* is better then *Egypt*, Paradife is better then a wildernefs, a Fathers Houfe is better then to ferve Swine, plenty is better then famine ; Now God fmiles on me, and fhall I raife his frowns ? Now confcience fpeaks peace, fhall I turn this oyle into a Sword ? O let me never unjoynt the Bones which mercy at leng h hath fet ; O let me never darken the Sun, which fhines fo comfortably ; O let me never feed on husks, who may ftill feed on bread ; O let me never run from a Pallace to a Prifon: It was Gods mercy, and my happinefs to be refcued out of a loft condition ; let it never be my fin and curfe, to throw my felf out of Heaven, to caft my felf out of Paradife again, for a fins fake which formerly loft me, to depart from mercy, which hath gracioufly found me.

7. *If a found perfon doth ftray, he cannot be quiet until he be found, and come back again to his God.* Pfal.119.176. *I have gone aftray like a loft fheep, feek thy fervant:* There is this difference twixt the ftrayings of the Godly, and of the wicked ; when a wicked man ftrayes he is then at home, (fin is his home, and finful paths are the paths in which he loves to wander ; the mire and dirt are the delightful home of the Swine) and therefore he delights to be abroad, and cares not to come back again : But a Godly man, if he ftrayes, if he fins, he is now from home, he feeth fome fteps of loftnefs in every ftep of finfulnefs, his heart is apt prefently to fmite him for it ; Alas ! what have I done? whether am I going ? fhall I go again from my Fathers Houfe? what ayled me thus to ftep afide ? I cannot reft thus, I will home again what ever comes of it. And back he comes with an afhamed heart, as *Ephraim* did ; and with a mourning heart, as *Peter* did ; and with a felf-judging heart, as *David* did: O my God, O my Father, I, even I have finned, finned again ; yet for Chrifts fake, accept of me again. 'Me thinks it 'is with him, juft as it is with a poor Child, whom evil com-'pany hath feduced from home ; his heart akes, and he flips 'from them, and under a Bufh he fits, and there bethinks him-'felf, and fighs, and weeps as if his heart would break; after which 'he rifeth, and home he comes, and fteals to the door, and liftens, 'and knocks foftly ; and the Servants comes forth, and, fay they, 'where have you been all this while ? O, your Father wonders 'at you ! and hath been much troubled that you have dealt

If he do ftray he is not quiet till he come back again.

'thus

Gods Gracious Acceptance

'thus with him : Now the child takes on, and is cut to the heart;
'and will not my Father be pacifyed? I know that I have offen-
'ded him, and dealt unkindly with him : Never had a Child so
'good a Father; I pray you, speak for me, and tell him, I am
'without. Let him come in, faith his Father : In he comes, and
'falls down, and with floods of tears acknowledges his strayings,
'and humbly intreats his Father to pass by this wandring, and to
'own him again, and to look on him as he was wont to do : O Sir,
'(faith he) I cannot live without your favour, nor will I live out
'of your house. Even thus is it with a found Child of God, if he
'happens to stray and sin, his heart smites him, and his heart akes;
'(O faith he) what have I done to deal thus with my good God
'and Father, I am ashamed and grieved; To one Minister he
'goes, and perhaps to another; Do you think that the Lord will
'be merciful to me again? Yea, to God he goes, and confesseth
'all, and beseecheth him to deal with him like a Father: Lord,
'(faith he) it hath been a woful and bitter time to me, I cannot
'stand it out; I come in unto thee, sin is my burthen, and thy
'displeasure is my burthen : I beseech thee to pardon the tres-
'pass of thy servant, and be reconciled unto me, and own me
'with thy favour and mercy once again.

He endesvours to find others. 8. *He who is truly found by Gods Grace and Mercy, doth desire and endeavour to find others, or that others may also be found;* Jo. 1. 43, 45. Christ finds *Philip,* and *Philip* finds *Nathaniel:* There is no good man who would pertake of Grace and Heaven alone; and there is no wicked man who would enjoy sin and hell alone: Wicked men are like those that are drowning, who catch hold on others; and every good man is like a Candle, which being lighted holds out light to others; or like a stick of fire, which being kindled, would kindle more sticks: Good Lord, the same Mercy, the same Grace, the same Christ, the same reconciled God, and Father for my poor Child too, and for my poor Husband too, and for my poor Parents too : O Lord, pity them too, they are lost, and they know not the misery of a lost condition, nay, the happiness of a found condition : Good Lord, open their eyes, and bring them home to thy self in Christ. And to his friends he goes;. O continue not in this condition, you are lost, I was so; Return to God, you know not the sweetness of his mercy, of his love.

9. If

Of the Returning Prodigal.

9. If God hath found thee indeed, *Then thou mayst be found in Gods wayes*: The wayes or courſe of life which a man leads, plainly diſcovers whether he be found or loſt; a man that is ſtill loſt, he continues in wayes which are looſe and loſt, which will bring him to everlaſting perdition and loſs: A man that is found by Grace, is now, in ſuch wayes as brings Glory to him which finds, and alſo brings him to Glory who is found; What! talk of being found by Gods mercy, and yet wallowing in thy luſts, ſtill running on in thy ſinful baſe wayes! what brought back to God, and ſtill running away from God! Aſſuredly, the found man is to be found in new wayes, in the paths of righteouſneſs and holineſs; he is aſhamed of his old wayes, and forſakes them: *Paul* is not perſecuting now, but humbling himſelf for it, and praying, and preaching, and living to Chriſt.

He will be found in Gods wayes.

The next Uſe ſhall be of Exhortation unto a twofold Duty. 1. To find out your loſt condition. 2. To get out of a loſt condition. 1. *Labour to find out your loſt condition*: Be convinced, that naturally you are loſt men. There are two Reaſons which may move you to this. 1. *The extream pride and ſelf-conceitedneſs*; the ſelf-conceit, and ſelf-deceit in every ſinner; there is no ſinner thinks himſelf ſo ſafe and well as the loſt ſinner: *I have need of nothing* (ſaid *Laodicea*.) *I was alive once* (ſaid *Paul*,) *We were never in bondage* (ſaid the Jews.) 2. *You will never ſeek unto the Lord to bring you out of a loſt condition, until you find your ſelves loſt*: Who ſeeks his bread but the hungry? or asks the way, who thinks himſelf in the way? or comes home, who is not gone abroad?

Uſe 2. Exhortation. To find out our loſt condition. Conſider. The extream pride and ſelf-conceitedneſs of every ſinner. We ſhall never ſeek to God, till we find our ſelves loſt.

Obj. But you will ſay, how may a man be convinced that his condition is loſt? *Sol.* I anſwer, there are ſeven ſpecial convictions of it. 1. *The fall of mankind in* Adam: Our nature was like a ſtock depoſited in his hand, what he had, we had; what he kept, we kept; when he fell, we fell; and what he loſt, we alſo loſt; his condition was not perſonal, but natural; not particular, but Univerſal: Oh, that Ship is ſplit, that Tree is fallen, that Stock is ſpent. 2. *The Obſervation of our wayes and pathes*: do but eye them, and judg of them: As when God opened the eyes of the Syrians, they ſaw themſelves to be in the midſt of *Samaria*; ſo if God ever open thine eyes, thou wilt ſee and confeſs that all thy wayes are but wandrings, and all

Seven Convictions of our loſt condition.

K k 2 the

the time of thy life hath been loſt in iniquity, and vanity. 3. *The ſtudy of the Law:* Ah! When wilt thou read thy ſelf in it! thou wilt find thy ſelf many a thouſand mile from home, and to have been a long, very long wanderer, a loſt and undone perſon. Rom. 7. 9. *When the Commandment came, ſin revived, and I dyed.* 4. *A conſcience inlightned and quickned:* There is no one faculty in man, which can diſcover his preſent condition to him, ſo certainly and ſo clearly as Conſcience; Men ſpeak, fancy ſpeaks, corrupted judgment, and reaſon ſpeak, yea, but what doth conſcience ſpeak, in private, on a ſick bed, in an imminent judgment? 5. *The judgment of Godly and experienced Chriſtians,* who have known experimentally a loſt condition, and a found condition. 6. *The un-inclination of his ſpirit to all Communion with God*: Nay, the very averſneſs of it thereto. 7. *The abſolute inexperience* of his ſoul, in the family of God, never yet knowing what ſuch a fathers houſe doth mean.

Strive to get out of this loſt Condition. Secondly, *When you have found out your loſt condition, then ſtrive to get out of it:* O, do not continue in it, either through preſumption, that you can quickly come home, or through deſpair, that God now will never look after you, nor regard you; But pray the Lord in mercy to turn thy heart, to give thee an heart to come back unto him. *Obj.* But I have wandered ſo long, that I ſhall never be accepted, nor welcomed, although I ſhould come back. *Sol.* Say not ſo: But conſider well of theſe enſuing particulars. 1. The Lord ſaith, *That he hath been found of them that ſought him not*; and will he not then be found of them that return and ſeek him? *Si peccanti, quid penitenti, ſi erranti quid quarenti?* If he looks after thee then, will he not look on thee now? 2. There was never a wandering loſt Soul, that ever returned back to his Fathers Houſe, but the door hath been opened to him, and he hath found mercy; the *Prodigal* here, *Manaſſes, Paul* &c. 3. If thou haſt a heart to turn home, it is a certain ſign that God intends thee mercy; he hath put returning thoughts in thee, becauſe he hath already contrived thoughts of mercy towards thee. *We love him, becauſe he loved us firſt*; we turn to him, becauſe he firſt turned to us. 4. The Lord God hath ſent *Jeſus Chriſt from Heaven, to look after, and to find, and to ſave that which was loſt:* Now, though thou canſt not expect to find

the

the door opened for thine own fake; yet thou fhalt fee the door open, and the Armes of Mercy open to thee, for Chrifts fake. 5. *How many meſſengers and ſervants hath God, and doth God ſtill ſend after,* which cry earneſtly unto thee, Come back, return and live? Thus the Gofpel cries, thus Confcience cries, thus all thy mercies cry, thus all thy afflictions cry: If God be yet feeking after thee, thou mayſt yet be found; and if thou wilt feek, and wait a while, thy poor loſt foul fhall alfo be found. 6. *God hath chalked out the wayes and ſteps of returning home to him.* 7. God hath found men in their blood, and hath faid unto them, Live. Ezek. 6.

For this my Son was dead, and is alive again.

Thefe words do hold forth a pithy defcription of a finners converfion; that is, a paſſage from death to life; or a mutation from a dead condition, into a living condition; the eftate of fin is a dead eftate, yea, a deadly eftate; and the ftate of Grace, is a living eftate, yea, a lively eftate. There any many Doctrinal Propofitions, which are couched in thefe words: As 1. That an impenitent, or unconverted man, is a dead man: [*This my Son was dead*] 2. That when a finner is converted, he is then made alive: [*And is alive*] 3. That God doth fometimes convert a very great and notorious finner: [*This, this my Son*] 4. That great afflictions are fometimes the means of a great finners Converfion: [*This my Son was*] 5. That there is an almighty power, required to convert or change a finner ⊦ As much as to make a dead man to live.] 6. That true Converfion is a very great and confpicuous alteration: (No change is like that from death to life.) 7. That true Converfion is an inward, or a foul-alteration; not of cloaths, or painting: (It is the putting of life into a dead man.) 8. That a finner contributes nothing at all towards his Converfion, but Converfion of a finner, is the fole work of a God; (for it is God only, who can quicken the dead, no dead man can make himfelf alive.) 9. That the Lord takes notice of every condition of man (of the *Prodigals* former condition, *he was dead,* and of his prefent condition, but *he is alive again.*) 10. That the Lord doth own every converted perfon, as a Father owns a Son: [*This my Son.*]

That

Doct. 1.
An unconverted man, is a dead man.

1. *That an impenitent or unconverted man is a dead man* [*This* is *my Son was dead*] The sinner is in Scripture sometimes stiled, A *fallen* man. *Hos.*14.1. *Thou hast fallen by thine iniquity* : Yea, but this fall is a deadly fall ; not like *Eutychu's* Fall, Acts 20.29. in whom yet there was life, *vers.*10. But like *Ahaziah's* Fall, which was deadly to him, 2 *Kings* 1.4. A *diseased* man, (*Isa.*1.6. *From the sole of the foot even to the head, there is no soundness*) but this disease is a deadly disease; and therefore sin is called the *Plague of the heart*, 1 *Kings* 8. No disease is so deadly as the Plague, and no Plague is so deadly as the Plague in the heart. A *wounded* man (*Luk.*10.30. *A certain man fell among Theeves, who wounded him.*) But this wound is a deadly wound, like that which the King of *Babilon* gave to *Pharaoh*, which made him *groan with the groanings of a deadly wounded man*, Ezek. 30.24. An *imthralled* man. 2 Pet. 2.19. *Of whom a man is overcome, of the same he is brought in Bondage* ; But this Bondage is a deadly Bondage; *whether of sin unto death* (saith the Apostle) of the servants of sin, *Rom.*6.16. A *dead* man ; and this is the highest, unless you say, a damned man ; frequently doth the Scripture Phrase this way. *Psalm* 106. 28. *They did eat the sacrifices of the dead*, because offered to dead Idols, and by dead Idolaters. *Prov.* 21. 16. *The man that wandreth out of the way of understanding, shall remain in the Congregation of the dead*, (.i.) of the ungodly, wicked, impenitent : The *Ephesians*, what were they before their conversion? See Chap. 2. 1. *Dead in sins and trespasses.* The *Colossians*, what were they before their conversion? See Chap. 2.13. *And you being dead in your sins*, &c. 1 Pet.4.6.*The Gospel was preached to them that were dead*,(.i.) to wicked and impenitent persons; nay, *Jude*,v.12. speaks of some that were *twice dead* ; dead in respect of *Original Sin*, and dead in respect of *Actual sin* ; or, dead in respect of corruption, and dead in respect to their former profession. I grant, that an unconverted sinner may be alive. 1. In respect of *his own opinion* : *I was once alive* (said *Paul* Rom. 7. 9.) *but when the Commandment came, sin revived, and I dyed.* 2. In the *opinion of men*. *Rev.* 3.1. *Thou hast a name that thou livest, and art dead* ; So Christ of the Church of *Sardis*. 3. *To sinful works* ; he lives in them, and lives with them, and lives to them; but this life is death, this life is a sign that he is dead, that unto spirituals he is dead. This is a great Point, of

which

which I am now difcourfing, and hath been the fubject of much difpute, as in former Ages, fo in this latter Age. There have been fome that have denyed (utterly) this death of a finner; others have held finful men to be wounded, and to be half dead: The *Pelagians* go this way, fo do all the *Papifts*, and verily the *Arminians* come not much fhort herein; yea, moft men prefume that though they be finners, yet that they are not altogether dead, but fome life ftill remains in them, or fome power. Favour me therefore, to open the point with fome diftinctions, and then I fhall confirm the truth delivered, both with Scripture and Arguments, and wind up the reft with fome profitable Applications to our felves. *Several Diftinctions.*

1. For the firft of thefe I diftinguifh thus; Man is confiderable under a threefold eftate. 1. *Of Inftitution, or Creation:* Wherein he was alive, and had a power to live or dye. 2. *Of Deftitution, or Degeneration:* In this eftate every man living is dead. 3. *Of Reftitution, or Regeneration:* And here he is born again, and is made alive again. Again, man in his degenerate or fallen eftate, may be confidered in relation to actions, and objects, either, 1. *Natural*: To thefe he is alive; the foul in man is no dead, but living thing, and is able to underftand, will, defire, difcourfe, and reafon; and this man can eat, drink, fleep, &c. 2. *Political:* Here alfo life is found in him; even a wicked man (deftitute of all Grace) is alive to trade, to bargain, to buy, to fell, to plant, to build. 3. *Theological*, or Spiritual: Now here the impenitent, or unconverted man is *plane mortuus*, ftark dead. An underftanding (I confefs) he ftill hath, but none that is able to know God aright, or Chrift, or any faving truth (without Divine aid or Grace.) 2 Cor. 3. 5. *We are not fufficient of our felves, to think any thing as of our felves,* If we (Apoftle and regenerate) be not fufficient, who is! if not to think, then to what! to think, is the loweft act of power, 1 Cor. 2. 14. *The natural man receiveth not the things of the Spirit of God, for they are foolifhnefs unto him; neither can he know them, becaufe they are fpiritually difcerned.* John 1. 5. *The light fhineth in darknefs; and the darknefs comprehended it not.* A Will alfo I grant unto the natural and unconverted man, for he could not be a man, if he had not a will, but this will (without Grace) cannot do any fpiritual good, nor chufe it, nor love it, nor defire it: *Non poteft homo aliquid velle nifi adjuvetur.*

Man confidered under a three-fold State.
Of Creation.
Of Degeneration.
Of Regeneration.
Man in his Degeneration confidered as to
Natural actions.
Political actions.
Or Theological.

adjuvetur ab eo, qui malum non potest velle: So S. *Austin* against *Pelagius,* Tom. 3. *De spiritu & Litera* cap. 3. *Without me* (faith Christ) *ye can do nothing,* Joh. 15.5. *No man comes to me, except the Father draw him,* Joh. 6.44. *It is God who works in us to will and to do* (faith the Apostle) *Phil.* 2.13. And *Works,* I grant unto this man, but spiritual work I deny to them. *Quid boni potest perditus nisi in quantum à perditione liberatus:* Austin *in Enchirid.* c. 30. *They that are in the flesh cannot please God,* faith the Apostle, Rom. 8.8. *An evil Tree cannot bring forth good fruit,* so our Saviour, Mat. 7.18. *Without faith it is impossible to please God,* Hebr. 11.6.

Reasons of it.

2. But let us proceed further, and search what Reasons may be produced to demonstrate the Assertion: That the natural, or unconverted man is spiritually dead, and as to spirituals altogether dead; Thus then,

He hath no communion with the principles of spiritual life.

1. *He who hath no Communion at all with the principles of spiritual life,* is (in a spiritual sense) altogether dead; for where there is no principle of life, there cannot be any thing but death: *Tolle animam, tolle vitam;* but the impenitent and unconverted sinner, hath no communion with any one principle of spiritual life: Therefore, &c. There is a twofold principle of this life. 1. *A primitive conjunction with God, in the estate of Innocency;* but this is lost. 2. *A renewed Conjunction with God by Christ;* but yet this is not attained to by an unconverted sinner. It is a confessed truth, that Jesus Christ is the Author of spiritual life to the sinner: *He that hath the Son, hath life, and he that hath not the Son, hath not life,* Joh. 5.17. And the sinner hath it partly by *Faith,* which taking Christ, takes life from him; by the *Spirit of Regeneration,* which renews, and makes him alive; but the unconverted sinner, hath neither the one, nor the other; had he either, he were then converted.

Original sin, is a compleat cause of spiritual death.

2. *Original sin (whilst reigning) is a compleat cause of spiritual death:* But original sin reigns in the impenitent and unconverted sinner, therefore he is dead. The Fathers have diversly Phrased Original sin; some call it *Venenum Syerpentis,* so *Cprian;* others *Plagam serpentis,* so *Ireneus;* others *Vitium parentum,* so *Paulinius* in *Austin;* the Apostle *Paul* calls it, sometimes, *the body of sin,* sometimes, *the body of death,* sometimes, *the Law of sin and death,* sometimes, *the Uncircumcision of the heart.* Our Divines generally conceive two things in it, *viz.* In Original sin, there is

1. *A*

Of the Returning Prodigal.

1. *A total deprivation of original righteousness:* The Faculties remain, but the Rectitude is gone. It is reported of an excellent Philosopher, that he fell into a Disease, which dashed out all the Learning that ever he acquired, so that he forgat even his own Name. Original sin is like the extinguishing of a Candle; the Candle remains still, but the Light is gone: Or like the quenching of red Iron; the Iron remains, but the fiery redness is all gone: Or like a Tree, the Limbs remain, but the Life is gone. It is an Universal spoil; it hath robbed us of all our supernaturals; worse to us than the Devil to *Job*, who took away all that he had, yet spared his Life: But Original Sin not onely took away Paradise and Righteousness, but all self-power so much as to desire to be good. 2. *A total depravation of all the man. Seges ubi Troia:* The Soul of Man was once like a Garden, fully set with the sweetest Flowers of Righteousness; but now it is become like a Wilderness run over and filled with Briars and Thorns: Or it is like a Face, which once was the most curious of features, (every part expressing most amiable sweetness;) now it is like the same Face, most deformed with the clusters of the Pox, and the very shame and reproach of it self. There is not a Faculty in the Soul, but it is like the Bough of a fruitfull Tree, thickly laden with Iniquity: It is a Spring, bubling out nothing but aversation, enmity, resistance to spiritual good; and readiness, inclination, eagerness, unsatiableness to all that is evil: *God saw that every imagination of the thoughts of the heart of man was onely evil continually,* Gen. 6. 5. The best of men complain of blindness, of dulness, of deadness; Alas then, what, or how is it with the worst of men? *Paul* could not do good, a wicked man would not do good: *Paul* complains for want of power; what then may an unconverted man do! By all this (I think) it manifestly appears, That the unconverted man is spiritually dead, because Original Sin reigns in him; (if in any, then in him;) and where Original Sin reigns, there is a total privation or absence of all spiritual Life, and total corruption or presence of spiritual Death in the Soul.

3. The Terms used in Scripture to express a sinners conversion, do seem sufficiently weighty, to prove, That before his conversion

The terms used in Scripture to express conversion.

L l

vesion he was spiritually dead: For it is set forth sometimes, By the *Resurrection of the dead*; Ephes. 5. 14. *Awake, thou that sleepest, and arise from the dead.* By the *Generation of a person. Of his own good will begat he us with the word of truth,* Jam. 1. 18. By *Creation.* 2 Cor. 5. 17. *If any man be in Christ, he is a new creature.* Now observe; if Conversion be a Resurrection, a spiritual Resurrection, then the soul before Conversion was spiritually dead; if Conversion be a Regeneration, then a new life is brought into the soul, which it totally wanted before: If Conversion be a Creation, and the converted man *qua talis* be a new creature, then he had no spiritual being before. If spiritual Life be a creature onely of Christ's making, then, *&c.*

The promises of giving a spiritual being and life.

4. To me, those *spiritual Promises which God makes, of giving a spiritual being and life,* do abundantly clear, that man is dead: As, of pouring forth the Spirit of Grace, giving his Spirit, taking away the heart of Stone, and giving the heart of Flesh, of giving Knowledge, Love, Fear, *&c.* Such kinds of Promises imply three things: 1. *Our total want* and need; 2. *Gods undertaking to bestow them;* 3. *A free and total donation* of them to us on Gods part.

The duty of Prayer.

5. S. *Austin* useth the Duty of Prayer, to prove this Assertion against the Pelagians; *Petenda à Deo bona omnia, ergo nihil boni ex nobis possumus.* And in an Epistle to *Vitalis*, he saith, *Prorsus non oramus Deum, sed orare nos fingimus si nos ipsos non illum credimus facere quod oramus.*

Man cannot prepare himself to life.

6. I will add but one Argument more, *viz.* That man is totally dead, (*quantum ad spiritualia,*) who cannot so much as prepare himself, no not remotely, no not in any degree unto the life of Grace: But, the Unconverted man cannot (*virtute propria,* and without supernatural aid,) in the least degree prepare himself, *&c.* for, without that aid, he cannot desire deliverance out of his sinfull estate, nor mourn over it, nay not feel it, nay not spiritually know it.

The Use which I desire to make of this Point, I shall reduce unto, 1. Information, 2. Trial, 3. Instruction.

Information. The unconverted man is in the saddest condition.

1. For *Information.* Is every natural and unconverted man a spiritually dead man? Hence we may be informed of several Truths. 1. *That the unconverted man is, of all men on the earth, in the saddest, vilest, miserablest condition:* Why? Because

Of the Returning Prodigal.

cause he is spiritually dead, dead, spiritually dead. A wounded man is in a tedious condition, and a diseased man is in a languishing condition; but what is a wound to death? what is a disease to death? *Me morienti mori*; Death is the Sun-set of all comfort; Death is the drowning of a little world; Death is the very Hermitage of forgetfulness and loathsome corruption: Death is the lowest and vilest condition; what then is a spiritual Death? No Death like the spiritual Death. O my friends, consider spiritual Death, either in comparison, or in its proper complexion, or in the consequents of it, surely, no Death, no condition is so dismal as it.   1. *In comparison with any other Death*: This is the worst, this is the heaviest. There is the Death of our *Goods* and *Estate*, (into which *Job* fell;) of our *Name* and *Reputation*, (into which *David* fell;) of our *Bodies* and *natural Life*, (into which *Lazarus* fell;) of the *Soul*, the immortal soul of man, into which every unconverted sinner is fallen: Now what is a dead Estate to a dead Soul? Or what is a dead Name to a dead Soul? Or what is a dead Body to a dead Soul? It is not so much as the death of a Dog to the death of a Man. Every unconverted man hath a dead soul; a converted man may have a troubled soul, but the unconverted man hath a dead soul, sin hath slain his precious soul; If the soul be dead, what is alive? What is that man whose soul is dead? In all other deaths, something is alive; if Goods be gone, the Name lives; if the Name be gone, the Body lives; if the Body be gone, the Soul lives: But if the Soul also be gone, what lives?

2. *In it self*: Why spiritual Death is a total privation of God, of Christ, of Grace; no life of God, no life of Christ, no life of Grace is there in any unconverted person; none at all. Ah poor wretch! what art thou, and what is thy condition, who art thus dead? A total corruption, diffusion, possession with sin. S. *Austin* affirms, That the very Vertues of the Heathens were but *splendida peccata*, meer flowers on a dead man: And *Solomon*, *The sacrifices of the wicked are an abomination to the Lord.* What a gastly sight would it be, to open a grave, and see the dead body run over with crawling worms, and a general putrefaction over all the parts! And truly, so it is with the soul of an unconverted person; it is the filthiest, nastiest, corruptedst, may I say, Carrion. *Luther* said once, So many sins, so many hells;

surely

surely, I may then say, So many Sins, so many Deaths. The unconverted man is full of sin: *his heart is full of evil,* so *Solomon*; He *is filled with all unrighteousnesse,* so *Paul* affirmeth. *Job* was filled with botches, yea, but he was not filled with sins; and *Lazarus* was filled with sores, yea, but he was not filled with sins; and *Davids* soul was filled with complaints, and *Chrifts* soul was filled with sorrow, yea, but it was not filled with sin. Every unconverted mans dead soul is filled with living sins, as a good mans soul is filled with dying and dead sins; and a soul full of living sins, is much like a soul filled up with Hel-fire. There is no evil so evil as sin, and no sin so evil as living sin, and no living sin so evil as a fulnes and an onlines of living sin.

In the consequents of it. 3. *In the consequents of it :* I will name but three of them, 1. All the guilt of all those sins lie on him alone. 2. All the wrath of God looks on him, the sentence of curse. 3. An eternal death may soon befal him.

No marvel that admonitions, reproofs, counsels, prevail not with most men. 2. Then no marvel, *that publick and private admonitions, counsels, reproofs, prevail not with the most of men.* We Ministers preach, and we think we preach Religion, and with evidence enough of Reason, and deliver things fairly and plainly and convincingly; and now we wonder at it, that men should hear such clear and undeniable truths, and not be moved and perswaded! And Parents give admirable counsels and instructions to their Children, and no good comes of them! &c. Why Sirs, are not unconverted men dead men? And what can all our undertakings (alone considered) do unto dead men? Assuredly, unless the Lord of Life himself will speak these counsels and these admonitions unto sinfull men, they will never hear them so as to be stirred, so as to be moved, so as to be converted by them; they will remain in their sinfull condition and obstinate wayes to eternity.

It Is Gods mercy that any soul is converted. 3. *Then it is of Gods meer mercy, and pity, and power, if ever thy poor soul be converted:* Never ascribe it to thy excellency, (what excellency is there in a dead man?) to thy power, (what power is there where there is no life?) to thy self preparations, (what active disposing or preparation can a dead man afford?) The dead sinner is the meer object of purest mercy, and the dead sinner is without all strength; if ever his souls lives, then to Christ must that life own it self, and to Divine Mercy, and Power, &c.

The

Of the Returning Prodigal. 261

The next Use shall be for *Trial* or Examination. Since every unconverted man is spiritually dead; let's therefore search our hearts, in what a condition they are : Are not many of us yet dead in sins and trespasses? spiritually dead men? There are four Tokens of a man spiritually dead. 1. *Unsensibleness:* Where there is no life, there is no sense; of all sinners, the unsensible sinner is in the most deadly condition. *Tanto pejor quanto insensibiliter,* saith *Austin*. Do what you will to a dead man, he is unsensible of it; ca'l to him, he hears not; put the sweetest perfumes to him, he smels not; kick him, cut him, burn him, he feels not; although he be full of loathsomness, he perceives it not. Now I beseech you mind this Trial; for verily, if spiritual unsensibleness prevail upon you, you are spiritually dead : If spiritual sense be the first evidence of Life, then *è contra*, spiritual unsensibleness is a sure evidence of Death : And what spiritual sensation is yet wrought in you? There are sins upon sins (mountains upon mountains) in your hearts, the least of them hath been an heavy burthen to a living soul; but what hast thou ever felt of thy sinfull heart and life? There is in the Ministry of the Gospel, no less than riches of Mercy, freeness of Love, glories of Heaven tendred to you; but what do you perceive in it? Didst thou never yet feel and cry out of a body of Death? O here, here is a dead heart, an ignorant heart, a proud heart, an unbelieving heart, an heart in which there is no good, in which is all evil. Ah poor man, thou art a dead man; no feeling, no complaining, no crying out of thy heart against all those many many vile and notorious sins.

Use 2. Trial, Whether we be spiritually dead.

Four Tokens of it.

Unsensibleness.

2. *An universal and constant coldness.* If life be gone, heat is gone; the Feet are cold, and the Hands are cold, and the whole Body is cold, and the very Heart is cold too: A living man may have cold hands and feet, but he never hath a cold heart; for life is there, and heat is there. Why! there is no one converted man under heaven, but he hath some heat in him; though not much in some of his actions, yet certainly some in his heart:O, saith he, I approve of what is good, and I would do good, and I delight in the Law of God after the inward man; I believe, Lord help my unbelief. But now, an unconverted man hath, 1. *A cold heart unto any spiritual good.* Suppose he be at Prayer, and at Sermon; why! but he hath no heart to or in these duties, he hath no mind to these works, no delight

An universal and constant coldness.

light in them, or in the Sabbath, or in a Fast; and though his body be present, yet his heart is afar off, it goes after his covetousness. 2. And this *Coldness is universal* : There is not any one spiritual Duty, unto which his heart is not dead or cold. He will tell you when he hears Catechizing, I should like Preaching; and so when he hears Preaching, I could like Praying; and so when Praying comes, I could like Reading; and when Reading comes, I could like Meditating; and when that comes, I could like Practising; and when Practising comes, I could like Understanding: But he dissembles, he loves not one Duty at all; his heart to these is like a sick stomack, that seems to like any thing but what it hath, but indeed likes no meat. 3. *And it is also constant*: I confess, even a good and converted heart may find sometimes more actual indispositions to good, than at other times; and sometimes a greater measure of dulness and deadness; but an heart constantly cold, from one end of the year to another, all the life long, still to loath spiritual services, never to attain unto a delightfull and affectionate communion with God, This is a Token of a dead soul.

Where the Word preach'd is but a dead Letter.

3. *Where the Word preached is but a dead Letter unto the hearer*, certainly that man is in a dead condition. *If our Gospel be hid, 'tis hid to them that are lost*, saith the Apostle: So may I say, If our Gospel be dead, it is so onely to them that are dead. The Gospel is the great Trumpet of Christ, the Silver Trumpet by which he raiseth the dead; as, at the last, he shall raise the dead by the Voice of the Trumpet; this is that by which Jesus Christ quickens and pulls a soul out of its sinfull condition. 1. It lets in light to see that condition: 2. It affects Conscience to feel it: 3. It puts in Faith to go to Christ to fetch life: Yet many men are not wrought on at all by the Gospel preached: Unmoveableness is the token of a dead man.

A delight in dead works.

4. *A delight in dead things, and in dead works, plainly declare a dead condition.* Paul, in *Ephes.* 2. 1. tels the *Ephesians*, that they were *once dead*; but how did that appear? See verf. 2. *In time past ye walked according to the course of this world.* And verf. 3. *Ye had your conversation in the lusts of the flesh, fulfilling the desires of the flesh and of the mind.* 1. *In dead things*: Dead men are heavy, and descend to the earth; worldly things are the *Optima* and the *Ultima* of an unconverted heart. *Who will*

Of the Returning Prodigal.

will shew us any good? Pfal. 4. If that *of Paul.* (*Col.* 3. 1, 2. *If ye be risen with Christ, then seek those things that are above, and set your affections on things that are above,*) be a true sign of a living railed man, then *e contra*, to seek, to settle affections on things below, is a true sign of a dead man. 2. *In dead works:* These *opera mortua & mortifera.* And truly, nothing doth more discover a spiritual death, than a delight, and a service of sin; certainly, such a man is yet an unconverted man.

The last Use shall be for *Instruction* unto several Duties. I will but glance a them. 1. *Have as little society with wicked men as may be*; for they are dead men: Would any man living have a dead man to be his companion? There is a two-fold Society with men: 1. One is *necessary*, in respect of our Relations, or of our Commerce and Trade, which cannot well be avoided: 2. Another is *arbitrary*, in respect of our Election; avoid this, do not make choice of wicked society. There are two Reasons to hearken to this advice: One is, *You shall never get any spiritual good by their society*; a wicked man is an unprofitable man; Can any one gather Figs of Thorns, or Grapes of Thistles? Who is the better for a dead man? Another is, *You shall receive much hurt by such society*: The Jews were unclean, if they did but touch a dead body. It was the practice of a Tyrant once, to tie a dead man to a living man, that the filthy savour of the dead man might infect and destroy the life of the living man. O you who are to marry your children, take heed of marrying them to the dead; and you who are Free-men, take heed of embracing society with the dead. There are three notorious mischiefs will ensue hereupon: 1. *Dead society will, by degrees, bring you into a deadness of heart;* wicked company will certainly abate your zeal and holy affections, as waters do the flaming fire: 2. *Dead society will quench your Life in spiritual Duties;* they will not onely interrupt, but mitigate your sweet and wonted society with God and good men: 3. *Dead society will, in time, corrupt you to dead works*: Remember Solomon.

Use 3. Instruction. Have as little society with unconverted men as may be.

2. Lament and bewail thy unconverted Friends and Kindred. You read that *David* wept for *Absalom, O Absalom, my son, my son,* &c. and you read, that Christ wept for *Lazarus,* being dead;

Lament thy unconverted friends.

dead; and you read, of both of these weeping also for those that were spiritually dead: *David*, Psal. 119. *Rivers of tears run down mine eyes, because men keep not thy Law*. *Christ* came near to *Jerusalem*, and *wept over it*, saying, *Oh if thou hadst known, even thou, at the least in*, &c. Wouldst not thou weep to see thy Fathers, or Mothers, or Sisters, or Brothers dead body carrying out to the grave? and say, *Alas my Father, alas my Brother*, alas my Child? How then canst thou refrain tears for their dead souls? Why doest not thou pity the dead and unconverted soul of thy Father? *&c.* At a Funeral Feast, there is no mirth, because the Master of the house is dead: Ah, weep over thy Father, over thy Son; the Master of the house is dead, his precious soul is dead: Thy pity can do a dead body no good, but it may do a dead soul some good, especially, if you take in the next Duty, which is,

Pray for the Dead.

3. *Pray for the dead:* I mean not in the Popish sense; they, you know, pray for souls departed, supposing them to be in Purgatory, where the pains, as they say, are intollerable, equal to them in Hell, and the souls are deprived of the vision of God; and therefore their Priests and others often pray for them; and upon the Graves they inscribe, Pray for the soul of such a one, and on his soul Jesu have mercy: But this is a wicked superstition. We acknowledge no Purgatory, and no need of Prayers for souls departed, yet we hold Prayers requisite for one another, whiles we are upon the earth. And because some are dead whiles they live, O pray to the Lord for them; Lord Jesu, have mercy upon the soul of my Husband, Child, Wife; O convert them, quicken them from the dead, suffer them not, their poor souls, to die for ever. When *Steven* was to die, he prayed for those that were spiritually dead: When *Christ* was dying, he also prayed for them: And *Monica*, the Mother of *Austin*, prayed for him; and all of them were heard. *Object.* But I have prayed, but yet no good comes of it. *Sol.* Pray still; as long as there is life, and as long as there is prayer, there is hope: It will be an excellent comfort to thee, and eternal happiness to thy friend, if thou canst, at length, by thy prayers, prevail with God to deliver that one soul from death.

Use the means by which you may be quickned.

4. If the Lord hath opened any of your eyes but to see what your spiritual condition is, that you are yet in your graves, yet dead

dead in trespasses and sins; my advice unto you is this, *Go, use the means by which your dead souls may be quickned.* *Object.* Why! but this is ridiculous, to bid a dead man do work, go, stir, do any thing. *Sol.* I answer, 1. There is a difference twixt a man corporally dead, and a man spiritually dead: The former can do no action whatsoever, neither spiritual, nor civil, nor natural; the latter, though he can do nothing in spirituals, yet for the other, he may, and can. 2. You must distinguish twixt a spiritual action, and an action which brings to a spiritual means: He cannot convert his own heart, yet he hath power to hear the Word, which can. 'Tis true, that a wicked unconverted man cannot exert any one spiritual action; nevertheless, he hath liberty and power to go to Church, and hear a Sermon: Why! use this power, and this liberty, to come to the *Pool where the Angel stirs*; to come to the Ordinances, where God is pleased to quicken and raise the dead. 3. When thou art under a spiritual Ordinance, thou art under the voice of Christ himself, who hath said, That *the dead shall hear the voice of the Son of God, and live.* And truly, let me tell thee, That the Voice of *Jesus Christ* in his Word, hath not only a power to find a lost man, but also to quicken a dead man.

I have finished the first Proposition out of these words, *viz.* Luk. 15.24. That the unconverted man is a dead man: I now proceed to the second, which is this;

That every converted man is a living man. When the sinner is converted, he is then made alive. Conversion is a Sinners Life. So the Text, *This my son is alive again.* It is reported of *Similis*, Captain of the Guard to the Emperour *Adrian*, that he retired from the Court into the Countrey seven years before his death, and caused this to be written on his Tomb, *Hic jacet Similis cujus ætas multorum annorum fuit, ipse septem duntaxat annos vixit:* For so many years only was he converted. *We count the length of our lives from the time of our birth, and we must count the life of our souls from the time of our new birth,* said *Hierom.* It is frequent in Scripture, to stile converted persons living persons, or persons made alive, *Rom.* 6. 13. *Yield your selves unto God, as those that are alive from the dead.* Chap. 8. v. 10. *If Christ be in you, the spirit is life because of righteous-*

Doct. 2. Every converted man is a living man.

righteousneß. Gal. 2. 20. *I live,* faith *Paul.* Col. 2. 13. *You who were dead in your sins hath he quickned.* For the advantagious discussion of this Point, I shall briefly open unto you, 1. What Life that is, which the converted sinner attains unto? 2. How it may appear that he is invested with such a Life? and why? 3. Then the useful Application of all this unto our selves.

<small>What is the life of a converted sinner,</small>
1. What Life that is, wherewith the converted man is invested? *Sol.* I speak only of that Life incident unto man, which is four-fold. 1. *Life natural,* which is a power to move and

<small>A four-fold life.</small>
act. *I count not my life dear unto me,* said *Paul,* Act. 20. 24.

<small>Natural.</small>
All that a man hath he will give for his life, Job 1. This is the Life of Nature, and every man, good or bad, enjoys it.

<small>Life connatural.</small>
2. *Life connatural;* which is a prosperous fruition of our Lives with peace, contentment, and comfortable successes, in the external matters and affairs of our life: This also is possibly inci-

<small>Preternatural.</small>
dent to all sorts of men. 2. *Preternatural;* which is a death, rather than a life: A sinfull life, a life acted under the power and motion of sinfull lusts. *I was alive once,* said *Paul,* Rom. 7.

<small>Supernatural.</small>
In this respect, wicked and ungodly men only are alive. 4. *Supernatural;* a divine life, a new life, a life in Christ, and from Christ, and to Christ: Of which there are two parts, and they are proper only to converted persons. 1. There is the *Life of Grace,* which they enjoy in this world: 2. There is *the Life of Glory,* which they enjoy in the world to come, called often in

<small>The life of Grace, is</small>
Scripture, *eternal life.* The Text speaks of the first of these; The converted sinner is invested with the Life of Grace: And this

<small>The life of Justification.</small>
again is branched into the life of, 1. *Justification;* for when a sinner is justified, he is then in the condition of life: The unjustified man is a dead man, (for he lies under the sentence of death;) and the justified man is a living man, he is passed from death to life; the Lord takes off the sentence of eternal death from him; He shall not die for the sins which he hath committed, for I have pardoned all his sins, and now he shall live, and not die,

<small>Of Sanctification. Which may be considered, In the cause of it.</small>
saith the Lord. 2. *Sanctification:* When a sinner is sanctified, he is then made alive. At this, I suppose, the Text doth principally aim. This Life is considerable, 1. *In the Cause of it,* which is no other but the Spirit of Jesus Christ, who unites Christ and the Soul together; and upon this union, the Soul is quickned with the life of Christ. *I live by the faith of the Son of God,* Gal.

Gal. 2. 20.   2. In the *Nature of it* ; it is a *novum & spirituale esse*, which doth regenerate the man, and, as it were, create him again. The Scripture stiles this quality, *a new creature*, and *the new man:* It is an holy living principle. In a word, this life is nothing else but the Grace of the Spirit, regenerating, and renewing the whole soul of a sinner. It is saving light set up in the Mind, and saving wisdome set up in the Judgment, and saving grace set up in the Will and Affections, which alter the old sinfull nature in man, and are a new spiritual inclination to matters that are spiritual, yea, and a new spiritual ability or power in the whole soul of man to work that is spiritual: Whereas the Understanding could not know the things of God, now it is enabled to know them, and to admire them, and to study them: whereas the Will was both unable to good, and unwilling to good, and only set on what was evil; now, being quickned by Grace, it is drawn off from that affectionate inclination to evil, and it is bent and inclined, and in some measure enabled to desire Christ, to love Jesus Christ, to fear God, to obey God, and to walk with God: And when this comes into the heart of a sinner, he is said to be alive again.
   In the nature of it.

   Shall I draw out my thoughts of this Subject more clearly unto you? Take me then thus.   When any sinner is made spiritually alive,   1. *Jesus Christ applies himself to the Soul, and he breaths into it the Spirit of Life.* He doth with a poor dead soul, much like as *Eliah* did with the *Shunamites dead child*; who lay upon the child, and put his mouth upon the childs mouth, and his eyes upon the childs eyes, and his hands upon the childs hands; and he stretched himself upon the child, and the flesh of the child waxed warm: So the Lord Jesus applies himself by his Spirit to the soul of a sinner, (to all the soul of a sinner,) and works mightily in it, producing knowledge in a blind mind, and feeling in an hard heart, and faith in an unbelieving spirit, and all his Graces in the whole Soul.   2. *Which gracious principles are all of them living principles*; and alter all the soul, and incline it spiritually: So that the man who cared not for God, nor Christ, nor Grace, nor holy Duties heretofore; now his soul bends to these, and he minds these, and he is never better than when he is thinking of God, and mourning for his sins, and thirsting for Christ, and praying to God, and hearing of the
   When a sinner is made alive. *Jesus Christ applies himself unto the soul, and breaths into it the breath of life.* *He puts in living principles.*

Word of God; this is his defire, and this is his delight. 3. *There is a power in these principles of spiritual life.* A power againſt his ſins; ſo that now he can hate them, and ſay, *What have I to do any more with Idols? Get ye hence.* And a power in his affections; ſo that now he is able to love God above all, and able to fear God, and not diſpleaſe him willingly. And a power in his will; ſo that now he is able to come to Chriſt, and cleave to Chriſt, as his onely happineſs. And a power to ſpiritual actions; ſo that he is now able to hear and underſtand, to pray and wreſtle, to pray and believe, to believe and repent.

There is power of ſpiritual life in theſe principles.

Queſt. 2. *How it may be evidenced, that the converted man is thus made ſpiritually alive.* Sol. Thus, 1. *Every converted man hath a living union with Jeſus Chriſt*; he is brought into fellowſhip with Chriſt. Now Jeſus Chriſt is a living Head, and all his members are living Members. 1 Joh. 5. 12. *He that hath the Son, hath life.* And Joh. 6. 51. *I am the living bread, if any man eat of this bread, he ſhall live for ever.* 2. *All true grace is of a living nature:* Falſe grace is a dead thing, it hath no life, and can give no life; but true grace is living. True faith is a living faith, *I live by the faith of the Son of God*, Gal. 2. 20. And true hope is a living hope; 1 Pet. 1. 3. *God hath begotten us to a lively hope.* True repentance is a living repentance, *a repentance unto life.* 3. *Every converted man is the child of the living God*; he is born of the Spirit, who is the Spirit of life. *God is not the God of the dead, but of the living*; and God as a Father never begets any dead Children: All his children are begot after his own image; they are partakers of the Divine nature, and that is a living nature. 4. *The converted man lives the reſt of his life unto God.* 1 Pet. 3: 2. *None of us liveth to himſelf; for whether we live, we live unto the Lord*, Rom. 14. 8. Can he poſſibly live unto the Lord, until he be made alive by the Lord? What glory can God get by the life of a dead ſinner? *The living, the living, he ſhall praiſe thee, as I do this day*, ſaid *Hezekiah*, Iſa. 38. 19. God muſt have much glory from the converted man; not only paſſive glory on him, (this he hath on wicked men,) but active glory from him, glory from his believing, and glory from his obedience, which cannot be unleſs he be made alive, ſpiritually alive.

How this may be evidenced.

He hath a living union with Chriſt.

True grace is of a living nature.

He is a child of the living God.

He lives the reſt of his life to God.

Of the Returning Prodigal.

The Use of this Doctrine shall be to draw you into a searching acquaintance with your spiritual condition. There is not a business which can possibly concern you more nearly than this, Whether you be children of Death, or of Life? Whether yet dead in sins, or quickned by the life of grace? Can it be said of us as here of the Prodigal, This my Son was dead, but is alive? So we were *sometimes disobedient, ignorant, proud, vile, serving divers lusts: but after that the grace of God hath appeared, we are alive*; we have put off those lusts, and have other Principles, other Natures, other Lives. Let me offer unto you four *Motives*, to try your souls about their spiritual Life.

Use. Trial of our selves about our spiritual life.

Motives to this Trial.

1. *You have enjoyed the means of Life.* The Gospel is often called, the *Word of Life*, a quickning and regenerating Word; it carries Christ in it, the Author of Life; and the Apostle calls it, the *Ministration of Life*: And perhaps it hath been so to some poor man and woman, and to some of thy children. But- O how long hast thou heard it? how often hast thou come to this Bread of Life? to these Waters of Life? What! and yet dead in thy sins? not yet quickned and made alive? Why! thou art a reproach to the Gospel; and thy sins have not only given death to thy soul, but death to the Gospel of Christ, the Gospel is made by them a dead Letter; it is not so in it self, but thou hast made it so: And how wilt thou answer God, for killing thy soul, and killing his Christ, and killing his Gospel?

You have enjoyed the means of life.

2. *Many have a name that they live, but* (like the Angel of the Church of *Sardis*) *they are dead*, Revel. 3. 1. Oh Sirs! Spiritual life, (the life of grace,) is a rare thing, and a difficult thing. Every man loves his life, but few love this life: No man hates his own life (almost,) but most men hate this life of grace, because it is destructive to this life of sin: And many think they have it, and others think so too, and yet they have it not. You know, it is one thing to put Flowers upon a dead body, and another thing to put life into a dead man: It is one thing for the Sun to convey light, another thing for the Sun to convey life. I might shew you, that men mistake spiritual life exceedingly : Education in a person may lead him far, and so may an enlightned and generous Conscience, and so may restraining

Many have a name to live, and yet are dead.

restraining Grace, and so may Art, and so may the common gifts of the Spirit; they may enable a man to strange conceptions, and strange affections, and strange actions, and yet the man may be spiritually dead: Not any of these flow from a gracious principle of spiritual life: Why! common Gifts may lead up the soul far, and Education may lead to Duties much, and Conscience may awe sin exceedingly, and Art or Hypocrisie may counterfeit the very life of Grace (as a Stage-player doth a King) wonderfully. O therefore, look to it, that you have more than a name of life; that you live indeed.

It would be very sad to be deceived in this.   3. *If you should deceive your selves*, and when you come to die, you find that you have been dead all your lives, and never were spiritually made alive; Oh! in what a condition will thy poor trembling soul be! To die, and see nothing but death! I thought there was life in my heart, and life in my strong faith, and life in my troubles of spirit, and life in my obedience; but alas, I never lived, I never enjoyed Christ, never enjoyed grace, *&c.*

To be alive, is cause of great joy.   4. If the *Lord hath made thee alive from the dead*, I do not know any man living on the earth, that hath *such cause of joy unspeakable and glorious*. I will mention but three particulars unto thee. 1. *Hereby thou mayest be assured of thy interest in the richest mercy, and greatest love of God to thy poor soul*. Read but the Apostle in *Ephes.* 2. 4. *But God, who is rich in mercy, for his great love wherewith he loved us,* v. 5. *even when we were dead in sins, hath quickned us.* 2. Thou mayest palpably discover *the tokens and vertues of Jesus Christ upon thy soul*, the very Effigies of the saving works of Christ; that which *Paul* so longed to know, even *the power of the death and of the resurrection of Christ,* Philip. 3. 10. In thy death to Sin, and in thy life of Grace, doth the power of Christs death, and of Christs resurrection appear. 3. *Thou mayest certainly know, that Heaven shall be the place of thy rest hereafter.* Spiritual life comes from Heaven, and bends to Heaven, and shall bring to Heaven: It prepares for Heaven, and it is a part of Heaven, and it shall be perfected and filled up in Heaven. O what things are these! who would miss of these! For Christs sake, search throughly whether you be made alive.

Now

Of the Returning Prodigal. 261

Now me thinks I hear some soul secretly longing to know how it may be cleared unto it, That God hath quickned it from the dead; That as it was once dead, yet it is now alive. *Sol.* There are many things which may clearly declare it; for indeed, life is such an active thing, (especially spiritual life,) that it may easily appear, sometimes or other, to him who hath it. 1. If sin be alive, then thou art still dead; and *if sin be dead, thou art certainly alive.* I will open both these parts. 1. *If sin be alive, then the man is dead*; for it is impossible that the same man should be alive and dead under the same consideration. Spiritual Life and spiritual Death are incompatible at the same time in the same subject: And therefore, if sin be alive, questionless you are spiritually dead. Now there are four things which manifest sin to be alive in any mans soul. 1. The flaming *bents*, and *infatiable desires of the heart, after things forbidden in the Word.* Ephes. 4. 19. We read of sin with *greediness* 2. The *universal* and *easie authority, law,* or *command* that it hath over the soul and body; that it can use them in the service of lusts, when, and as it pleaseth, *Ephes.* 2. 2, 3. 3. The *joyfull contentation and satisfaction* which the heart takes in evil things; as we do in meat and drink. 4. *The customary trade and course of our life* in sinfull ways; a walking in them, a living in them. O, if these be yet found in thee, sin is alive still, and thou art dead still. 2. But *if sin be dead, thou art certainly alive.* I confess, sin may be restrained, and a man not alive; and sin may be troublesome in some respects, and a man not yet alive: But if it be dead, the man is spiritually alive; for sin in thee can never come to be dead, but by spiritual life. Now sin is dead in thee, if thou canst find two things. 1. *If it hath lost thy affections*: If love to sin be gone, and hatred of sin be come; if delight in sin be quenched, and sorrow for sin be implanted. Oh Sirs! the love of sin is the life of sin; and if the hatred of sin doth live, then the love of sin is dead. 2. *If it hath lost its Authority*, its free and uncontrolled power; although it molests still, and tempts still, yet it rules not, thou art not a slave to it, and subject to it, thou wilt not serve it, obey it any longer: If thou hast Christ for thy Lord, the Law of Christ for thy Rule, and Sin for thy Enemy, thou art alive.

Signs of spiritual life.

If sin be alive, the man is dead.

If sin be dead, thou art alive.

2. *A second sign of spiritual life is, a spiritual sense of spiritual wants.* This is an undoubted truth, That where there is life, there is sense; and where there is sense, there is life: If the life be a spiritual life, then the sense is a spiritual sense, a feeling of our spiritual wants. When the *Prodigal* began to live, he began to feel; to feel his nakedness, to feel his poverty, to feel his wants: And when *Paul* began to live, he began to see his wants; *Rom.* 7. 14. *The law is spiritual, but I am carnal, sold under sin: I know that in me there dwelleth no good thing; how to perform that which is good, I find not.* O when God gives grace unto the heart, that grace, though never so weak, affords two operations.: 1. It gives you *a clearer sight of sin*; 2. it gives you *a fuller sight of your wants.* It is Learning which makes us to see how much Learning we want; it is Health which makes you see how much Health you want; it is Grace which makes you see how little Grace you have, and how much you still need: No man rightly feels the want of more Faith, but by some Faith; the want of more Softness, but by some Softness.

Object. But now the Question may be, How a man may know, that the sense of his wants be a spiritual sense of them? for many men say that they want such and such spiritual Graces, and yet they have not a spiritual life in them. *Sol.* I answer, There are four things which declare the sense of our spiritual wants to be a true spiritual sense: 1. Ordinarily, *it follows after a deep Conviction of sin*; that man deceives himself, who talks of spiritual wants, and yet never saw his spiritual fulness of sin. The Lords ordinary way in Conversion is, To strip us wholly of our selves; and therefore, 1. He opens our eyes to see how rich we have been in sin; 2. To see how poor and nothing we are in Grace. 2. If it be a spiritual sense, *it is an humbling sense:* He who can see much sin in himself, and not be troubled, is not rightly sensible of sin; and he who can see much want of grace in himself, and not be humbled, is not spiritually sensible of his spiritual wants. What! and yet so little Knowledge! yet so little Faith! and yet so little Love of Christ! yet no more strength to pray, to deny my self, to overcome my sins! And now he mourns and weeps.

3. If

Of the Returning Prodigal.

3. If it be a living spiritual sense, *it is an humble sense.* The prefence of Grace (though little) breeds an high conflict with all sin, and a lowly spirit under all wants. This man admires at other Christians Graces, and prizes them, and goes home, and confesseth, Lord, *I am less then the least of all Saints.*   4. If it be a spiritual sense, then it is *a careful and an active sense*: It would have these wants supplied; it is full of inquiry, what shall I do? and it is full of Prayer, *I believe, Lord, help my unbeliefe*: The sense of want will not cease but in the sense of supply. *[It is an humble sense. It is a careful and an active sense.]*

3. *A spiritual appetite is a sign of spiritual life*; You know that life seeks its own preservation; the living man must have food, and will have food: As soon as ever a child is born, if it be living, nature prompts it to crave the brests; and verily, so it is with every new born Christian; *As new born babes desire the sincere milk of the word,* 1 Pet. 2. 2. As soon as the *Prodigal* began to be spiritually alive, he presently thought of food; O, (saith he) *there is bread enough in my Fathers house, and to spare:* As there is bread for life, so there is bread of life; and as there are waters for life, so there are waters of life; there is spiritual bread, and spiritual water: *Corpus Christi est pabulum fidei,* The Lord Jesus and his Ordinances are the spiritual food of the soul; and when a man receives a spiritual life, he cannot live without them, but depends on them as for the nutrition and preservation of his life. *[There is a spiritual appetite.]*

Here again it may be demanded, How a Christian may know that his appetite is a truly spiritual appetite, flowing from life? To which I answer thus: If it be an appetite flowing from spiritual life, 1. Then it is a *strong appetite*; the Scriptures call it an *hungring* and *thirsting*, the strongest and fiercest of all appetites: O Sirs, There is an appetite dainty, and there is an appetite hungry; there is a difference twixt a wanton empty desire, and an hungring, or an appetite for life. *Give me children, or else I dye;* the word is to such a man, more *then his appointed food.*   2. It is an *Universal Appetite*: Some men have a stomack to the Word, but not to the Sacrament; and some have a stomack to the Sacrament: (O, that they must have) but not to the Word; and some have a stomack to this part of the Word, not to that part of the Word, and to it as thus dressed, and another way dressed; New Dishes for dainty stomacks: But a Christian in whom the life of Grace is wrought, why! he is for the Word, *[Signs of appetite flowing from life. It is a strong appetite. A Universal appetite.]*

N n   and

and he is for Sacrament, and he is for all Chrifts Ordinances, and all Chrifts truths: Why! (faith he) I have a proud heart, and such a truth will humble it; and I have a troubled heart, and such a truth will comfort it; and I have a doubtful heart, and such a truth will direct it; and I have a weak heart, and such an Ordinance will strengthen it; so that he sees food in all of them, and he hath an appetite to all of them   3. *It is a conftant appetite*: Give a living man food in the morning, and Life looks for some at night; he can feed to day, and he can feed to morrow too. Thus it is with a living man; though when a man is dying, his ftomack dies in him, and leaves him: One Sermon a moneth, or a year, will satisfie. A living Chriftian, he takes in provifion every market day (every Sabbath) for his foul, and he longs for the market day again: O, when will the Sabbath come again! O, when shall I appear before God again! O, when shall I fit down, and be entertained at Chrifts Table again! O, I could hear of Chrift, of Faith, of Mortification, of the Love of God, of newnefs of Obedience, &c. ftill I need more heavenly nourifhment for my Graces, &c.

A conftant appetite.

There is spiritual growth.

4. *Spiritual Growth is a fign of Spiritual Life:* You know that living men do grow, until they attain unto that proportion and meafure, which Nature (fay the Philofophers,) God (fay we) allots unto them. Therefore living Chriftians are compared to a fucking and thriving child, which fucks and growes by fucking: And to living branches that grow into more ftrength; and in Scripture, True Grace (which is the fame with fpiritual life) it is of an increafing and growing nature; Chrift compares it to *a grain of Muftard-feed*, which is little at firft, but in time growes and fpreads exceedingly; and *Solomon* compares it to the *Sun,* which rifeth more and more to the perfect day. *Paul* commends the *Corinthians,* that they did *abound in all Grace*; and praies for the *Philippians,* that their *love might abound yet more and more in knowledg, and in all Judgment*; And he himfelf *forgat what was behind, and preffed forward, and counted himfelf not to have apprehended.* O you! who take your felves to be alive, do you grow in grace? Many men grow worfe and worfe under the means of Grace; many grow in notions, but they do not grow in Grace; many grow into new opinions, but they do not grow in holy affections. But do you grow in Grace? and do you grow in all Grace?

Of the Returning Prodigal.

Grace? and do you grow according to the means of Growth? Alas! many men decay apace, and many men, like pictures, retain the same dimensions; sin is no more weakned after forty years living, then at the first; their old sins retain their old strength, and their faith receives no augmentation; they are no more able to trust on God for their bodies, nor to rely on Christ for their souls then heretofore. The barrenness and unfruitfulness of Christians, is an unspeakable dishonour to the Gospel, and an evident testimony, that they have but a form of Godliness without the power of it; I might now have shewn you, that true spiritual Growth is 1. Especially an inward Growth. 2. And a general Growth. 3. And the Growth comes in by the Growth of Faith. 4. And appears best in the Growth of humility.

5. *A spiritual cry or breath, is another sign of spiritual life:* If a man can but groan and breath, that man is a living man. When *Paul* was converted, *Ananias* was sent unto him, as to a chosen Vessel, *Behold* (said God unto him) *he prayeth*: in Zach. 12. 10. *The Spirit of Grace, and of Supplication* are joyned, for the one never goes without the other: But will some reply, This cannot be a sure sign of spiritual life; for a wicked man may pray, and cry to God; we read of their Prayers and cries in Scripture often. I grant it, But 1. There is a difference twixt a spiritual cry, and a natural cry; their cries arise from natural principles, but not from a spiritual principle. 2. It is the cry of a distressed man, but not of a renewed man. 3. It is a cry for natural and outward good, but not for spiritual and everlasting good. 4. And when they cry for mercy and heaven; it is not that mercy may bring them into an holy communion with God, but only that mercy may keep them from wrath and Hell. *There is a spiritual breath.*

6. Lastly, *A spiritual manner of working is an infallible evidence of a spiritual quickning:* When the Lord converts a man and makes him spiritually alive, he now works spiritual work. 1. By Spiritual Rules. 2. From Spiritual Principles in the strength of Christ, by Faith, and from love. 3. With Spiritual Affections, willingly, cheerfully, and delightfully. 4. For Spiritual ends. 1. *By Spiritual Rules; To as many as walk according to this Rule, peace be on them,* Gal. 6. 16. A dead and unconverted man lives by the Rules of his sensual Lusts, or the customes of the World, or the wisdome of carnal policy; sin *There is a spiritual manner of working.* *By spiritual rules.*

rules him, and men rule him, and his profits and pleasures rule him: But when the man is converted, now God rules him; he stands in *awe of Gods Word, and lives*, as 1 Pet. 4.2. *To the Will of God*: His actions, intentions, desires, steps are measured by the word; tis not *An libet*, but *An licet*; The word lets him out, and brings him in: *Whether the living Creature went, thither the Wheeles went*, so, &c. 2. *From spiritual Principles*: O Sirs, a man may do much work (which we call spiritual) from a Carnal and low principle; self-Love, vain-Glory, Education, a quick Conscience, may set out much: But the living Christians work arises from union with Christ; all is done in the strength of Christ, and Faith fetcheth strength from Christ to pray, and to preach, and to mourn, and to repent, &c. 3. *With spiritual affections*: There is a connaturalness twixt a spiritual heart, and a spiritual work. Thy word was the rejoycing of my heart; *I was glad* (said *David*) *when they said unto me, let us go to the House of the Lord*. *I delight* (saith *Paul*) *in the Law of God after the inward man*: *It is good for me to draw near to God*: There are affections in the works of a living man; his works drop out of his heart, another mans fall out of his parts. 4. *For spiritual ends*; So that Christ may be glorifyed: we live unto the Lord, unto him that dyed for us; *Whatsoever ye do, do it to the Glory of God; that God in all things may be glorified through Jesus Christ*, 1 Pet. 4.11.

Obj. But will some say, if these be signs of the life of Grace; of one being made spiritually alive, then I am in a sad condition: For 1. I find much sin still living in me. 2. And I find very dull, if not dead affections; and I find, 3. Exceeding impotency to what is good. 4. And I cannot find that old appetite, and those old fervent cries of Prayer which heretofore I found. 5. And as for growth under spiritual means, O, my heart sinks to behold the rich seasons of Grace, and my barrenness and unfruitfulness under them. *Sol.* I should be loath that any truly living Soul should go away with a sad heart; therefore give me leave to answer thy fears, 1. Generally. 2. Then distinctly.

1. *Generally* thus: 1. *Such complaints as these* (*ordinarily*) *are the language not of the dead, but of the living*: When shall you hear such inditements from a base, lewd, sin-loving, and serving person?

perſon? O no, theſe are the complaints of an heart that is ſpiritually ſenſible, and ſpiritually tender, and ſpiritually jealous, and which would not be deceived in its ſpiritual condition. 2. *If ſuch complaints as theſe be attended with inward humblings, and abaſings of the heart, and with deſires and endeavours of help*, aſſuredly they are the Teſtimonies of a living man: *Who ſhall deliver me, O wretched man!* was the complaint of living *Paul*. 3. *If thou canſt not at all times find every one* of the forenamed *Symptomes of life*; yet if at *any time thou canſt find any one of them*, it is a ſign that thou liveſt; if the child doth not go, yet if it ſucks, this ſhews life; if it doth not ſpeak, yet if it cry, it is alive; if it doth not cry, yet if it breath, it is a ſign of life: If there be groanings under the burden of ſin, and ſighings, for help, for grace, for Chriſt, &c. they are a ſign of life. O Chriſtian, the ſpiritual life is ſometimes more open, and full, and lively, and quick in actions; and ſometimes it is reduced to deſires, to a will, to a complaint, to a tear, to a ſigh, to a groan; O, that I could pray, O, that I could believe.

2. Diſtinctly to the particular Caſes.

Obj. 1. *Thou feareſt that thou art not alive, becauſe much ſin is yet living in thee:* To which I anſwer. 1. *It is with the Chriſtian made alive by Grace, as it was with* Lazarus *made alive by Chriſt*, who had for a while his grave cloathes on him, and he was bound hand and foot, and yet he was made alive; ſo there may be many ſinful corruptions, yet cleaving to that ſoul, which is indeed quickned with ſpiritual life. Nay, if thou didſt feel no ſinful corruptions, I ſhould queſtion whether yet thou wert made alive, for ſpiritual life or grace doth give unto the ſoul, 1. *The cleareſt ſenſe of ſin*. 2. *And the greateſt grief for ſin*. 3. *And the ſtrongeſt combate and conflict with ſin*. 2. *There is a difference twixt a feeling of ſin ſtill ſtirring in us, and of the life of ſin ſtill ruling in us:* Thou feeleſt ſin living in temptation, but doſt thou feel ſin living in thy affection; Thou feeleſt ſin moleſting of thee as a Tyrant, but doſt thou acknowledg ſin ruling over thee as a King. 3. *And what doeſt thou, when thou findeſt ſin thus working?* Doſt thou dye daily? If thou feeleſt ſin as if it were alive, doth not this humble thee? and doth not this

278 *Gods gracious Acceptance*

this haften thee by Faith unto Chrift, for more crucifying virtue?

There is much dulnefs and deadnefs in my affections and operations. Anfwered.

Obj. 2. Thou feareft that yet thou art not alive, becaufe *thou difcerneft much fpiritual dulnefs, and deadnefs in thy affections and operations.* Sol. I anfwer. 1. *Even the living have found too much fpiritual deadnefs in their hearts:* Davids foul was heavy, and caft down, and indifpofed, and a deadnefs poffeffed him, and he prayes often; O Lord quicken me. 2. But is there not a *difference twixt deadnefs and death*; death is the total privation of life (where there is fpiritual death? there is not fo much as the habit of grace) but deadnefs is fome diminution, or fome damp upon the habit of grace, that it fteps not out to its acts, with that liberty, and that alacrity as it was wont, and fuch a deadnefs may be in a living foul. And thirdly, *Thou feeleft this deadnefs, and thou diflikeft it,* and thou bewaileft it, and thou prayeft, how often, how earneftly: Lord quicken this dead heart of mine: Is it thus where death prevails? do dead men do thus? 4. *The actions of life are various*; Let the action for the quantity be what it will, greater or leffer, quick or dull, free or checked, and interrupted; yet if what thou doft be done in the ftrength of Chrift, if it be wrought with an humble and an upright heart; affuredly, thou art not a dead finner, but a living (though perhaps troubled) Chriftian.

I have no power to do any good. Anfwered.

Obj. 3. But *I have no power to do any good*; I cannot believe, I cannot pray, I cannot mourn. Sol. 1. *What, no Power at all?* never any power, no power from thy felf, nor any power from Chrift; no power perhaps to this work; but what, no power to any fpiritual work? no power (perhaps at this time) to an eminent act, but then is there not a power to pray for power? Though power appears not in the work, doth not power yet appear in the will and defire? *Rom.* 7.18. *I know that in me (that is in my flefh) dwelleth no good thing. For to will is prefent with me; but to perform that which is good I find not:* I cannot do it, but I would do it. 2. *If there be a power living in the will, it is the beft fign of life:* A wicked man doth often the good which his will is againft, and the good man often doth not the good, cannot do the good, which his will is yet for. Now God looks upon the will, more then upon the work: If gracious acts be couchant in the will, life is in thee. 3. However, *although thou*

of the Returning Prodigal.

thou haſt not power (ſometimes) let down *for ſpiritual work*; yet thou hast *ſo much power ſtill remaining, as to lift up weak hands for more power:* Though thou canſt not believe, nor repent, nor mourn as thou thinkeſt, yet there is an heart to ſeek unto God in Chriſt for this power to believe, *&c.*

*Obj.*4. But *my old lively affections are gone,*my old eſtimations, my old hungrings and thirſtings, my old delightful communion with God in prayer, and in his ordinances. *Sol.* To this I would only ſay thus much. 1. *There is a difference twixt the intenſive ſwiftneſs,* or *flaſh of affections,* and the *intenſive ſtrength,* and *weight of the affections.* A young Chriſtian is moſt in the former, an old Chriſtian (who acts more upon Judgment and Faith) is moſt in the latter. 2. *The caſe ſeems rather to be of a living man, like to dye, then dead:* Of a man decaying in Grace, rather then totally deprived of grace; of a ſick Chriſtian, rather then of a dead Chriſtian. 3. And therefore *ſeriouſly ſearch the cauſes of the remiſſion of thy firſt love,* of thy ancient favour in holy communion: O, look whether a dead flye be not fallen into the ointment, whether ſome inſnaring luſt, fleſhly, or worldly hath not robbed thee of thy ſtrength. 4. If ſo, *Be humbled greatly, and repent, and do thy firſt work.*

*Obj.*5. But where *there is life, there is growth,* but I find it not. *Sol.* A word to this: The denial of growth may be either 1. *Negative,* Never any at all; this is impoſſible if life be wrought. 2. *Comparative*; Not ſo much as another, not ſo much as I have found under ſuch, or ſuch means; not ſo much as I deſire; and this may be where there is life.

I have finiſhed two Propoſition from this Text: One reſpecting the death, and the other reſpecting the life of a ſinner: I now proceed to a third, which is, *That a very great and notorious ſinner may be (at length) converted and changed.* [*This my Son was dead, and is alive again:*] This Son! and who was he, or what was he; in the precedent Verſes, you may ſee his picture, you may read the Hiſtory of him; he was one, who would be gone from his Fathers Houſe, and into a far Country he went, and there he did waſte his ſubſtance with riotous living. He made an end of all of it, and in the baſeſt of wayes, amongſt Harlots; and then betakes himſelf to ſordid ſhifts: He offered himſelf to feed Swine, and would have fed with the Swine, nay, would have

My old lively affections are gone. Anſwered,

I finde no growth. Anſwered,

Doct. 3. A very great ſinner may be converted.

have lived upon the Offals and Husks which the Swine left: He stood it out to the laſt; if he could poſſibly have ſubſiſted, if he could but have lived, he would never have come back to his Father: Yet this Son, this Son at length comes back, at length is converted, and is alive again. *But I obtained mercy* (ſaid *Paul*, 1 *Tim*.1.13.) *Miſericordiam donantem*, mercy of Converſion; *miſericordiam condonantem*, mercy of remiſſion: I obtained mercy! Why! what was he more then another, that he does ſo emphatically ſpeak of himſelf, I obtained mercy! Yea, there was reaſon to ſet it off thus with an Emphaſis; for he was a notorious ſinner, *I was* (ſaith he) *a Blaſphemer*, and a *Perſecuter* and *Injurious*, *yet I, I obtained mercy*! Some of you know that it hath been an ancient queſtion and debate about the equality or inequality of ſin; I think thus, 1. *That Original ſin* (*quantum ad ſe*) *is equally divided amongſt all men*, there is *æqualis carentia debiti*, and *æqualis inhærentia Indebiti* (as touching the nature of Original ſin) in every man; in reſpect of it, one ſinner is not a greater ſinner then another. 2. *Yet the actual exerciſe of that ſin, may be more in one man, then in another*; and hence it is, that ſome ſinners we call them leſſer, and others we call them greater: By a great ſinner, I mean one who exceeds another very much in ſinful wayes and guilt. And one may be called a great, a very great ſinner in four reſpects; neverthelefs they have not hindered converſion.

One may be called a great ſinner in four reſpects.

1. One may be called a very great ſinner, *whoſe ſingle ſin is of an amazing quality*; ſuch as not only Scripture condemns, but even nature ſhrinks at it, as *Inceſt* and *Sodomy*; there is a kind of reluctancy, and abhorrency in nature againſt thoſe, and the very Heathens ſtart at them: Yet God hath converted ſome men guilty of theſe ſins. *The inceſtuous Corinthian, whom* Paul *would have delivered to Satan*, was wrought upon, and converted, and repented; and 1 Cor. 6. 9. *Some of them who were abuſers of themſelves with mankind*, v. 11. *Were yet waſhed, and ſanctifyed and juſtifyed*. 2. One may be called a very great ſinner, *whoſe kinds of ſinning are very many, and all of them exceedingly provoking*: When they are as a volly of poyſoned arrowes, all of them levelled at, and ſhot into the very face of God; every one of them, like *Saul*, is higher by the head then other ſins, which in compariſon are of a lower ſtature: Such a

When a ſingle ſin is of an amazing quality.

Whoſe kinds of ſinning are very many and provoking.

great

Of the Returning Prodigal.

great sinner was *Manasses*; he was one of the *highest Idolaters* that ever we read of, and a *witch*, and *dealt with the Devil*, and *offered some of his children to the Devil*, 2 Chron. 33. 3, 4, 6. *and shed much innocent bloud:* Yet this notorious sinner at length humbled himself greatly, and was converted: See verf. 12, 13. 3. One may be called a very great sinner, *who hath continued a long time in the course and practise of great sins*, perhaps twenty, forty, fifty years: *Abraham* continued a long time in his Idolatry, and at length was called and converted: The *Ephesians walked according to the course of this world, and had their conversation in times past in the lusts of the flesh, fulfilling the desires of the flesh, and of the mind*, Chap. 2. verf. 2, 3. yet at length were quickned and converted, *verf.* 5. 4. One may be called a great sinner, *whose sinnings are very greatly circumstanced :* Circumstances, you know, give a very great accent unto moral actions.

Quest. But how may it appear, that a very great sinner may be converted? *Sol.* There are four Reasons of it, or Demonstrations for it. 1. *Because some great sinners belong to the Election of Gods Grace : Paul* was (as you have seen) a very great sinner; yet faith God of him, *Act.* 9. 15. *He is a chosen vessel unto me.* There are two things (amongst many other) which belong to the Divine Election. 1. *It is a free Act*, and if I may use the word without offence, an Independent Act, raised only from the good pleasure of the Divine Will, and not from the condition of the Object. *Rom.* 9. 15. *I will have mercy on whom I will have mercy, and I will have compassion on whom I will have compassion.* Verf. 16. *It is not of him that willeth, nor of him that runneth, but of God that sheweth mercy.* If God will choose foolish things, and base things, &c. 1 Cor. 1. 27, 28. 2. *It is an infallible Decree :* I mean, such a Decree which God will certainly fulfil. In Election, God doth decree or ordain a person unto salvation; and this person God will certainly bring unto salvation, by those means which he hath appointed for that purpose: And therefore, if a great sinner be within the compass of Gods Election, him in time will God convert; *Act.* 13. 48. *As many as were ordained to eternal life, believed.*

Who hath continued a long time in a course of great sins.

Whose sins are greatly circumstanced.

Demonstrations it.

Some great sinners belong to the Election of Grace.

2. *Because*

The conversion of a sinner is an omnipotent work.

2. Because *the Conversion of a Sinner is an omnipotent work*: It belongs to God, to whom nothing is too hard; he can pardon great sins as well as little, and convert great sinners as well as ordinary sinners. There is as much power put forth to convert a sinner, as there was to make a world, yea, and more: For in Creation, there was nothing in the Subject created to resist and withstand; but when a Sinner is to be converted, there is an exceeding great resistance, such a resistance, as is able to put by all the strength and power of a moral Agent. No created and finite power can convert a sinner: An infinite power is required; and if that be put forth, the stoutest and strongest sinner must and doth yield. If the Sun riseth, then the thickest darkness flees away and vanisheth: If Christ speaks the word, then *Lazarus*, who *had been dead four dayes, lives again*. *Steven* preaches, and not only *Paul* slights his Sermon, but *consents also to his death:* But when Jesus Christ spake only a few words unto him, *Paul* now quakes, and trembles, and yields, *Lord, what wilt thou have me to do*.

God hath the absolute dominion over the heart.

3. Because *the Lord God hath the absolute dominion over the heart*; he can dispose, fashion, alter, turn it, as he pleaseth, and when he pleaseth: He hath the command of the heart and grace. Take the heart (as usually we do) for any or all the faculties of the soul, yea, as corrupted by nature and custome, yet God hath a dominion over it, and he can make new impressions, and divine alterations and inclinations upon it. The Understanding naturally is blind and dark, unable to unfold and apprehend the morality of conditions, actions, objects; but God can turn it from darkness to light; he can imprint on it the clearest light, whereby it shall be able to behold what is good, and what is evil. The *Judgment* naturally is erroneous, it mistakes good for evil, and evil for good; judgeth sinfull evil as the best and sweetest way, condemneth good as most contrary to us, to our delights, courses, ends: But God is able to imprint on mans Judgment, a discerning and righteously sentencing ability, that a man shall not only see his sinfull nature and life, but condemn it (*I was mad*, saith *Paul*; such a fool, a beast was I. *They shall remember their evil wayes, and loath themselves*, Hos. 2. 7.) as his greatest evil and misery; and conclude, that a new holy penitent life is the best of all lives, and that for himself. The

Conscience

Conscience is either sleepy or seared naturally: But God can awaken it, and imprint on it a power to feel sin; to complain, accuse, indite, wound, and slay the sinner, that he shall have no rest as long as he lies in his sinfull condition: *Sin revived and I died*, Rom. 7. The *Will* is naturally averse, and perverse; it is set against all spiritual good, and set upon evil: But cannot God alter this Will? He can easily turn it about; let him but drop in the least degree of Grace, and the Will presently wheels about, and is as ready, and desirous, and cleaving to good, as ever it was to evil: *Lord, what wilt thou have me to do?* Act. 9. So for the *Affections*, the Lord hath the dominion over them: He can make them to love him as much and more than ever they loved sin; and to grieve, and to hate, and to fear sin, &c. *Get thee hence; what have I any more to do with Idols?*

4. The Lord doth *sometimes convert a great sinner to glorifie his own Grace.* 1. The *power of it*, that it is able to cure great and strong diseases. If ordinary sinners onely were converted, men would imagine but a common and vulgar power lay in converting Grace; where there is a lesser opposition, there a weaker strength may suffice to do the work: But if sin be strong, now the power of Grace appears, in rescuing the soul even from the Gates of Hell, and from the Powers of Darkness. 2. *The riches of it*: When all the world knows, and the man himself knows, That there was nothing in him, but a vilest heart, and lewdest course, and yet Divine Grace hath converted him; O, saith he, this was rich Mercy and Grace indeed. The Apostle saith, That God quickned the dead *Ephesians*, that *he might shew the exceeding riches of his grace*, chap. 2. vers. 7. O, saith the great sinner, (now converted,) never was there such a gracious and such a mercifull God, such a kind and loving God; I was dead, and he hath made me alive; I was the greatest of sinners, and I have yet obtained the sweetest of mercies; I was the greatest Enemy, and yet God would be my kindest Friend; overcome by Sin, and now overcome by Grace; falling down into Hell, and now lifted up to Heaven; so bad, that Justice might have had much Glory to damn me, yet God hath been so good, that Mercy shall have the Glory to save me.

The first Use of this Point shall be, *To relieve any troubled and distressed Conscience.* You shall find by experience these two

God doth this to glorifie his own grace.

Use 1.
To relieve the troubled Conscience.

two Truths: 1. That whiles men are in a dead, lost, vile, and unsensible condition, they then imagine that their sins are little, and mercies great, and they have power to turn to God when they please: 2. That when they come to be truly sensible of their hearts and ways, then their sins appear exceeding great, and the mercy and grace of God seem little; O! they have withstood the offers of grace, and all self-power is gone, and the greatness of their sinning is an absolute bar to their conversion.

Reasons why a man sensible of his great sin, thinks God will not convert him.

And there are eight Reasons, why a man (made sensible of his great sinnings) inclines to think that God will never convert him. 1. *Because he hath been one who hath exceedingly provoked God to wrath against him*: He sees great wrath in God, and that he hath, by his continual sinnings, incensed the Lord. O, saith he, it is mercy that must convert; but I have turned a mercifull God into a just God, and a kind God into an angry God; my great sins have put me into the hands of his great wrath. 2. *Because such a person sees his condition lying under the threatnings of God, and out of the reach of the promises of God;* God threatning him, Warrants issued out to take and arrest him, an Arrow levell'd at him; God hath said, That *he will wound the hairy scalp of him that goes still on in his iniquities*; and that *he who hardens his heart, being often reproved, shall be destroyed without remedy*; Now I have been that sinner. 3. *Because such a person feels the impressions of Gods displeasure on his Conscience:* He is in the very hands of wrath; Conscience tells him, Thou art the man, and these have been thy sinnings, these have been thy ways and thy doings; and Conscience condemns him for one who hath delighted himself in evil, and secretly goes and smites him with unavoidable fears and terrors. Now when a man feels wrath, 'tis an hard thing to perswade him, that God hath any thoughts and intentions of mercy and grace for him. 4. *Such a person ordinarily looks more upon the examples of destruction, than upon the instances of conversion;* rather what God hath done against them, than for any of them. O, saith he, God in Scripture hath often left such and such great sinners to their own hearts lusts, and he hath given them up to Satans delusions, and to a reprobate mind and sense, and would not have mercy on them, he would deal with them no more. 5. *The distance twixt his greatly sinning soul, and converting grace,* seems to him

As the Israelites Psal. 81. 12. 2 Thes. 2. Jer. 13. 14.

wondrously

wondrously large: If I had been but sick and weak! but can a dead man live? should a Rebel be embraced? can a Blackmore be made white? It is great grace to convert a little sinner, but what grace is sufficient to convert so great a sinner? 6. *He measures the disposition of Divine Grace, by the indisposition of his own heart.* O, saith he, I have been, how long, how stubbornly unwilling to receive grace, how violent to oppose grace! If I had neglected it only, but I have rejected it; I have been so long unwilling, despising, will Grace be pleased and so willing to one so unwilling? Grace will not be willing to smile on him who hath frowned on it; Grace will not stoop to him who hath trampled upon Grace: Can Divine Grace and I be so easily friends! What, forty years lying in Hell, and now to think I shall go to Heaven! all my life to serve the Devil, and yet now to think that God will take me, or make me his servant! 7. *Such a man sees his sins in another manner than ever before:* The face of sin is unvailed, like so many spears in the heart of Christ, like so many wounds given to sweetest Mercy, like so many cups of poyson that he hath drunk, and so many cups of wrath which he hath made Christ to drink, and as so much dung cast upon the Beauties of Holiness. 8. *Yea, and he feels his sins in another manner.* O, saith he, I feel my proud heart still, and my adulterous heart still, and my covetous heart still; and when any good ariseth, it is surprized, it it resisted, it is quenched by a thousand evil motions: And though I hear, and though I seek God, yet it is thus with me. O! my sins have been so great, that God will never undertake my conversion, my change; had I been more civil, had I been less evil, perhaps he would.

Now I would say six things to this great sinner. 1. *Great sinnings should be reasons of great humblings, but they should never be the causes and helps of unbelief.* Grandia delicta, fletus grandes. Because thou hast found an heart which could sin exceedingly, beseech God to give thee an heart to mourn exceedingly; and think not, that God cannot do much good, because thou hast done much evil. 2. *Great sinnings should work a self-despair, but they should never work a God-despair.* Great sinnings shew a great fulness of sin, which cannot be overcome, but by a great God. Thou art a great sinner, but God is a great God; there is no sinner like to thee, and there is no God like to him: He

Six things to this great sinner.

Great sinnings should be reasons of great humblings, but not of unbelief.

Great sinnings should work a self-despair, but not a God-despair.

He is great in power, (if he were not able to convert a great sinner, he were not great in power;) and he is great in mercy and love, (he were not great in mercy to pardon, nor great in love to save, if he did not pardon great sinners, and convert great sinners:) Therefore, as the least sinner should despair of his own power, so no sinner, no not the greatest, should despair of Gods power. 3. *God hath converted great sinners.* Usually, the sinners whom God hath converted, they have been of the greatest rank of sinners: He hath passed by many an hundred civil righteous persons, and his converting Grace hath laid hold on the notorious sinner. Thou art not the first Idolater, the first Thief, the first Whore, the first Adulterer, the first Drunkard, the first Swearer, the first Sodomite, the first Persecutor, the first Unbeliever and refuser of Grace, that Divine Grace hath assayed and converted: They had no more power to contribute towards their conversion; there was no more reason in them to move the Lord to look upon them, than there is in thy self; yet God did convert them. 4. *Though a person can say, that God hath not hitherto converted him; yet no sinner* (living under the means of Grace) *can safely say, that God will never convert him:* For no sinner can know his eternal Reprobation, this is a secret counsel which is reserved in the bosome of God; can know the season, the very designed season when God will convert him; for the Lord reserves the power of conversion, and the season of conversion to himself; he converts some at one time, some at another: God never revealed to any man, that at such a time, at such an hour he would convert him; *Consequenter,* a man may know the hour of his conversion, but *Antecedenter,* he could not know that God would then (just then) convert him. 5. *There is more probability that God will convert thee* (thus *sensible,* &c.) *than that he will not.* For 1. The clearing of thy great sinfulness unto thee, and the setting of thy great sins in order before thine eyes; 2. The quicknings of thy Conscience to feel the burthen and weight of thy great transgressions; 3. The great perplexities and fears in thy heart because of these great sins, are no evil signs at all: Of the two, the troubled Conscience is much more hopefull than the seared Conscience. *Vicinior saluti est dolor patientis quam stupor non sentientis,* as *Austin* well. Though trouble in Conscience be not alwayes an

infallible

God hath converted great sinners.

No sinner can say, God will never convert him.

There is more probability of thy conversion, being thus sensible, than not. Reasons of it.

of the Returning Prodigal.

infallible Argument of Life, yet it is an ordinary Antecedent unto Spiritual Life: The still Voice came after the Whirlwind, and Christ came after the storm, and *Canaan* came after the Wilderness; the Spirit of Adoption comes after the Spirit of Bondage. 6. *But what if the Lord hath already converted thee?* What if God have done that work in thee which thou fearest he will never work further? 'Assuredly, if thou art great-
'ly ashamed of thy great transgressions; if thy soul can now
'loath it self for all its abominations; if thy heart can remember
'them, and bitterly mourn over them; if thy cries be great to
'be delivered from them; if thy fears be great to sin no more;
'if thy heart will not be content without a new heart; if thou
'and God must be reconciled; if thou hast received an heart wil-
'ling to be converted; What shall I say? Thou art indeed con-
'verted.] Remember two supports which I leave with thee:
1. No poor sinner can be so ready and willing to be converted by God, but God is much more ready and willing to convert him;
2. A willingness to be converted, is conversion begun; the first stroke of conversion lights upon the Will of a sinner, and the greatest part of conversion appears in the change and conversion of the Will; it is from the will of Gods grace, that thou art willing to have grace.

What if the Lord have already converted thee.

A second Use shall be of *Caution. Let no man presume to continue in great sins*, or to remain secure and careless, because he hears that a great sinner may be changed and converted: For Although *God doth convert some great sinners*, one *Abraham*, one *Paul*, one *Mary Magdalene*, yet there are *many of them whom he never converts*. 2. *Perhaps he may convert, perhaps he may not*; and what if he doth not? It is but contingent to thee: Perhaps he will convert thee, this should move thee to seek him; perhaps he will not, this may affright thee to stand out any longer against him. Therefore, to be bold in sin, because God can, and sometimes doth convert a great sinner, may move thee rather to conclude, he will not, he intends not to convert thee, than that he doth. When Divine Goodness is made encourageable to sin against that Goodness; when it is not a melting Sun, but an hardning Sun; it is a presage rather of a mans subversion, than of his conversion. 3. *Though God can, and doth sometimes convert a great sinner, yet usually the greater sinner*

Use 2. Caution. Let no man presume to continue in great sins.

comes

comes off with the sharper conversion. The great Malefactor sometimes hath his Book and his Life too, but he is burned in the Hand, and in the Shoulder. *Paul* was a great sinner, and was converted; but his great sins, which were a troubling to Christ, did prove a trembling to his heart. God puts such a sinner upon the Rack; he strikes and wounds him, that all the Countrey shall hear of the troubles which his Conscience feels for his sinnings against God: God doth, as it were, singe him with the flames of Hell, before he meets him with the kisses of Heaven. 4. *Most usually, those great and notorious sinners whom God converts, are such who have thus sinned under their ignorance. I was a blasphemer,* &c. saith *Paul, but I did obtain mercy, for I did it ignorantly, and through misbelief.* He did not know what he did, he thought he had been in the right: You seldome read of one knowing Pharisee, who persecuted Christ, that was converted; yet you read of many of the Jews, and of the Elders, that were converted; for they did not know Jesus Christ to be the Lord of Glory. I will not say, that no knowingly notorious sinner shall ever be converted; but certainly, Conversion is very rare, where Knowledge holds the Candle to long and great works of Darkness. Those sinners who go on against the workings of an enlightning Spirit, fall very rarely within the favour of the converting Spirit: Therefore let no man gather poyson from this honey, &c.

Use 3. Direction to such converted sinners.

Take pains to be assured of pardon.

Keep conscience tender.

The last Use shall be a word of *Direction* to any *great and notorious sinner, whom God hath been pleased mightily and graciously to convert.* I would commend these Advisoes unto him. 1. *Let him take much pains to get his Acquittance fairly writ and sealed;* I mean, to be well assured that his sins are pardoned. Believe it, no man shall find his title so questioned, his heart so assaulted with often doubts and fears of pardon, as one who hath been a great sinner: The Provocations have been great, and Conscience hath been boistrous, and Satan can lay in shrewd exceptions, &c. 2. *Let Conscience be exceeding tender:* O awake it not, displease it not by new adventurings; all the old wounds will bleed afresh: A little new sin committed, will raise up the old ghosts; it will revive the sense of all the old great sins, which although they be pardoned, yet thou wilt now think they are not. A person who before his Conversion lived as if he had been

Of the Returning Prodigal.

been in Hell, should after his Conversion live as if he were in Heaven. 3. *Love much*, *and do much*; do some great thing for Gods Glory.

Love much, and do much.

This my Son was dead, and is alive again.

Alive again! but how came this about? what was the occasion of this Prodigals Conversion? look back unto *v.* 15, 16. he was brought so low as to feed Swine, and would have been glad of the Husks, but no man gave unto him, and he is ready to perish with hunger; and now returning thoughts came into his mind; now he resolves to come back again unto his Fathers house: Whence observe,

That great afflictions are sometimes an occasion of the Conversion of a great sinner. There are two sorts of afflictions, 1. *Inward*, which set upon the conscience; these are sometimes an occasion of Conversion: A troubled conscience doth many times end in a renewed conscience; troubles of heart are oftentimes closed with change of heart. The great storms occasion the Traveller to come in for shelter: *The biting Serpents* occasioned the *Israelites to look to the brasen Serpent;* the *avenger* of *blood* made the guilty person to *flye to the City of refuge;* and a condemning conscience oftentimes makes a poor troubled Soul to come in unto Jesus Christ for ease and rest. 2. *Outward,* which light upon the body and estate of a sinner; these also sometimes serve to fetch in a sinner; as he once said, *periissem nisi periissem*, I had perished unless I had perished. *Josephs brethren* had never found *Joseph,* and craved food of him, unless a famine had befallen them. If God had not deprived some men of their worldly goods, they had never come in to seek heavenly Treasures: We may say of them that if they had been fed, they had been famished; and if they had not been famished, they had never been fed with the bread of life.

Doct. 4. Great afflictions are sometimes an occasion of great sinners conversion.

Again, these outward afflictions may be considered two wayes, either 1. *Simply*, and nakedly in themselves; so they cannot convert any sinner, no more then the *pool of Bethesda* (alone) could heale a diseased Person, or *Elijahs salt could heal the Waters.* 2. *Concomitantly,* as accompanied with, and sanctifyed by Gods Spirit: It is not the hammer, but the fire which softens the Iron,

P p

iron; It was not the Water, but the Angel that stirred the water, which made the water medicinal: It is not the Rope, but the strength of the hand upon the Rope, which draws in the Boat. Afflictions in themselves are privations of a comfortable good; but if God sanctifies them, they may then be a means of our everlasting good: God can use them as a bridle, not only to stop us running out of the way, but also to turn us into the right way. *Hof.* 2. 14. *I will allure her, and bring her into the wildernefs.* By alluring, he means a gracious and effectual perswasion, a prevailing even to Conversion; but then he will bring her into the wildernefs; God brings men into the Wildernefs (into a barren, desolate miserable condition) and then allures or converts them. *Manaffes* was a great sinner, and yet *God humbled him greatly*, and (as it is thought) converted him; but what means did he use for this? See 2 *Chro.* 33. 11. *The Lord brought upon him the captains of the hoft of the King of* Aſyria, *who took* Manaſſeh *among the Thorns, and bound him with fetters, and carryed him to* Babylon. v. 12. *And when he was in affliction, he befought the Lord his God, and humbled himself greatly.* *Nebuchadnezzar* was a proud and lofty sinner, and therefore God puld him down; *he did drive him from men, and he did eat Grafs as Oxen, and his body was wet with the Dew of Heaven;* and having thus abafed him, he wrought upon him to acknowledg and praife the true God, *Dan.* 4. 33, 34.

How this may appear.
Afflictions sanctifyed are the souls Looking Glaſſes.

Queſt. How may it appear that, &c. *Sol.* There are four things attending upon sanctifyed afflictions, and all of them contribute to Conversion. 1. *Afflictions (sanctifyed) are the souls Looking-Glafs,* wherein a man may see his sins, which are the causes of afflictions; there are divers Glaſſes in which we may see the face of our sins. 1. The Glafs of the Word. 2. The Glafs of Reproof. 3. The Glafs of Conscience. 4. The Glafs of Afflictions: Affliction is a Glafs wherein a person firſt *sees his own sins*; *Ocules quam culpa claudit pena aperit.* *We were verily guilty of the blood of our brother* (said Joſeph's Brethren;) *and as I have ſerved others, ſo the Lord hath ſerved me* (said *Adonibezeck*.) 2. *Sees them as ſinners*. In proſperity we see the pleaſures of ſin, but in adverſity the bitterneſs of ſin; in the one we ſee them as our friends, in the other as our enemies: *An evil and bitter thing that we have forſaken the Lord* (so *Jeremiah* speaketh.) 3. *Sees them with a ſerious look;*

Of the Returning Prodigal.

look; sees them, and thinks of them; sees them, and layes them to heart: *Thy wickednefs hath procured thefe things unto thee.* Now when a person is brought to a right sight of sin, to see his own sins, and as sins, and seriously considers of them; this is a way tending to his Conversion: *I confidered my wayes* (said *David*) *and turned my feet unto thy teftimonies.*

2. *Afflictions* (*fanctifyed*) *work much upon the Confcience*; they are the rods of God upon the Soul; they are the Waters of *Marah*, bitter Waters, and they stir up conscience to speak bitter words unto us: These were thy wayes, and these were thy doings; thou wouldst not be warned, thou wouldst not hearken, and now see whither thy sins do tend, now see into what straits they have brought thee, now thou wilt believe that God is displeased with thee: When conscience is stirred, when the burden of afflictions turn into the burden of conscience, two things ordinarily ensue thereupon. 1. *A mans carnal fecurity is broken*: The man thought himself safe and secure before; but now he sees his condition to be very sad, unsound, unsafe, and miserable; not only my goods are gone, but my God also is gone. 2. *The heart comes to be humbled*: O, A working conscience, a smiting conscience is the Hammer of God, by which he breaks and bows the soul. Afflictions now stir up the Gall and the Wormwood, and the soul is humbled by them; and when the soul is brought to see sin, and to consider of sin, and to be humbled for sin, it is now in a fair way of Conversion.

3. *Afflictions (if fanctifyed) are gales to Prayer:* Lord, *in trouble have they visited thee; they powred out a Prayer, when thy chaftening was upon them,* Isai.26.10. *In their afflictions, they will feek me early,* Hosea 5. It is almost natural for an afflicted man to pray, and afflictions put an edge of zeal on Prayer; we are seldome more frequent and more fervent in that duty, then in the times of our diftrefs. But then observe, that as afflictions are apt to quicken prayer; so if they have occasioned a sense and trouble in the heart for sin, Then 1. *Usually they ftir up Prayer for pardon of sin*, and for conversion from sin. *Blot out my tranfgreffions*, praies afflicted *David. Turn thou me, and I fhall be turned*, praies diftreffed *Ephraim,* Jer.31.18 These are the two great defires of a diftreffed soul. 2. *Usually God hears*

Gods Gracious Acceptance

hears these Prayers, *The sacrifices of God are a broken spirit; a broken and a contrite heart, O God, thou wilt not despise,* Pf. 51.17. A poor sinner cannot put up a more acceptable request unto God then this: Lord, I beseech thee, change and turn my heart, subdue mine iniquities! let not sin have dominion over me! I beseech thee, suffer me not to dishonour thee any more! So that now you see that afflictions have brought the Soul and God together; the afflicted Person sees a need of Mercy and Grace, and unto God he applies himself who is the only Author of a sinners Conversion, the only Physician of a sinful soul.

They incline us to converting ordinances.

4. *Afflictions (if sanctifyed) incline us unto converting Ordinances:* You shall observe that men under their afflictions are 1. *More willing to hear.* 2. *More attentive in hearing.* 3. *More tractable and pliable,* (.i.) more easie to be wrought upon in hearing: *When a man is chastned with pain, and his flesh consumed away, and his soul draws near to the Grave; then he will make use of a Messenger, of an Interpreter, of one among a thousand to shew unto him his uprightness,* Job 33. 19. to 23. Oh, what a Divine influence and authority hath the Word over such a man? he can be content to have his sins ript open, and he can hear and weep, Oh, a sinner! and he longs to hear of some word of hope, and when he hears it, Oh, how good is God! and he catcheth greedily at the word of direction; and when he hears it, Oh, when shall I be this! when shall I do this! Lord, give grace, give strength unto thy poor servant; the man in his prosperity would not know the Lord, nor hearken to him; he was above counsel and instruction, but now his *ear is opened to discipline, and instruction is sealed unto him,* Job 33.16. Now it is, *Lord, that which I see not, teach thou me; and if I have done iniquity, I will do no more,* Job 34.32.

Use.

Trial, what the fruit of our affliction is.

The first Use shall be for *Trial* of our selves, *what the fruit of all our afflictions is*; I think there is no man almost in all the Kingdome, but God hath of late some way or other afflicted him. Many have lost all their estates, not an House is left to them, nor Land, nor a Rag to their backs; many have lost their Husbands or their Children in the War; many have lost some of their Family with the Plague lately; who hath not been some way or other afflicted? Now consider, 1. *It is the saddest affliction, to be no way bettered by afflictions*; No misery like that, to love the sins, and continue still in the sins which brought our misery:

It is the saddest affliction, not to be bettered by affliction.

Of the Returning Prodigal.

misery : Oh, to be as far from our friends (as before) and as far from our God as before ; to be thrust out of an earthly possession, and not yet to get an heavenly inheritance ; to lose our Lands, and not yet to get Christ; to have no home to go to here, nor any home to go unto hereafter; to lose our estates, and keep our sins; to lose the world, and to lose the soul too; to lose all our comforts, and yet not to lose the cause of all our discomforts. It was a miracle that *the three children were in a fiery furnace, yet not one hair of their heads was singed* ; It was a miracle that *Moses bush was burning, and not consumed* : Oh, it is a sad wonder that so many afflictions are upon men, and not one sin troubled, not one sin consumed, mortifyed !

2. *Many persons, though much afflicted, and long afflicted, yet are not converted* ; God complained of old, *they return not to him that smites them* ; and in another place, *yet have ye not returned to me*, saith the Lord. There are eight sorts of men, whose Afflictions have not been effectual to their Conversion. 1. *Stupid Sinners*, who know not from whom afflictions are sent, nor for what end : *Wherefore hath all this evil befallen us*, said they. 2. *Desperate Sinners*, who forsake God in their afflictions : *They cry not when he bindeth them*, Job. 30. 1 3. *This evil is of the Lord; why should I wait upon the Lord any longer ?* said he in 2 Kin. 6. 33. 3. *Bold sinners*, who grow worse and worse under their affliction; as the Anvile by blows is more hardened ; like *Ahaz in his distresses who sinned yet more*, 2 Chr. 28. 22. 4. *Proud Sinners*, who repine, and murmur, and complain against God, fretting against him, and perhaps cursing of God, as they in *Is*. 8. 21. 5. *Careless Sinners*, who regard not the operations of Gods hands, and lay nothing to heart : *The unjust knows no shame*, Zep. 3. 5. 6. *Politick Sinners*, who think to make up their losses by any temporizing compliances. 7. *Despairing Sinners*, who sink under the burden of worldly losses and crosses ; a worldly sorrow doth seize on them, even unto death, and crush them as *Rachel*, &c. 8. *Hypocritical Sinners*, who seem to turn unto God in Prayer and Fasting, but it is like *Judah, friendly not with their whole hearts* ; at the best they doe but stop in sinning, but they do not forsake their sins ; their righteousness is but as the morning dew, *Hos*. 6. I will but say three things to all these men. 1. *It is a sure sign, that the afflictions are whips of wrath, and not rods of love*, they come not from a Father, but from a Judg. 2. *It is a sure sign that greater afflictions are*

Many persons though much afflicted, are not converted.
Eight sorts of persons.
Stupid sinners.
Desperate sinners.
Bold sinners.
Proud sinners.
Careless sinners.
Politick sinners.
Despairing sinners.
Hypocritical sinners.

are to follow, *I will chastise you seven times more*, Lev. 26. 21. or else, which is worse, eternal destruction. *Reprobate Silver shall they be called: Because I would have purged thee, and thou wast not purged, thou shalt not be purged till I cause my fury to rest upon thee.* 3. It is a sign that men are very wicked, drowned in the love of sin, or the World, or that a spirit of Atheism prevails and reigns in them.

I now proceed to another Proposition, which is implyed in these words:

Doct. 5.
There is an almighty power required to convert a sinner.

That there is an *Almighty Power required to convert or change a sinner*, no less then is requisite to quicken a dead man : (This my Son was dead, and is alive again;) To awaken a man out of sleep, needs no great power ; (a word, a call, a cry, a little stirring may do it ;) but to quicken a dead man, here calls, and cries, and stirrings will not do it, all the power of Men and Angels will not do it. In *Acts* 2.41. you read of *three thousand converted at one Sermon.* And in *Acts* 4. 4. of *five thousand converted at another Sermon*, so many, so quickly converted ; certainly the Power that wrought this must be Almighty. Jesus Christ himself must come, and he must cry, and he must *cry with a loud voice*; Lazarus, *come forth*, Joh. 11.43. The Apostle speaks of the *exceeding greatness of Gods Power, towards them that believe, and of the working of his mighty Power*, Ephes. 1. 19. *Even such a Power as God wrought in Christ, when he raised him from the dead*, v. 20.

The power put forth in conversion. Not moral only.

There is a twofold opinion about the power which is put forth in a sinners Conversion. 1. Some hold it to be *Moral only*, because this is most congruous to the will of man, which is a moral subject. God (they imagine) doth offer and propound such Objects, with such Arguments which do wooe, and allure, and prevail with the will of a sinner. *Sol.* It is true that the outward means work only after a moral way. The word (which is the ministry for Conversion) it doth offer to the sinner Arguments of life, and death ; It reveales, and commands, and promiseth and threatneth : But a moral suasion (as they call it) is not sufficient to convert : And there are four Reasons which

Proved.
to me seem very strong and unanswerable against it, 1. *The very Phrases by which a sinners Conversion is expressed in Scripture, do surmount a moral suasion :* There is no less power to convert

convert a sinner then there was 1. To create man at the first. 2. There shall be to raise the dead at the last; when a sinner is converted, he is said to be created again, to be born again, to be regenerated; his heart is said to be opened, and circumcised; his strong heart is taken away, an heart of flesh is given unto him; surely all this is more then a moral power. 2. *This moral suasion must necessarily presuppose some power and abilities in him with whom it deals*; as if you counsel a man, you suppose something in him to incline him to hearken; if you do not suppose such a power, then it must be supposed that your counsel is in vain; as if you should counsel an *Ethiopian* to change his skin, or a blind man to see; this were in vain, for there is no power in them to do these. 3. *The conversion of a sinner in respect of God should be then contingent*; It might be, and it might not be; Though God intends to convert a man, yet he may fail and miss of the event, for as much as a moral work is resistible, and may easily be put by. *How often would I have gathered your children, and you would not; yee alwayes resist the Holy-Ghost.* 4. *Yea, the Conversion of a sinner should in the event depend more upon the will of man, then on the will of God.* The grace offered is common, and it is made peculiar, and differential by mans will; the right use of grace is not of grace, but of free will; so that *discrimen filiorum Dei & seculi*, is a *natura*, not *ex gratia*. The moral suasion is presented unto two sinners, the suasion is alike; why doth it bring this man and not the other man to Conversion? There can be no reason given but this, that the one would hearken to it, the other would not; so that the effect of Conversion (by this opinion) is manifestly placed in the liberty of a sinners will, whereas the Scripture plainly ascribes it to the will of him who calls, not to the will of him who is called. 2. Others hold it to be much beyond this; *To be a most High Power,* a *Creating Power*, a Divine Power, an Almighty Power, such a Power as overpowers all the sinful power in man, bears it down, and overcomes a proud, stubborn, resisting heart; though it doth not *totaliter eradicare*, yet it doth *actualiter predominari & vincere resistentiam voluntatis.* Now that no less power is sufficient, effectually to convert a sinner, may be cleared by these Arguments. 1. *If you consider the nature of Conversion it self,* there are two things which Conversion doth denote; One is an immediate work of

I. is a most high power, a creating power.

Proved.

From the nature of conversion.

of God, renewing man, or giving unto him a new birth; this cannot be done without an almighty Power. Our Divines in the Synod of *Dort*, call this *Mirabilem operationem*; *Prosper* calls this Grace *Bonorum in nobis creatricem*: This is the creating work, to bestow a Soul upon the Soul, a Spirit of life upon a spirit; this must be the work of an almighty God indeed, *Omnipotentissima potestas inclinandi humanorum cordium*: Austin *de Cor. & Gra. c.* 14. No man nor Angel can make a creature, only a God can make creatures, and new creatures: The *Ethiopian* cannot change his skin, and can any but a God, change the heart, the nature of a sinner? Another is, *A work of man by Faith, and Repentance*, turning himself unto God; some term the former *conversionem primam*, and the latter *conversionem secundam*; these two in the order of time cannot scarce be distinguished, but in order of causality they are, the work of God converting man is before, and it is a cause of the action in man converting unto God: Now Conversion in this sense depends upon an almighty Power; even the believer cannot believe without Gods mighty Power; there is a wonderful Power required to draw out the act of believing: Oh, how much power is necessary to make any troubled broken heart actually to come unto Christ, actually to believe, to embrace Jesus Christ! how many Seas must be divided first? how many Mountains levelled and removed out of their places first? It must come from the Father, if any do come unto the Son. See *Jo.* 6. 37. 45. *Unto you it is given to believe*, (τὸ πιστεύειν) Faith is the gift of God, and the act of Faith is the gift of God too; a renewed will is from God, and when it is renewed, even now to will is from God: God works in you to will and to do of his good pleasure, *Phil.* 2. 13. there must be his good will to make us will good, and his ὁ ἐνεργῶν for our τὸ ἐνεργεῖν, his work to make us to work. 2. If you consider *the strength of sin in mans nature*: we look upon two things in sin; the *guilt* of it; Oh, this was so great, so mighty that it could never be expiated but by an almighty satisfaction, even the blood of the Son of God; the *filth* and corruption of it, why! thus considered, it is of that strength in the Soul, that no Power but what is Divine can overcome it, an almighty Power is necessary to this, it must be a stronger then the strong that must dispossess this strong man;

From the strength of sin in mans nature.

Of the Returning Prodigal.

man; they are no weak weapons, but mighty weapons; and mighty through God, which muſt pull down theſe ſtrong holds; *the heart of man is full of evil*, ſaith Solomon; *it is deſperately wicked*, ſaith *Jeremy* : I beſeech you pauſe a while upon two Conſiderations. 1. *There is an exceeding ſtrength in Sin, even in the Regenerate, and converted Perſon:* *Paul* cries out, *I am ſold, I am led captive.* *David* is weeping for no leſs ſins then of *Adultery*, and *Murder*: *Peter* weeps bitterly for no leſs ſin then denying *of Chriſt*, then for ſwearing and curſing. In the very beſt *the fleſh luſteth againſt the Spirit* ; *So that they cannot do the Good they would*, and cannot overcome the evil that they hate. Now mark, if there be ſo much ſtrenghth in ſinful nature dying, how great is the ſtrength in ſinful nature living ? If there be ſo much power in a broken arm, how great is the power in a perfect, ſtrong unbroken arm ? If all the Chriſtians Grace he hath be ſometimes too weak for his ſinful inclination, aſſuredly then all external counſels, adviſes, reproofs are too weak to alter the whole ſinful nature; for the quality of *Grace* is much more ſtrong, then the exhortation unto Grace.

2. That *there is ſuch a ſtrength in ſin, that all the degrees of Grace unto which a converted perſon can poſſible attain in this life, are not able totally to rid the ſoul of it.* Till the mud-wall be quite pulled down, ſome of the Ivy will ſtick unto it ; *Jacob* went halting unto his grave. Till death makes an end of our lives, Grace cannot make an end of our ſins. Is it thus with the converted perſon, that neither Counſels, nor Exhortations, nor Grace received can utterly extirpate ſin ? nay is ſometimes too weak for ſin ? verily then there can be no converſion of a ſinner without an Almighty power : the power of ſin in an unconverted man being in fulleſt ſtrength, in every faculty and making higheſt reſiſtance to Grace, becauſe naturally of deepeſt contrariety thereunto.

3. Nay thirdly, conſider as there is a mighty ſtrength in ſin, ſo *there is a mighty ſtrength joyned with ſin, to oppoſe the ſinners Converſion* ; and the ſinner cannot be converted until both theſe armies be conquered : 1. *Satans ſtrength is* joyned with the ſtrength of ſin; the ſinner is under the dominion of ſin, and he is likewiſe under the dominion of Satan; and as ſin is a powerful Lord, ſo Satan is a powerful Prince ; he is the *God of this world, he works mightily in the Children of diſobe-*

From that ſtrength joyned with Sin, to oppoſe the ſinners Converſion.

Q q *dience,*

dience, Ephef. 2. 2. He takes them captive at his pleafure; and as *Pharaoh* raifed all his hoft, when the Children of *Ifrael* were to go out of *Egypt*; fo doth Satan ftir up all his policy, and put forth all his power, to withhold a perfon from being converted. He arms the Judgment with reafons, exceptions, fhifts, difputes; and he arms the Will with averfnefs, unreafonablenefs, ftubbornnefs, pride; And he arms the Confcience, and he arms the Affections. O what corrupt reafonings? how many proud denials? what hideous reprefentations of the wayes of Grace? what delights, what profits we have had by fin? what impoffibilities, what difputes, what feares, what terrors, what dampings of the Word, what diftractions in Prayer, what agonies, and continual, and vehement, and violent conflicts, doubts, fcruples, &c? 2 *All thefe muft be anfwered,* and all thefe muft be conquered, if the foul be converted. And can all this be done by a morall power? O no; it muft be an Almighty power, which muft refcue a poor foul out of the hands of two fuch mighty Lords. The people of *Ifrael* could not be delivered from one King, and with a temporal deliverance, but by the exceeding greatnefs of Gods power, and by an high and infuperable working of divine Grace. 4. There is more then an ordinary power required *for effects which fall fhort of Converfion:* and if no lefs then an almighty power be required for thefe (which are at the beft but fubordinate and preparative workes to the main work of Converfion,) queftionlefs then, the work of Converfion depends, and muft depend on an almighty Power. Such a quantity of power cannot be denied for the greater, which yet muft be granted for the leffer works, in the fame Order. There are fome good and learned Divines, who handling the preparatives to Converfion, do conceive four precious acts or works, wrought before it. *v. g.* 1. *Notitia divinæ voluntatis,* a knowledg of the Divine will. 2. *Senfus peccati,* a fight and feeling of our fins, and finful condition; 3. *Cogitatio de liberatione,* fome thoughts and defires of deliverance; 4. *Spes veniæ,* an hope at laft of a poffibility of mercy and pardon: all which God works by the preaching of the Word. As upon *Peters fermon,* they came to a fenfe of their fin, and fear, and trouble, and defire, and had fome hope of deliverance preached unto them, the promife being made to them and unto their Children; upon which God converted

From the effects which fall fhort of Converfion.

Synod. Dordr. pag. 169.

of the Returning Prodigal.

verted them. Now mark me; There is a necessity of an almighty Power to produce these antecedaneous, and inferior works. None but the *God of our Lord Jesus Christ, the Father of Glory, can inlighten the eyes of the Ephesians,* c. 1. 17, 18. Surely then, none less then he can open the heart of the Ephesians; for which is the greater work, to open an eye, or to open an heart? Is it not more to give life to the dead, then to give sight to the blinde? None but God can make a sinner sensible of his sins; *When the Commandment came, sin revived, and I died,* Rom. 7. 9. Now which is the greater work, to make me feel my sins, or to make me forsake my sins? to trouble my heart, or to alter my heart? to feel my disease, or to heale me of my disease? to shew me my fetters, or break off these fetters?

5. It is (at least) as great a *work to convert a sinner, as it is to preserve a sinner converted*; and one would think a greater work; for to the one man is dead, to the other he is living. Is it not more to make the house, then to repair the house? but to preserve or keep a converted person stedfast to the end, there needs no less then the power of a God: (*We are kept by the power of God through faith unto Salvation.* 1 Pet. 1. 5.) therefore to convert a sinner doth require no less power then that of a God. Now put all these things together; the nature of Conversion, the Power of a sinful heart, the Strength of Satan, the Power required for lesser works then conversion, the Greatness of making, then keeping, and then I think it wil manifestly appear, That no less then an almighty Power is necessary to a sinners Conversion.

From the power required to preserve a sinner converted.

Is there an almighty power required to convert a sinner, as great a power as to make a dead man alive? how may this *humble all our thoughts,* and all our hearts! you may *judg of the depth of the disease, by the bredth of the Remedy*; so may we of the greatness of our fall, by the greatness of the power which is required to raise us up. O who can utter the sinfulness of a sinner! who of us would believe that there is so great a strength in one of his sins! that all the powers in heaven and earth (less then Gods) are not able, are not sufficient to turn his heart from it! That one lust of Pride, that one lust of Uncleanness, that one lust of Covetousness, that one lust of vain-Glory, &c. is too strong for thee, and it is too strong for all the men on earth, and it is too strong for all the Angels in heaven.

Use 1.

To humble us from the consideration of the Depth of our disease.

Though

Though one puls and the other puls, and all of them pull together, they cannot pull it from thy heart, nor thy heart from it: you read in 2 Kings 4. 31. that *Gehazi* went before *Elisha* and *laid the staff upon the face of the Child*, but there was neither voyce, nor hearing; wherefore he went again to meet *Elisha*, and told him saying, The child is not awaked: Why! thus it is with thy heart under all the means of life and Grace; they may all turn back to God and say, This sinner is not yet awakened, he is not yet turned; The word of God may say, I cannot with all my Instructions, with all my Reproofs, with all my Exhortations convert him: nor can I, saith Conscience; nor I, saith Affliction; nor I, saith the Minister; nor I, saith the Father. The proud Pelagians, Papists, Arminians dream in this Point of a sleeper, but think not of a death; they talk of a prison, and opening the doore, but think not of the chains wherewith the prisoner is bound and fettered: they talk of a Counseller, but forget the Physitian; they write, as if a sinner were to be converted with Logick and Rhetorick; but alas! if any word converts a sinner, it must be an almighty word; God must quicken, as well as call; God must heal, as well as speak; God must work as a God, or else the sinner will remain an eternall sinner.

It is foolish presumption to defer Repentance upon a pretence of turning when we list.

2. If such an almighty Power be necessary to convert a sinner, then what a *foolish Presumption is it to defer to beg Repentance, supposing a lurking dormant power in the heart to turn when we list*? But, O vain man! why yet a little sleep more, and yet a little slumbring more! and why to morrow, or why hereafter? what is thy power, or what is thy strength to come off from thy sins, or to overcome and turn thy sinful heart? Why! Go and try some lesser thing, change the Leopards spots, turn night into day, raise thy dead child out of the grave, stop the course of the Sea, and sweeten it: Read the word, and make thy self to understand it; Read thy heart and make thy self to humble it; if thou canst not do the lesser, the weaker, why wilt thou endanger thy self with a presuming to do the greater, the stronger? Is it credible, that a sinner is able to do the work of a God? thou canst not break the thred, and shalt thou be sufficient to break the Cable? thou canst not pluck up the plant, and shalt thou be able to pull up the Oak? thou art not able to extinguish the rising of a sinful thought, and wilt thou ever be able to convert

vert a sinful nature? And tel'me serioufly, doth thy sinful power decreafe by sinful actings! In civil trading the stock is sometimes diminished; but in sinful tradings, sin increafeth the more in strength, by how much the more is it laid out in sinning; and the more that sinful power increafeth, the more need is there of a greater power to convert the heart. If the weakest sinner doth need an almighty power to convert him, O what an almighty, almighty power doth the strong sinner, doth the long sinner need for his Converfion!

3. If an almighty power be required to the Converfion of a sinner; *then, if ever you would be converted, look to that which is more then a finite power.* If thou wouldst have thy self converted, or any who belong to thee converted, do not expect it from men or means; Friends may defire converfion, and Minifters may preach the doctrine of Converfion, but it is God only who can effect the work of Converfion. *I spake unto thy Difciples* (said that troubled man about his poffessed child) *to caft him out, and they could not*, Mar. 9. 18. I confefs, we must use spiritual means, we must hear, we must pray, we must confer, but if you think that any of thefe (*nuda virtute*) by their own natural power can convert, you are deceived. It is not the word, but God by the word; (*the power of God to falvation*:) it is not prayer, but God to whom ye pray; it is not the minifter, but God who fends the minifter, who is able to enlighten thy mind, to quicken thy confcience, to convert thy heart; *Turn thou mee, and I shall be turned*, said *Ephraim*, Jer. 31. 18. So say thou, O Lord, thou art the living God, thou only art the Lord of life, I come to thee to convert mee unto thee; I hear, I read, I confer, I meditate on arguments, I purpofe, and yet I am not converted; Minifters deal with me, and Friends deal with me, and Mercies deal with me, and Afflictions deal with me, and Ordinances deal with me, and yet I am not converted! O Lord, I am without strength, and they are without strength; but thou art not without strength. No power lefs then thine will be sufficient for my Converfion: Now, O Lord, reveal thine arm; stretch out thine hand; O pity, fpeak, quicken, turn, fave one sinner more; nothing is too hard for thee, thou didst make a world by thy mouth, and thou wilt raife the dead, by thy word; O fpeak but one word, and my dead soul shall live. 4. Doth the converfion

If you would be converted look after an almighty Power.

Despair not of a mighty sinner. version of a sinner depend upon an almighty power? then *let us not despair, of a mighty sinner*; nor yet let a mighty sinner despair of a possibility of Conversion. God hath an almighty Power to condemn a sinner, therefore let him not presume; God hath an almighty Power to convert a sinner, therefore let no sinner despair.

Bless God for our conversion. 5. Then if any of you be converted, *Bless God for it*: we could never do it; it is God, and God alone, who hath done it: there are reasons why God reserves the power of a sinners Conversion to himself alone; 1. That men should seek to him alone for it; If God alone had not all the power of giving, he should lose of all the duty in praying, and asking. 2. That he alone may have all the glory, and praise.

Comfort to us that God converts by an almighty Power. 6. This is of exceeding *Comfort to us, That it belongs to the almighty power of God to convert a sinner*: For 1. That power is power sufficient: 2. It ever abides in God: 3. It is accompanied with an exceeding willingness; if thou seekest to him, thou shalt find his will to be as great as his power; he is as willing as he is able to convert thee; thou canst not come with a more exceptable petition.

Luke 15. 24.

This my son was dead, and is alive again.

These words comprehend in them (if I mistake not) a most exact discription of a sinners conversion; both 1. In the general nature of it, that it is a (perfective) change; [*Was, and Is; was dead, and is alive*:] 2. And in the differential or proper ingredients of it, which are couched in these words [*is alive again.*] In which three distinguishing ingredients of conversion are espiable; namely, That it is a *Change*: 1. Very *great*, and *notable*: The inlivening of a dead man is so. 2. Very *secret* and *internal*; the puting of life into a dead man is so. 3. Very *spreading* and *universal*; when a dead man is made alive, it is so. I confess that every one of these particulars doth merit a full and large discourse; but because I desire to open unto you the true nature of conversion, at the first, in as narrow a compass as I can, I shall therefore endeavour to draw all these goodly truths into one little Map, that so you may be the better able to understand and remember them. With your favour, I will

grasp

of the Returning Prodigal.

grasp them into this one Proposition.

That *true Conversion is a change, a very great, and inward,* Doct. 6. *and universal change.* You plainly see four things in this Assertion which offer themselves to our consideration. 1. TrueConversion is a *change* ;(*was dead and is alive*;)certainly here is a change. *Ego sum ego,* said the Harlot, here was no Conversion. *Ego non sum ego,* answered the young man ; here was conversion, for here was a change ; There may be a *was,* and an *is,* without a change. Christ was God, and is God, *Revel.* 1. 8. And in many men the *was,* and the *is,* are without a change; They were ignorant, and are ignorant still ; they were filthy, and are filthy still ; *Rev.* 22. 11. But if a man be converted, *the was,*and *the is,* are different, they are changed : *I was a Persecutor,* said *Paul,* but being converted he is not so ; *such were some of you,* said *Paul* of the Corinthians, *but ye are washed, but ye are sanctified.* Now when I say, that Conversion is a change, you must know that there is a two-fold Change : One is, *Substantial,* which alters the substance of man, as in Generation, and in Corruption, of which the Philosophers speak:Conversion is no such change ; the soul and body of a man remaines the selfe same substance before and after Conversion: It was the same *Paul* who Was a Persecutor,and Is a Preacher of Christ : As in the Sacrament, it is the same Bread for substance after Consecration, which it was before Consecration ; So is it the same man, for the Philosophical substance, before and after conversion.

Another is accidental, which alters the qualities of man. *Naaman* was the same man when he was a Leper,and when he was cured of his Leprosie ; he was the same for substance, (of it there was no change,)but he was not the same for the accidental quality, (because his leprosie was changed.) Such a change is there in conversion ; the sinfull Leprosie is changed, and a fair beautiful form of holinefs is put into his soul ; the Glove is now perfumed, the bitter water is now seasoned, another nature contrary to his former nature is now infused ; *old things are past away, all things are become new,* 2. Cor. 5. 17. Againe observe, that the accidental change, or alteration of a person, is likewise two-fold ; 1. One is *Corruptive,* which is from good to evil ; such a change was there in the *Angels that fell,* (they fell from heaven to hell, from being Children of Light, to be the Princes of darknefs) and

True conversion is a change,a great, inward,and universal Change. It is a Change.

and such a change was there in *Adam* that fell. O what a change! what a sudden loss of great possessions, of unspeakable perfections. O how good once he was, O what a sinner now he is! 2. Another is *perfective*, which is from evil to Good: Such a change is Conversion: Why! it is from sin to God: It is more then for *Joseph* to leave the prison and be made a Prince: when a man is converted, he is now raised and enabled with the nature, and life, and excellencies of God and Christ; true Conversion is a perfecting change.

One distinction more I cannot omit; It is this, The perfective change is likewise two-fold 1. *Relative* and *forinsecal*, as in the Justification of a sinner: when a sinner is Justified, the state of this sinner is changed; before it he was in the state of death and condemnation; after it he is in the state of life and absolution. 2. *Inherent* and *intrinsecal*; as here in the conversion of a sinner, which is a change within a man; a change not so properly of his *condition*, as of his *disposition*; even from one contrary to another, and that *à Genere ad Genus*, from one kind of quality to another kind. A sinner hath sometimes a contrary motion of good to evil put into him, but this is not Conversion; for it is not a mutation, but a motion: A sinners inclination is sometimes withheld, that he doth not sin; yet this is not conversion, for it is a chaining only, not a changing of his disposition; the Lyon is a Lyon in chains. A sinner goes from one sin to another; he leaveth his riotousness, and turneth to covetousness; he leaveth profaneness, and turneth to hypocrisy; yet this is not Conversion, for his sinful disposition is not altered from kind to kind: It is but a shifting from one evil to another evil; as the wind from one poynt to another; it is not a change from evil to good. If a man could leave all the sins in the world, and yet he loved and served but one, this man is not a converted man, because conversion is a change from one kind to a contrary kind, which the man comes short of whose heart is still set on any one sin.

It is a very great and notable change.

2. True Conversion is *a very great and notable Change*; there is no change, I think, in all the world of that height and depth as the conversion of a sinner. No not that from Grace to Glory; because it is but *ab imperfecto*, and this is *à contrario*.

of the Returning Prodigal.

trario. The Scripture doth frequently parallel it even with thofe changes which are miraculous: When Chrift made the *blind to fee*, and the *deaf to hear*, and the *dumb to fpeak*, and the *dead to live*, and *difpoffeffed Devils*; thefe were very great and notable changes, take them fingle and they were fo. Now all thefe miracles are wrought in any one converted perfon; 'Tis called a *Creation*, a *Refurrection*, &c. becaufe God puts out as much Power in the Converfion of a finner, as he did in creating the World. It is the prime work of the Spirit of Chrift, the top, the very higheft; when any one man is converted, the blind is made to fee, and the deaf is made to hear: (Ifai. 29. 18. *In that day fhall the deaf hear the words of the Book, and the eyes of the blind fhall fee out of obfcurity, and out of darknefs,*) and the dumb is made to fpeak, and the lame is made to leap: Ifai. 35. 5. *The eyes of the blind fhall be opened, and the ears of the deaf fhall be unftopped.* v.6. *Then fhall the lame man leap as an hart, and the tongue of the dumb fing:* Yea, and the dead is made to live; [*This my Son was dead, and is alive again;*] and fo many fins as there are from which the heart is converted, of fo many Devils is that heart difpoffeffed; thy filthinefs was an unclean Devil, and thy perfecution was a raging Devil; every fin that poffeffed thee was a ftrong Devil within thee: Oh, what a great change is it to behold a ftone turned into flefh! and yet in Converfion, *The heart of ftone is turned into an heart of flefh*, Ezek. 36. 26. What a change were it to fee a ftone changed into a Son of *Abraham*! and yet in Converfion a ftony hearted finner is changed into a Son of God; what a change were it to fee darknefs turned into light! yet in Converfion it is fo; *Ye were once darknefs, but now are ye light in the Lord*, Eph. 5. 8. What fhall I fay? in Converfion, the Bramble becomes a Fig Tree, and the Lion becomes a Lamb, and the Wildernefs is turned into a Paradife, and Hell is turned into Heaven; the Extortioner turns liberal, fo did *Zacheus*; the Perfecutor becomes a Martyr, fo did *Paul*; the hideous finner become a Saint, fo did the *Corinthians*; the blafphemer now fears an oath. There are four things which fet out the greatnefs of the change in a finners Converfion. 1. *There is a change of nature in nature*; there is a man, and a man, in the fame man; an old man, and a new man, in the fame man; two judgments in one judgment, two wills in

Four things fet out the greatnefs of this change. There is a change of nature in nature.

R r one

one will, like two Armies in one Field, or like the Twins in Rebecca's Womb. 2. There is the *strangest unlikeness to a mans self in a moment that ever was*; in a moment to hate Christ exceedingly, and the next moment to love Christ above all; to crucifie Christ because he said he was the Son of God, and presently confess that he is the Son of God; to mock the Apostles as drunkards, and presently cry out, what shall we do? &c. this moment to love sin, as if it were my only Heaven; and the next moment to loath sin, as if it were my only Hell: Now to count all truth and holiness, but as dung to the World; and presently to count all the World but as dung to Grace and Christ. 3. *There is the highest contrariety in actions and courses that ever was*; to see a man pull down what he built up, and to build up what he pulled down; to be mad against Christ, and then presently even besides himself for Christ; to scourge and revile *Paul* and *Silas*, and presently after, honour and embrace, and almost adore them: To reproach the Saints and their wayes, and suddenly to admire them, and value them and their paths, as worthiest of our dearest love and society. 4. *And a little, very little Grace to produce all this*: That one drop should sweeten the great bitter Ocean; that one little spark should cause all this flame; A very little Engine should move all the World, and level the Mountains; a little Grace to enter the Throne, and to turn all the soul round about. That *Moses* little *Rod should divide the Sea*, and melt the Rock; a little Ant tumble down a Mountain; that the *Grain of Mustard-seed*, which is the least of seeds, should grow into a Tree: That a very little Grace should transform the most rebellious heart, humble the most proud heart, quicken the dead, purifie the most vile affections, conquer the Gates of Hell, overthrow sin, dispossess Satan; should beget such a River of Grief, kindle such a flame of love, such a zeal for God, tendernefs in Conscience, such a strength to do, and suffer, to believe, life in death, joy in sorrows, hopes in despair; raise so high as to love them that hate us, bless them that curse us, pray for them that despightfully use us, and do good for evil. 3. True Conversion *is an inward change*: When a dead man is made alive, this is done by the infusion of an inward principle of life; the cloathing of a dead man is one thing, and the quickning of a dead man is another thing; it is one thing

Of the Returning Prodigal.

thing to plaister an old house, and it is another thing to build a new house; Conversion may be considered two wayes; either 1. *Extensively*: So it is a change even of the life, and outward actions of men; it is a cleansing of the flesh, as well as of the spirit; it is a sanctifying of the body, as well as of the soul: *It is a putting off the former Conversation*, Eph. 4. 22.   2. *Denominatively*: So it is an inward change; the Prophet calls it a washing of the heart, *Wash thine heart, O Jerusalem*, Jer. 4. 14. The Apostle calls it a *transformation by the renewing of the mind*, Rom. 12. 2. and a *Circumcision of the heart*, Rom. 2. 29. St. *John* calls it, *a laying the Ax to the root of the Tree*, Mat. 3. 10. *Ezekiel* calls it, the *giving of a new heart, and of a new spirit*, Ezek. 36. 26. Every converted man hath a changed heart; we say in nature, that *Cor est primum vivens*: It is true also in Grace, the first work of quickning and converting Grace begins in the heart of a sinner. The heart first fell from God, and it is the first that turns unto God. The heart is the first Seat of Sin, and it is the first Throne of Grace: Sin is the wound and disease of the heart, and Grace must bring the Plaister thither; sin is first in the heart, and most in the heart; dominion is there, the poyson is there; bring in the heart, prevail with it, and you bring in all the man: An outward change without an inward change, is   1. But *Hypocrisie*:   The Hypocritical *Pharisees made clean the outside of the Cup, but not the inside*; a golden profession and a rotten heart, this is but Hypocrisie.   2. But *Vanity*; it is to lop the Boughs, and leave the Roots which can send out more; it is to empty the Cistern, and to leave the Fountain running, which fills it again.   3. *But self and soul-deceit*:   What a foolish fancy is it to think my self a converted man, because my Tongue is quiet, and yet my heart doth curse God? because my body is honest, when yet my heart burns and boils with lust? because my hands strike not, and yet my heart is full of malice, and revenge, and murder?

Quest. But here a single scruple may be propounded, *viz. Whether every internal change be an evidence of true Conversion.* To which I answer, it is not; there are four Internal changes which may be in a man unconverted.   1. *A change from ignorance to knowledg*: The man who was an ignorant sinner, may become a knowing sinner, and yet remain still an unconverted sinner;

Whether every internal change be an evidence of true conversion.

Four internal changes may be in man unconverted.

A change from ignorance to knowledg.

sinner; for a man may hate the good which he knows, and love the evil which he knows; neither of which can consist with true Conversion. 2. A change *from error to truth.* Many a man forsakes the Popish Religion, and embraceth the Protestant Religion; his opinion and judgment of things may be altered, and yet his sinful heart may not be altered; he may hold justification by faith only, and yet his heart be utterly void of saving faith; he may deny merit unto the works of Repentance, and yet his heart never truly repent; he may hold the true and right Government of Christ in his Church, and yet that Government of Christ may never be set up in his own heart. 3. A change *from security to trouble* and perplexity: It is possible that a great sinner who was as senseless as the Rock, may now be as trembling as the Leaf, and his conscience troubled as the Sea, and yet his heart not converted; *Cain* was troubled, so was *Pharaoh*, so was *Saul*, so was *Judas*, yet none of them converted: There is a trouble which riseth from a quick conscience, and there is a trouble which riseth from quickning grace; this latter is an evidence of true Conversion, the other is not. 4. *A temporary change*, or rather a transient diversity in the affections. It is possible for some scornful person to hear the Gospel preached by some *John Baptist* (as *Herod* did) with joy, and to hear some *Paul* (as *Felix* did) with trembling, who formerly scorned all preaching; yea, this man may be in a great changeablenefs, yet never be truly changed; divine truths may fall upon him with that evidence and efficacy, as to shake his heart, stir his affections, excite his resolutions, and yet after a little while, as the cold doth on Water that is heated, all these workings expire into nothing, his old incorporated, familiar lusts prevail over them, and work them wholly out; till the inward change be a change of the heart, it is not a truly converting change.

4. Lastly, true Conversion is *an universal change*: When a dead man is quickned, the soul is not only infused, but also diffused, it is *tota in toto, & tota in qualibet parte*, the whole made alive; so is it in true Conversion, that grace which converts a sinner, doth change all the sinner, every faculty of the soul for the quality of it, and every member of the body, for the spiritual use of it; Therefore, converting grace

grace is compared to the *Light* which runs through all the body of the aire, every part whereof is inlightned; and it is compared to *Leaven* which spreads and infinuates it felf into every part of the Lump. You cannot dip into any leaf of this Book, into any parcel of a converted man, but you shall find a divine and spiritual change, a spirit of grace on it. He is sanctifyed throughout, *in foul, spirit and body* : I confefs, it were a work worthy of the deepest study of the exacteft Minifter to find out, and deliver two things unto us :   1. One is, the *Minimum quod fic*, the leaft breath or life of converting grace. 2. Another is, *The fpecifical operations of converting grace, in all the faculties of the foul*, fo that one may fay fafely, this faculty is changed, and that faculty is changed by grace and nothing elfe. This I make no queftion of, that converting grace doth make the whole man alive. For 1. It is a *new* and *renewing quality*. 2. It is of a *diffufive virtue*, being a good in *Genere optimorum*. 3. It muft be *Co-extenfive with fin*, which hath perverted the whole man : But yet to fet out its changing work in every faculty of the foul, I cannot undertake it in the exquifitenefs thereof; yet if you will favourably accept of my endeavours, I fhall attempt towards it, that fo you may the better conceive of that univerfal change wrought in a finner upon his Converfion.

Concerning this univerfal change,

1. I premife a few Propofitions which I take for granted truths, (*v.g.*)   1. That *converting Grace*, (which changeth the foul) *is a Concatination of all particular faving graces* : It is not Faith only, nor Repentance only, nor Hope only, nor Love only, *&c.* but all of them, a Link or Golden Chain, as it were, of them.   2. That *all thefe are fimultaneous in their birth*; they are not implanted one before another, or one more than another, (habitually confidered) but are of a fimultaneous and coexiftent production, although in the order of working and manifeftation of work, there be a precedency.   3. *All thefe graces concur in their fpecifical nature*, and immediate operation, as to a change of the foul. The change wrought in the mind, is of the fame nature with that which is wrought in the will; and the change in the will, is of the fame nature with that in the affections ; every faculty is renewed and changed with the fame kind of Grace in Converfion ; for all true

Premife fome things.

Co verting grace is a concatination of all faving graces.

All thefe are Simultaneous in their Birth.

All thefe congraces cur in their fpecifical nature, as to this change.

Graces

Graces are of the same nature, and all of them concur to work a like saving change; though one grace be seated in one faculty, and another grace in another faculty; all of them are like so many streams flowing from the same Fountain, and coming into diverse Rooms, and washing, or cleansing of them all, so that the whole house is made clean by them.

2. These things being premised; I shall now briefly shew unto you the Universality of change wrought by converting Grace. 1. In the *mind* or *understanding* of a sinner (when he is converted) there is implanted an heavenly and saving light or knowledg, which removes the power and dominion of darkness or ignorance, and now inables the person to behold the saving truths, and will, and wayes of God in Christ, in a spiritual, clear, serious, and delightful manner; all which he looks upon, not with a naked or meerly intuitive apprehension, but with admiration, but with application, but with delight, and singular desire, and a certain kind of transformation. 2 Cor. 3. 18. *But we all with open face beholding as in a glass the Glory of the Lord, are changed into the same image from Glory to Glory:* When the mind is renewed, it hath now a spiritual light to see and conceive of spiritual things in their spiritual excellency and worth. Jesus Christ appears as an excellent Object to *Paul*, Phil. 3. 8. and the Statutes of God an excellent Object to *David*, Psal. 119. 4, 5.

2. In the *Judgment* of a sinner (when he is converted) there is also a saving and a gracious change; for there doth converting Grace cast down the high imaginations of a sinner (as touching himself) and his carnal reasonings, and fleshly disputes against God and Christ, and holiness, and so captivates the judgment of a sinner, that he confesseth and acknowledgeth, and approveth of all the methods, truths, causes, means, and wayes of salvation, as best, and best for him, and now best for him; Oh, *none but Christ, none but Christ* (said *the Martyr:*) It it wonderful to behold how the judgment of a converted man condemns what he formerly approved most, and how it approves what he condemned most; the man now judgeth of his sin, as the only evil, and of Christ as his only good: Oh, how foolish, how vain, how vile, that I have lived in, and served, and followed my sinful lusts! Oh, how glorious, how happy, how desireable is a part in Christ and Grace; yea, and the judgment now is as fruitful and vigorous

vigorous in forming Arguments to forsake sin, as it was once to draw the heart to sin, and sees a thousand times more reason to embrace Christ, and love holiness, then to slight and refuse them. 3. In the *Will* of a sinner (when he is converted) there is also a change wrought by Grace; the resisting, proud, unreasonable stubbornness and enmity of it is subdued, and an holy pliableness, yieldingness, willingness is conveyed into it. Tis rare to behold how the Needle with one touch of the Adamant wheels about, so to behold the admirable inclinations of the will of a sinner, upon one touch of Grace from Christ; not long since deaf, but now hearkening; not long since resisting of Christ to the death, and now following Christ as for life; a little while since shutting the door, and barring it, and now unlocking the door, and opening it; erewhile I will not, and now Lord, what wilt thou have me to do? I should be tedious unto you to discourse of the new inclinations and aversations, of the new elections and rejections, of the new purposes and resolutions, of the new conformableness and subjections which are plainly evident upon Conversion in the will of the sinner. 4. *In all the affections* of a sinner, which in Conversion are so metamorphosed or changed, that you can hardly perswade your self, this is the man to day, whom you knew yesterday; one affection seems to be changed into another, love into hatred, and hatred into love; joy into grief, boldness into fear; Lately, the desires were, who will shew us any good; now the desires are, what shall we do to be saved? Lately, the delights were in sin, in sensualities, in vain societies; now they are in the favour of God, in Jesus Christ, in pardon of sin, in heavenly communion: Lately, the love was set on that which was most unlovely, now it is set on the most lovely object indeed, Christ is the center, &c. Lately, the grief was a turbulent Sea for worldly losses, but now it is a running River for sinning against God: Lately, the affections were wings for iniquity, but now they are springs for duty: I may not inlarge; by what you have heard, it may plainly appear that true Conversion works an universal change in the sinner: Demonstrations that there is a notable change in Conversion. 1. *The person converted, he is made pertaker of the Divine Nature,* 2 Pet. 1.4. He is *a new Creature,* 2 Cor. 5.7. He is *quickned from the dead,* Eph. 2.1. He is *born again,* Jo. 3.3. 2. *The work*

In the will.

In the affections.

Demonstrations of a notable change in Conversion. From the person converted. From the work of Conversion.

work of *Converfion*: It is the effect of the great and good will of Election; and in it, God difplayes the glory of his great Love and Grace, and Mercy; And Chrift fees of the travel of his foul, fome fpecial fruit of his wonderful fufferings and purchafes; And the holy Ghoft doth manifeft his almighty Power, and the nobleft act thereof; and converting grace is a new contrary nature, a new man. 3. *The end of Converfion*: Converfion is the firft inward work for heavenly glory. It is wrought to *make us meet to be partakers of the inheritance of the Saints in light*; Naturally we are oppofite to God, and to all Communion with him; *Without holinefs no man fhall fee the Lord*; no unclean thing can enter there; finning Angels were caft out of Heaven; God qualifies thofe whom he will dignifie; he qualifyed *Saul* for an earthly Kingdome, much more the finner for an heavenly Kingdome: Heavenly glory is abfolutely inconfiftent with a gracelefs heart; the promife of it is fo, and the nature of it is fo, and the work of it is fo, and the reward of it is fo. 4. *Converted perfons are to live other lives*, and to do other works; therefore, there muft be a change of their Forms, and Principles, and Powers.

Ufe I. Is true Converfion a change? a great change? an internal and cordial change? an univerfal change? Why! then this one truth palpably *convinceth multitudes of people, to be (as yet) not converted.*

1. There are fome men *in whom there appears no change at all*, neither inward nor outward; the Leopards fpots remain, and the Blackmores skin is unchanged; they were ignorant, and fo are ftill; they were drunkards, fwearers, railers, fcoffers, mockers of godlinefs, and godly men, Sabbath-breakers, unclean, proud, and fo are ftill. The Prophet fpeaks of fome, *whofe fcum departed not from them*, Ezek. 24.12. And the Apoftle, of fome *who cannot ceafe to do evil*, 2 Pet. 2. 14. And *David*, of fome who *hate to be reformed*, Pfal. 50. 16. And *Steven*, of fome *who alwayes refift the holy Ghoft*, Acts 7. 51. And *Paul*, of fome *who wax worfe and worfe*, 2 Tim. 3. 13. Although changes go over their age, they were young, and now are old, yet no change goes over their hearts and lives; although changes go over their bodies, (their ftrength is changed into weaknefs, and their health is changed into ficknefs;) although changes go over their eftates, (their wealth

of the Returning Prodigal.

wealth is changed into poverty, and their abundance is changed into want;) although changes go over the times, (peace is changed into war, and safety is changed into danger:) nay although sometimes changes goe over their consciences, (Stupidity is changed into horrour, and pleasure into terrour:) yet their hearts are not changed: (they approve, love and delight in their sins as much as ever:) and their Conversations are not changed; they drive the same trade, run on to the same excess of Riotousness, wallow in the same mire of Ungodliness; despise converting Ordinances, converted Persons, converting Graces. Now what shall I say to these Persons? They are unchanged sinners, and so is God an unchangeable God; who hath threatned them, and swore his Wrath against them. Thou wilt not repent of thy sins, nor will God repent of his Wrath; thou wilt not turn to him, and therefore will he turn away his mercy from thee, and will *overturn, overturn, overturn* thee, as the Prophet phraseth it.

2. There are some *whose change is only outward, but it is not inward* and cordial: they stand off from many sins, and come on to many duties, and yet their hearts are not changed. There are six things which may convince a man, that his heart is not changed; 1. When a man seems *to be tender least he should commit a sin,* but yet *his heart* was *never tender and humbled for all the sins which he hath committed.* Jer. 31.19. *I was ashamed, yea even confounded, because I did bear the reproach of my youth.* If Repentance begins not in tears, it will end in tears. When I look forward and see sin with a trembling eye, (O I dare not offend my God:) and when I look backward and see sin with a mournful eye; (O I have sinned, I have sinned:) these indeed do shew a converted and changed heart. But I fear it is rather a policy, then a change, and a regard more to my credit, then my conscience, when I expostulate with a sin in Temptation, and never mourn for many sins in Commission.

2. When a man *leaves* many sins, but yet he doth not *loath any sin.* Many a man sometimes abstains from meat, yet loves it; but a good heart abstains from sin, as from a serpent, which he hates. He turnes his face from them, but he turnes not his heart from them; he doth not act the sin, nor doth hate the sin; he doth not let sin out of door, nor yet crucify it within door;

Such whose Change is only outward not inward.

Six things convince a man his Heart is not changed.

S f

door; he seems not to be a friend, and yet is not an enemy to sin; this mans heart is not changed. 3. When *a man acts from an awing Conscience* and *not from a renewing Spirit*; flies from sin, only, when conscience flies upon him for sinning, and doth good only when conscience is unquiet; when not Grace (which works uniformly,) but terour (which works accidentally) is his Principle; though a while there be some diversity and diversion too in this man, yet there is no change of heart in him; even Pharaoh under a Judgment yielded, who yet upon a respite hardned his heart again; and Iron, whiles hot, becomes malleable, neverthelefs, it is not changed in its Intrinsecal disposition. 4. When a man is *Formal* in duties, but *not Spiritual* in duties; he holds a customary course, but not a conscientious course; this mans heart is not changed: *Judas* was as busie about Christ as the other Disciples, yet he was not changed; Some unconverted man may be as frequent in religious duties as converted persons are, yet their hearts unchanged. There are four things which prove a formal Christian to have an unchanged Heart; for though he doth good duties, yet he doth them, 1. From *carnal Principles*, of Custome, Education, Example, not from Faith, Love and Spiritual Principles. 2. For *Carnal Ends*, with a respect to his Estimation with men, not with God; or he doth some good, to blind and cover more evil. 3. As a *Carnal* or *Natural* work, not as a Communion with God or Christ; if he doth them it is sufficient, but whether he meets with God in them, or God with him in them; whether he pleaseth God, and God accepts of him and them, or what heavenly revenues come into his soul upon them, he regards not. 4. *Without any Delight*; A good man hates the sin which he doth, an evil man hates the good which he doth; he delights not in the Law of God after the Inward man; he is glad when the work is done, but not to do the work: It is his Task, it is not his Pleasure; It is a Heavinefs, but not an Heaven to him; his Spirit is weary, as much as his Body; he cannot take hold of God, Be importunate in prayer for any Grace; he doth not put out a Might, a Power, a Zeal in holy Services; but acts them with a sleepy, faint, wearisome undelightful Spirit. 5. *When a man hath been and still is a stranger to Inward Conflicts*, certainly that mans heart was never changed: there may be

Four things prove a formal Christian to have an unchanged Heart.

of the Returning Prodigal.

be two conditions, wherein all may be quiet: One is in another life where grace stands alone; in heaven there is no sin, but holiness is grown unto its utmost perfection, and therefore it is above contrariety and conflict. Another is in this life, where sin stands alone, it hath the dominion, and blinds the mind, sears the conscience, and hardens the heart; there is neither a contrary light, nor a contrary grace, to raise any stirs and conflicts. But then there is a third condition, which hath *medium participationis* in it, in which the soul is partly flesh and partly spirit, sin is there, and grace is there; there are two contrary Natures, two contrary Lawes, two contrary Inclinations and workings; two Adamants as it were, one drawing the soul to evil, the other drawing the soul to good, one willing, the other unwilling, one yielding, the other resisting, one putting on to faith, to love, to mourning, to praying, to repenting, the other putting off the soul from all these; *when I would do good, evil is present with me*, saith *Paul*. And verily it is thus with every converted and changed man: *The flesh lusteth against the Spirit, and the Spirit lusteth against the flesh; and these two are contrary one to another, so that they cannot do the good that they would*, Gal. 5.17. And if no such thing be in thee, thy heart was never changed: That man who never finds an unbelieving nature, opposing and conflicting with a believing nature; hardness conflicting with softness, &c. his heart was never changed, for converting grace is in us but in part; and if but in part, then some sinfulness still remains; and believe it, there are not two more active, more contrary, more conflicting principles then grace and sin in the same subject. 6. When a man is constantly formal in the same rode and posture, all his dayes like a Picture, never better nor worse.

7. There are many men who seem to be changed without and within, yet the change is not a total or universal change; and there are two things which do manifest a partial change only to be in many men. 1. *When they do not come up fully to God, in respect of his commanding will*; they cannot come up to the Will of God, when his *Will is most spiritual*, when his will is most strict as self-denial, when his will is most difficult; Oh, to sacrifice *Isaac* that beloved Child, to part with *Benjamin*, this is against them; to pluck out the right eye, and cut off the right hand, this is

Such who seem to be changed without and within, but it is not total. Two things manifest a partial change. When they do not come up fully to the commanding Will of God.

is an hard saying, when his *will is most suffering*: For the *young man* to forsake all his riches, this is a sorrowful Injunction; to renounce all our honours with *Moses*, and to suffer reproaches with the people of God; to leave Friends, and Father, and Mother, and Brethren, and Sisters, and Children, and Lands, and Life too, as the Apostles did. When a man is converted, he is now so changed that his will and Gods Will are not sutable, but also coextensive; It is pliable, and it is parallel: Gods Will is my will, and what he wills I will; *the Law of God is written in his heart*, every command of God is ingraven upon it; there may you read the Masters Copy, and the Scholar writing after it. This is to be done (saith God,) this I desire to do, saith the Godly heart; this I would have thee to believe, *Lord I believe, help my unbelief*; Thus much I would have thee to suffer; Lord strengthen me, and give me not only to believe, but to suffer for thy sake: But in a partial change it is otherwise.

Nor to the forbidding Will of God. 2. *When they do not fully come up to God in respect of his forbidding will*; You know that God forbids all sin, he forbids spiritual sins, (pride, ambition, &c.) as well as fleshly sins, 2 Cor. 7.1. little sins (faith and troth, vain thoughts) as well as great sins; secret sins (alone) as well as open sins; heart sins (heart-adultery, revenge, malice) as well as life sins; Gospel sins (unbelief and grieving of the Spirit of God) as well as Law sins; sins of Omission as well as sins of Commission; breeding or original sin as well as actual.

How a man may know that God hath indeed changed his heart? Some things premised. There are many abortive changes.

Quest. But some may say unto me; If the case be so, How may one know that God hath indeed converted and changed his very heart, so that he may confidently say, that although I was once dead, yet I am now alive? This Question deserves a serious Resolution. For 1. "There are many abortive changes, "deluding changes, rising from false and insufficient Principles, "from a terrifyed conscience, or from politick parts, or from "the power of restraint, or from denial of occasions, or from "prevalent passions, or from the contrariety of one sin to another, or from a present and sudden apprehension of matters, "or from the defect of strength, or from judicial impressions, "by the appearing of death, or from education, or from respect "to our superiours and friends, and hopes which we have from

If the heart be never changed, "them, &c. 2. *If the heart should never graciously be changed,*

(as

of the Returning Prodigal.

(as sure as God lives) *the man will be damned* ; though the man may have parts, abilities, honours, be civil, ingenuous, candid and punctual with men, and in-offensive in his dealings : O friends! the Heart (or Soul) is that which God looks on, and every man is as his heart is ; as that is, so the man is ; he is so for the present, and he is so for eternity. *Except a man be born again he cannot enter into the Kingdome of God*, said *Chrift* to *Nicodemus*, Joh. 3.3. *If any man be in Chrift, he is a new creature,* faith the Apostle 2 *Cor.* 5. 17. *Old things are past away, all things are become new. Chrift you know is the way, the truth, and the life:* Can the Chriftlefs man ever be a heavenly man? afluredly no Chrift, no Heaven : But then if a man be in Chrift he is a new Creature *(.i.)* Chrift doth change him, and forms him a new ; he ftrips him of his old heart, and puts into him a new heart.

the man is damned.

These things being premised : I now come to answer the Cafe propounded ; Only I muft crave favour to acquaint you with two things. One, that I fpeak not of *fuch a change as implies perfection,* but only of that which although it be *true* and *faving,* is *neverthelefs imperfect,* for fo is all the work of grace in this life. Another is, that I intend not to give you *Characters of a progreffive change,* which may be found in Chriftians whom God hath called, and converted, and changed for many years, in whom the work of Converfion is come to much maturity and ftrength ; but only of an initial change, as it ftands in truth and fincerity, although newly wrought, and perhaps it be very feeble and weak, yet it is to be found in every man whom Divine Grace doth convert. Now this *Initial change* may be evidenced by the feveral contrary habitudes and fixed carriages in the converted perfon, as to time paft, and time prefent, and time future ; in refpect of all which you fhall clearly difcern a fingular alteration, if the Converfion be true.

The cafe anfwered.

The initial change evidenced by the feveral contrarieties.

1. The firft contrariety or alteration, refpects *the time paft :* Before the finner was converted, there were four unhappy qualities poffeffing of him, as touching his finfulnefs.   1. *A marvellous blindnefs,* and reflexive unfenfiblenefs of his finful condition, *dead in trefpaffes and fins,* Eph. 2.   *Paft feeling,* Eph. 4. 19.
2. *A wonderful erroneoufnefs* and falfe judgment of his eftate ; thinking highly and proudly of himfelf, as once *Laodicea* did, and

As to the time paft.

the

the Jews and Pharisees did; *We are* Abrahams *seed, and never in bondage,* Joh. 8. 33. 3. *A miserable security of spirit,* extreamly carelefs and negligent about the internal and eternal concernments of his foul; *alive once without the Law,* Rom. 7. 9. *Soul, take thine ease,* &c. They fay, *peace and safety,* 1 Thef. 5. 3. 4. *A remorseless pursuing of his sinful lusts,* without any heart-smiting troubles for his sinning and provoking of God. *No man repented, saying, What have I done? every one turned to his course,* Jer. 8. 6. 5. *Alienation from the life of God,* Eph. 4. 18. Thus it was with the man, before God converted him, and changed him; but now behold the alteration and contrariety. 1. *There is a graciously quick and active quickning light* fallen into him, which opens his eyes, and affects his confcience to a clear and right fight of his sinful heart and life. Rom. 7. 9. *But when the Commandment came, sin revived,* &c. As if the light of the Sun brake into a dark room, and reprefented all the naftinefs in it. Acts 26. 18. *To open their eyes, and to turn them from darkness to light, and from the power of Satan unto God.* His fins are fet before him, and confcience acquaints him with his forepaft evils, fo that he is convinced, and can make no defence, but cries out with the Leper, *I am unclean, unclean.* 2. *All his erroneous and proud conceits of himself are tumbled down*; the Mountains are laid low, and the man judgeth of himfelf, as if he were the greateft and vileft finner that ever lived; he abhors himfelf, Oh, how wicked! Oh, how vain! Oh, how vile! Oh, how mad! Oh, how foolish! Oh, how beaftly! I have been a tranfgreffor from the womb; I have lived without God, againft God; none fo ignorant, none fo proud, none fo filthy, none fo froward and rebellious againft the Will of God, againft the goodnefs of God as I: *In me there dwelleth no good thing*; I am without ftrength: No man living hath fuch proper thoughts, fuch humble thoughts of himfelf as he. Oh, unfit to dye, unworthy to live, undone if mercy be not free mercy, and abundant mercy. 3. *His Caftle of fecurity is demolished,* and the fecure negligent man becomes now a moft anxious and folicitous and careful man about the condition of his foul. 2 Cor. 7. 11. *What carefulness it wrought in you*; this now takes him up. *What shall we do?* fay they to *John the Baptift*: And *what shall we do?* fay they to *Peter*: And *what shall I do to be sayed?*

of the Returning Prodigal.

saved? Acts 16. 30. O my Soul (my poor lost, wandring, sinful, undone Soul) what shall I do? what will become of me? and what will become of thee for all these sins? And now the man inquires, and hears, and confers, and prayes, as for his life: Oh (saith he) I need mercy, and mercy I must have; I need Christ, and Christ I must have; I need grace, and grace I must have; and as that impotent person lay at the Pool for cure, so doth this converted sinner; he lyes at the pool of the word, and at the gates of heaven day and night; and there he cries out, God be merciful to me a sinner; and there he *wrestles with God*, as *Jacob* once; *I will not let thee go unless thou bless me*; until thou be reconciled, until I have Christ, until my heart be sanctifyed. 4. *His hardned remorselesness is now turned into a singular brokenness* and grief of spirit; the Rock is smitten, and the waters gush out; a Fountain is opened within him: He who made but a sport of sinning before; he who could grasp the nettles, and tread on hell, and vex mercy, and shoot through the heart of Christ, and not be moved or troubled at all: Oh now, how is the man altered? I see him *trembling* and quaking with *Paul*, I see him bitterly *weeping* with *Peter*, I see him *washing his Couch, with David*; I see him in heaviness and bitterness for his sinnings, as one for his first born. One while he meditates, and then weeps; thus, and thus, and thus have I dishonoured my God. Another while he hears, and reads, and weeps, I am that man, O Lord; I am he of whom thou speakest, I am that sinner; I am he who hath out-faced thy Law, out-stood thy offers of grace, and resisted (Oh how often) thy good Spirit. 5. *He is now for the life of God to be wrought in him*: This he now prizeth as the most excellent life; and for this, he praies, Lord, another heart, a new spirit.

2. The second contrariety respects *the time present*: And As to the time there are four things for the time present, in a truely changed and present. converted person which never were in him before. 1. A present hatred of sin. 2. A present flying unto Christ. 3. A present love of God. 4. A present course of new obedience. 1. When the Lord hath converted and changed the heart of a sinner, there is wrought in him *a present hatred of sin*; the man loved his sins before, and took pleasure in unrighteousness, held it fast, and defended it; sin is now seen as the greatest

evil,

evil, and the more he sees it, the more he hates it: As soon as ever the heart is changed, immediately it is a sin-hating heart; I do not say there is no sin, but I say the heart hates sin: *The evil that I hate*, said *Paul*, Rom. 7. 15. and in *Ezek.* 36. where God promiseth to give them *a new heart*, he saith, *Then shall ye remember your own evil wayes, and shall loath your selves in your own sight for your iniquities, and for your abominations.*

How a man may know that he has e: sin. *Quest.* But here now is a great Scruple, how a person may know that he hates sin? Many think they do so, and are deceived, it proves only a passion.

Sol. In true hatred there are six things. 1. *An extream detestation*: Every dislike is not hatred, but true hatred is an extream loathing. *Thou shalt cast them away as a menstruous cloath; thou shalt say unto it, Get thee hence*, Isai. 30. 22. 2. *An earnest separation*: He that hated his wife did sue out a Bill of divorce from her in the Law. 3. *An irreconcileable alienation*: Two angry men may be made friends; but if two men hate each other, friendship is everlastingly broken betwixt them. 4. *A constant and perpetual colluctation*: If they cannot be severed one from the other, they still oppose and conflict one with the other. 5. *A deadly intention* and destruction; for nothing satisfies hatred, but death and ruine; *Saul* hated *David*, and sought his life, *Absalom* hated *Amnon*, and killed him. 6. *An impartial aversation*; hatred is of the whole kind, *I hate every false way:* Wilt thou now know whether God hath changed thy heart, then ask thy heart; What is it that thou abhorrest as the superlative evil? what is that which thou wouldst have separated as far from thee, as heaven is from hell? what is that thy heart will never renew league or friendship with any more? what is that against which thy soul doth rise, and with which (as *Israel* with *Amalek*,) thou hast war for ever? what is that which thou wilt be avenged of, and daily dost endeavour the mortifying and crucifying of? what is that which thou sets thy heart against, in the comprehensive latitude thereof, whether great, or little, open, or secret? If it be sin, if it be thy sins, assuredly here is true hatred of sin, and assuredly here is a most distinguishing Character of a sound Conversion and change. It was not wont to be thus with thee, nor

is

Of the Returning Prodigal.

is this findeable in any unconverted person whosoever. Sin was once to thee as *Dalilah* to *Samson*, and now is it to thee as *Tamar* to *Amnon*. It was a sweet morsel once which thou heldst fast, but now it is the menstruous cloath which thou dost cast away, and say, get thee hence; what have I to do any more with Idols? If it be thus with thee, bless thy God who hath shewed grace to thy soul.

2. When the Lord hath changed and converted the heart of a sinner, *the sinner presently flies unto Jesus Christ:* The first stroke of Grace is on the heart, and the first breathing of Grace is for Christ; as the new born babe flies unto the brests, or as any creature doth to its center, and place of rest. For when the heart is changed by converting grace, 1. It breeds the most exquisite discovery and sense of sin, and consequently of the souls need of Christ. 2. It is most impatient of distance or difference with God, and prizeth his reconciled favour superlatively, cannot live without it. 3. It seeth nothing more valuable in it self, or more sutable to its condition then Christ, *Christus amor meus pondus meum.* And therefore, if you take notice of it, you may experimentally find upon the first impressions of Grace, that the soul is mostly taken up with Christ, and with Faith: Oh, that I might be found in him! Oh, that I could believe on him! It sees excellency in Christ, and Peace in Christ, and Redemption in Christ, and Righteousness in Christ, and Grace in Christ, and Kindness in Christ, and Help, and Life, and Heaven, and all in Christ. In Conversion, Christ secretly draws the Soul to himself; and being converted, the soul strives to draw Christ to it self; It would have Christ, it must have Christ; it is never well, it is never satisfied until it hath Christ.

3. When the Lord hath converted and changed the heart of a sinner, there is wrought in him *a present love of God:* It is wonderful to see how the Tide turns upon Conversion. There was once one found weeping very bitterly; and being demanded, why! O, said he, all other things are loved, but *Amorum amatur,* Love it self is not loved. So before Conversion, a man could find love for his Parents, and love for his Relations, and love for his Recreations, and love for his Profits, and love for his Sins; but no love for God. But after Conversion, the man can

scarce find any love for any, unless it be for his God, and in his God. A graciously changed Heart is enabled to see, 1. The glories in God; those most Pure and Amiable Excellencies in God. 2. The Transcendent Love of God to it, in the Eternity of it, in the Freeness of it, in the Sweetness and Goodness of it. 3. The Unspeakable Communications and Bounties of God towards it in Jesus Christ; for the present, and for the future: It is Grace which makes us to see what a gracious God he is: It is Grace which makes us to see what a Royal gift Jesus Christ is; It is Grace which makes us apprehensive of all the Love in God, and from God; and therefore no marvel that the changed heart fals presently in love with God; (*O Love the Lord all ye his Saints*) into a *Love of Friendship*, and into a *Love of Complacence*, as they speake; that it admires God, and prizeth Communion with him; and takes its full and highest delight in him: *Plusquam mea, plusquam meos, plusquam me*, said *Bernard*.

4. When the Lord converts and changeth a person, the man presently *Steps into the path of new Obedience*; when Grace hath changed the Heart, the Heart instantly changeth its Master and its service; O it will not live as it hath done, for a thousand Worlds; It is a servant of sin no more, but a servant of righteousness: look on any converted man (since the Word began,) as soon as ever Grace dropt into his Heart, a newness of Obedience dropt into his Life, against all Ease, Pleasures, Profits, Encouragements, Discouragements, Threats, Dangers; It was so with *Abraham*, with *Paul*, with all those *thousands* in the Acts, with all those *Ephesians*; And indeed it cannot be otherwise, forasm ch as al' their external course is but the pulse of the Heart. The *Pondus* of the will is changed, it is at the command of the Heart; which being brought into God, the services of the heart are also brought in with it. O, that you would peruse your selves in this second Tryal, what present contratiety you find in your Hearts; It is a very neer Tryal, and a most Infallible discovery of the truth or falshood, of your Change.

As to the time future. 3. The last Contrariety or Change (which I shall but touch) respects *the time Future*: there are five admirable Properties for the time future, which may be found in every truly Changed and Converted person. 1. He is very tender and

and fearful, least he should sin against his God: *Keep thy servant from presumptuous sins ; cleanse thou me from secret faults :* Psal. 19. 12, 13. *Should we again break thy Commandments !* said Ezra, c.9.14. *How can I do this Great wickedness, and sin against God !* said Joseph, Gen. 39. 9. There is in a Changed and Converted man, 1. A tender Jealousy over a Deceitful heart. 2. a tender Watchfulness, against Alluring temptations. 3. a tender Conscience, which feels the first Risings of sin. 4. a tender Diffidence of his Own strength. 5. a tender Fear, and aweful Regard of Gods Presence and Goodness. He is afraid to sin, although the sin be Secret ; and although it be Commodious ; and although it be Pleasant. I will but name the rest. 2. He is very Zealous and Active for God ; *Paul* even besides himself. 3. He is very Faithful and Constant unto God. 4. He is very Serious and Industrious, to get assurance of Gods love, and of his inheritance in the highest heavens. Give all diligence &c. 2 *Pet.* 1.10. 5. He strives for the Conversion and change of others.

The next Use must be of *Comfort* and *Support*, to *all such who find this change wrought in their hearts* by converting Grace. There are four Adjuncts which make this Converting change unspeakably Comfortable and Joyous. 1. *Next to Christ it is the choicest and chiefest gift that the heart of man is capable of in this life.* The gifts of God are of several Orders and several Natures, uses and ends ; some are in order to a natural preservation, as food, and raiment, and Health. Some are in order to an extrinsecal condition or State of Life, as Honours and civil Authority ; Some are in order to private society and relation, as Wife, and Husband, and Children ; Some are in order to secular converse, as Father and Friends, politick wisdome, and parts, &c. These are all of them good in their kind, but as it is said of diverse Captaines belonging to *David*, although they did great matters, yet they attained not to the acts of the three first Worthies : So none of these rise or mount either to that intrinsecal Dignity, or to that supernatural and ultimate End, which the change by Grace doth ; The least drop of Grace is more then all the Ocean of the World. The Apostle *Paul* saith, it is *a change from Glory to Glory* ; the work is a work of Glory and the man becomes

Use. 2.
Comfort to those who are changed.
Next to Christ it is the choicest gift the heart is capable of.

becomes glorious who is a converted man. S. *Peter* faith, *He is now made partaker of the Divine Nature*: The excellencies of God are stamped on thy soul; the Sun is now risen within thee as the Glory of God filled the Temple: so when a man is converted, the beams of grace do fill his soul; thou art precious, the filthy rags are taken away.

<small>It is an evidence of great love.</small>

2. *It is an evidence of great love and rich mercy*, Eph. 2. 4. *But God who is rich in mercy, for his great love wherewith he loved us when we were dead, hath quickned us*, &c. It is a testimony of the greatest love, as it is of the greatest hatred in God, to be left to our sinful lusts and wayes.

<small>It is the first visible distinction betwixt hell and heaven.</small>

3. *Converting grace it is the first, visible and sure characteristical distinction twixt Hell and Heaven*, twixt Death and Life, twixt a Goat and a Sheep, twixt a wicked condition, and a Godly condition. There is a twofold distinction of persons touching their everlasting estates: One is *in decreto*, which lies in the brest and counsel of God; the other is *in objecto*, which is to be found in the heart of man. Now *quoad nos & quantum ad objectum*; Converting grace makes the difference, it shews who is loved, and who is hated; it shews who is for Heaven, and who is for Hell. It is not honour, nor wealth, nor strength, nor parts, nor civility, nor meannefs, nor poverty, nor education, nor knowledg, nor trouble of conscience, nor restraint, nor profession, nor external action, which is the partition wall which divides and decides the state for the present and future. If Ministers or Angels should assure thee of an interest in Christ, and of remission of thy sins, and of future happiness while yet thy heart is unconverted, they do certainly delude and deceive thee; for if any man be in Christ, he is a new Creature: But if God hath converted and changed thy heart, thou art assuredly past from death to life, thou art among the first born of God: No sorts of wicked men are in this changed and converted condition, no prophane person, no hypocritical person; as soon as any is converted, it may be said of him, as Christ of *Zacheus*, *This day is salvation come to him, for as much as he also is a child of* Abraham.

<small>It never goes alone.</small>

4. *It never goes alone*, it is alwayes accompanied with justification, pardon, interest in Christ, reconciliation with God. *Jesus was sent to bless them in turning them away from their iniquities*,

of the Returning Prodigal.

quities, Acts 3. 26. *Be converted that your sins may be blotted out*, Acts 3. 19. *Come now, and let us reason together*, Isai. 55. 7. 1 Cor. 6. 11. *But ye are washed, but ye are sanctifyed, but ye are justifyed*, &c.

5. *It is the most comfortable and joyful condition*; for now there is a change of all, without and within you. The converted souls are *glad*, Acts 2. 47. the converted *Jailor rejoyced*, Acts 16. 34. the *Eunuch rejoyced*, Acts 8. 6, 8. The first work of the Spirit is *grace*, the next is *joy*; Heaven now stands open for you to see all, &c. Threatnings are turned into promises, curses into blessings, enemies unto friends, aliens into sons, accusing into an excusing conscience, voice of terror into a voice of peace, hell into heaven.

6. *It is the only unprejudicial change on earth*: In all other changes there is either diminution or danger. If a rich man becomes poor, there is a diminution of his Condition; if a poor man becomes rich, there is a danger to his spirit, lest he becomes covetous or proud. If a man be lifted up to greatness and authority, there is a danger, lest he forgets God, and be injurious; if an healthy man becomes sick and weak, here is an impairing, a loss and danger of life: Only, when a wicked man is converted, and becomes holy, there is neither diminution nor danger; converting grace is no thief in the Candle: It is no preternatural heat which sucks away that which is vital; thou losest nothing at all by it, no spot to thy credit, no burden to thy conscience, no eclipse to thy honour, no gall in thy Cup, nor waft to thy Lands: It doth not darken thy name, nor weaken thy strength, nor diminish thy coffers, nor imbitter thy comforts: No loss but the losing of sin, which we cannot keep but to our loss; all that it doth is this, that it decreaseth and destroyeth thy sinful lusts; it roots out those weeds, it pulls out hell, it heals thy wounds, and is the deadly enemy to thy deadliest enemies.

7. *The converting change is an unchangeable change*: The next change is into Heaven. A wicked man may be changed into a Godly man, and a Godly man may be changed into Heaven, but the Godly man shall never be changed again into a wicked man; the state of grace is an unchangeable state, a better condition them *Adams* in Paradise; his was perfect but mutable, this is imperfect, but not changeable: Once a Son, and ever

ever a Son; *the Son abides in the house for ever* (sayes Christ;)once converted, and for ever blessed. Gods converting Grace is an abiding seed, and it is immortal seed, and it is a gift which God never repents of, although much of the strength of it may be abated by our falls, as fire is raked up under the ashes; although the sense of it doth sometime fail us, and the comfort, and the liveliness of operation appears not, yet as there is life in the root, though there be not leaves on the Tree, and as there is a soul in the man, though sickness be in his body, so the truth and state of grace continues under all a Christians eclipses, weaknesses, failings; for converting grace comes from an unchangeable will in God, the will of his love, whom he loves once, he loves to the end.   2. *It depends upon an everlasting Communion with Christ*, who marries the soul to himself for ever.   3. And it is given as a *pledg and pawn of eternal glory*.   4. And it is *assisted with an everlasting arm*, and power of God.

<small>No other change shall hurt us, but further us.</small>

8. *No other change shall hurt you, but further you*: Afflictions, Death, it is gain unto you, it is the last stile, and then you are at home for ever.

Object. But now some distressed person may reply, These are comforts indeed, but not to me; for I fear that my heart is not changed, nor yet truly changed; I am not indeed altogether what once I was, but this I fear is but a stop of conscience, or <small>I fear I am not truly changed.</small> but the fruit of hypocrisie. Oh, I feel such changes on my spirit! it is not alwayes alike, and so much sinfulness, so much unbelief, so much hardness, so much difficulty to good, so much weakness under temptations; surely my change is not true, a great, an inward, a total change, and therefore none of these comforts appertain unto me.

Sol. Shall I speak a few words to such a person, (surely some such there may be.)

1. *The change by Conversion is but imperfect in this life*; it is a <small>This change is but imperfect in this life.</small> total change, although it changeth us not totally: A converted man is sanctifyed throughout, but not perfectly throughout; when the day breaks, there is a change that one may truly say, the night is past, and yet many degrees of darkness stick in the air; as soon as ever God infuseth grace into the soul, there is immediately a change as to the denomination of the estate, though not as to the consummation of the estate; *Paul's* estate was a converted

of the Returning Prodigal.

verted and changed estate, and yet there was a *Law in his Members*, as well as a *Law in his Mind*, Rom. 7. Conversion is a change from the dominion of what was contrary, not from the absolute being of a contrary. Though a Tyrant dwell and stirs in a Kingdome, yet if a lawful Monarch rules, the Kingdome is changed: Many sins are in a converted man still; but if grace doth rule the heart now, which formerly was ruled by sin, that man is a changed man.

2. *Converting grace, although it be wrought at once, yet it is brought on by degrees*: The truth of it begins in an instant, but the strength of it comes in time. It is a very curious question why God gives Grace by degrees, or successively in this life, and not all at once, but still leaves some sinful corruption behind. Divines conjecture three reasons of it? 1. *Our present incapacity of a present fulness*: The Bottle cannot be filled but by degrees, though the Ocean be full; there is as much grace given at first as to make a new creature, but not a strong creature. 2. *Our estate on earth, must be a combating estate*, to difference the estate of grace and glory; that in heaven only is the crowning and triumphing. 3. And it is an *estate of faith*, which is a continual dependance, and a continual drawing of help, and a continual recourse to the fountain: In Creation, Perfection of being was at once, and in Glorification at once; but not so in Sanctification, this rises like *Ezekiels* Water, or like the light of the Sun. This may yet satisfie thee, though grace be imperfect and not full at once. 1. Justification is perfect. 2. Though you find but little, yet you cannot be satisfyed without more. 3. You have perfecting means of holiness, though you have not perfect holiness; a word to build you up. 4. That God who hath begun, has promised to finish, and your little is a pledg of more. 5. Truth of grace may lye in a little compass.

Converting grace, though wrought at once, yet is brought on by degrees.

3. *There may be many changes upon the spirit of a man, which yet are not inconsistent with the saving change of his Spirit*: Sometimes he may be lively and quick, sometimes he may be flat and dull, sometimes he may be confident and cheerful, and at some other times he may be afraid and mournful; sometimes he may be full, and enlarged; and at some other time he may be aukard, and streightned; sometimes he may have more sense of Gods Love, and sometimes more sense of his own sins: None of these

There may be many changes not inconsistent with the saving change.

these things are essential to the converted estate; a mans heart may be truly changed by converting grace, notwithstanding many crosses and afflictions on his outward estate, many eclipses in his comforts, many varieties in his spiritual actings, many contrarieties twixt his sence and his faith, many temptations upon his spirit, to many doubts and fears in his heart.

Sinful corruptions work with more sensible strength when the heart is truely changed.

4. *Sinful corruptions never work with a more sensible strength, then when the heart is truly converted and changed:* Before Conversion, our sins do work more mightily, but we do not then perceive the workings, because your delight was then in sinning, and nothing is burthensome to delight; and nothing was in us contrary to our sinnings; the strong man kept all the house, and every faculty was a friend and servant to sin; the river ran all one way: But when the heart is converted, there is now laid into it 1. The quickest principle of feeling. 2. The contrariest principle of resisting. 3. The properest principle of destruction to sin; and therefore no marvel that we feel our sinful natures more than formerly; for all qualities are most active, and most felt in cases of resistance and destruction; nevertheless none of these must conclude against our Conversion, but rather for it, because 1. The greatest work of grace is inward. 2. The sense of sinful workings joyned with an hatred of them, and humbling of the heart under them, and with addresses to God for subduing power, is certainly a sign of converting grace: Therefore hearken unto me thou distressed soul: 1. Though the *Glory of Grace* consists in *Victory*, yet the *Truth of Grace* appears in *Combats*; the fighting Souldier is as right to the cause, as the conquering Souldier: there is fire in the *smoaking flax*, as well as in the flaming furnace. 2. That *great corruptions still remaining in temptation, are the burdens of a weak Christian, but are not the Characters of a false Christian.* 3. Jesus Christ can by a *little grace weaken strongest corruptions*: The least true grace will help thy soul to Christ, through whose strength thou who art now in conflict shalt ere long be made more than a Conqueror. 4. *True grace begins in weakness,* goes on with *combat,* but ends in *victory:* There is but little light at the first, and more darkness for quantity; but the light of the Sun is rising, and dissipating, and at length remains alone. Conquering grace hath comfort, conflicting grace hath strength, and

even

Of the Returning Prodigal.   329

even mourning grace hath truth; *Peter's* tears shewed truth of Grace, as well as *Paul's* Triumph.

But how may I defcern my *change to arife from the power of converting grace*, and not from the power only of a troubling confcience? *Sol.* I conceive thus, in four particulars.   1. *When the change is made only from the fting of confcience, that change goes off, and vanifheth*, when the trouble of confcience goes off, and continues only while that doth continue: whiles the trouble of confcience is on the man, the man will hear, and the man will pray, and the man will confult, and profefs, and purpofe, and refolve, yea, and now too, to become a new man; yea, and he will cry out againft his fins, and will not come near his fins. But when that trouble is off, all is off again; the Water which was heated, grows cold again; *Saul* is purfuing *David* again, and *Felix* is covetous again. But if the change be from grace; though trouble be off, yet the heart is againft fin, and is for good; for grace fets us againft fin, as it makes us unholy, and evil, and not only, or principally, as it makes us uncomfortable and miferable.   2. When the change arifeth only from a troubling confcience, not from a contrariety to God, but to us: *It doth not arife from a hatred of fin, and a love of good; but only from a hatred of torment, a felf-love*, and a love of eafe; the man loves that fin, that he dares not now commit, and hates the good which now he doth; he doth the good, only as a means to take off his trouble; he doth it not as a work in which he delights, nor doth he flie fin as an evil which he hates; he flies fin as it is *malum fenfibile*, not as it is *malum fpirituale*: But in a gracious change, trouble doth not caufe hatred, but hatred caufeth trouble of fin.   3. When the change is only from a troubling confcience, *then when the trouble is gone, the mans heart is more hardned*, and he growes more wicked then ever before, and in after finnings, lefs fenfible, and lefs troubled; as Iron growes more hardned after it hath been in the fire, or water that is ftopped more violent. *If they be again intangled, and overcome, the latter end is worfe with them then the beginning*, 2 Pet. 2. 10. But where the heart is changed by grace, the more grace, ftill the more fenfe of fin, and ftill the more fear to fin, and ftill the more love of God.   4. When the change comes only from the trouble of confcience, *the change extends no further then to*

How it may be difcerned, that this change is from converting grace, and not from the power of a troubling confcience. Anfwered.

V u   *that,*

that, or those particular sins for which the conscience doth trouble the man; if the other sins trouble not, they are not left: But when the change is wrought by grace, this change extends to all sins. *I hate every evil way* (saith *David*;) *they do no iniquity*, Psal. 119. *'Let us cleanse our selves from all filthiness of flesh and spirit*, 2 Cor. 7. 1.

How it appears, this change is not the fruit of Hypocrisie. Answered.

Quest. How may a man know that his *change is not the fruit of Hypocrisie*, but of Converting grace? *Sol.* This may be discerned thus. 1 The change by Hypocrisie 1. *Is not Cordial*; no Hypocrites heart is changed: *In heart ye work wickedness*. The Hypocrite dares to give way to heart sins: Judah *turned not with her heart but feignedly*. 2. *Is not Universal*: The Prophet tells the hypocritical Israelites, that they were as a *Cake half baked, and not turned*; an hypocrite, though he forsake many sins, yet he loves some sin; *Jehu* cannot part with the golden Calves, though he did destroy *Baal*. 3. *Is not lasting*, but changeable; sutable occasions are too strong for an heart falsely changed. 4. *Is not able to abide three Trials*, of the *Word*, of *Conscience*, of *Death*.

Use 3. Exhortation to beg of God to work this change.

The third Use shall be to *exhort* and entreat us to stir up all our hearts, *to beg of God to work in them this admirable change by Conversion*. I read in Scripture that the *blind man* cryed out, *Jesu! thou Son of* David *have mercy on me*; and again, Thou Son of *David*, &c. and all this was for a change in his eyes; and I read that *Naoman* took a great journey into the Land of Israel, and all was to *be cleansed of the Leprosie* of his body. And why will we not take a little pains to have our hearts and souls changed by grace: Consider seriously, 1. *That a man is not excluded from heaven, for any other want*; not for want of wisdome, or parts, or riches, or dignities. 2. *Thou art certainly excluded from heaven*, the door is shut up against thee, if thou be not converted and changed; the holy God will never look upon thee, and thou shalt never look upon that holy God in his holy place. The unclean person was shut out of the Camp, and no unclean thing shall ever enter into heaven. 3. *It is thy duty*, thou art bound to be a converted and changed person; every man is bound to hate and forsake his sins, and to come back, and love, and serve his God; did God make thee to serve thy lusts? hath he preserved thee all this while to sin against him? Is this the

No other want excludes from heaven. This want certainly excludes us.

It is thy duty to be changed.

fruit

of the Returning Prodigal.

fruit of thy dreadful Covenant which thou haſt made with him? 4. *What wilt thou get by keeping thy ſins,* or any one of them? *Be perſwaded* therefore at leaſt unto two things. 1. *To beſeech the Lord to change and convert thy heart*, even thine alſo, remember well. 1. *None can change a ſinner but God:* The Muſician muſt tune the Inſtrument. 2. *It is no ſin to beg of God a Converſion from ſin*; No, no, thou canſt not put up a more acceptable requeſt: Lord, I am weary of my ſins, I would diſ-honour thee no more, I would be good, I would ſerve thee; thou only canſt change me, and enable me; for thy Mercies ſake do ſo, and heal, and turn me, ſo ſhall I be healed and turned. 3. *God hath changed and converted great ſinners*; was not *Manaſſes* ſo! *M. Magdalen* ſo! *Paul* ſo! the *Corinthians* ſo! Why, venture toward his mercy ſeat; who can tell but he may do ſo to thee? 4. *He hath changed ſinners, who have not ſought him*; and will he refuſe it for them, who do ſeek it of him? if he many times be found of them that ſeek him not, will he deny to them, who ſeek? 5. *You have his promiſe to do this very converting work for you*; *He will give his holy Spirit to them that ask him,* Luk. 11. 13. *I will give a new heart, and a new ſpirit,* Ezek. 36. 26. Behold he calls thee, he tells thee that he is willing to convert thee, why, then art thou not willing to receive it, to have it done? do not ſay, thou art a ſinner; God never did convert any but a ſinner, nor does he promiſe to convert any, who is not a ſinner. 6. *Did ever any beg this, and failed of it?* Lord (ſaid one to Chriſt) *If thou wilt, thou canſt make me clean,* (what, ſaith Chriſt to him? doth he not anſwer him at all? Doth he ſay, I cannot? Or doth he ſay, I will not? O no, his anſwer is (and it is a pre-ſent anſwer,) *I will, be thou clean.* 2. *To come to the Word, and come for this end,* that God may convert and change; many came to the *Pool of Betheſda,* to look on it; and an *impotent man* came thither to be cured in it, and there he was cured; many come to hear the Word, to mock at it; and many come to get ſome notions from it, and many come to catch the Miniſter at it, but he who comes for this very end to be converted and changed by it, I believe he ſhall firſt or laſt attain his end; the word ſhall convert and change him. The word is ſometimes compared to a *Glaſs*, which diſcovers; *Jam.* 1. 29. and ſome-times to a *Laver* which waſheth and cleanſeth, *Pſal.* 119. 9. even

Vu 2

the young man (who of all other is moſt unruly and wild) is converted by it. The Power of God, goes with the Word of God; and the Grace of God, comes by the Word of God; it is *Vehiculum Spiritus, & canalis Gratiæ*; Thouſands have been converted by it, and ſo maiſt thou.

Uſe 4.
Counſels to the converted.
Hath God converted and changed thy heart? hearken then to a *few counſels*. 1. *Take heed of ſinning after Converſion*; Do not ſin againſt grace received; if thou doſt, thou wilt weaken and lame thy ſtrength, wilt darken thy heaven, wilt perplex thy conſcience, wilt ſhew thy ſelf more ungrateful then any man; no wicked man can have ſuch an aggravation of ſin upon him, as thou haſt. 2. *Honour God with that Grace which thou haſt received:* Converſion fits and enables a man for Gods Service and Glory.

Luke 15.24. *And they began to be merry.*

Theſe words are as the Banquet after the Feaſt; they are the cloſe, and the reckoning that is brought in upon the loſt Son being brought home. The caſe is wonderfully altered with him, (all is altered, when the ſinner is altered) when he was wandring from his Father, he ran up and down the Country, and waſted all his eſtate among Harlots; he ſhifted himſelf to his very skin, and out he is turned amongſt the Swine, and no man regarded him; the poor wretch wanted Father, and Houſe, and Cloaths, and all Comforts, and was upon his laſt Leggs, at the very point of ſtarving and famiſhing. But now being found and returned home, all mercies come in unto him; there's a Father to embrace him, and an Houſe to entertain him, and Raiment to cloath him, and Friends to welcome him, and a feaſt to rejoyce him. [*And they began to be merry:*] As formerly you have had the nature of Converſion, ſo in theſe, you have the *fruit of Converſion*. When Jeſus Chriſt was born, there was great joy; and when a ſinner is born again, hereupon alſo ariſeth great joy. The Propoſition on which I intend to inſiſt, is this:

Doct. 7.
Converſion brings the ſoul into a very joyful condition.
That *Converſion brings the Soul into a joyful, a very joyful condition*; [They began to be merry] Mirth is the accent of joy, it is an emphatical joy; but when did they begin to be merry? why! as ſoon as it was ſaid, This my Son is alive, and this my Son is found; now they begin to be merry. Converſion may be

be confidered three wayes. 1. *Antecedenter*: For the precious qualities and works, which immediately go before, and ordinarily usher in Conversion; so it is sad, and bitter, and sharp; for there the law imprints a sense of sin, and of wrath, and a spirit of bondage to fear; the Needle pricks, and the Sword cuts and wounds, and the Hammer bruiseth, and the Plough rents and tears. 2. *Formaliter*: as it is a perfective change, and alteration, even from hell to heaven, from basest lusts, to sweetest holiness; and thus it is (at the least) a fundamental, radical, and virtual joy. 3. *Consequenter*: For the Crop and present harvest, which results out of Conversion; thus it is the Musick after the tuning of the strings; the fruit of righteousness is peace, so the fruit of conversion is joy and delight. There are three things unto which I desire to speak about this point. 1. That upon Conversion, the condition becomes very joyful and pleasant; *quod sit*. 2. What kind of joy and pleasure Conversion doth bring; *quale sit*. 3. Reasons why so; *cur sit*: and then the useful Application.

Quest. 1. For the first of these; that Conversion doth bring the soul into a very joyful condition.

Sol. There are four things which demonstrate the *quod sit* of this. 1. *Many pregnant places of Scripture*; Psal. 52. 11. *Shout for joy, all ye that are upright in heart*, Psal. 132. 9. *Let thy Saints shout for joy*, Isai. 35. 10. *The ransomed of the Lord shall return, and come to Zion with songs, and everlasting joy upon their heads; they shall obtain joy and gladness, and sorrow and sighing shall flee away*. Isai. 65. 13. *Behold my servants shall rejoyce, but ye shall be ashamed*. v. 14. *Behold my servants shall sing for joy of heart, but ye shall cry for sorrow of heart*. Isai. 61. 10. *I will greatly rejoyce in the Lord, my soul shall be joyful in my God*. Rom. 14. 17. *The Kingdome of God consists in righteousness, and peace, and joy in the Holy Ghost*. Prov. 3. 17. *Her wayes are wayes of pleasantness, and all her paths are peace*. 2. *Many pregnant testimonies and instances*: When *Zacheus* was converted, *he came down joyfully*, and received *Christ*, Luke 19. 6, 9. When the three thousand were converted, there ensued singular *gladness* and *joy*, Acts 2. 41. When the *Eunuch* was converted, *he went home rejoycing*, Act. 8. 39. When those in *Samaria* were converted, the Text saith, *There was*

The *quod sit* demonstrated.

By Scripture.

By Instances.

was great joy in that City, Acts 8. 5, 6. When the *Jailor* was converted, *He re,oyced, believing in God with all his houfe*, Acts 16.34. When they to whom *Peter* wrote were converted, they did rejoyce with joy *unfpeakable*, *and full of Glory*, 1. Pet. 1. 8.

By Comparifons.

3. The many *Comparifons*, by which converting grace is expreffed, doth comfirm it, that it makes the fouls condition very joyful, and delightful: The eftate of grace is fet forth by all the things which are efteemed pleafant, and delightful, and joyful. Men take Deligh, and Joy, in Honour, Beauty, trength, Youth, Riches, Pearls, and Jewels, in Birth, in Wifdome, and Knowledg, in Springs, Orchards, Spices, Perfumes, Buildings, Victories, Life, Duration, Friends. Why! when converting grace is conveyed into the heart, the man now is honourable, and of high dignity; now the beauties of Chrift are on his foul, all his graces are more precious then Pearls, and Gold, and Silver; he is rich in fpiritual treafures, he is one born of the Spirit of God, never truly knowing and wife, till now, *&c.* Nay, grace is phrafed by fuch things, which yield a general and univerfal contentment and delight to the whole man: It is fometimes called *Light*, which is pleafant to the eye; *Oyntment*, which is pleafant to the fmell; *Wine*, which is pleafant to the taft; *Mufick*, or the joyful found, which is pleafant to the ear. Nay, yet again, it is fometimes called *Truth*, and that is pleafant to the underftanding; *Goodnefs*, and that is pleafant to the will; a *Kingdome*, and that is pleafant to defire; an *Inheritance*, and that is pleafant to hope; *Communion*, and that is pleafant to love; a *Poffeffion*, and and that is pleafant to joy; a *Victory*, and that is pleafant to hatred; a *Security*, and that is pleafant to fear; *Heaven, the Kingdome of Heaven*, and that is pleafantnefs it felf; and all this even under fears and combates, when at the firft, and weakeft, and loweft: Nay, yet once more, it is fet out by all the occafions, and by all the times of joy, to the *birth of a man-child*; for joy that a man-child is born (faid Chrift;) A converted man is a new-born. *To the day of Marriage*, which fome call the only day of joy; a converted man is marryed to Chrift: To a *Feaft*, Ifai. 25. 6. Every difh is filled with mercy. To a *Coronation day*, which was a day of gladnefs of heart to *Solomon*, Cant. 3. 11. There is a crown of life for every converted foul. *To the time of Harveft*, when the Husbandman reaps with joy, *Ifai*. 9. 3. To the *returns of*

of the Returning Prodigal.

of *Merchants* upon the increase of Wine and Oyle; Psal. 4. To a *ransome* and release from bondage and captivity; a converted man is set at liberty, he is a freeman in Christ 4. Consider Conversion in the Causes of it, or in the very Nature of it, or in the Acts flowing from it; certainly by all of them you may be induced to believe that it makes the Condition joyful and pleasant. 1. *The Causes of it*, which are four, 1. *The Radical cause.* Why! Conversion drops out of the Eternal Love of God to a mans soul. *Behold what manner of Love*, 1 Jo. 3. 1. *as many as were ordained to eternal life* believed, Acts. 13. 2. *The Meritorious cause*: *Who loved us and gave himself for us*, Gal. 2. It is one part of Christs purchase, he merited Grace and Glory for his. 3. *The Efficient cause*; (immediately efficient) it is the first breath of Gods sanctifying Spirit, the Spirit of true Comfort and Joy. 4. *The Instrumental cause*; the word which is called sweet, and sweeter then the Hony, and the breasts of Consolation, is the instrument of Conversion, Jam. 1. 2. *Its owne Nature.* Converting Grace hath three things intrinsecal unto it. 1. *Goodness*; it is good, and it only makes us good: Now Goodness is the foundation of Delight; Nothing is truly pleasant, but what is truly good. 2. *Suteableness*; There is nothing so suteable either to the nature of the soul, or end of the soul, as true Grace. 3. *Perfection*; it is the Glory of the Soul.

3. *The acts flowing from it*; If the acts flowing from Conversion be such as God himself takes delight in, (*He takes delight in the prayer of his servants*, in the broken hearts of his servants, in the Faith, and in the Fear, and in the Hope of his servants; all their services are a sweet savour unto him, as *Noahs* sacrifice was:) Surely then Conversion is able to make the converted Soul joyful and delightful. Againe, there cannot be a greater delight and joy then when an Active and Actual intercourse is maintained twixt an immortal Soul and perfect Blessedness; when my Soul hath a free converse with Blessedness it self, and Blessedness it self hath a Gracious converse with my soul, this is as if two deeply in Love conversed with each other: this is as if *Jonathan* and *David* met together; this is as if *Jacob* and *Joseph* met together, and infinitely more: But upon Conversion, the soul and God have mutual communications. (And is not God

By the Causes of it.

By the Nature of it.

By the acts flowing from it.

God the blessedness of mans soul, and is not blessedness a joyful and pleasant sight) God speaks to that soul, and that soul speaks with God; the soul opens its self to God, and God opens himself to that soul. *Ergò.*

By the dishonour that otherwise would redound to God. 5. It were a mighty dishonour to God that his *Wayes,* his *Image,* should be barren of *Joy,* and yet the Divels wayes and sin, pleasant. 6. A Great motive to draw in a soul were lost. 7. Grace doth spiritualize our joyes, it doth not nullify true joy.

What kind of Joy Conversion brings. *Quest.* 2. What kind of Joy and Pleasure doth Conversion bring unto the Soul. *Sol.* There are five properties in the joy which Conversion lets into the Soul.

A Lawful Joy. Quædam.
1. *Nec bona nec Jucunda.*
2. *Bona sed non jucunda.*
3. *Jucunda sed non bona.*
4. *Jucunda et Bona.* so *Bern.rd.*

1. It is *a lawful Joy* and Pleasure. There are many things which are pleasent, but they are not Lawful: *Stollen waters are sweet,* saith *Solomon,* but God allowes them not; the Tree in the garden was Pleasant, but it was not Lawful for *Adam* and *Eve* to taste of. Sinful wayes afford some kind of joy, but that joy is forbidden fruit; God hath cursed sin and all that comes out of sin. *Agrippina* poysoned her husband with the meat he most delighted in. Wicked men delight and rejoyce in sinful things, but this is only sweet Poyson, God allowes it not; nor is it safe: But conversion yeilds a Joy, which the soul may safely feed on; It is lawful to rejoyce in the Lord, and to rejoyce in Christ, and to reioyce in the pardon of our sins, and to rejoyce that our names are written in the book of Life.

A Spiritual joy. 2. It is *a Spiritual Joy*; A Joy that reacheth to the spirit of Man, and that becomes the spirit of man, and that raiseth the spirit of man. 1. Many men have joy in their faces, and yet not joy in their hearts; A man in a feaver hath a lively colour, when yet he hath a dying heart; and many have joy in their tongues and mouthes, and yet no joy in their consciences. As he said to one that commended his fine shoe, But you doe not know where it pincheth me; a wicked man hath an hell in his conscience, who yet hath a smile in his countenance; But a Converted mans joy, is an heart joy; *My servants shall sing for joy of heart,* Isa. 65. 14. *My Spirit rejoiceth in God my Savior,* said Mary, Luk. 2. 2. And it is a spirit becoming joy. *Laughter is not seemly for a fool,* said *Solomon*; There are joyes which are not seemly nor becoming an Immortal soul: *Agesilaus* said of some pleasures, that they were fit for slaves, not for Freemen

men: a wicked man takes joy either in Vile things, which fight against the Soul; or in vain things, which are below a Soul; his joyes are fetcht out of hell, or out of the Creature; either such joyes as delight the Devil, or delight the beasts, or delight the basest and vainest of men; in Whoring, and Drinking, and Cursing, and Dicing, and Dancing, and Gaming, and Mumming, and Masking &c. But Conversion feeds the Soul with the joyes of the Holy Ghost, with Divine joy, joy drawn out of the wells of Salvation, Ifa. 12. 2. And it is a Spirit-raising joy: when the soul is cast down, and all the comforts on Earth cannot lift it up and chear it, yet Conversion can let in a fetching Cordial; It can open a window to see the light of Gods countenance and favour, which can turn night into day, and troubles into peace, and heaviness into an exceeding joy; even Davids, *Why art thou cast down O my Soul?* into *Praise the Lord O my Soul* 3. It is *a wonderfull Joy*; There are two cases wherein men do wonder, how a man can possibly be joyful. 1. One is, when all the comforts of the Creature fail him; not a Candle but is without light, not a Well but is stopt; not a Spring but is dry; No friend to look on and pity, no maintenance, no subsistance: Yet in such a case (which is wont to be a time Sighs and Tears) can a converted man rejoyce. Hab. 3. 17. *Although the Fig-tree shall not blossome, neither shall fruit be in the Vine, The labor of the Olive shall faile, and the field shall yeild no meat, the flock shall be cut off from the fold, and there shall be no Herd in the stals; Yet I will rejoyce in the Lord, I will joy in the God of my salvation.* 2. Another is, when all outward miseries are upon him: as when all his outward estate is taken away, yet then converted persons have taken *joyfully the spoyling of their Goods*, Heb. 10. 34. When Afflictions, Derisions, Reproaches, Bonds, Imprisonments, Scourgings, cruel Torments, are laid on him; Yet faith Paul, *Wee rejoyce in Tribulations also*, Rom. 5. 3. Yet faith Christ, *when men shall revile you, and persecute you, and say all manner of evill against you falsly for my sake, Rejoyce and be exceeding glad*, Mat. 5. 11,12. And the Apostles when they were imprisoned and beaten, *rejoyced that they were counted worthy to suffer shame for his name*, Act. 5. 41. *My Brethren count it all Joy, when ye fall into diverse Temptations*, Jam. 1. 2. When he is going to endure a cruel

A wonderful Joy.

a cruel death, as burning in the Fire, devouring by wild Beasts, roasting on the Gridiron, boyling in Oil, breaking of the Bones, tearing out the Bowels; All these have converted persons sustained, with unspeakeable Courage, clapping of the Hands, kissing of the Stake, and Glorious Rejoicings. Why, the truth is that though all the Candles on Earth be put out, yet he hath Light and Comfort, still the Sun shines, nothing can dissolve, nor yet interrupt the souls sweet Communion with God. 4. It is *a Firme, and Pure, and Unclogged Joy*; an unconverted man hath his joy, and his delights, and his mirth, and pleasure; but there are three doleful burdens under which all this while he lies. 1. Notwithstanding all his joyes, he lies under the hatred of God. 2. Notwithstanding all his joyes, he lies under the dominion of his sinful Lusts. 3. Notwithstanding all his joyes, he lies under the power of a Guilty, and Accusing, and Condemning Conscience; but now the Converted mans joy is a Perfect joy, a Wel-grounded joy; God loves him, Christ hath satisfyed for him, his heart is sanctifyed, and his conscience pacified. 5. It is *a well ending joy*; A joy which ends in joy: an unconverted man hath his joyes and pleasures, but they end in Griefe and horror. O my poor Soul, said *Adrian*, when he was dying, whither art thou now going? all thy Mirth, and Joy, are at an end: *nec ut soles dabis jocos*, thou art going away, and all thy joyes are going away: Luk. 16. 15. But *Abraham* said to *Dives, Remember that thou in thy life time receivedst thy good things, and Lazarus evill things; but now he is comforted, and thou art tormented.* Dives fared sumptuously every day, he had pleasure on earth, but after them his soul went into hell torments: he never had pleasure more. Babylon, it is said of her Rev. 18. 7. *how much she hath glorified her self, and lived deliciously, so much torment and sorrow give her*: Job speaking of the Wicked, chap. 21.7. saith, *That they take the Timbrel and Harp, and rejoyce at the sound of the Organ*: v. 12. *they spend their dayes in wealth, and in a moment go down to the Grave*: *Solomon* speaks ironically to the Voluptuous Youthes, Eccles. 11. 9. *Rejoyce O young man in thy Youth, and let thy heart cheer thee in the dayes of thy Youth, and walk in the wayes of thine heart, and in the sight of thine eyes; But know thou, that for all these things God will bring thee into Judgment*: So then the

Un-

A firm and pure Joy.

A well ending Joy.

Of the Returning Prodigal.

converted man's joy, is a short joy, and a joy that ends in bitter-est sorrow: But a converted man's joy, is a lasting joy, and it ends in perfect joy; when he dies, yet his grace dies not, yet his joy dies not: *Well done good and faithful Servant, enter into thy Master's joy*; the end of life, is the beginning of all joy.

6. It is a transcendent joy; it exceeds all worldly joyes. *Psal.* 4. 7. *Thou hast put gladness in my heart, more then in the time that their Corn and their Wine increased.* Psal. 60. 3. *Thy loving kindness is better then life*. A transcendent joy.

Quest. 3. Why doth Conversion make the souls condition so joyful? *Sol.* It cannot but be so, if you consider Conversion, either as to God, or as to Christ, or as to Conscience. Reasons of it.

1. *As to God.* As to God.

1. *True Conversion is the certain effect of Gods gracious election*; Although Conversion be not the cause of election, yet it is the fruit of election, it is the counterpane of election. Act. 13. 48. *As many as were ordained to eternal life, believed.* 1 Thes. 1. 4. *Knowing, Brethren, Beloved, the election of God.* v. 5. *For our Gospel came not to you in word only, but in power also, and in the Holy Ghost.* 2 Pet. 1. 10. *Give diligence to make your calling and election sure.* When the word comes to the person, in the Letter only, this is no sign of his election, but when it comes in power, and in the Holy Ghost it is; for to come in power, and in the Holy Ghost, is mightily, and effectually to change and convert a person, and this the Apostle makes an evidence of election; and questionless, a copy of a man's election cannot but be a cause of great joy; *Rejoyce* (saith Christ to his Disciples) *that your names are written in heaven:* Oh, what a comfort is it to know that God from all eternity hath written and recorded it down, This is the man whom I will have mercy on, and will glorifie to all eternity! Conversion is the certain effect of Gods election.

2. True Conversion, *It is the singular fruit of God's great Love*, and of his rich mercy to a mans soul, the sure token of great love: God hath a common love and mercy, and God hath a choice love and mercy; there are some to whom he hath a great love, and unto whom he shews rich mercy: Now Conversion is a drop out of that great Ocean; the man is greatly beloved of God, who is converted by God. 1 Joh. 3. 1. *Behold what manner of Love the Father hath bestowed on us, that we should be called* It is a singular fruit of Gods Love.

X x 2

called the Sons of God. Eph. 2. 4, 5. *But God, who is rich in mercy, for his great love wherewith he loved us,* v. 5. *Even when we were dead in sins, hath quickned us.*

It brings a soul under all the smiles of God. 3. True Conversion *brings a soul under all the good and kind Language of God, under the smiles of God.* All the Ordinances are as Milk, and Honey, and Wine, and Oyle to a converted man. The Word is a good Word to him, and the Sacrament is a good Sacrament to him; Why! when an unconverted man hears of all the mercy, and kindness, and happiness which God portions out for a converted sinner; I say, when he hears of all this, and gets but a lick or a taste of it upon the top of his Tongue, it effects him, and makes him glad. Herod *heard* John Baptist *gladly*, and the stony ground *received the seed with joy*; and shall not the converted man, whose due portion all this is, shall not his heart have joy and gladness? shall a stranger who peeps over into the Garden, and is a spectator only at the Feast, shall he find a relish? and shall not he who hath the Posie at his Nose smell the sweetnesse? shall not he who eates at the Table, be filled with the goodnesse, and fat, and marrow, and rejoyce, and blesse God?

It is the clasp of the Covenant of Grace. 4. True Conversion, *It is a Claspe, the Golden Claspe of that everlasting Covenant of Gods Grace.* Note here two things. 1. All the desireable delicacies of the soul are treasured up in the Covenant of Gods Grace; in it are contained all the gracious attributes in God, all the gracious affections of God, all the gracious relations of God, all the gracious promises and engagements of God. There you find the reconciled God, the merciful God, the pardoning God, the sin-subduing God, the strengthning and helping God, the guiding and upholding God, the blessing and comforting God; you cannot think of a mercy for the soul, of a mercy for the body, of a mercy for this life, of an happiness after this life, but there it is, but there it is for you, but there it is assuredly for you. 2. Every converted person is in this Covenant; Why! the new heart, and the new spirit, (is not this Conversion?) are a very part of it; Ezek. 36. 26. *I will give them a new heart, and a new spirit:* If this be so, then certainly Conversion brings a person
into

into a very joyful condition. Mark a little: If the mercies which many receive only from Providence do delight and pleafe them, fhall not the mercies which men receive from Gods Covenant pleafe and rejoyce them? Bread is fweet to an hungry man, out of whatfoever hand it comes; and is it not more fweet when it comes out of the hand of love and kindnefs? O Sirs! even the ordinary mercies to a converted man, have a fweet diftinction in them; they are fo perfumed, they are fo diftilled, they are fo carved, they are all of them the kiffes of a father, the gifts of a gracious God. Every bit of Bread thou eateft, and every draught of Beer thou drinkeft, and every piece of Cloath thou weareft, it is the fpecial provifion of thy moft gracious God, and thy loving Father: If fome one royal mercy in the Covenant be able fometimes to fweeten an Ocean, to turn hell into heaven, to wipe off all tears, and put the foul almoft into an extafie of joy; what rivers of joy then can the whole Covenant afford? If the lifting up of the light of Gods countenance upon the foul, (which is but one beam of the Covenant) if his faying to a man, Soul, I am thy Salvation; if one word, *Son, be of good cheer, thy fins are forgiven thee,* imprints a fuperlative comfort, a joy unfpeakable and full of glory; if one drop be fo fweet, how fweet is the Fountain? if one Grape, what is the clufter of Grapes? Now not only this or that mercy in the Covenant belongs to a converted man, but every mercy, the God of all mercies, and all the mercies of God; the God of all comforts, and all the comforts of God.

5. True Converfion, *It is the infallible fore-runner, the earneft, the pawn of Glory :* the pledg which God leaves in hand, the firft fruits of thy eternal Glory in the higheft heavens; and is not this a caufe of great joy? if I look back, and fee a love from all eternity; if forward, and fee a glory to all eternity. Truly, if I fhould never tafte Honey on earth; if all the Wells of a prefent comfort were ftopped up; if my Father fhould never fmile on me in the way, if all my Life were a fayling on brinifh tears, and my Ship were ftill to be toffed with troublefome waves; yet, if I were fure at length to put in at this Port, to come fafe to Heaven at length, to appear before

It is the infallible forerunner of glory.

before the God of Gods at the laſt, to ſee him in Glory, and enjoy his face, and the pleaſures at his right hand for evermore, even this confidence and aſſurance were enough to make me to rejoyce in the hope of the Glory of God. Oh Chriſtian, beſides all that joy which ariſeth from converting grace (which is it ſelf a ſweet Roſe) and beſides all thoſe Honey dewes which fall upon the ſoul in the exerciſe of grace, in the way to Heaven, (*Thou meeteſt him that rejoyceth and worketh righteouſneſs, thoſe that remember thee in thy wayes,* Iſai. 64. 5.) There is alſo reſerved in the higheſt heavens, that moſt perfect happineſs, that moſt perfect tranquillity, that moſt perfect joy; Oh, I cannot expreſs it, I cannot comprehend it. 1 Pet. 1. 3. *He hath begotten us again unto a lively hope.* v. 4. *To an inheritance incorruptible, and undefiled, and that fadeth not away, reſerved in heaven for you.* "Ponder the words; an inheritance, the beſt of poſſeſſi- "ons; incorruptible, the beſt of inheritances; undefiled, "the beſt of incorruptibles; unfading, the beſt of undefileds; "and reſerved in heaven, the beſt of unfadings: Nothing "is ſo ſurely kept as that which is kept in heaven for us, and "born unto all this, and a lively hope of all this: Oh, what comfort! Oh, what joy comes out of all this! If I had all the world, and lookt up towards heaven, but my heart ſhould tell me, that goodly *Canaan* will never fall to thy portion; it would be now with me, as once with *Ahab*, who, though he enjoyed a Kingdome, *yet was very ſad, becauſe the heavens were as Braſs to him.* But in the midſt of all diſtreſſes to look up to Heaven, to think of God, and the future Beatifical Viſion, and upon infallible grounds, to ſay, that God is my Father, that Heaven is my inheritance, that place of Glory is my home, there ſhall I be ſhortly, there ſhall I be to eternity, I have the earneſt of it, the pawn of it in my heart, the firſt fruits, &c.

As to Chriſt.
2. Secondly *As to Chriſt*: The converted condition cannot but be joyful, becauſe the converted perſon hath. 1. *A neer relation to Chriſt*; Bone of his Bone. 2. *A ſingular propriety in Chriſt*; *my beloved is mine*, &c. 3. *An admirable revenue by Chriſt*; wonderful riches, of and by Chriſt *all are yours, for ye are Chriſts.* 4. *He is bought by Chriſt*, and reconciled by Chriſt, and loved by Chriſt, and diſcharged by Chriſt, and owned

of the Returning Prodigal. 343

owned by Chrift, and defended by Chrift, and kept by Chrift, and fhall one day be faved by Chrift.

3. *As to Confcience* : As a mans confcience is, fo is his comfort or difcomfort, fo is his joy or forrow : One drop of an evil confcience (faith *Luther*) doth imbitter the whole Sea of worldly joy : an evil confcience is an hell in the breft, and in hell (faid *Latimer*) there is no mirth: and on the contrary, a good confcience it is a kind of heaven ; one good word from it will fweeten all our miferies, and caufe us to rejoyce under all forrows. *Solomon* faith *it is a continual feaft*, it is the year of *Jubilee*; confcience fpeaks the trueft joy, and the ftrongeft joy, and the higheft joy, and no man hath a good confcience but a good man : Confcience cannot fpeak peace till a man be converted ; and when he is converted, confcience hath then a commiffion and authority to look on the man, and fpeak to the man as God doth. When thou heareft of pardon of fins, Oh, faith confcience, hearken and be of good cheer, that's thy portion : when thou heareft of Jefus Chrift, and of his fufferings, and of his fatisfactions, and merits, hearken, faith confcience, and take hold, for all this alfo is thy portion ; when thou heareft the Covenant of Grace gracioufly explained, and all the glories in heaven ; Oh, faith confcience, all this alfo is thy portion : when thou art about to pray, and fears are intruding themfelves ; do not fear, faith confcience, thou art fpeaking to thy Father : when thou art about to dye, and tremblings are upon thee, do not doubt or tremble, faith confcience, thou art going to thy God : when Satan fuggefts thou haft nothing to do with the mercy-feat, what, fuch a finner ? thou haft, faith confcience; when unbelief fuggefts, Chrift will have nothing to do with thee, he will, faith confcience.

As to Confcience.

Now, againft all that hath been faid ; it is objected, That the affertion of joy for a converted perfon cannot be true : Becaufe 1. No perfons are fo expofed to afflictions, and perfecutions, and infamies as converted perfons. They are appointed to them, 1 *Thef. 3.* And they that will live godly in Chrift Jefus, muft fuffer perfecutions ; how can that condition be fo very joyful, which may, and oftentimes doth deprive a man of all his comforts. 2. Converfion brings the perfon into a narrow path, and under the ftraiteft rules, even fuch as condemn, and cut off a world of pleafures, and delights ; can that condition be very joyful which denies us the

fruition

fruition of many joyes and delights. 3. Conversion breeds the deepest sense of sin, and the greatest mourning for sins: Nothing makes the heart more mournful then converting grace. See *Zach.* 12. 10. Can that condition be so very joyful, which makes the heart so exceeding mournful? 4. We see no persons walk more uncomfortably then (at least) some converted persons: Yet the estate is joyful, though the man is not alwayes so; God is a God of comfort, and they can pray for comfort; comfort, O Lord, thy servants soul! But more fully.

How can this condition be joyful that is so exposed to afflictions. Answered.

Object. 1. No persons are so exposed to afflictions and persecutions as converted persons, and these do deprive us of joy and comfort.

To this I answer, 1. It is a truth that Conversion doth expose a person to most afflictions and persecutions; *Many are the afflictions of the righteous,* saith *David,* Psal. 34. 19. *All that will live godly in Christ Jesus, must suffer persecution,* saith *Paul,* 2 Tim. 3. 12. *Filii lucis,* are *Filii crucis,* and *Christianus* is *Crucianus* (said *Luther.*) *In the World you shall have troubles* (said Christ to his Disciples) *and the Disciple is not above his Master;* if the Master dyed upon the Cross, is it much that the Disciple take up the Cross? Nevertheless in the second place, as it was emblem'd in Reverend *Hoopers* Motto, There was a Lamb in a flaming Bush, with the Sun shining upon it; or as it was with the three Children, though they were in a fiery Furnace, yet the Son of God walked with them, and preserved them: So, though converted persons meet with many afflictions, there is yet a spring of joy, a Sun of comfort open unto them; therefore heed me.

Afflictions only take away their outward comforts.

1. *Afflictions and persecutions do only take away the Christians outward comforts*: The Shell, not the Kernel; the Case, not the Jewel (which neither make nor marr the joy and comfort of a converted person) they do not take away the true principles of comfort. There are three sorts of comforts; *Sensual*; which are drawn out of our sinful lusts; Conversion is an enemy to these: *Sensitive*; which are drawn out of the creatures; affliction is an enemy to these: *Spiritual,* which are drawn out of the favour of God, the blood of Christ, the Testimony of a good conscience; afflictions cannot hinder these, and only a sinful unconversion is an enemy to these: The Winter freezeth up the Ponds

of the Returning Prodigal.

Ponds, but not the Ocean; the winds blow out the Candle, but not the Sun: An Unconverted man may have an exemption from all outward Afflictions, and yet have no inward Joy; for although he hath peace with men, yet he hath no peace with God; and although he hath no trouble upon his Estate, yet he may have terror upon his Conscience. But a Converted man, although he be compassed with outward Sorrows, neverthelefs he hath inward Joy; though all the Candles be blown out, yet I am Comforted as long as the Sun doth shine. There are two sorts of evils; there are *mala tristia, & mala turpia*: afflictions are only Sorrowful evils as to our sense, they are not Sinful evils as to our conscience. Now no evil is able to take away spiritual comfort, unless it be a sinfull evil; I confess, that did a godly man look upon creature comforts as his *bonum ultimum*, as that which made him happy, then afflictions would be inconsistent with his joy, he might well cry out, as *Micah* once, *Ye have taken away my gods, and what have I more?* But he doth not so: It is not the Creature, but the Creator, which is the foundation of his Happiness and joy. A man may be Bad who hath them, and Good who wants them: *If we had hope only in this life* (faith the Apostle, 1 *Cor.* 15.) *we were of all men the most miserable.* I wish that you would or could give credit unto two things, one is, That that only makes the estate comfortable which denominates it to be good; for nothing can be truly delightful, but what is truly good. The other is, That there is a greater power in the presence of the chiefest good to make the Soul joyful, then there can be in the recess or absence of the least kind of good to make it uncomfortable. Were Afflictions the greatest evils, and were Creatures the best good, then joy could not consist with afflictions; but God is the chiefest good, and the Christian enjoyes him under all afflictions as his inseparable good; *Ergo.*   2. As Afflictions do not take off the Christians true joy, *so the times of afflictions are oft times the most proper seasons for joy and comfort to his soul.* There are three seasons of special comforts which God is pleased to reserve for his servants, one is *after great temptations*, or to prepare against them; as that Voice, *This is my well beloved Son*, came to Christ immediately before his temptation. The second is, *after*

Times of afflictions are his most proper seasons for joy.

Y y *great*

great *Humiliations*. God who *comforts them that are cast down*, faith *Paul*, 2 *Cor*.7.6. The Angel comforted Christ after his Agony; the Cordial comes after the Physick. The third is, before and under great afflictions and tryals: *Paul* was to appear before *Nero*, but first *God appeared to him saying, Be of good cheer* Paul. *He is come, he is come*, said the Martyr when he saw the stake; and *Stephen saw heaven opened* before he dyed. The comforts of heaven came into his heart just before the stones were thrown at him to dash out his brains. 2 *Cor*. 1. 3. *Blessed be God, even the Father of our Lord Jesus Christ, the Father of mercies and God of all comforts, who comforteth us in all our tribulations; for as our sufferings abound, so our Consolation aboundeth through Christ*. Is not the night a season to light a Candle? and is not weakness the season to give a Cordial? and is not the winter a season to make a Fire? When doth or can the Christian more need the comforts of God, then when all comforts on earth do fail him? 3. As afflictions deprive not the Christian of the true principles of Joy, so neither can they hinder those *principles in himself from acting in a way of comfort*. There are two principles (especially) in the Christian which enable him to joy and comfort: One is *Faith*: It is still Day, and never Night with Faith; the Star shines best in the night; *(Believing ye rejoyced with joy unspeakable and full of Glory*, 1 Pet.1.8.) Now Faith can act very comfortably in uncomfortable times; it can see the same God, with the same Love, and in the same Covenant, and in the same Relation, in Adversity as in Prosperity: *Hab*.3.17. *Although the Fig-tree shall not blossome, &c. yet I will rejoyce in the Lord, &c.* Rom. 5.3. *And not only so, but we glory in tribulation, &c.* 1 Sam.29.6 the people spake of stoning him, *but David encouraged himself in the Lord his God.* Rom.8. 35. *Who shall separate us from the love of Christ? &c.* If even in afflictions I can go unto the same armes of Christ, and unto the same brests of divine Love, and into the same chamber of Presence; if I can look upon God as my God, and see him to be my Father, that I can make known my heart to him, and he can make known his favour to me, what should hinder me now to be joyful, who still do enjoy him who (alone) makes all my joy? Another is, the

Testimo-

Afflictions cannot hinder his principles of Joy from acting in a way of comfort.

Testimony of Conscience: This is the Friend in adversity. *This is our rejoycing, even the testimony of our Conscience*, 2 Cor. 1. 12. Conscience is a mans night or day, his Hell or Heaven, his Palace of delight or Jail of bitternefs: If Conscience be sanctified or pacified, it can speak a peace or joy that none can crush; none can hinder, but under the greatest afflictions and persecutions a converted man may and doth enjoy the testimony of a good Conscience: *Thou art upright*, faith Conscience to *Hezekiah* on his fick-bed; *Thou fearest God*, faith Conscience to *Job* under the lofs of all; *Thou lovest Christ*, faith Conscience to *Paul*, even in the Prifon.

Object. 2. Now to the second Objection, That converting Grace brings the perfon into a narrow path, and under the strictest rules, even such as condemn a multitude of joys and delights; how can that condition be so joyfull, which denies and abridgeth, &c? *Sol.* To this I anfwer.

1. It is granted, That converting Grace brings the perfon into a very narrow path, and under very strict rules. A converted man must not walk as other men; he must not allow himself to think, and defire, and love, and speak, and act as formerly: He must fear to fin, he must love the Lord with all his heart, and with all his foul, and with all his might; he must order his steps by the Word of God; he must deny himself, and crucifie his deareft lufts, and not shun the hardeft duty, nor delight in the leaft iniquity.

2. But then, *This strictnefs is no adverfary to his true joy*. *In keeping of thy commandments there is great reward*, faith *David*, Pfal. 19. 11. *Great peace have they who love thy law*, Pfal. 119. 165. *As many as walk according to this rule, peace be on them, and mercy upon the Ifrael of God*, Gal. 6. 16. I befeech you to confider four things: 1. *Let thine own Conscience judge, whether it be not a more comfortable courfe to obey God, then to difobey God?* to have grace to ferve God acceptably, then to have an heart still free and ready to difhonour and provoke God? Who hath most true comfort, the bones found and in place, or broken? to walk on the Land, or to be troubled at Sea? the Child who runs away from his Father, or the Child who waits upon his Father? the Child that defires to pleafe, or the Child that continues to grieve and vex? the wandring and famifhed Prodigal, or the returning

But conversion brings us into a narrow path, is an enemy to many delights.

Anfwered. There is a strictnefs required.

This strictnefs is no adverfary to true joy.

and embraced Son. *Hof.* 2. 7. *I will return to my firſt Husband; for then it was better with me then now.* 2. Rightly underſtand what it is ſtrictly to walk with God: It is an endeavour in your affections and duties to draw near to God in all well-pleaſing, and to anſwer the will of God. The Chriſtians courſe of obedience, it is his daily communion with his God in this life: When thou prayeſt, what is Praying, but a divine conference of the ſoul with God? and when thou heareſt, what is this but a divine conference of God with the ſoul? and when thou repenteſt, what is that but a recovery and return of the ſoul to God? and when thou believeſt, what is that but the recumbency of the ſoul on the goodneſs of God? and when thou receiveſt the Sacrament, what is it, but a communion, a feaſting with Jeſus Chriſt? If a ſtrict walking be nothing but a divine and heavenly communion with God, why doeſt thou, how dareſt thou to judge of it as the onely Bar to ſhut out all joy and comfort? Was there ever any affectionate Wife, that thought it an injury to her Joy to ſpeak with her Husband, or to enjoy the ſociety of her Husband? Was there ever any faithfull Friend, who thought it a miſery, a burthen to enjoy the ſociety of his Friends, to open his heart unto his Friend? How then can it be a prejudice to any mans joy, to enjoy communion with his God? 3. Conſult with experience, which hath travelled in the ſtrict ways of God; either thine own experience, (if any,) which day of thy life hath been cloſed up with heartieſt joy? whether the day of licentiouſneſs, or the day of ſtrictneſs? That day which thou haſt let out to thy luſts, hath made the night a trembling to thee; that day which thou haſt redeemed for walking with God, hath always given unto thee the ſweeteſt reſt and repoſe at night: The experience of godly people; have any of them ever found more ſoul rejoycing then when they have abounded in ſtricteſt obedience? This is thy burthen, but it is their delight; the pureſt walking hath diſtilled the ſweeteſt joy, and their looſer walking hath been the cauſe of their greateſt ſorrows. It is with a ſtrict Chriſtian as with the Sun, which ſtill keeps to the Ecliptique Line, and is of all the Stars the moſt glorious and comfortable when it is at the higheſt; and the higher Sun, the purer and warmer light: And it is with the looſe Chriſtian as with the uneven foot, the wry ſtepping is the cauſe of unjoynting, or pinching and paining.

Of the Returning Prodigal.

paining. 4. *The strict walking*, what is it but *a path to everlasting life?* every step of it is a step to heaven. *Strait is the gate which leads unto life*, faith Christ: There is an easie way for men to walk in, but that's the way to hell, and what comfort is it, after all to go to hell, to go to hell with ease. There is a strict way for men to walk in, but it is the way to life, to eternal life: Now even that alone is sufficient to create joy, that these steps after a while will bring me to appear before the God of Gods in Sion; and truly, there is no end whatsoever, the which if it be (in it self) amiable and comfortable, but it darts also an amiableness and comfortableness upon all the steps and paths which tend unto it.

3. Lastly, *Converting Grace doth not condemn or deny any lawfull joy and comfort* : It doth onely two things ; 1. It absolutely condemns and abridgeth the soul of man of all sinfull joys, of joys and delights which arise from his sinfull lusts and ways ; and is it not the great goodness of God, to deny us leave to drink cups of poison, and glasses of hell ? Or is it possible that any Christian should set up sinfull lusts for his souls delight ? The Lord be mercifull to thee, that sin should be thy delight, which is a departing of the poor soul from God, which is an incensing of the wrath of God, which was such a dreadfull burthen to Jesus Christ, which puts the soul under the wrath and curse of God ; one act whereof must cost more then all the world is worth to pardon it. 2. It doth onely order our outward lawfull joys and delights, for the seasons, for the measures, for other circumstances ; so that they may be our sauce, not our food ; our helps to Godliness, not damps thereto : It is but the Bridle on the Horse, the Pale for the Garden, the Finger on the Dial. Conversion abridgeth us of no delight, but of that which to want is a true delight; and so orders the rest, that you may not lose delight.

Object. 3. Conversion breeds the quickest sense of sin, and the deepest mourning for sin, yea, a continual mourning for sin, makes the clouds to drop, never mournfull till converted ; and can that condition be so joyfull which makes the heart so mournfull ?

To this I answer, 1. It is certain, that true grace. 1. doth *make the clearest discovery of sin: 2. It yields the tenderest sense of*

Converting grace denies not any lawfull joy.

Conversion mournful for sin, and how can it be so joyfull.

Answered.
True grace makes the heart more mournfull.

of sin, (for it takes away the heart of stone, and gives an heart of flesh,) and nothing makes the heart more mournfull, then true grace.

But this is not inconsistent with joy. 2. But then know, that *mourning for sin and joy in the heart are no way inconsistent.* Isai 12. 3. *With joy shall ye draw water out of the wells of salvation.* Three things I would grant, 1. That love of sin and true joy are inconsistent ; 2. Worldly sorrow and spiritual joy are inconsistent ; 3. That terrour for sin and joy of heart are inconsistent ; Legal terrour and Evangelical joy are so, but Evangelical sorrow and Evangelical joy are not so ; for as one grace is consistent with another grace, so one heavenly affection is consistent with another heavenly affection. And there are three things which (to me) fully convince, That Evangelical mourning is consistent with Spiritual joy : One is, That such a mourning is but a drop out of the eye of faith ; *They shall look upon him whom they have pierced, and mourn,* Zach. 12. 10. and certainly, nothing comes from faith, but what is comfortable ; all is Gospel that Faith trades in. Another is, That the mourning heart is a renewed heart, and verily the gracious heart is a joyous heart. The third is, That the mourning sinner is a pardoned sinner : (*Cum intueor flentem, sentis ignoscibilem,*) if the fountain of sorrow be set open in the heart, the fountain of mercy is set open in heaven, Zach. 12. 10. compared with chap. 13. 1. Yea let me add to this also three experiences : 1. One is this, *That the Christian is never more sad and mournfull, then when he feels his heart least mournfull* : He is then cast down ; O (saith he) into what a condition am I brought ? I was wont to find a tender, sensible mourning spirit ; but me thinks now my heart is grown hard again :- O Lord, why am I now hardened from thy fear ? And the man never gives over with God and himself, until tendernefs be renewed in his heart again. 2. *That the Christian is never more joyfull, then when he is most mournfull :* Blessed are they that sow besides all *Waters*, saith the Prophet. *Blessed are they that mourn, for they shall be comforted*, saith Christ. *They that sow in tears shall reap in joy,* saith *David*. Godly sorrow is the Water that is turned into Wine ; One drop of a guilty Conscience is able to turn all our Joyes into Bitterness, and one drop of godly

of the Returning Prodigal.

godly sorrow is able to turn all our bitternefs into joy. *I rejoyce, faith Paul, that I made you sorry*; what caufe then had they to rejoyce who were forry? *forry after a godly fort*; forry with a forrow that bred repentance unto falvation, never to be repented of. 3. *That the Christian is never more mournful then when he is moft joyful*: The time of a Christians higheft joy, is the time of his greateft affurance: Sealing and affuring times are the foul-raifing and reviving times. And the times of greateft affurance, are the times of our greateft mournings: The more manifeftation of Gods Love, and the more affurance of Gods Mercy, do ever caufe in the heart more Humility and more forrow; here is now the greateft joy for mercy, and here is now the greateft mourning for finning againft mercy.

Object. 4. We fee no perfons to walk more fadly and more uncomfortably then (at leaft) many do who are converted perfons, *Ergo*. To this give me favour to anfwer more fully: 1. This is a *Falfe Charge*, and a very unjuft Calumny: take the divifions of the fons of men according to the diverfity of their fpiritual conditions, compare men with men, according unto them, and I dare confidently affirm, That no condition is more dreadfully fad then the condition of men Unconverted; and no condition is more comfortably cheerful, then the condition of men truly Converted; let's a while perufe the phrafes and inftances of fuch. Me thinks the terrible paffages in Scripture may abundantly convince us of the dreadfulnefs of an Unconverted and wicked perfon, Ifa. 57. 20. *The wicked are like the raging fea that cannot reft, whofe waters caft up mire and dirt.* ver. 21. *There is no peace, faith my God, to the wicked.* Job 20. 16, 17, 23, 24, 25. there *Zophar* fets him out: *He fhall fuck the gall of Afps, and the Vipers tongue fhall flay him. He fhall not fee the Rivers, nor the floods and ftreams of Honey and Butter. When he is about to fill his belly, God fhall fend upon him the fiercenefs of his wrath, and fhall caufe it to rain upon him. The bow of Steel fhall ftrike him through, the gliftring fword cometh out of his gall, terrors are upon him.* Pfal. 11. 6. *Upon the wicked he fhall rain fnares, fire and brimftone, and an horrible tempeft; this fhalt be the portion of their cup.* Again, did you ever read of any one godly and converted perfon who fell into that horrible defpair

I, but no perfons walk more fadly then converted perfons.
Anfwered, It is a Falfe Charge.

as

as *Cain* or *Judas* did? But take the hardest agonies incident to true converts, they are 1. rather fears then horrours; 2. rather doubts then despairs; 3. effects of a mistaking Conscience, then a rightly condemning Conscience; 4. They can look towards the Promises, as *Jonah* did in the deeps towards God; 5. Faith doth doth act for relief, and will hold some communion with God; 6. They are abated by the Ordinances; 7. They are but for a time; 8. They end in fullest setling and glorious comforts, and likewise with advantage to their gracious condition. And truly, it is impossible that wicked and ungodly men should ever enjoy that serenity and peace as the godly do, for as much as all the principles and causes of uncomfortableness abide on the wicked. 1. *Sin is in them in all its strength:* They have a thousand hells and arrows of guilt sticking in their hearts; they have souls full of plague sores, the deadly strokes of death, the restless motions of evil spirits. 2. *They carry a roaring Lion in their brests*; I mean, an evil, accusing, smiting, wounding, racking, condemning Conscience; which if it once awake, it will tear the caul of their hearts, and crush them with the flames of unavoidable, unsupportable and continual wrath. 3. *They have no City of Refuge open to their succour,* no land or shore, no place to cast anchor, no portion in Christ; and therefore the Law of God stands in full force against their souls, and under its curse they lie, and at that Bar of Justice must they be tried. 4. *They end in an eternal and perfect Hell.* 5. Take them at their best, *God is their Enemy,* (they never yet made peace with him,) *and all their outward blessings are steeped in gall, and drenched in Wormwood* ; as their sorrows, so their blessings are distributed in wrath.

Many converted persons are not really sad, they onely seem so.

2. Many converted persons are not really sad and uncomfortable, but onely seem so to the mean and childish opinions of vain men, 2 Cor. 6. 10. *As sorrowfull, yet always rejoycing.* The joy of Christians is an hidden joy, (*Hidden Manna,* Revel. 2. 20.) it is a spiritual joy to which thou art a stranger, meat to eat which thou knowest not of. Suppose that thou rejoycest not in a fine Baby, and a Toy, which is a Childs great delight, art thou therefore sad? All objects yield not contentment to an high mind, nor joy to a good man; he cannot take pleasure in an Alehouse and Tavern, in swaggering and masking, in dicing and

of the Returning Prodigal.

and carding, and swearing, and whoring; but yet he can take delight in a reconciled God, in a Christ, in the Word of God, in praying to God, in gracious returnes from God, in expectation of the Glory of God. A swine delights in mire, but a man doth not. The Moon is oft times dark to the world, when yet that part which faceth to the Sun is beautiful and lightsome: The countenance and carriage of a Christian, as to the world, seems dull and uncomfortable, but if you could look into the heart of him (which faceth towards heaven) O there is Righteousness, there is Peace, there is Joy in the Holy Ghost!

3. *If any converted persons be sad, and want actual joy and comfort, yet their Conversion is not the cause thereof.* Can the Sun be any cause of darkness? But, amongst others, these are the Causes of it; Either 1. *Thy unconversion.* It is the unconverted husband, child, master, which makes sadness in the heart of the converted wife, father, &c. It is thy drunkenness, thy cursing and swearing, thy scorning and scoffing, thy resisting and shifting the offers of Grace, thy lying and slandering, thy pride and loosness which makes the hearts of Ministers ready to break, and the hearts of thy godly friends ready to sink in them: O they tremble at thy condition, and they grieve to see God so extremely dishonoured. *Psal.*119.136. *Rivers of tears run down mine eyes, because they keep not thy Law.* ver.158. *I beheld the transgressors and was grieved, because they kept not thy Word.* 2 Pet.2. 7,8. *The wicked deeds of the ungodly Sodomites vexed the soul of righteous Lot.* Luke 19.41. It was *Jerusalems* proud obstinacy, that *would not know in her day the things which concerned her peace,* that *made Jesus Christ to weep.* 2. *Their Captivities to sin. Pauls* conversion did never trouble him, but this did trouble him, that *he did the evil which he would not;* his Corruption, not Conversion; *That the Law of his members led him captive against the Law of his mind.* It was not *Peters Conversion,* but *Peters transgression,* that made him *go forth and weep bitterly.* It was not *Davids Conversion,* but *Davids great sinning,* which made him go so heavily, and roar so greatly, *Psal.*32. 3. *The Fears and Suspitions* that they are not yet truly converted. *O wretched man that I am, who shall deliver me from this body of death!* O they feel so many working Corruptions still, and so little of the strength of Christ still, and so much unbelief still, and so many indispositi-

If they be sad, Conversion is not the cause of it.

Gods gracious Acceptance

ons still, and so many failings still, and so many doubts about these; This Grace is not right, the saving Work is not begun; and these things make them to sigh, and weep, and go heavily all the day long.   4. *They are but newly crept out of the shell*: The Spirit of Bondage is yet hardly worn off, some legal Dints stick on them: they are either still in travel, or but newly delivered; Or if they be got out of the state of Bondage, yet they are for the present under spiritual conflicts; and as spiritual Bondage before Conversion, so spiritual conflicts after conversion suspends the taste of a present and actual joy: Or if that be not the damp, then perhaps it is some ignorance or unexperience; they are not yet come to read their Fathers Will and Christs Testament, what portion is left and laid out for the Children of God: Or if that be not it, then perhaps it is a present fit of unbelief, they cannot yet be perswaded that God means so much mercy, and so much love, and so many great things for them.

Use 1.
Information.

Is it so, That Conversion brings the person into a very joyful condition? Hence then   1. We may be *Informed* of four things,

They are enemies to their joy, who are enemies to Conversion.

1. *That they are enemies to their joy and comfort, who are adversaries to their Conversion.* Prov. 1. 22. *How long ye simple ones will ye love simplicity, and ye Scorners delight in scorning, and fools hate knowledg?*   Six things shew one to be in an unconverted condition; Unsensibleness, Love of sin, Path of evil, hatred of Reformation, despising the Means of Conversion, loathing of Converted-Persons.   There are some persons who hate to be reformed, who hold fast their sins, and will not let them go; they are like those stiff-necked Jewes, who *alwayes resisted the Holy Ghost*; a disobedient people to the Call of God, they refuse to put their necks into the yoak of Jesus Christ, and will not be bound with his cords; They love their sinful wayes, and will not return to the Almighty: Why! *Write that man childless*, said God of *Coniah*; So I say of these men, Write them comfortless: Will the Lord lye for you? Or will he misplace his hands for you? Peace is the effect of righteousness, and Joy is the fruit of Conversion. And shalt thou have pleasure, who takest pleasure in unrighteousness? Shalt thou know the wayes of Peace, who wilt not know the path of Holiness? Did ever God smile on him who hated God? Or clasp him with joy, who despised his grace with hatred?

hatred ? Go enquire and search all the Springs of joy, and knock at all the Gates of pleasure, diligently ask, What of delight they contain for thee ? Knock at the *mercy-seat*, which is the Gate of God, and ask ; Lord, hast thou not joy for one who will go on in his sins, and will not return unto thee ? No (saith God) not any; *but he who forsakes his sins shall have mercy, and he who hardens his heart shall fall into mischief*, Prov. 28. 13, 14. Knock at the *Gospel*, which is the gate of Christ, and ask ; Blessed Jesu, hast thou no word of comfort for him who resists thy spirit, and will not come in unto thee ? No not I (saith Christ) not any ; thou despisest the goodness of God, *and by thy impenitency and hardness, treasurest unto thy self wrath against the day of wrath*. Knock at *conscience*, which is the gate of thine own soul, and ask ; O conscience, hast thou not a word of peace to speak to one who loves his sins, and is an enemy to God and godliness ? Who, I, saith conscience! not I ; thou art an enemy of righteousness, and in the gall of bitterness, and except thou repent, thou shalt certainly perish. Knock at the *Scriptures*, which are the Gate of truth, and ask ; May not the wicked and unconverted person suck at the brests of your consolation ? are not those wells of salvation open for me to draw joy and comfort out of ? Oh no, say the promises, we are childrens bread, and legacies for sons ; if thou be a believer, we are a Fountain opened for thee ; if thou be an unbeliever, we are a Fountain sealed against thee. Knock at the *Creatures*, which are the Gate of Providence, and ask ; Have ye no Commission of Comfort for one who cares not to remember his Creator ? O no, say all the Creatures, Sin long ago hath cast thee out of Paradise, and turned the earth into a curse, and thy blessings are cursed, and thy sinnings do poison all the flowers in our Garden unto thee. Nay, Knock at thy very *Sins*, which are the Gate of Hell, and ask them ; Ye of all other are my dearest friends, and choicest masters, and have ye no Joyes and Comforts for me ? O yes, say they, we have, but they are forbidden fruit, but they are pleasures of sin for a season, but they will end in everlasting torments and sorrow. Thus is every wicked and unconverted man in *Cains* condition, who cryed out, *Behold, thou hast driven me out this day from the face of the earth, and from thy face shall I be hid, and I shall be a fugitive and a vagabond in the earth*, Gen. 4. 14.

4. That

Gods Gracious Acceptance

They are slanderers of the sweetness of Gods ways, who thus reproach the state of Conversion.

2. *That they are enemies and slanderers of the goodness and sweetness of the wayes of God, who load the estate of Conversion with all the ignominious reproaches of sadness and heaviness;* and mopishness, and melancholy, and bitterness, and grave of all joy and pleasure: As the *Spies* of old traduced the good and pleasant land of *Canaan,* which abounded with milk and hony, O it was a land that did eat up the Inhabitants thereof; But as God spake once to *Aaron* and *Miriam, How were ye not afraid to speak against my servant Moses?* So I to these; How are ye not afraid to reproach the wayes of the living God? Is not God the God of comfort? Is not Christ the consolation of Israel? Is not the Holy Ghost the comforter? are not the Scriptures written for our consolation? are not the Promises the breasts of Consolation? are not all the pathes of Wisdome pathes of pleasantness? are not the Graces of God the very beds of Spices? Is not the peace of Conscience a peace that passeth all understanding? Doth *David* find the Word *sweeter then the hony comb?* Doth *Job* find it *better then his appointed food?* Doth *Jeremiah* find it *the Rejoycing of his heart?* Doest thou read of so many Converted persons in Scripture full of joy and gladness, rejoycing in Christ, *rejoycing in the hope of the Glory of God, rejoycing in Troubles,* in *Persecutions,* yea, in *Death it self;* and yet darest thou to revile and scandalize the converted mans condition as the only sea of Bitterness, and darkest night, eclipsing all joy and comfort? I pray thee to consider, 1. *This doth arise from the gall of thy wicked and imbittered Spirit,* hating and despising the goodly excellencies of holiness and holy persons. 2. It doth shew a cursed heart to *call good evil,* as it doth to *call evil good;* and as he *that justifies the Wicked,* so he that *condemns the just,* is *an abomination to the Lord;* How much more then, he who condemns Righteousnes it self. 3. This doth shew an *Universal rage against Gods glory* and *mans happiness;* So heavily dost thou load the pathes of Conversion, that so much as in thee lies, thou disswadest and discouragest all the men on earth from leaving off their sins, so that God shall have no Glory from them; nor they any true happiness from God. 4. And lastly: Take heed least God deal with thee, as once he did with the lying spies; shut them out of Canaan, and destroyed them with a remarkable Judgment.

3. That

Of the Returning Prodigal.

3. *That they have hitherto deluded and deceived themselves with false joy, in stead of true joy, who as yet never saw a converted condition.* All thy mirth and joy hath been but false fire; a madness, not a joyfulness; sparkles of thy own kindling; thou hast fed on the husks all this while, on a fancy, on a Dream; thou hast never in all thy life took in one draught of true joy, nor ever shalt thou, till God convert thy soul. Take heed of setling your souls, or resting your souls on any works, or on any affections which are antecedent to conversion, even the sorrows and troubles before conversion are no matter of joy and comfort; if any joy depends on them, it is rather because conversion hath followed them; and the joys which many men take before their conversion, certainly they are false joys, poor joys, they are not pleasures of Gods right hand. There are three properties of true Joy: 1. It is not the *Usher* which goes before, but the *Handmaid* that follows after Grace. 2. It is not a *Surfet* to dead, but a *Cordial* to strengthen; and it is not a *Feast* to satisfie, but a *Sawce* to quicken communion with God. 3. It is not a *temptation* to sin, but *upholds* against the new temptations of sin. True Joy never goes before true Grace, but follows it. Do you use to gather fruit before you plant, or reap before ye sow.

4. *Then if ever you would have joy, and live joyfull lives, get converted hearts.* Every man desires joy; and as the Bee hunts for honey, so do men naturally hunt for delight; ἢ ἡδέα ἢ ἡκιστα aut jucunde aut non omnino. Let the thing or condition be what it will, if we take no delight in it, it is a burthen to us: Heaven would not be Heaven to him who cannot find delight in it. Now Conversion is the true path to true joy. If God would be pleased (once) to convert thy soul, his converting Grace would lick thy sores, and pull out the stings in Conscience, and sweeten the bitter Springs, and clear the Heavens to thee; it would make thy bed to be easie, and thy bread to be sweet, and thy condition to be a Paradise; even the Wilderness should drop honey to thee, and thy heart should sing for joy. It is a witty passage of *Bernards*, (*de bonis deferendis*) *Be willing to sacrifice thy Isaac, and thy Isaac shall live. Isaac*, you know, signifies *laughter*; do but sacrifice thy sinfull pleasure, and then thy true pleasure shall not die, but live. *Caius* gave

unto

They who never were converted, delude themselves with false joy.

If you would have joy, get converted hearts.

Gods gracious Acceptance

unto *Agrippa* a Chain of Gold which was as heavy as the Chain of Iron that he endured in the Prison: Sins do put upon us a Chain of Iron, which if we would forsake, Conversion would put upon us a Chain of Gold; thou shalt not lose, but better thy pleasures, by forsaking of thy sins and the pleasures of them. O! that all the joys which you have heard attending a converted condition, might allure all our hearts to become converted persons. I observe five things about the converted condition in Scripture. 1. *The invitation unto it*, and there joy presents it self; *Turn and live*, turn and live; *hearken diligently unto me, and eat ye that which is good, and let your soul delight it self in fatness*, Isa. 55. 2. 2. *The entrance into it*, and there joy embraceth the person: As soon as the Prodigal Son returned, *his Father saw him a far off*, (O how quick is Mercy to espy a Convert!) and *had compassion*, (O how tender is Mercy to yern over a Convert!) and *ran*, (O how swift is Mercy to receive a Convert!) and *fell on his neck*, (O how how out-stretching is Mercy to embrace a Convert!) and *kissed him*, (O how kind is Mercy to entertain a Convert!) 3. *The motion or course of it*, and there joy attends the person: *I have rejoyced*, saith David, Psal. 119. 14. *in the way of thy testimonies, as much as in all riches*. When a converted man doth *Meditate*, his meditation is stiled sweet: *Hear*, he hears with joy; *When they heard this they were glad*: *Pray*, this is a sweet incense to David; *And I will make them joyfull in my house of prayer*, Isa. 56. 7. *Believe*, he doth believe and rejoice: *Mourn*, there is appointed the *oyl of joy for mourning*, Isa. 61. 3. *Do the will of God*, it is his delight to do the will of God: *Suffer*; *Rejoyce*, saith the Apostle, 1 Pet. 4 13. *in as much as ye are partakers of Christs sufferings*. 4. *The conclusion or end of it*, why! there also doth joy accompany him: Psal. 37. *Mark the perfect man, and behold the just, for the end of that man is peace.* 5. *The reward and recompence of it*, and there also joy doth clasp the converted person: *Enter into thy Masters joy*, saith Christ to the good servant: Gaudium supra omne gaudium; *At thy right hand are pleasures for evermore*, said David.

O! that all these things might so affect our hearts this day, as to forsake our sins, and turn back to God   Pleasure is the great bait which is laid forth to catch the soul of man; Satan draws us to sin by pleasure, and God draws us to grace by pleasure; shall pleasure move thee to damn thy soul? and shall not true pleasure move thee to save thy soul? Our Aversion from God depends much upon pleasure, and our Conversion unto God depends much upon pleasure; me thinks that Gods promise should be more accounted then the Divels temptation; is it not more probable to buy a better pennyworth from heaven then from hell? and is it not more reasonable to traffick at the gates of life for joy, then to trade at the gates of death for comfort? Return, return, O sinner! yet, yet, come back to thy God, and do not for lying vanities any longer forsake thine own mercies,——— But God must perswade Japhet.

Use 2.
Try whether you are in a converted condition or no. There are two sorts of persons. 1. Some plainly unconverted. 2. Some deceiving themselves about it. Nine things do shew that a man is as yet absolutely in an unconverted condition.

Try whether converted or no. Nine things shew a man is unconverted.

1. *Unsensibleness*: God promiseth to take away the stony heart; *quanto insensibilior, tanto pejor*. This is the Stone upon the Grave.

2. *Love of sin*: Wicked men are described by this in Scripture.

3. *Walking in the path of sin*: It is his work, his trade; when a man chuseth an evil way, and sits in the Chair, is a servant of unrighteousness, walks in the way of wicked men.

4. *Hating to be reformed*: It is an abomination to him to be good, that will rather be damned then reformed, breaks the Cords, will not have Christ to reign.

5. *Despising of the means of Conversion*: The word of the Lord is a reproach to him; his heart rageth when the word finds out his sins, and would separate him and his lusts.

6. *Loathing of converted persons*; cannot endure the sight of grace; his special dislikes are of the godly, and disgraces, and discountenancings of them; he is exceedingly displeased and grieved at the estimations of godliness, and rejoyceth in the cloudings, and setting of it.

7. *In communion with God*: It is a note of a wicked man, that God is not in all his thoughts, and that he calls not upon God, but is a stranger to him, the stil-born child is a dead child.

8. *Disva-*

8. *Disvaluations of Jesus Christ*, and of all the precious seasons of grace, and opportunities of mercy; the Swine tramples upon the Pearl, the dayes of the Son of man are of no account with him.

9. *An earthly rest and satisfaction*: When he is a man only for this life, and for this present world, sets up his staff on this side Jordan; all his hopes are in this life.

Secondly: Five things which do shew that a man flatters and deceives himself about his condition, that it is converted, when yet it falls short thereof.

<small>Five things shew a man deceived about his conversion.</small>

1. *Meer knowledg*; though a man knows never so much, yet if he be but a knowing man, he may be a learned man, but he is not a converted man. It is one thing to know controversies, another thing to know Conversion: If the knowledg be without 1, *Experience*; know what sin is, but feel it not; know what Christ is, but never feel the virtues and powers of his death and resurrection: 2. *Propriety*; know Christ as a purchase, but not as an inheritance; what he is, and hath done, but not what he is to me, or hath done for me: 3. *Power*; as a candle that lightens, but not as fire to burn, as an Ornament on a Tomb, not as a Soul to the Body; as a Star which shines in the night, not as the Sun which makes day; new knowledg, but still an old heart: 4. *Affections*; know sin, but hate it not, nor mourn for it; know Christ, but love and desire him not: 5. *Practise*, like a Scholler, who knows Countries, but never travels to them; reads the Copy, but writes not after it, know the way to heaven, but never walks the way to heaven.

2. *Meer trouble of conscience*: A troubled condition is one thing, a converted condition is another; *Cain* and *Judas* were troubled, yet not converted; many things may suffice to trouble us, which yet are not sufficient to convert us; the Law, the Wrath of God, the quickness of conscience, fear of death and hell and shame may suffice to trouble us, yet not to convert us. The Sea may be troubled, and yet remains brinish; the Iron may be broken, and yet it is hard; the Water boils, and yet it is Water: There is a difference twixt passive trouble, and active trouble; twixt a trouble that I would get off, and godly sorrow which I would get up; twixt trouble in *ratione pœna*, and in *ratione gratia*; twixt being troubled for sin as it is *malum sensibile*, and as *malum spiri-*

of the Returning Prodigal.

spirituale, twixt *malum* as *causa mali*, and *malum* as *affectus mali*. The Land-flood is high, but it leaves the mud and dirt behind; the Wells water is less, but it cleanseth.

3. *Limited Reformation*: When only external; if internal, yet partial, will stick with Christ for some one tHing. True Conversion is an invisible work, it is seed under ground, tis a child formed in the womb, it is the hidden man of the heart, tis Christ formed and living in us, it is a new Creation of the heart, the new heart, a law written there. The Pharisees were good at Outworks, all fair to the eyes of men: Outward abstinence from sin may consist with an inward love of it; and a man may do much good, who yet is not good: Self-grounds, and ends, of profit, of esteem, of hopes, of compliance with others, besides those workings of conscience, &c. may lead us out to visible conformities, when yet, &c.

4. *Accidental resolutions*: When a person will on a sudden grow good altogether, only upon mutable occasions; 1. As in an exigence of Conscience, 2. In a fit of Sickness, 3. Some present conviction of the Word, 4. Some imminent judgements, 5. Some present hopes; not upon solid Conviction, consideration, fervent prayer to God to work the change, &c.

5. *Passionate Joyes*: If taken by the Word upon the discoveries of Grace, and Mercy, and Love of Christ, and of future glory; like one who is taken with the Ware, yet will not come up to the Price: The young man would have heaven, but will not sell all, take up the Cross and follow Christ. But when a man is truly converted, he is like the *Wise Merchant*, *who found the Pearl, and rejoiced, and sold all, and bought it*. He will part with all his Lusts, and Friends, and Pleasures, and World, to enjoy Christ.

Doth Conversion bring the soul into a joyful condition? Then let *every converted person take his due portion*, and live as becomes himself, joyfully. Psal. 32. 11. *Be glad in the Lord, and rejoice ye righteous*. Phil. 4. 4. *Rejoice in the Lord alway, and again I say, rejoice*. I wish that converted persons would consider

1. *That God doth not reserve all their joyes unto another life*: O no, spiritual joy is an allowance also for this life; a good bit

Use. 3. Let every converted person take his portion of joy.

God doth not reserve all their joy to another life.

bit and bait by the way. Nay, it is not a meer Toleration or Permission, but it is an express Command and Injunction; and as a man doth sin who refuseth Grace, so some man may sin who refuseth Joy. 2. *God would have the life of Grace to be a primordial shadow* (at least) *of the life of Glory*: and indeed our estate of Grace is an Epitome of that in Glory; only that is a fuller and larger Volume: We have the same God, the same Christ, the same Spirit, the same Communion in this as in that; only here it is more Mediate, there more Immediate; here Imperfect, there Perfect; here Mixt, and there Pure. And doest thou so poorly conceive of God, that He who is able to make an heaven full of joy to Eternity hereafter, is not able or willing to let fall a few drops of joy upon thy soul on earth? Or that there can or should be any Communion with such a God, which should not be joyful and delightful? The Emperor would have none to go away sad. 3. *God would have the Christians life, as to be the fruit, so to be the credit of Grace.* Grace is an ornament to the soul, and spiritual joy is an Ornament to grace: It testifies to the world, that conversion quits all costs: What! shal madness be found in the habitations of the wicked, and shall not joy be found in the tabernacles of the just? Shall the worldly man rejoice in a Creature, and shall not the godly man rejoyce in his God? Shall the condemned malefactor take delight, and shall not the acquitted person take comfort? Shall wicked men suck pleasure out of bitter waters, and shall not good men draw joy out of the wells of salvation? *Joy is not comely for a fool*, saith *Solomon*, but it *becomes the upright to rejoice*, saith *David*. 4. *As spiritual joy is an ornament, so it is an improvement to grace.* It is a certain truth, that grace is the Mother of joy, and true joy is the Nurse of grace. Spiritual comforts are inlargements to spiritual graces; look as it is with sinful pleasures, they do add to our sinful principles; the more delight that any man finds in sinful wayes, this adds the more love, and the more desire, and the more earnestness for to sin; so is it in spiritual wayes, the more joy and delight any man takes in them, this adds a new quickning to his graces, a fresher edge unto them; nothing makes either a communion, or an action more frequent, or more fervent then delight; didst thou

of the Returning Prodigal.

thou ever find thy heart more apt to pray, or more fixed in prayer, then when thou foundest most delight and comfort, in, or upon praying? So for other duties.   5. *Spiritual joy will exceedingly facilitate the way and work for heaven:*   It is our *facundus Comes*, which is pro *Vehiculo*.   As the *fear of the Lord is our treasure*, Isa. 33. 6.   So *the joy of the Lord is our Strength*, Neh. 8. 10. An heavy, dull, sad spirit, is a burden of it self, and is very apt to make every thing else a burden: Now spiritual joy, it takes off dulness and deadness, and enables us to run the way of Gods Commandments, and to run the race that is set before us. *Amanti nihil difficile*, it makes our spiritual work to come off; the Wheels run if oyled.

It will exceedingly facilitate the way and work to heaven.

Quest. This is true, will some reply; but what should converted persons do, that they may walk joyfully?   *Sol.* There are two sorts of converted persons: *Incipientes*; who are newly called, newly wrought on, newly brought home;   and these ordinarily are full of fears, of doubts, of temptations, of conflicts, of heaviness: *Proficientes*; who are long standers in the wayes of grace.   Will you favour me to speak a few words to either of these.

What should converted persons do to walk joyfully?

1. To persons newly converted: I would humbly present these directions, as proper means or Conduits of joy and comforts to their souls.

Directions. To persons newly converted.

1. *Draw up your spiritual condition to some issue:*   Do not live with a doubtful suspicion; perhaps you are converted, perhaps you are not converted: As ignorance is an enemy to grace, so doubtfulness is an enemy to comfort.   That man who is still in suit, whether his Conversion be true, will not dare to lay claim to the joyes which result from Conversion: If I fear my grace, I shall much more fear my comfort;   *Give all diligence to make your calling and election sure.*   Therefore do this; bring thy souls estate to the word, (that is the rule, that is the fire, that is the touchstone;)   if the Word of God will approve and decide for thee, bless God, and maintain the truth of thy spiritual estate, against all the suggestions of Satan, and cavils of thine own heart; when once that doth say, truth of grace is in thee; conscience will say, truth of comfort belongs unto thee.

Draw up your Spirituall condition to some Issue.

2. *Get-*

Gods Gracious Acceptance

Get a little more faith.

2. *Get a little more faith*; one dram more would turn the scale, and settle thine heart. Faith trades with the Fountain, with the God of Comfort, and of Peace, and with Jesus Christ: It is Faith that lets you into Christ, and it is Faith which lets comfort into you. *The God of hope fill you with all joy and peace in believing*, Rom. 15. 13. There are five priviledges of Faith: It hath the first *look* of Mercy, it hath the first *kiss* from Christ, it hath the first *news* of acceptance unto Life, it hath the first *answer* of Peace, it hath the first *draught* of Joy: Oh, get a little more faith; a little more faith would weaken the grounds of thy fears, quell the motions of thy doubts, clear thy way to the fountains of comfort, imprint on thy heart a most joyful Communion with thy God and Christ; no life of joy, but that of faith.

Learne to live by faith.

3 And *Learn to live by faith*, and then you will have more joy and comfort. Four things would make a mans life very joyfull and comfortable. 1. If he were eased of all burthens. 2. If he were secured from all prejudices. 3. If what he had were good, and enough. 4. If he were assured, that whatsoever good he should need, of that he should not fail, but be supplied with it in due time. Now the life of faith, 1. *Easeth you of all your burthens*: There are but two burthens upon us; 1. The *sinfull*, Faith sees this taken off by Christ, *He bare our sins*: 2. The *earthly*, of cares; Faith sees Gods providence taking that off, *The Lord is a Sun*, &c. Psal. 84. *I will never leave thee*, Heb. 13. *Bread shall be given to him, his waters shall be sure*, Isa. 33. 16. *Cast your care on him, for he careth for you*, 1 Pet. 5. 7. 2. *Secures you against all prejudices and hurts*: Faith finds us still in Gods hands, and in a safe custody: Though there be evils in the world, yet they shall not come nigh you; and his work goes on, though ours do not: God is with you, who can be against you. There's a Deluge, but *Noah*'s in the Ark; a storm, but you are in an hiding place: He holds you in his hand, and covers you under his wings; makes all things to work for good. Faith sees the Trouble and the Sanctuary both, Occurrences and Providence both, ruling, carrying on, observing, watching, preserving: If Earth won't keep you safe, Heaven shall. 3. *It renders the present possession as good, and enough:*

Your

Your portion is so: For what is a Christians portion? Is not God? is not his favour? And is not God enough? is not his favour better then life? He who cannot be contented with a God, and a Christ, and a Covenant of Grace, and Heaven, will be satisfied with nothing. You have but little of Earth, Ai but you have God and Christ. If a man have but a little Garden, yet if he have a large field, &c. A little of Earth, and much of Heaven, makes a fair Estate. 4. *It assures you of supplies universal and seasonable.* *Universal*; I shall not want, *Psal.* 23.1. *No good thing will he withhold,* Psal. 84.11. No good for soul, no good for body, (you have his Bonds for both;) and this is for life; *Surely goodness and mercy shall follow me all the days of my life,* Psal. 23. Nay, for everlastingness; *I will marry thee to my self for ever,* Hos. 2.19. 2. *Seasonable*; In an acceptable time, &c. *In the mount God will be seen.*

4. *Get a little more understanding and judgment about your converted and gracious condition.* Shall I help thee a little with a few Considerations and Informations? Know then, 1. *The great Fountain of thy Joy lies more in thy Justification then in thy Sanctification.* Thou hast not so much Holiness as another, but thou hast of Christs Righteousness; thou canst not apprehend so strongly, but thou art apprehended as strongly, Christ lays as fast hold of thee. 2. *That Grace and Weakness may dwell together.* It may be very true, though very weak, *the smoaking flax,* and *the bruised reed,* and the *grain of mustard-seed*; A Father hath one Child in the Cradle, and another in the Shop; a Shepheard hath Lambs in the flock, as well as Sheep; the Gardiner hath Plants, as well as Trees; and Christ hath Babes, as well as strong Men, belonging to him. 3. *That the least Grace, and the great Love of God do go together*: The little drop of Grace comes out of the Ocean of his great Love; the Peny, as well as the Shilling, bears the Superscription. 4. *That the least degree of true Grace denominates the condition to be converted:* I would believe, is Faith; I would love thee, is Love; I desire to do thy will, is Obedience: Not Strength, but Truth denominates. 5. *True Grace and many Conflicts go together:* Let the motions of sin be never so vile, but I hate them; never so many, but I resist them; here Grace is the Lord which rules me, though

Get more understanding and judgment about your converted condition.

though sin be the Enemy which molests me. Why am I thus Alas, there are contraries in thee, Light and Darkness, Flesh and Spirit. 6. *True Grace and some Failings may lodge together:* I may at the same time be a Captive to Sin, and yet a Servant to Grace; sin may sometimes be too strong even for him who hates sin. 7. *All services to God are interpreted and accepted by God according to the will of a converted person:* Although thou canst not pray so freely, so fully, so uniformly, yet if God see a will in thee desirous so to do, it shall pass for currant; groans, and sighs, and chatterings, and desires, and tears, &c. 8. *Thou never doest any Duty, but Jesus Christ gives acceptance unto it by his Intercession;* his sweet Incense takes off the ill favour: The greatest work done by thee, if it comes in thy own name, is rejected; the weakest, if presented in his Name, a sigh or groan, is graciously accepted; as the Sacrifices by the Priest. 9. *God never expects thou shouldest buy out thy own pardon,* or bring from thy self any satisfaction for any of thy sins; he hath designed that work onely to Jesus Christ, in whom he hath accepted thee, and for whose sake alone he doth and will discharge thee: You trade in Heaven upon gracious terms; when you come for any grace and help, thy Reasons and Motives are in God, who gives, and freely gives. 10. *As soon as ever converting Grace prevails upon thy heart, Salvation is come to thy soul:* Thou art now a Believer; and if a Believer, a Son; and if a Son, an Heir of all the comfortable Promises now, and a Co-heir with Christ hereafter. 11. *The Lord will bless thy buds, and increase thy stock of Grace:* He will water, as well as plant it. 12. *That little Grace shall never fail thee,* never leave thee, till it brings thee to Heaven: The greatest Grace is imperfect, and the least Grace is invincible; the greatest Grace is weak, and the weakest Grace is immortal.

Now if Christians did believe all these Truths, and would consider of them, would not their condition be more joyfull? Here's a Weakness, I but it is Grace; that Grace is little, I but it comes from Graciousness, and makes me gracious: O how many conflicts! I but 'tis 'twixt Grace and Sin; yea, and many sinnings, I but not love of sin, no voluntary service: But how poor in Duties! I but God regards the Will: But what will become

of the Returning Prodigal.

become of me for my former sins? Why! Christ hath satisfied, and God hath pardoned: But if I had strength of Grace, I might take comfort; Why! the weakest Convert is a Believer, and the weakest Believer hath Christ; *Ergo*.

Secondly, to *Persons long since converted*; What should they do to walk with joyful hearts? I answer, 1. *Often examine and review your Spiritual condition*; this will keep you and God friends: often look upon the evidences of Gods favour to your Souls, and maintaine and cleare them if blotted; Such experiences are bathes of Comfort: Remember the days of old. 2. *Be upright*; maintain the Oyl, and you maintain the light. *The work of Righteousness shall be peace; and the effect of Righteousness, quietness and assurance for ever:* Isai. 32. 17 A stable Spirit will further a stable Joy; one wry step puts the bone out of joynt, That man loseth his Spiritual pleasure, who steps out for sinful pleasure; remember *Davids* swarving, and *Peters*, and *Jacobs*. 3. *Live by faith*: We never meet with more troubles then when we shift for our selves. That man who can trust God most, him doth God trust with most Grace and peace: see Habak. 3. 17, 18. 4. *Hold up close communion with God and his people*; he who trades most at heaven, gets the greatest stock of Grace and comfort; even the neglect of one prayer may lose a man much comfort; be satisfied with God alone, and let not out your minds to earthly things; And that one sermon which thou didst overslip, brought in exceeding Joy to thy fellow Christian. 5. *Walk in the fear of God all the day long*: Self-confidence makes the person to lye down in tears; but he who feares to sin, fortifies his Graces and comforts; expose not your selves to Temptations. 6. *Renew a solemn and speedy Peace upon every fall*; Light may quickly be restored to a candle newly blown out, and the bone displaced may presen ly be set again; Let not a disease settle. 7. *Engage not thy mind to vain and new Opinions*. Mind the maine things of Life and Salvation, and not unprofitable strifes. He who hath not more Grace to get, hath assuredly much comfort to lose; an Unsetled Judgment will quickly raise an uncomfortable heart. 8. *Preserve an humble and contented Spirit*. Pride is the father of discontentment, and Discontentment is a prison to our Graces, and a Sea to our com-

To persons long since converted,
Often examine and review your Spiritual condition.
Be upright.
Live by faith.
Hold up close communion with God.
Walk in the fear of G.d all the day long.
Renew peace upon every fall.
Engage not to new opinions.
Preserve an humble and contented Spirit.

Be active and thriving.

comforts. Thy Graces will not be pleasant to thee, if thy outward condition please thee not. 9. *Be active and thriving.* That man who doth most for God, doth also most for his own comfort; Barrenness is no good sign of Life, and therefore no good way for comfort; the travelling Bee is laden with hony: Thriving Grace is a clear evidence of truth, and adds to our excellency and our joy.

FINIS.

www.ingramcontent.com/pod-product-compliance
Lightning Source LLC
Chambersburg PA
CBHW032042220426
43664CB00008B/814